An Introduction to Applied Linguistics

Edited by

Norbert Schmitt
University of Nottingham

1 6

ARNOLD

A member of the Hodder Headline Group
LONDON

Co-published in the United State
Oxford University Press In

D0277368

First published in Great Britain in 2002 by
Arnold, a member of the Hodder Headline Group,
338 Euston Road, London NW1 3BH

http://www.arnoldpublishers.com

Co-published in the United States of America by
Oxford University Press Inc.,
198 Madison Avenue, New York, NY10016

The advice and information in this book are believed to be true and
accurate at the date of going to press, but neither the author[s] nor the publisher
can accept any legal responsibility or liability for any errors or omissions.

British Library Cataloguing in Publication Data
A catalogue record for this book is available from the British Library

Library of Congress Cataloging-in-Publication Data
A catalog record for this book is available from the Library of Congress

ISBN 0 340 76418 X (hb)
ISBN 0 340 76419 8 (pb)

1 2 3 4 5 6 7 8 9 10

Production Editor: Jasmine Brown
Production Controller: Iain McWilliams
Cover Design: Terry Griffiths

Typeset in 10/12pt Sabon by Phoenix Photosetting, Chatham, Kent
Printed and bound in Great Britain by MPG Books Ltd, Bodmin, Cornwall

What do you think about this book? Or any other Arnold title?
Please send your comments to feedback.arnold@hodder.co.uk

If you want peace, work for justice

Contents

Preface

This book is intended to give you a broad overview of Applied Linguistics. It will introduce you to important areas in the field, and familiarize you with the key issues in each of those areas. The book is written at the 'sophisticated introduction' level, where the most current ideas in the field are presented, but explained in language that is accessible and direct. After having engaged with the knowledge in this introductory book, you should be able to move on to more advanced books and articles, such as those recommended at the end of each chapter in the 'Further Reading' section.

In addition to helping you become familiar with the issues in Applied Linguistics, the book will also help you become familiar with some of the research methodology currently being used in the field. Knowledge of this methodology is important in order to be able to read and understand original research studies in Applied Linguistics books and journals. A number of chapters show you how research in their area is carried out (for example, Chapter 9, *Sociolinguistics*, and Chapter 11, *Listening*), which should enable you to gain a greater awareness of various research approaches. In addition, each chapter has some data for you to analyse and interpret, with the authors' suggested solutions at the end of the book. These 'Hands-on Activities' will help to understand the information in each chapter better, because you will use some of it in your own analyses.

Applied Linguistics is a big field and one person cannot be an expert in all areas. To ensure that each chapter contains an authoritative treatment of an area, it is co-authored by two (and sometimes three) leading international specialists. By having two specialists writing together, the chapters can represent an expert consensus of the most important issues in that area. The various teams of authors working in their own separate areas have naturally developed different ways of discussing issues, and I have decided to let each team retain their own 'voice' and style, rather than trying to homogenize the chapters into a single style throughout the book. I hope you will find the result illuminating and engaging.

Although teams of authors will retain their individual identity, there is a common format for the chapters. First, each chapter opens with an

'Introduction' or 'What is X?' section which briefly explains what the area is and why it is important. The following section will be the heart of each chapter, where the key issues pertaining to the area are discussed. Next, the pedagogical implications of the area will be considered. Of course some chapters, such as Chapter 3, *Vocabulary*, may have more tangible pedagogical implications than others, such as Chapter 8, *Psycholinguistics*, but all will address pedagogical concerns. Each chapter has a 'Further Reading' section, with approximately six reading suggestions, complete with brief annotations. Finally, each chapter has a 'Hands-on Activity', where some data are presented for you to analyse and interpret. The authors present their suggestions in Chapter 16, *Suggested Solutions*.

The areas of Applied Linguistics are related to each other in various ways. This means that certain ideas will inevitably appear in more than one chapter. I have built a certain amount of this repetition into the book, because I believe a good way to learn key ideas is to see them approached from slightly different perspectives by several authors. When an idea is discussed in another chapter, it will usually be cross-referenced, for example: (see Chapter 4, *Discourse Analysis*, and Chapter 5, *Pragmatics*).

This book has been a team effort with 31 authors contributing their expertise. Writing sophisticated ideas in an accessible way is no easy task, and I thank them for their efforts. I also wish to thank the team at Arnold publishers, in particular Christina Wipf Perry, who have worked hard to ensure that all stages of the publishing process were academically rigorous, but refreshingly expedited. I learned a lot about Applied Linguistics by editing this book. I hope you will be able to say the same thing after reading it.

Norbert Schmitt
University of Nottingham
November 2001

An Overview of Applied Linguistics

Norbert Schmitt
University of Nottingham

Marianne Celce-Murcia
University of California, Los Angeles

What is Applied Linguistics?

'Applied linguistics' is using what we know about (a) language, (b) how it is learned and (c) how it is used, in order to achieve some purpose or solve some problem in the real world. Those purposes are many and varied, as is evident in a definition given by Wilkins (1999: 7):

> In a broad sense, applied linguistics is concerned with increasing understanding of the role of language in human affairs and thereby with providing the knowledge necessary for those who are responsible for taking language-related decisions whether the need for these arises in the classroom, the workplace, the law court, or the laboratory.

The range of these purposes is partly illustrated by the call for papers for the American Association of Applied Linguistics (AAAL) 2002 conference, which lists 18 topic areas:

- language and its acquisition
- language and assessment
- language and the brain
- language and cognition
- language and culture
- language and ideology
- language and instruction
- language and interaction
- language and listening
- language and media

- language and policy
- language and reading
- language and research methodology
- language and society
- language and speaking
- language and technology
- language and translation/interpretation
- language and writing.

The call for papers to the 2002 AILA conference goes even further and lists 47 areas in applied linguistics. Out of these numerous areas, the dominant application has always been the teaching and learning of second or foreign languages. Around the world, a large percentage of people, and a majority in some areas, speak more than one language. For example, a survey published in 1987 found that 83 per cent of 20–24-year-olds in Europe had studied a second language (Cook, 1996: 134). Also, in some countries, a second language is a necessary 'common denominator' ('lingua franca') when the population speaks a variety of different L1s. English is the main second language being studied in the world today with an estimated 235 million L2 learners (Crystal, 1995: 108), so it is perhaps not surprising that this book is written in that language, although the concepts presented here should be appropriate to non-English L2 teaching and learning as well. Figures concerning the numbers of people learning or using second languages can only be rough estimates, but they still give some idea of the impact that applied linguistics can have in the world.

Due to length constraints, this book must inevitably focus on limited facets of applied linguistics. Traditionally, the primary concern of applied linguistics has been second language acquisition theory, second language pedagogy and the interface between the two, and it is these areas which this volume will cover. However, it is also useful to consider briefly some of the areas of applied linguistics which will not be emphasized in this book, in order to further give some sense of the breadth of issues in the field. Carter and Nunan (2001: 2) list the following sub-disciplines in which applied linguists also take an interest: literacy, speech pathology, deaf education, interpreting and translating, communication practices, lexicography and first language acquisition. Of these, L1 acquisition research can be particularly informative concerning L2 contexts, and so will be referred to in several chapters throughout this book (*see* Chapter 7, *Second Language Acquisition*, and Chapter 8, *Psycholinguistics*, in particular, for more on L1 issues).

Besides mother tongue education, language planning and bilingualism/ multilingualism, two other areas that Carter and Nunan (2001) did not list are authorship identification and forensic linguistics. These areas exemplify how applied linguistics knowledge may be utilized in practical ways in non-educational areas. Authorship identification uses a statistical analysis of various linguistic features in anonymous or disputed texts and compares the results with a similar analysis from texts whose authors are known. When a match is made, this gives a strong indication that the matching author wrote the text in question. The search for the anonymous author of the eighteenth-century political letters written under the pseudonym of Junius is an example of this. A linguistic analysis of the vocabulary in the letters (for example, whether *on* or *upon* was used) showed that it was very similar to the use of vocabulary in the writings of Sir Philip Francis, who was then identified as the probable author (Crystal, 1987: 68). Similar analyses are carried out in forensic linguistics, often to establish the probability of whether or not a defendant or witness actually produced a specific piece of discourse. Crystal (1987) relates a case where a convicted murderer was pardoned, partially because a linguistic analysis showed that the transcript of his oral statement (written by the police) was very different stylistically from his normal speech patterns. This discrepancy cast strong doubts on the accuracy of the incriminating evidence in the transcript.

In addition to all these areas and purposes, applied linguistics is interested in cases where language goes wrong. Researchers working on language-related disorders study the speech of aphasic, schizophrenic and autistic speakers, as well as hemispherectomy patients, in the belief that we can better understand how the brain functions when we analyse what happens when the speaker's language system breaks down or does not function properly.

The Development of Applied Linguistics

Early History

Interest in languages and language teaching has a long history, and we can trace this back at least as far as the ancient Greeks, where both 'Plato and Aristotle contributed to the design of a curriculum beginning with good writing (grammar), then moving on to effective discourse (rhetoric) and culminating in the development of dialectic to promote a philosophical approach to life' (Howatt, 1999: 618). If we focus on English, major attempts at linguistic description began to occur in the second half of the eighteenth century. In 1755, Samuel Johnson published his *Dictionary of the English Language*, which quickly become the unquestioned authority on the meanings of English words. It also had the effect of standardizing English spelling, which until that time had been relatively free (for example, the printer William Caxton complained in 1490 that *eggs* could be spelled as 'eggys' or 'egges' or even 'eyren' depending on the local pronunciation). About the same time, Robert Lowth published an influential grammar, *Short Introduction to English Grammar* (1762), but whereas Johnson sought to describe English vocabulary by collecting thousands of examples of how English words were actually used, Lowth prescribed what 'correct' grammar should be. He had no specialized linguistic background to do this, and unfortunately based his English grammar on a classical Latin model, even though the two languages are organized in quite different ways. The result was that English, which is a Germanic language, was described by a linguistic system (parts of speech) which was borrowed from Latin, which had previously borrowed the system from Greek. The process of prescribing, rather than describing, has left us with English grammar rules which are much too rigid to describe actual language usage:

- no multiple negatives (I don't need no help from nobody!)
- no split infinitives (So we need to really think about all this from scratch.)
- no ending a sentence with a preposition (I don't know what it is made of.)

These rules made little sense even when Lowth wrote them, but through the ages both teachers and students have generally disliked ambiguity, and so Lowth's notions of grammar were quickly adopted once in print as the rules of 'correct English'. (*See* Chapter 2, *Grammar*, for more on prescriptive versus descriptive grammars.)

Applied Linguistics during the Twentieth Century

An Overview of the Century

The real acceleration of change in linguistic description and pedagogy occurred during the twentieth century, in which a number of movements influenced the field only to be replaced or modified by subsequent developments. At the beginning of the century, second languages were usually taught by the 'Grammar-translation method', which had been in use since the late eighteenth century, but was fully codified in the nineteenth century by Karl Plötz (1819–1881), cited in Kelly (1969: 53, 220). A lesson would typically have one or two new grammar rules, a list of vocabulary items and some practice examples to translate from L1 into L2 or vice versa. The approach was originally reformist in nature, attempting to make language learning easier through the use of example sentences instead of whole texts (Howatt, 1984: 136). However, the method grew into a very controlled system, with a heavy emphasis on accuracy and explicit grammar rules, many of which were quite obscure. The content focused on reading and writing literary materials, which highlighted the archaic vocabulary found in the classics.

As the method became increasingly pedantic, a new pedagogical direction was needed. One of the main problems with Grammar-translation was that it focused on the ability to 'analyse' language, and not the ability to 'use' it. In addition, the emphasis on reading and writing did little to promote an ability to communicate orally in the target language. By the beginning of the twentieth century, new use-based ideas had coalesced into what became known as the 'Direct method'. This emphasized exposure to oral language, with listening and speaking as the primary skills. Meaning was related directly to the target language, without the step of translation, while explicit grammar teaching was also downplayed. It imitated how a mother tongue is learnt naturally, with listening first, then speaking and only later reading and writing. The focus was squarely on use of the second language, with stronger proponents banishing all use of the L1 in the classroom. The Direct method had its own problems, however. It required teachers to be highly proficient in the target language, which was not always possible. Also, it mimicked L1 learning, but did not take into account the differences between L1 and L2 acquisition. One key difference is that L1 learners have abundant exposure to the target language, which the Direct method could not hope to match. *more input*

In the UK, Michael West was interested in increasing learners' exposure to language through reading. His 'Reading method' attempted to make this possible by promoting reading skills through vocabulary management. To improve the readability of his textbooks, he 'substituted low-frequency "literary" words such as *isle, nought,* and *ere* with more frequent items such as *island, nothing,* and *before*' (Schmitt, 2000: 17). He also controlled the number of new words which could appear in any text. These steps had the effect of significantly reducing the lexical load for readers. This focus on vocabulary management was part of a greater approach called the 'Vocabulary Control Movement', which eventually resulted in a book called the *General Service List of English Words* (West, 1953), which listed the most useful 2000 words in English. (*See* Chapter 3, *Vocabulary*, for more on frequency, the percentage of words known in a text and readability.) The three methods, Grammar-translation, the Direct method and the Reading method, continued to hold sway until World War II.

During the war, the weaknesses of all of the above approaches became obvious, as the American military found itself short of people who were conversationally fluent in foreign languages. It needed a way of training soldiers in oral and aural skills quickly. American structural linguists stepped into the gap and developed a programme which borrowed from the Direct method, especially its emphasis on listening and speaking. It drew its rationale from the dominant psychological theory of the time, Behaviourism, that essentially said that language learning was a result of habit formation. Thus the method included activities which were believed to reinforce 'good' language habits, such as close attention to pronunciation, intensive oral drilling, a focus on sentence patterns and memorization. In short, students were expected to learn through drills rather than through an analysis of the target language. The students who went through this 'Army method' were mostly mature and highly motivated, and their success was dramatic. This success meant that the method naturally continued on after the war, and it came to be known as 'Audiolingualism'.

Chomsky's (1959) attack on the behaviourist underpinnings of structural linguistics in the late 1950s proved decisive, and its associated pedagogical approach – audiolingualism – began to fall out of favour. Supplanting the behaviourist idea of habit-formation, language was now seen as governed by cognitive factors, in particular a set of abstract rules which were assumed to be innate. Chomsky (1959) suggested that children form hypotheses about their language that they tested out in practice. Some would naturally be incorrect, but Chomsky and his followers argued that children do not receive enough negative feedback from other people about these inappropriate language forms (negative evidence) to be able to discard them. Thus, some other mechanism must constrain the type of hypotheses generated. Chomsky (1959) posited that children are born with an understanding of the way languages work, which was referred to as 'Universal Grammar'. They would know the underlying *principles* of language (for example, languages usually have pronouns) and their *parameters* (some languages allow these pronouns to be dropped when in the subject position). Thus, children would need only enough exposure to a language to determine whether their L1 allowed the deletion of pronouns (+pro drop, for example, Japanese) or not (–pro drop, for example, English). This parameter-setting would require much less exposure than a habit-formation route, and so appeared a more convincing argument for how children learned language so quickly. The flurry of research inspired by Chomsky's ideas did much to stimulate the development of the field of second language acquisition and its psychological counterpart, psycholinguistics.

In the early 1970s, Hymes (1972) added the concept of 'communicative competence', which emphasized that language competence consists of more than just being able to 'form grammatically correct sentences but also to know when and where to use these sentences and to whom' (Richards, Platt and Weber, 1985: 49). This helped to swing the focus from language 'correctness' (accuracy) to how suitable any use of language was for a particular context (appropriacy). At the same time, Halliday's (1973) systemic-functional grammar was offering an alternative to Chomsky's approach, in which language was seen not as something exclusively internal to a learner, but rather as a means of functioning in society. Halliday (1973) identified three types of function:

- *ideational* (telling people facts or experiences)
- *interpersonal* (maintaining personal relationships with people)
- *textual* (expressing the connections and organization within a text, for example, clarifying, summarizing, signalling the beginning and end of an argument).

This approach to language highlighted its communicative and dynamic nature. These and other factors pushed the field towards a more 'communicative' type of pedagogy. In the mid-1970s, a Council of Europe project (van Ek, 1976) attempted to create a Europe-wide language teaching system which was based on a survey of L2 learners' needs (*needs analysis*) and was 'based on semantic categories related to those needs, including the relevant concepts (*notions*) and uses of language (*functions*)' (Howatt, 1999: 624). The revised 1998 version (van Ek and Trim: 27) lists six broad categories of language function:

- imparting and seeking factual information
- expressing and finding out attitudes
- getting things done (suasion)
- socializing
- structuring discourse
- communication repair.

In addition, eight general categories of notions were listed, which are shown here with representative examples of their sub-classes:

- existential (existence, presence, availability)
- spatial (location, distance, motion, size)
- temporal (indications of time, duration, sequence)
- quantitative (number, quantity, degree)
- qualitative (shape, colour, age, physical condition)
- mental (reflection, expression of ideas)
- relational (ownership, logical relations, effect)
- deixis (anaphoric and non-anaphoric proforms, articles).

The materials from this project were influential (for example, *Threshold Level English*), and textbooks based on a notional–functional syllabus became widespread. In the early 1980s, a theory of acquisition promoted by Krashen (1982) focused attention on the role of input. Krashen's 'Monitor theory' posited that a second language was mainly unconsciously acquired through exposure to 'comprehensible input' rather than being learnt through explicit exercises, that it required a focus on meaning rather than form and that a learner's emotional state can affect this acquisition ('affective filter'). The pedagogical implications of this theory were that classrooms should supply a rich source of language exposure that was meaning-based and understandable, always including some elements just beyond the current level of learners' ability (*i+1*).

The methodology which developed from these factors emphasized the use of language for meaningful communication – communicative language teaching (CLT) (Littlewood, 1981). The focus was on learners' message and fluency rather than their grammatical accuracy. It was often taught through problem-solving activities and tasks which required students to transact information, such as information gap exercises. In these, one student is given information the other does not have, with the two having to negotiate the exchange of that information. Taken further, students could be taught some non-language-related subject, such as history or politics, in the L2. The assumption was that the learners would acquire the L2 simply by using it to learn the subject matter content, without the L2 being the focus of explicit instruction. Taking the communicative approach to its logical extreme, students could be enrolled in 'immersion' programmes where they attended primary or secondary schools which taught subject matter only in the L2.

Results from this kind of immersion programme, such as those initiated in Canada but which now also exist elsewhere, showed that learners could indeed become quite fluent in an L2 through exposure without explicit instruction, and that they developed excellent receptive skills. However, they also showed that the learners continued to make certain persistent grammatical errors, even after many years of instruction. In other words, a communicative approach helped learners to become fluent, but was insufficient to ensure comparable levels of accuracy. It seems as if a certain amount of explicit instruction focusing on language form may be necessary as well. The current focus-on-form movement (for example, Doughty and Williams, 1998) is an attempt to inject well-considered explicit instruction back into language lessons without abandoning the positive features and results of the communicative approach.

Just as language pedagogy developed and advanced during this time, so did the field of language assessment. Until the 1980s, tests were evaluated according to three principal criteria:

- 'Validity' (did the test really measure what it was supposed to measure?)
- 'Reliability' (did the test perform consistently from one administration to the next?)
- 'Practicality' (was the test practical to give and mark in a particular setting?).

These criteria focused very much on the test itself, and took little notice of the effects it might have on the people ('stakeholders') involved with it. Messick (1989) changed this with a seminal paper which argued that tests could not be considered 'valid' or 'not valid' in a black and white manner by focusing only on test-internal factors; rather, one needed to argue for the validity of a test by considering a variety of factors: for what kind of examinee was the test suitable; what reasonable inferences could be derived from the scores?; how did the test method affect the scores?; what kind of positive or negative effect ('washback') might the test have on stakeholders? and many others. Now, tests are seen in the context of a complete assessment environment, which includes stakeholders (for example, examinees, raters, administrators, government officials), test conditions (for example, can everyone hear the tape recorder clearly), the intended use of the scores (for example, will they be used for relatively 'high-stakes' purposes (university admission) versus relatively 'low stakes' purposes (a classroom quiz)) and characteristics of the test itself (Are the instructions clear? What kind of tasks does the test employ?). Within this framework, tests are generally seen as being suitable for particular purposes and particular sets of learners, rather than 'one size fits all'. Since every classroom and group of learners is somewhat different, there has been a move towards exploring the value of alternative types of assessment which can be individualized to suit particular situations. These include structured observation, progress grids, portfolios, learning journals, project work, peer-assessment and self-assessment. (*See* Chapter 15, *Assessment*, for more on these issues.)

Technology was advancing throughout the century, but the advent of powerful and affordable personal computers probably has had the greatest impact on applied linguistics. Of course, language laboratories had utilized technology since the mid- to late-1940s, but the relatively recent development of very capable personal computers made quite sophisticated language programs available to the individual user, whether learner, teacher or researcher. Pedagogically, this opened the door to 'computer-assisted language learning' (CALL), where learners could work on individual computers truly at their own pace. Computer technology has also facilitated the incorporation of audio and video input into learning programs on a scale previously unimaginable. The best of the current programs are starting to become inter-active, tailoring their input and tasks to individual learners' progress, although it must be said that much remains to be done in this area. With new learning programs arriving regularly, today CALL is one of the more dynamic areas in applied linguistics.

Computing technology also made it possible to analyse large databases of language, called 'corpora'. Evidence from corpora have provided numerous insights into the workings of language (Egbert and Hanson-Smith, 1999; *see also* Chapter 6, *Corpus Linguistics*). Perhaps the most important revelation is the vast amount of lexical patterning which exists; in fact, it is so great that some scholars have suggested that it is more important than grammar in con-tributing to the organization of language (Sinclair, 1996). Corpora are now a key tool in lexicography, and have been consulted in the development of most current learner dictionaries. Evidence from corpora of spoken discourse has also highlighted the differences between spoken and written discourse (McCarthy and Carter, 1997). Happily, corpora have now made truly descrip-tive grammars possible, with writers having numerous authentic examples of many grammatical structures at their fingertips. The best studies in this area can even distinguish varying language usage between different registers, for example written fiction versus academic prose (Biber, Johansson, Leech, Conrad and Finegan, 1999). It is likely that evidence from corpus linguistics will continue to have a major influence on applied linguistic thinking well into the new millennium.

Incorporating Social/Cultural and Contextual Elements into Applied Linguistics

Before the early part of the twentieth century, the mind and mental attributes such as language were largely studied as part of philosophy, but some scholars held a desire to study the mind independently of the philosophical paradigm. One way to break away from philosophy was to study the mind on a scientific basis, using empirical evidence. This led to the genesis of the modern field of psychology. Before this, the study of the mind and individual and the study of social influences were not separated. But Wundt (1877), in his early pioneering work, split psychology into two strands: a physiological psychology which concentrated on 'elementary' functions, such as sensory experience, and a 'higher' psychology which included processes such as 'deliberate remembering, reasoning, and language' (Cole, 1996: 28). This higher psychology necessarily included elements of human interaction and knowledge gained from society, and became known as 'Völkerpsychologie' ('social psychology'). The two strands were complementary; however, they required different research methods: the 'physiological' strand would largely rely on experimental research (often in the laboratory), whereas social psychology required 'descriptive' methods, such as ethnography and interview, which could capture the social elements.

Wundt (1877) argued that both approaches were essential and interrelated, but the division between strands became mutually exclusive to a great degree, largely because of the growing influence of experimental science in psychology. In the attempts to make psychology 'scientific', only elements which could be easily quantified were eventually accepted into the orthodoxy of the field. Social influences could not be counted easily and so effectively were excluded. In essence, scholars wanted to look at the mind as an 'object' uncontaminated by outside factors which were messy and could not be conveniently controlled. Social issues were not totally ignored, but they went on to influence other fields, such as sociology and anthropology, much more than psychology.

This separation of individual and society soon became firmly entrenched. The mid-twentieth century domination of behaviourism as the overriding psychological paradigm (at least in English-speaking countries) meant that only stimuli (that is, teaching input) and reactions (student responses) which could be observed were considered worthy of discussion in the area of psychology. In linguistics, a similar dichotomy occurred when Saussure (1857–1913; *see* Saussure, 1966) split language ('langue') from the actual use of language ('parole'). Chomsky's (1965) ideas had a similar effect as they distinguished what was happening inside the learner ('language competence') from what was observable outside the person ('language performance').

There were some voices speaking out against these divisions, such as Vygotsky (1896–1934; *see* Vygotsky, 1987), but political and academic factors kept their influence in check until the latter part of the twentieth century. In the late 1960s, Labov (1970) began exploring how social factors influence L1 language use, and Tarone (1979) and others later did the same for L2 usage. The study of the interface of social factors and language use eventually developed into the field of 'sociolinguistics'. Similarly, it was acknowledged that the context in which language is used (for example, for what purpose, the relative power relationship between interlocutors) also affects the language of communication. The study of these factors blossomed in the area of 'pragmatics'. Together, these fields, along with the closely related area of 'discourse analysis', have shown that social and contextual influences cannot be divorced from individual learners when language learning and use are studied.

This realization has not yet been fully integrated into second language acquisition models, partially because of the continuing dominance of the Chomskyan Universal Grammar perspective. However, alternative views of language acquisition are starting to surface (for example, connectionist and exemplar-based models in which grammatical structures are learnt by repeated exposure to recurring patterns in language, *see* Ellis, 1998, in press (a), in press (b)), and in some cases these models are better able to embrace social and contextual influences than approaches focusing on innate knowledge. Also, the availability of vast amounts of corpus evidence now encourages the direct study of both native speaker and learner output (Chomsky's 'performance') rather than relying on indirect evidence of what a person intuitively 'knows' (Chomsky's 'competence').

In addition, a new view of cognition, called 'sociocultural theory', is starting to influence thinking in applied linguistics. It emphasizes individual–social integration by focusing on the necessary and dialectic relationship between the sociocultural endowment (the '*inter*'-personal interface between a person and his or her environment) and the biological endowment (the '*intra*'-personal mechanisms and processes belonging to that person), out of which emerges the individual. Sociocultural theory suggests that in order to understand the human mind, one must look at these two endowments in an integrated manner, as considering either one individually will inevitably result in an incomplete, and thus inaccurate, representation. For it is only through social interaction with others that humans develop their language and cognition. Furthermore, most language interaction is co-constructed with others and not the product of one individual acting alone. In many ways, sociocultural theory may be seen as re-integrating individual and social factors.

Themes to Watch For in this Book

This book includes a broad selection of the major applied linguistics areas. But this diversity does not mean that each area can be isolated and dealt with on its own. On the contrary, true understanding of any individual area can only be gained by understanding others which are related. For example, to truly understand the information in Chapter 3, *Vocabulary*, one must take on board the insights given in Chapter 6, *Corpus Linguistics*. In fact, if we look deeply enough, nearly all of the areas are related to each other in some way. This being the case, there are several themes that run through the various chapters. These underlying currents are important because they add coherence to the overall discussion and represent an entry point to understanding and critiquing the ideas in this book.

The Interrelationship of the Areas of Applied Linguistics

There is a story from India about the five blind men of Hindustan who went out to learn about an elephant. They all felt different parts of the elephant's body and came to very different conclusions about what an elephant is like. The man who felt the trunk thought an elephant was like a snake, the one who felt a leg thought elephants were like a tree, the one who felt the ear thought elephants were like a fan, and so on. Similarly, language is a big, complex subject and we are nowhere near to being able to comprehend it in its entirety. The best any person can do at the moment is to study a limited number of elements of language, language use and language learning, and try to understand those elements in detail. Although we strive to connect this understanding with insights from other areas in the applied linguistics field, we can only be partially successful. Thus we end up with scholars becoming specialists in areas of applied linguistics, but with no single person able to master the whole field. (That is why this is an edited volume and not a book written by a single author.) This is inevitable and happens in every field, but it does mean that applied linguistics is compartmentalized to some extent. We must be aware of this and realize that this compartmentalization is an expedient which enables us to get around our cognitive limitations as human beings; it is not the way language works in the real world. Language, language learning and language use are a seamless whole and all of the various elements interact with each other in complex ways. Each chapter in this book looks at one area of specialization, but when reading them, it is useful to remember that they make up only one part of the larger 'complete elephant'.

The Move from Discrete to more Holistic and Integrative Perspectives

Despite the above-mentioned caveat about compartmentalization, we are getting better at being able to grasp larger and larger bits of the language elephant. Up until the middle of the last century, language was viewed in very discrete terms: it was made up of grammar, phonology and vocabulary, each of which could be separately identified and described. (In fact, phonetics was the first area within linguistics to become well-developed [late nineteenth century] and the Reform Movement in language teaching, led by phoneticians, was very influential in encouraging a focus on the spoken language.) The last 30 years have seen a move towards viewing language in much more integrative and holistic terms. We now know that language use is not just a product of a number of individual language 'knowledge bits' which reside completely within 'interlocutors' (language users); it is also profoundly affected by a number of other factors, such as the social context (who you are communicating with and for what purpose), the degree of involvement and interaction, the mode of communication (written versus spoken) and time constraints. Taking these and other factors into account gives us a much richer and more accurate account of the way language is actually used and leads to a better description of the knowledge and skills which make up language proficiency. A trend worth watching for in this book is how the various areas of applied linguistics now embrace integrative perspectives which acknowledge the complex interplay of numerous factors.

Lexico-grammar and Preformulated Expressions

The areas of vocabulary and grammar provide a good example of this new integrative approach. Traditionally, vocabulary was viewed as individual words which could be taught and used in isolation. With grammar being highlighted in most theories and pedagogical methodologies, vocabulary items were seen merely as 'slot fillers' necessary to fill out syntactic structures. This conception saw vocabulary and grammar as two discrete entities which could be taught and learnt separately. This view is starting to change and one of the most interesting developments in applied linguistics today is the realization that vocabulary and grammar are not necessarily separate things, but may be viewed as two elements of a single language system referred to as 'lexico-grammar' (Halliday, 1978). This term acknowledges that much of the systematicity in language comes from lexical choices and the grammatical behaviour of those choices. For example, you can use the word *plain* in many ways and in many grammatical constructions, but once you choose the collocation *made it plain* you are more or less constrained to using the following structure:

SOMEONE/SOMETHING *made it plain that* SOMETHING AS YET UNREALIZED
(often with authority) WAS INTENDED OR DESIRED
(Schmitt, 2000: 189)

This structure should not be viewed in terms of being first generated with grammar, and then the words simply slotted into the blanks. Rather, this structure is likely to reside in memory as a sequence which is already formed, that is, it is a 'preformulated expression'. Since it is preformed and 'ready to go', it should take less cognitive energy to produce than sequences which have to be created from scratch (Pawley and Syder, 1983). Evidence from corpora show that much of language is made up of 'multi-word units', many of which are likely to be preformulated in the mind (*see* Moon, 1997). Because we now believe that a great deal of language is stored in peoples' minds as these 'chunks', it makes little sense to attempt to analyse those chunks as if they were generated online according to grammar rules. This insight is forcing a reappraisal of both how we consider language itself and how it is processed.

Bringing the Language Learner into the Discussion

Previously, much of the discussion about language learning focused on the best techniques and materials for teaching. In other words, it had a focus on the teacher. There seemed to be an unexpressed view that the learner was somehow a 'container' into which language knowledge could be poured. This view fitted well with teacher-fronted classes and behaviourist theories which suggested learning was merely the result of practice and conditioning. However, in the early 1970s, it was realized that learners are active participants in the learning process and should be allowed to take partial responsibility for their own learning. This led to interest in the various ways in which individual learners were different from one another and how that might affect their learning. It also led to the development of the area of 'learner strategies'. If learners were, in fact, active participants then it followed that what these learners did would make a difference in the quality and speed of their learning. Studies were carried out to find out what behaviours differentiated 'good' from 'poor' learners (Naiman, Fröhlich, Stern and Todesco, 1978). From these studies, lists of learning strategies which good learners used were developed and it was suggested that all learners could benefit from training in these strategies. Of course, nothing in applied linguistics is so straightforward, and it was eventually discovered that the correspondence between strategy training and use, and higher language achievement was less direct than previously assumed. It is clear that effective strategy use can facilitate language learning (Oxford, 1990), but it is still an open question as to how to best train learners to use strategies, or indeed whether strategy training has any effectiveness. Looking beyond learner strategies, the broader area of 'learner autonomy' (Littlewood, 1996; Wenden, 1991) also includes various self-learning and self-direction aspects. Insights from this area are particularly important to develop in learners, as they can help to ensure continued learning after classroom instruction ends. Overall, acknowledgement of the centrality of the learner has grown stronger in applied linguistics, and is reflected in most chapters. However, these issues will discussed in detail in Chapter 10, *Focus on the Language Learner: Motivation, Styles and Strategies*.

New Perspectives on Teaching the Four Skills

The teaching of the four language skills (*see* Chapter 11, *Listening*, Chapter 12, *Speaking and Pronunciation*, Chapter 13, *Reading*, and Chapter 14, *Writing*) has long been an important concern in second language pedagogy. Language use inevitably involves one or more of the four skills, thus this text devotes a chapter to each language skill. Although it is useful to give attention to the unique sub-skills and strategies associated with each skill, it is also important to consider the overlaps in mode (oral versus written) and process (receptive versus productive):

	Oral	Written
Receptive	LISTENING	READING
Productive	SPEAKING	WRITING

Furthermore, each skill may usefully be described in terms of the top-down and bottom-up processing required. Listeners and readers work to decode and construct meanings and messages, whereas speakers and writers use language resources to encode and express meanings and messages. These meanings and messages occur at the level of text or discourse; thus, discourse analysis is highly relevant to understanding the four skills. Top-down processing utilizes shared knowledge, pragmatic knowledge and contextual information to achieve an appropriate interpretation or realization of textual meanings and messages. Bottom-up processing depends on language resources – lexico-grammar and phonology (pronunciation) or orthography – as aids to the accurate decoding or interpretation, or encoding or realization, of meaningful text.

Typically, more than one language skill is involved in any communicative activity (for example, we take turns at listening and speaking in conversation, we write notes while listening to a lecture, we read a passage carefully in order to write a summary, etc.). If teachers focus on one skill for purposes of pedagogy and practice, that is, to improve learners' use of that skill, the ultimate goal should always be to move from such practice toward the types of integrated skill use that the learners are likely to need when using the target language for communication.

The Lack of 'Black and White' Answers

Because language is created and processed both between interlocutors and within the human mind, much of what is of interest in applied linguistics is hidden from direct view and study. We cannot yet look into the human brain and directly observe language, which means that most research has to rely on indirect evidence observable through language processing and use. The results of such indirect evidence needs to be interpreted, and usually more than one interpretation is possible. This makes it difficult to say much with complete certainty about language learning and use. You will notice that throughout the book there are a number of theories and hypotheses and that different scholars hold different positions on key issues. Until 'neurolinguistics' allows us to directly track language in a physiological manner (it is already taking its first steps in this direction, *see* Schumann, 1988; Brown and Hagoort, 1999), a degree of controversy and multiplicity of views seems inevitable. It thus remains the responsibility of researchers, teachers and you the reader to evaluate the various proposed positions and decide which makes the most sense. Readers looking for easy, tidy and absolute answers are probably working in the wrong field.

Conclusion

From the discussion in this overview, it should be obvious that our field's views on language, language learning and language use are not static, but are constantly evolving. At the point in time when you read this book, they will still be changing. Thus, you should consider the ideas in this book (and any book) critically and remain open to future directions in the field.

Further Reading

- Howatt, A.P.R. (1984) *A History of English Language Teaching*. Oxford: Oxford University Press.
- Kelly, L.G. (1969) *25 Centuries of Language Teaching*. Rowley, MA: Newbury House.

Two books which give a historical background to the key applied linguistics area of second language teaching and learning (focusing primarily on English as a second language).

- Larsen-Freeman, D. (2000) *Techniques and Principles in Language Teaching* (second edition). New York: Oxford University Press. A very accessible book which describes and gives examples of the various major teaching methodologies used in the twentieth century.

- Spolsky, B. (ed.) (1999) *Concise Encyclopedia of Educational Linguistics*. Amsterdam: Elsevier.
- Carter, R., Nunan, D. (eds) (2001) *The Cambridge Guide to Teaching English to Speakers of Other Languages*. Cambridge: Cambridge University Press.

The above two reference books cover a more comprehensive range of subjects than the present one, although each area is generally covered in less depth. These are principally meant as teacher reference volumes where teachers can look up a range of topics and obtain a brief overview of that subject.

- Celce-Murcia, M. (ed.) (2001) *Teaching English as a Second or Foreign Language* (third edition). Boston, MA: Heinle & Heinle. A comprehensive introductory volume intended for preservice teachers focusing on teaching language skills and pedagogical issues.
- Crystal, D. (1987) *The Cambridge Encyclopedia of Language*. Cambridge: Cambridge University Press. A lively table-top reference book which gives interesting snippets on a wide variety of language issues, the vast majority of them focusing on the L1 (but including an L2 section).

I DESCRIPTION OF LANGUAGE AND LANGUAGE USE

2

Grammar

Jeanette DeCarrico
Portland State University

Diane Larsen-Freeman
School for International Training

Introduction: Grammar and Grammars

When it comes to definitions of grammar, confusion abounds. One problem is that the word 'grammar' means different things to different people. For many, the term suggests a list of do's and don't's, rules that tell us we should say *It is I*, not *It is me*, that we should not say *ain't*, or that we should avoid ending a sentence with a preposition. For others, the term may refer to the rules of grammar found mainly in written language, for example, rules that label sentence fragments as incorrect even though they are often found in spoken language (for example, '*Working on a term paper*' as a response to the question '*What are you doing?*'), or that admonish us not to begin sentences with *and* or *but*, though again, this usage is common in spoken English. For still others, it may simply mean an objective description of the structures of language, with no comment concerning correct versus incorrect forms.

Grammars with rules that make distinctions between correct and incorrect forms are defined as 'prescriptive' grammars. They tell us how we ought to speak, as in *It is I*, and how we ought not to speak, as in *It is me*, or *He ain't home*. This approach codifies certain distinctions between standard and non-standard varieties, and often makes overt value judgements by referring to the standard varieties as correct, or 'good' English and the non-standard as incorrect, or 'bad' English.

Grammars that do not make these distinctions and that aim to describe language as it is actually used are called 'descriptive' grammars. The rules are more like a blueprint for building well-formed structures, and they represent speakers' unconscious knowledge, or 'mental grammar' of the language. Taking this unconscious knowledge into account, this approach focuses on describing how native speakers actually do speak and does not prescribe how they ought to speak. No value judgements are made, but rather, the value-neutral terms 'grammatical' and 'ungrammatical' are used to distinguish between patterns that are well-formed, possible sentences or phrases in the language and those that are not. For example, *The cow ate the corn* is a grammatical sentence in English, but *Ate the corn the cow* is ungrammatical. (An asterisk indicates a form that is ungrammatical or inappropriate.) Grammar in this sense consists of rules of syntax, which specify how words and phrases combine to form sentences, and rules of morphology, which specify how word forms are constructed (for example, present and past tense distinctions: *love*, *loved*; number distinctions: *word*, *words*) and so on. For linguists, a descriptive grammar may also be a more detailed look at language, including not only syntax and morphology but also phonetics, phonology, semantics and lexis (that is, vocabulary).

For applied linguists, the focus is more on 'pedagogical grammar', the type of grammar designed for the needs of second-language students and teachers. Although teaching grammar in a second language does involve some of the prescriptive rules for the standard varieties, a pedagogical grammar resembles a descriptive grammar much more than a prescriptive one, especially in terms of the range of structures covered (Odlin, 1994). And while certain linguistic grammars tend to be narrowly focused, pedagogical grammars are typically more eclectic, drawing on insights from formal and functional grammars (*see below*), as well as work on corpus linguistics, discourse analysis and pragmatics, addressed in other chapters in this volume. For after all, applied linguists must be concerned that students not only can produce grammatical structures that are formally accurate; students must be able to use them meaningfully and appropriately as well.

Issues when Describing Grammar

A descriptive approach to grammar may seem a simple matter, but in practice it is somewhat more complicated than it may first appear. The outcome will be different depending on which parts of the grammar are included and on what the focus of the description is.

Which Rules to Describe

For one thing, we tend to expect grammars to state rules in terms of general statements, to describe how structures behave in a predictable, rule-governed way. Yet a moment's reflection tells us that some rules apply more consistently than others. For example, whereas the ordering rule for auxiliaries is invariant (modal auxiliaries such as *would*, *might* and so on, always precede the primary auxiliaries *have* or *be*, as in, *would have tried*, *might be trying* but not **have would tried*, **be might trying*), the subject–verb agreement rule admits exceptions (verbs take the suffix *-s* if their subject is third person singular, as in *He leaves*, but there are exceptions such as subjunctive forms, *I insist that he leave now*). Plural titles of books, plays, films, etc. are also sometimes exceptions to the subject–verb agreement rule (Angela's Ashes *is a novel about growing up in an impoverished Irish family*).

As these examples indicate, grammar must include both rules that are invariant and rules that admit variations. Notice that these examples fall under well-established categories of acceptable, standard English. But what about different varieties? Some descriptive grammars may include only standard varieties as spoken and written on formal occasions by educated speakers of the language, whereas others may focus more on standard forms but also include certain non-standard, or 'informal' variants. Grammars intended for use by students of writing, for instance, typically include only those forms acceptable in formal writing. Pedagogical grammars, on the other hand, may focus on standard formal patterns but also include a number of informal alternatives, with explanations of the situations in which each is acceptable, for example, class assignments, job interviews and the like typically require formal writing or speaking (*How do you do?*, *I would like to enquire about X*), whereas casual conversation with friends tends towards informal expressions (*Hi there, What's up?*).

These examples illustrate that issues of what to include can often be decided on the basis of the intended audience. Some issues, though, are much more crucial, depending on a particular view of what grammar is and on what type of description accords with that particular view. These include formal versus functional approaches to grammatical description, considerations of type versus token, sentence versus discourse grammar and the role of spoken versus written forms. Choices based on these issues have far-reaching implications, not only for the particular framework of the grammar itself but also for applications that influence the design of pedagogical grammars, of syllabuses and of teaching approaches. The remainder of this section addresses these issues in more detail.

Form and Function

Models of grammar differ greatly, depending on whether they are formal grammars or functional grammars. Formal grammar is concerned with the forms themselves and with how they operate within the overall system of grammar. The most influential formal grammar in the latter half of the twentieth century has been the generative (transformational) theory of grammar (Chomsky, 1957, 1965), the general principles of which are still the basis for Chomsky's own more recent versions (1992) and for dozens of other competing variants developed within some version of the generative framework. The focus is primarily syntax and morphology.

Generative theory is based on a rationalist approach, the central assumption being that language is represented as a speaker's mental grammar, a set of abstract rules for generating grammatical sentences. This mental grammar, or internalized, unconscious knowledge of the system of rules is termed 'competence'. The rules generate the syntactic structure and lexical items from appropriate grammatical categories (noun, verb, adjective, etc.) are selected to fill in the corresponding grammatical slots in the syntactic frame of the sentence. The interests of generative linguists focus mainly on rule-governed behaviour and on the grammatical structure of sentences and do not include concerns for the appropriate use of language in context.

Hymes (1972), an anthropological linguist, developed a functional model that focuses more on appropriate use of language, that is, on how language functions in discourse. Although not rejecting Chomsky's model entirely, Hymes (1972) extended it and gave greater emphasis to sociolinguistic and pragmatic factors. A central concern of his model is the concept of 'communicative competence', which emphasizes language as meaningful communication, including the appropriate use of language in particular social contexts (for example, informal conversation at the dinner table versus formal conversation at the bank). For Hymes (1972), communicative competence is defined as 'the capabilities of a person', a competence which is 'dependent upon both [tacit] *knowledge* and [ability for] *use*' (Hymes, 1972: 282). In other words, it includes not only knowledge of the rules in Chomsky's sense (grammatical competence) but also the ability to use language in various contexts (pragmatic competence). For example, it includes knowing how to formulate a yes/no question (Operator–NP–VP) and knowing that only certain types (for example, *'Could you VP?'*) function as polite requests and knowing how to use them appropriately (*see also* Halliday, 1973).

In applied linguistics, the influence of these theoretical models is evident in various areas. For example, the approach to grammar as abstract linguistic descriptions is found in learners' grammars such as Quirk *et al.* (1972), a descriptive grammar that deals with abstract forms as syntactic combinations of words. On the other hand, a functional approach is evident in Leech and Svartvik (1975), a communicative grammar based on correspondences between structure and function. In this learners' grammar, each section is built around a major function of language, such as denial and affirmation, describing emotions, and presenting and focusing information.

Influence of different models of grammar can also be seen in syllabus design. Many ESL or EFL grammar texts are based on a structural syllabus design defined in formal terms, with lexical items and grammatical patterns presented according to structural categories such as nouns and noun phrases, verbs and verb phrases, verb tense and aspect, and clause and sentence types. In contrast, notional syllabuses are defined in functional terms such as the speech acts of requesting, *'Could you VP?'*; offering, *'Would you like X?'* and so on; these notional syllabuses developed at a time when linguistic interest had begun to shift to the communicative properties of language (Widdowson, 1979).

Various teaching approaches also draw on insights from these differing approaches to grammar. Approaches influenced by formal theories such as generative grammar tend to view language learning as rule acquisition and, therefore, focus on formalized rules of grammar. Those that evolved from functional considerations, known as communicative language teaching, view language as communication and tend to promote fluency over accuracy, consequently shifting the focus from sentence-level forms to discourse-level functions such as requests, greetings, apologies and the like.

More recently, some applied linguists have argued for an approach that draws not on one or the other, but on both (Rutherford and Sharwood Smith, 1988; Widdowson, 1989). Widdowson (1989) is particularly insistent that it is a mistake to concentrate solely on functional considerations while ignoring form altogether. He observes, for instance, that just as approaches that rely too heavily on achievement of rules of grammar often lead to dissociation from any consideration of appropriateness, so approaches which rely too heavily on an ability to use language appropriately can lead to a lack of necessary grammatical knowledge and of the ability to compose or decompose sentences with reference to it. There is, he says, 'evidence that excessive zeal for communicative language teaching can lead to just such a state of affairs' (Widdowson, 1989: 131). What is needed is an approach that provides a middle ground in that it neglects neither.

Celce-Murcia and Larsen-Freeman (1999) also give strong support to the view that, in teaching, one approach should not be taken to the exclusion of others. These authors aim for a middle ground that gives prominence not only to both form and function but to meaning as well. In keeping with an attempt to view grammar from a communicative perspective, they recognize that grammar is not merely a collection of forms 'but rather involves the three dimensions of what linguists refer to as (morpho)syntax, semantics, and pragmatics' (Celce-Murcia and Larsen-Freeman, 1999: 4). They illustrate the importance of all three dimensions by means of a pie chart divided into equal parts labelled 'Form', 'Meaning' and 'Use' (Figure 2.1). They feel this chart is

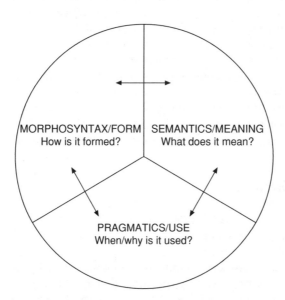

Figure 2.1 Interconnected dimensions of grammar.

useful as a conceptual framework for teaching grammar as it serves as a reminder that learners need to achieve a certain degree of formal accuracy, but they also need to use the structures meaningfully and appropriately as well (*see also* Larsen-Freeman, 1991a).

Type versus Token

In terms of descriptive grammars, there still remain questions about what it is, exactly, that should be described. Descriptions of language will also have different outcomes depending on whether they account for types of linguistic element in the abstract, or for tokens of linguistic element as they actually occur in contexts of use. Descriptions that deal with forms in the abstract describe a range of category types, but those that deal with actual tokens (instances) of language use reveal more than category types: they also reveal the relative frequency of forms and their habitual co-occurrence in different contexts. Whereas a type description might present a broad array of structures and give each equal weight, a token description 'might well reveal that some of these were of rare occurrence, or restricted to a realization through a limited range of lexical items, almost exclusively confined to certain contexts, or associated with certain meanings' (Widdowson, 1990: 75).

With the development of computers and computer analysis of language, token descriptions are now possible on a massive scale, and such descriptions have revolutionalized the way we view language (*see* Chapter 6, *Corpus Linguistics*). A well-known example is the COBUILD Bank of English Corpus, which contains more than 300 million words (mostly from written texts). Sinclair (1985) notes that type descriptions lacking attested data do not provide an adequate source of reference for language teaching. Instead, he believes that language for pedagogical purposes should be a projection of what actually occurs as recorded by the computer analysis of text.

Projects based on analyses of this and other corpus studies have produced various dictionaries and grammars, including the *Collins COBUILD English Grammar* (1990), of which John Sinclair is the Editor-in-Chief. This grammar attempts to make statements about English that are accurate, as attested by the corpus. It does so by picking out the main patterns and describing the important correspondences between these structures and their functions in discourse.

Discourse Grammar

Corpus studies have also led to an increased interest in analyses of 'discourse grammar', that is, analyses of the functional roles of grammatical structures in discourse.

Speakers and writers make grammatical choices that depend on contextual features and how they wish to position themselves in the world (Larsen-Freeman, forthcoming). In the tense–aspect system, for example, the past perfect tense–aspect combination is often used, not to indicate the first of two past events but to give a reason or justification for the main events of the narrative. These events are not the main events themselves but, rather, are felt to be an essential background to what happened (*see* McCarthy and Carter, 1994; Hughes and McCarthy, 1998). The italicized structure in the following excerpt, from an illustration given by Hughes and McCarthy (1998), occurs in a conversation between two young women who are talking about mutual friends from their days together at Brunel University.

> Speaker 1: Got on better with Glynbob I think and John Bish let me and Trudie sleep in his bed last time we went up to Brunel or the one time when we stayed in Old Windsor with them cos erm *Ben had given us his room cos he'd gone away for the weekend* and erm it was me and Trudie just in Ben's room and John Doughty had a double bed so he, John Bish had a double bed so he offered us this double bed between us and then slept in Ben's room cos *Ben and PQ had gone away* for the weekend. (Hughes and McCarthy, 1998: 270)

Hughes and McCarthy (1998) note that the italicized past perfects seem to give a reason or justification for the main events. In a similar vein, Celce-Murcia (1998) argues that the vast majority of grammatical choices that writers make represent 'rules' that are discourse-sensitive, including position of adverbials, passive versus active voice, indirect object alternation, pronominalization across independent clauses, article/determiner selection, use of existential *there* and tense–aspect–modality choice. The ordering of adverbial clauses, for instance, is not simply random. Rather, it has been found that sentence-initial adverbial clauses serve an important discourse-organizing role by linking up information in the main clause with information in the previous discourse; sentence-final clauses, in contrast, generally only expand the local main clause (Thompson, 1985; DeCarrico, 2000). The following example, from DeCarrico (2000), illustrates this point. It is an excerpt from a description of the painter Winslow Homer.

> Thoreau had called the seacoast a 'wild rank place . . . with no flattery in it.' Homer, in his later years, consciously cultivated a briney persona that matched [the seacoast] roughness. *When he was not communing with the roaring sea from his studio, on Prout's Neck, Maine*, he was off in the Adirondacks with his brother, Charles, angling for trout. (DeCarrico, 2000: 194)

The first sentence establishes, as the discourse topic, the ruggedness of the seacoast and Homer's deliberate cultivation of a rugged persona to match. DeCarrico (2000) notes that, given this context, the initial placement of the when adverbial clause not only functions within the sentence to indicate a time relation between the events within the two clauses themselves, but it also serves as a discourse link between the previously established topic, that of the wild seacoast and the pursuit of a briny persona, and the idea of being off in the

Adirondacks angling for trout. If normal word order had been used, with the adverbial clause in final position, the linkage with the previous discourse would be much less clear, if not entirely lost.

Spoken and Written Grammar

Corpus studies also reveal important distinctions between spoken and written grammar. Comparisons of spoken and written corpora have raised some basic questions concerning descriptions of grammar, such as how different types of spoken language can be classified, how features of written and spoken grammar are differently distributed and what the status of the spoken language is, as an object of study within applied linguistics (McCarthy 1998).

Carter and McCarthy (1995) believe that the differences between spoken and written grammar are especially important for pedagogical grammars, since 'descriptions that rest on the written mode or on restricted genres and registers of spoken language are likely to omit many common features of everyday informal grammar and usage' (Carter and McCarthy, 1995: 154). For instance, grammars these authors surveyed gave examples of the reporting verb in the simple past tense (*X said that* Y), and yet in their spoken corpus they found various examples of the reporting verb in past continuous (*X was saying* Y).

Limitations of Grammatical Descriptions

Previous sections have reviewed issues in describing grammar, issues that were mainly concerned with what to describe, how to describe it and how to account for differing approaches and their implications in terms of theory and pedagogy in applied linguistics. But however precise and thorough researchers may attempt to be in addressing these issues, there are certain limitations to descriptions of grammar given in isolation from all other parts of the language system.

The Interdependence of Grammar and Lexis

Regardless of the type of description or the approach taken, when we try to make general statements about grammar that neatly identify broad patterns, we are abstracting away from the overall system in ways that are somewhat artificial. One reason is that it is very difficult to isolate grammar and lexis into completely separate categories, because grammar does not exist on its own. It is interdependent with lexis, and in many cases, grammatical regularity and acceptability are conditioned by words.

A commonly cited example is the past morpheme *-ed*, which applies only where the verb happens to be 'regular', as in *walked, traded, wondered*. Irregular verbs, on the other hand, take various past forms, such as *drank* or *ate*. However, the choice of lexical item may restrict grammatical structures in other ways. The progressive aspect, for instance, is often used to indicate a temporary activity, but certain lexical items may act upon the grammar to constrain this sense of temporariness. We easily recognize that a sentence such as *Mary is taking a bath* indicates a temporary activity, whereas *Mary is taking a class* indicates an activity of extended duration.

Lexicogrammar: The Problem of Defining Boundaries

A more striking instance of the interdependence of lexis and grammar is that of prefabricated 'chunks' of language, in which the boundary between the two becomes even more blurred. Native speakers tend to use a great many expressions that are formulaic in nature (Pawley and Syder, 1983), fixed expressions that act as single lexical units used as wholes. That is, they are not composed each time from scratch by the rules of syntax. As fixed units, they appear to be intermediary between lexical words and grammatical structures.

Many of these prefabricated units, often referred to as lexical phrases, are 'multi-word lexical phenomena that exist somewhere between the traditional poles of lexicon and syntax, conventionalized form/function composites that occur more frequently and have more idiomatically determined meaning than language that is put together each time' (Nattinger and DeCarrico, 1992: 1). As form/function composites, lexical phrases differ from other formulaic language, such as idioms (*kick the bucket, hell bent for leather*), in that they have associated discourse functions. They range from completely fixed, as in *by the way*, which functions to shift a topic in discourse, to relatively fixed frames with limited slots for fillers, as in *a___ago*, used to express time relationships (for example, *a day ago, a long time ago*), to frames with slots allowing considerable variation, as in *I'm (really) (very) sorry to hear that X* (where X may be an entire clause, such as, *you flunked the test, your father died*, etc.), used to express sympathy.

The descriptive part of the problem is that these phrasal units, which are pervasive in language, cannot be adequately accounted for by models consisting of abstract rules of sentence syntax, supported by a lexicon of single word items that are inserted into abstract categories such as NP, VP, PP, etc. Although much of language is undoubtedly generated in this way, there is considerable evidence that the mind also stores and processes lexical phrases as individual wholes, including evidence from first language acquisition studies indicating that they are learned first as unanalysed chunks and, only later, analysed as to particular grammatical patterns (Peters, 1983).

At present, there is growing interest in investigating the implications of formulaic language for descriptions of grammar, in particular, implications for how we view the components of syntax and lexicon and for how the components interact with each other and with discourse level (pragmatic) concerns (DeCarrico, 1998). A closer look at the limitations of various grammatical models may help us to reexamine previous assumptions and to look for new directions in resolving issues and problems in the description of grammar. As this essential work on arriving at more comprehensive descriptive grammars continues, applied linguists must also get on with the tasks of explaining the learning, and improving the teaching, of grammar.

Learning Grammar

Over the history of applied linguistics, different theories of learning have been proposed to account for how grammar is learned. During the middle of the previous century, for instance, grammar learning was thought to take place through a process of verbal 'habit formation'. Habits were established through stimulus-response conditioning, which led to the 'overlearning' of the grammatical patterns of a language. In order to help students overcome the habits of their native language and inculcate those of the target language, teachers conducted pattern practice drills of various types: repetition, transformation, question and answer, etc. Teachers introduced little new vocabulary until the grammatical patterns were firmly established. Language use was also tightly controlled in order to prevent students making errors that could lead to the formation of bad habits, which would later prove difficult to eradicate.

With the rise of generative grammar and its view of language as a system of rules, grammar learning was seen to take place through a process of 'rule formation', which itself was brought about when students formulated, tested and revised hypotheses about grammatical structures in the target language. Thus, students were seen to play a much more active role in the classroom than they had earlier. Consistent with this perspective, students' errors were not to be feared, but rather welcomed as evidence that students were attempting to test their hypotheses and receive feedback, with which they could then revise their hypotheses. In the classroom, students were given written grammar exercises so they could induce the grammatical rules that would allow them to generate and understand novel sentences.

With the shift toward a more communicative approach to language teaching, views of grammar learning changed once again. Some held that grammar learning took place implicitly and most effectively when students' attention was not on grammar at all. In other words, they said that grammar was best learned subconsciously when students were engaged in understanding the meaning of the language to which they were introduced (Krashen and Terrell, 1989). Those that adhered to a Chomskyan universal grammar (UG) perspective felt that target language input alone or input with negative evidence (that is, evidence that a particular form is ungrammatical) might be sufficient to have learners reset the parameters of UG principles in order to reflect the differences between the native language and target language grammars (White, 1987). Others felt that explicit grammar teaching had a role; however, as we mentioned before, its role was diminished because fluency was deemed more important than grammatical accuracy.

Second language acquisition (SLA) research in both naturalistic and classroom environments has informed modern perspectives of grammar learning (*see* Chapter 7, *Second Language Acquisition*). SLA research tells us that an analysis of the language that learners use, their 'interlanguage', reveals that grammar is not acquired in a linear fashion, one structure being mastered after another. Further, with regard to any one structure, learners use a lot of intermediate forms before conforming to the target language. It can easily be seen that many learners' utterances are overgeneralizations of target language rules. For example, learners of English produce 'eated' for *ate*, thereby offering evidence for the rule-formation point of view. Even utterances that bear little resemblance to target grammatical structures can be seen as rule-governed in the sense that learners apply the same strategy consistently, such as using pre-verbal negation during early English language acquisition (for example, 'no want'), regardless of the native language of learners.

It is also clear, however, that rule formation does not account for all of grammar learning. It cannot account for the acquisition of formulaic language, for example. With the use of connectionism to simulate the way that neural networks in the brain function (*see* Chapter 7, *Second Language Acquisition*), new ways of conceptualizing grammar learning are coming to the forefront. For instance, attention is being given these days to associative learning (Ellis, 1998), in which repeated exposure to target language forms contributes to the strengthening of connections in neural network models. The models simulate rule-like grammatical behaviour even though no rules or algorithms are used in constructing the model. Instead, patterns are abstracted from the way structures are statistically distributed in massive amounts of input data.

Regardless of which type (or types as is more likely the case) of process is responsible for learning, SLA research makes clear to most researchers that some attention must be given to grammar by second language learners. However, it is also clear that the attention to form should not come in the shape of decontextualized drills or isolated grammar exercises. If it does, little transfer to use in communication results. Learners will be able to complete the exercises satisfactorily when their attention is focused on the grammar, but when their attention shifts to a more communicative interaction, the grammar will be forgotten. Further, for new forms to be incorporated into the inter-mediate language, or 'interlanguage', that learners speak, it is thought that students must first notice what it is they are to learn (Schmidt, 1990). Until they do, the target form may merely remain as part of the 'noise' in the input. Then, too, even when they are able to produce grammatical structures accurately, students still need to learn what they mean and when they are used. In other words, learning grammar does not merely entail learning form.

In fact, as we noted earlier, what needs to be learnt about grammar can be characterized by three dimensions: form, meaning and use. We have seen in Figure 2.1 that the dimensions are interconnected, but nonetheless can be described discretely. For example, in learning the rule of English subject–verb agreement discussed above, students would have to learn the form that an 's' is added to the verb stem and that the orthographic 's' may be realized in pro-nunciation as one of three allomorphs /s/, /z/ or /əz/. (The slashes indicate sounds; *see* Chapter 9, *Sociolinguistics*, and Chapter 12, *Speaking and Pronunciation*.) They would also have to learn what it means, that is, that it signals the present tense and that the subject is third person and is conceived of as a single entity. This being the case, usually, singular subjects go with singu-lar verbs and plural subjects with plural verbs. However, to show that the meaning contribution is independent from form, we only have to think of a case where there is a departure from this convention. For example, a sentence such as *'Ten miles makes for a long hike.'* shows us that even a plural subject can be conceived of as a single entity.

Finally, again, as we showed earlier, there are times when the rule of subject–verb agreement does not apply. Knowing when to use it and when not to, then, becomes essential for students to master.

The same analysis holds for a formulaic utterance. A greeting, such as *'Good afternoon'*, for instance, can be described in terms of its form, a noun preceded by an attributive adjective. Its meaning is a greeting at a particular time of day. Learning to use it would involve, for example, students' learning when to use it as opposed to learning to use a more informal greeting such as *'Hi'*.

More than likely, the dimensions of form, meaning and use are learned differently (Larsen-Freeman, 1995). It follows then that they should be taught differently.

Teaching Grammar

As mentioned above, the prevailing view today is that students must notice what it is they are to learn. Although this has traditionally been accomplished by a teacher presentation, often of an explicit rule, a greater variety of means, some far more implicit or interactive, is favoured these days. An example of an implicit means of promoting student noticing is the use of some sort of input enhancement (Sharwood Smith, 1993). It might take the form of 'input flooding', that is, increasing the number of times that students encounter the target structure in a particular text. Another possibility for enhancing the input is for the teacher to modify the text features in some fashion, such as bold-facing the target structures to make them more salient to students. An example of encouraging noticing through interaction is accomplished through guided participation (Adair-Hauck, Donato and Cumo-Johanssen, 2000), in which the teacher carefully leads students to awarenesses that they did not have before – it is neither an inductive nor deductive process, then, but rather teacher and students collaborate to produced a co-constructed grammar explanation. Awareness may also be heightened through peer interactions, as research by Donato (1994) and Swain and Lapkin (1998) has shown.

Peer interaction has also been used effectively in promoting noticing through the use of specific 'consciousness-raising' tasks (Fotos and Ellis, 1991) in which students are given data, such as a set of grammatical and ungrammatical sentences, and are encouraged to discover the grammatical generalization for themselves. For example, they may be given the following sentences in order to figure out the rule about English word order with regard to indirect and direct objects.

Sandy bought Margaret a gift.
Sandy bought a gift for Margaret.
Sandy bought it for her.
*Sandy bought her it.

Also included in the promoting noticing category would be Van Patten's (1996) input-processing tasks, in which students are guided to pay attention to particular aspects of the target language input rather than working on explicit rule learning and application. For example, if students are directed to accomplish a certain action by the teacher (for example, *Point to the window*), they have an opportunity to associate the imperative form with its use in a meaningful way.

Although not all would agree, we feel that teachers cannot be satisfied with merely promoting their students' noticing. Since language use is a skill, overt productive practice is also needed. It is important to point out, however, that the practice must be meaningful, what Larsen-Freeman (1997, 2001a) has called 'grammaring'. Grammaring may be accomplished by asking students to engage in a communicative task where it is necessary to use certain structures to complete it (Loschky and Bley-Vroman, 1993). An example might be where students have to read maps in order to give directions to someone. By so doing, they naturally would receive meaningful practice in using prepositions.

Depending on the learning challenge, that is, the grammatical dimension with which students are struggling, the nature of the productive practice activity will differ. If the students need to work on form, for instance, meaningful repetition is useful. For example, students might be asked to talk about their family members' or friends' daily routines, in which they will have ample opportunity to use the third person singular form of verbs. Meaningful repetition would also be useful for helping students learn the form of lexical phrases or other prefabricated structures. If the students' learning challenge is meaning, they will need to practise bonding form and meaning together, such as practice associating certain phrasal verbs with physical actions (*Stand up*, *Turn on the light*, *Sit down*, etc.). If the challenge is use, students will need to make a choice. For example, asking students to role-play a situation that calls for advice to be given to a supervisor versus to a friend invites those students to select the appropriate form of modal or other structure with which to offer such advice. To practise use of discourse grammar, students might be asked to choose between use of the active or passive voice after a given prompt.

Feedback is also seen to be a necessary part of grammar instruction. Feedback mechanisms span the gamut from direct correction by the teacher to recasts, in which the teacher reformulates correctly what the learner has just said erroneously, to giving students the space to correct themseleves (Aljaafreh and Lantolf, 1994; Lyster and Ranta, 1997). In a total turnaround from the view that learner errors are to be prevented, some applied linguists have even suggested that students should be encouraged to make errors by being 'led down the garden path'. For example, students might be given a rule without being told that it has exceptions. It is assumed that when students do over-generalize the rule and commit an error, the negative feedback they receive will be more successful in their acquiring the exceptions than if they were given a list of exceptions in advance (Tomasello and Herron, 1989). Of course, all of this is in vain, if learner noticing and uptake do not occur after the feedback.

Earlier we made the point that learners do not master grammatical structures one after another like beads on a string (Larsen-Freeman, 1991b). Indeed, the learning of grammar, as with the learning of many aspects of language, is a much more organic process (Rutherford, 1987; Larsen-Freeman, 2001a). This suggests that a traditional grammatical syllabus that sequences structures one after another may result in a mis-match between learnability and teachability (Pienemann, 1984). For this reason, many have recommended the use of a 'spiral syllabus', where particular structures are recycled from time to time during a course (Ellis, 1993). A helpful guideline in the construction of such a spiral syllabus might be to focus on a different dimension of a grammar structure each time it is revisited. An alternative some have recommended is not to adopt a grammatical syllabus at all, reckoning that the grammar that students need to learn will become apparent as they work on meaningful content. However, to leave the grammar to chance overlooks an important function of a 'focus on form' which is to 'fill in the gaps in the input' (Spada and Lightbown, 1993). That is, work with students on structures that do not normally arise in the course of every day classroom discourse or even content-based or task-based instruction.

Perhaps the best solution, therefore, is to employ a grammar checklist – to ensure that students have worked on particular forms by the end of a course – but leaving the sequence indeterminate so that students can work on structures as they emerge naturally from classroom tasks and content (Larsen-Freeman, 2001b). When they do not emerge, teachers can create supplementary tasks and activities to ensure that they receive attention when the teacher has determined that the students are ready to learn them. In this way, the risk of focusing on forms in isolation is minimized (Long, 1991).

Conclusion

Views of grammar have changed over the years. With the awareness that formulaic language is as prevalent as it is, it is clearly the case that we should be thinking more in terms of lexicogrammar, rather than thinking solely of morphology and syntax. Similarly, owing to contributions from SLA research, we can appreciate the fact that the acquisition of lexicogrammar is not likely to be accounted for by one type of learning process. Finally, due to the multi-faceted nature of grammar and the learning processes, we must recognize that the teaching of grammar itself is complex and multidimensional and may require a variety of teaching approaches.

Further Reading

- Bygate, M., Tonkyn, A., Williams, E. (eds) (1994). *Grammar and the Language Teacher*. Hemel Hempstead: Prentice Hall International. This anthology features a collection of papers that looks at grammar from a variety of perspectives. The authors challenge the conventional view that grammar consists of forms that operate only at the sentence level.

- Celce-Murcia, M., Larsen-Freeman, D. (1999). *The Grammar Book: An ESL/EFL Teacher's Course* (second edition). Boston, MA: Heinle & Heinle. Celce-Murcia and Larsen-Freeman have written their book to help prospective and practising teachers of English as a second or foreign language (ESL/EFL) enhance their understanding of English grammar, expand their skills in linguistic analysis and develop a pedagogical approach to teaching English grammar. Each chapter deals with a major structure of English, analysing its form, meaning and use. Each chapter concludes with teaching suggestions.
- DeCarrico, J. (2000). *The Structure of English: Studies in Form and Function for Language Teaching.* Ann Arbor, MI: University of Michigan Press. This book presents a descriptive overview of grammatical structures in English, but it differs from most grammar books in that the focus is not only on form but also on function (both sentence level grammatical function and discourse function). The underlying philosophy is that a better understanding of how grammar works and why it works that way will enable teachers to be more effective in teaching grammar in the classroom.
- Doughty, C., Williams, J. (1998). *Focus on Form in Classroom Second Language Acquisition.* Cambridge: Cambridge University Press. Doughty and Williams argue for incorporating a focus on form into the communicative approach to language teaching. They believe that focusing on form respects students' 'internal linguistic syllabus', drawing their attention to problematic linguistic features during communicative activities. This approach recognizes the need for accuracy and provides an alternative to methodologies that treat accuracy and fluency separately.
- Larsen-Freeman, D. (2001). Teaching grammar. In Celce-Murcia, M. (ed.), *Teaching English as a Second or Foreign Language* (third edition). Boston, MA: Heinle & Heinle. In this article, Larsen-Freeman makes a case for teachers' systematically addressing the three dimensions of grammatical structures: their form, meaning and use, depending on which of these dimensions presents the greatest learning challenge to ESL/EFL students. She also suggests that the three dimensions need to be taught differently since they are likely learnt differently.
- Larsen-Freeman, D. (2001). *Teaching Language: From Grammar to Grammaring.* Boston, MA: Heinle & Heinle. Larsen-Freeman proposes that grammar is, as with other naturally occurring systems, best conceived of as a non-linear, dynamic system. Seen in this way, the complexity of grammar is respected, especially as manifest at the discourse level, the non-linear nature of language and its learning is best understood and the organic nature of language/grammar is appreciated. As a consequence of this way of viewing grammar, Larsen-Freeman has proposed that grammar teaching be thought of as 'grammaring', to reflect the dynamic nature of grammar and its learning.
- Rutherford, W. (1987). *Second Language Grammar: Learning and Teaching.* London: Longman. Rutherford's approach to pedagogical grammar is closely tied to a premise of universal grammar namely, that

learners bring from their L1 experience an idea of what the target language may look like and the ability to make good guesses about what they don't know, within the bounds of universal grammar. The role of consciousness-raising is thus a central one. Pedagogically, this means that teachers decide which aspects of the grammar will provide learners with material to make the most powerful generalizations and then choose content that ensures the timely appearance of those aspects and that maximizes the probabilities for learner receptivity.

Hands-on Activity

Analyse the following interlanguage productions by ESL/EFL learners. Say what the problem is. Next, diagnose the error as an error of form, meaning or use in terms of Standard English. Finally, plan one promoting noticing and one practice activity for dealing with the problem as you have diagnosed it.

1. *Allyson is a 13-years-old girl.
2. *I am boring in algebra class.
3. *A goal was wanted by the other team.
4. *There are a lot of mountains in the West; on the contrary, there are few in the Midwest.
5. Would you hand me that book?
   *Of course, I would.
6. *Although he had few close friends, he was very lonely.
7. *I will buy for my parents a house.

3

Vocabulary

Paul Nation
Victoria University of Wellington

Paul Meara
University of Wales, Swansea

What is Vocabulary?

One of the most difficult questions to answer in vocabulary studies is 'What is a word?' and there are a variety of only partly satisfactory answers depending on the reasons for asking the question. If we want to count how long a book is, or how fast someone can speak or read in words per minute, then we need to count 'tokens'. The sentence 'To be or not to be, that is the question' contains ten tokens. Even though the same word form *be* occurs twice, it is counted each time it occurs. When counting tokens, it is necessary to decide if we count items such as *I'm* or *we'll* as two tokens or one. If we are counting tokens in spoken language, do we count *um* and *er* as tokens, and do we count repetitions such as *I ... I ... I said* as tokens? We can only answer these questions by examining our reasons for counting.

Often, we are interested in how many different words someone knows or uses. For example, if we are interested in how much 'sight vocabulary' a learner has (words that are known well enough to be recognized quickly and accurately) then we would count word 'types'. The sentence 'To be or not to be, that is the question' contains eight word types. Both *be* and *to* occur twice, and so they are not counted after their first occurrence. Some of the problems with counting types include deciding what to do about capital letters (are *High* and *high* two types or one?). And, what do we do with identical types that have different meanings (*generation* (of electricity) and (the younger) *generation*).

If our reason for counting is related to vocabulary learning then we need to choose a unit of counting that reflects the kind of knowledge that language users draw on. There is evidence (Nagy *et al.*, 1989) that language users see closely related word forms (*mend, mends, mended, mending*) as belonging to the same word family and it is the total frequency of a word family that determines the familiarity of any particular member of that family. In other words, the regular word-building devices create items that are seen as being very closely related to each other. A major problem with counting word families is in deciding what should be counted as a member of a family. The most conservative way is to count 'lemmas'. A lemma is a set of related words that consists of the stem form and inflected forms that are all the same part of speech. So, *approach, approaches, approached, approaching* would all be members of the same lemma because they all have the same stem, include only the stem and inflected forms, and are all verbs. A less conservative definition of a word family would also include items made with derivational affixes, such as *un-* and *non-*, and suffixes, such as *-ness* and *-ly*. Bauer and Nation (1993) suggest that as learners become more proficient, the number of items included in their word families will also tend to increase.

There are some groups of words, such as *good morning* and *at the end of the day*, which seem to be used like single words. Some of the groups may be items that have not been analysed into parts but are just learned, stored and used as complete units. Others may be constructed from known parts but are used so often that it is more efficient to treat them as a single unit. Pawley and Syder (1983) suggest that native speakers speak appropriately and fluently because they have stored very large numbers of these 'multi-word units' (MWUs) which they can draw on when using the language. These MWUs go by several names:

- 'Preformulated language' (emphasizing how MWUs can be stored as single units which are 'ready to go').
- 'Formulas' (emphasizing how MWUs can be repeatedly used instead of having to generate new ways of saying things).
- 'Lexical phrases' (emphasizing how certain phrases are typically used to achieve particular functions in everyday life, for example *Have you heard the one about* _____ is commonly used to introduce a joke).

A key feature of these MWUs is that the words in the unit cannot be freely substituted with other words; rather they have strong partnership connections, a property called 'collocation'. Although we have always been aware of some MWUs, for example idioms, research into MWUs has only blossomed with the advent of corpus analysis, which has brought extended lexical patterning into the light (*see* Chapter 6, *Corpus Linguistics*). Because this is a new area, counting these MWUs is still difficult, as no defining criteria have yet gained general acceptance. So, what is considered to be a MWU will depend on the purpose of the counting. If the goal is to count items that would require learning for comprehension then the MWUs would need to be to some degree non-compositional (the meaning of the unit could not be inferred from the meaning of its parts). This criterion would result in a rather short list of high-frequency items, if the frequency cut-off point was the same as that for single words. That is, MWUs are much less frequent than single high-frequency words. If the goal of counting is to come up with a list of items that could contribute to fluency and a native-like turn of phrase then the MWUs need at least to be frequent and grammatically coherent. Only a small list of such items would get within the most frequent 2000 words and phrases of English (Nation, 2001).

What Vocabulary Should be Learned?

What vocabulary to focus on should be determined by two major considerations – the needs of the learners and the usefulness of the vocabulary items. The traditional way of measuring the usefulness of items is to discover their frequency and range in a relevant corpus. The most striking features of the results of a frequency-based study are:

- The very wide spread of frequencies, with some items occurring many many times and some occurring only once.
- The relatively small number of words needed to cover a very large proportion of the tokens in a text.
- The very large number of low frequency items that account for a very small proportion of the tokens in a text.

These three points are illustrated in Table 3.1 and Table 3.2. Table 3.1 is the result of a frequency count of a 500-token section of this chapter. The 500-word section contained 204 different word types which made up 169 word families. Table 3.2 lists the frequency, the number of words with that frequency, and the cumulative coverage of the tokens. In Table 3.1 not all the words occurring once or twice are listed because there were too many of them to show here.

Table 3.1 A frequency list of a 500-word text

The	22	Family	6
Of	18	What	6
To	17	If	5
And	16	Same	5
Is	16	Types	5
A	14	Vocabulary	5
That	12	All	4
We	12	Do	4
Word	11	I	4
Or	10	It	4
Are	8	Occurs	4
Be	8	Related	4
In	8	With	4
As	7	Words	4
Count	7	Counted	3
Counting	7	For	3
Tokens	7	Forms	3

Table 3.1 – *continued*

How	3	Each	2
Include	3	Form	2
Items	3	. . .	
Language	3	About	1
Like	3	Affixes	1
Not	3	After	1
One	3	Also	1
Only	3	Anderson	1
Question	3	Answers	1
Stem	3	Any	1
Then	3	Approach	1
Twice	3	Approached	1
Would	3	Approaches	1
Answer	2	Approaching	1
Can	2	Asking	1
Closely	2	Bauer	1
Conservative	2	Because	1
Contains	2	Being	1
Deciding	2	. . .	
Different	2		

Table 3.2 Number of words and coverage for each frequency

Frequency	Number of types	Cumulative coverage of text (%)
10 and above	10 word types	29.6
8 occurrences	3	34.4
7	4	40.0
6	2	42.4
5	4	46.4
4	8	52.8
3	16	62.4
2	32	75.2
1	125	100

By making frequency counts of large relevant corpora, it is possible to come up with lists of words that will be very useful for people in the early stages of learning a language. Several such lists exist and they provide a very useful basis for course design. The classic list of the most useful words of English is Michael West's (1953) *A General Service List of English Words* (GSL) which contains 2000 high-frequency words. There is plenty of evidence that 2000 words is an appropriate size for such a list, but the list needs to be based on a corpus where spoken language is well represented. The GSL is based on written language, and so needs to be updated by a new list based on both spoken and written discourse.

The information from frequency studies suggests a cost–benefit approach to dealing with vocabulary. If we use frequency counts to distinguish high-frequency from low-frequency words then it seems clear that the high-frequency words need to be the first and main vocabulary goal of learners. These words are so frequent, so widespread and make up such a manageable group that both teachers and learners can usefully spend considerable time ensuring that they are well learned. The low-frequency words are so infrequent, have such a narrow range of occurrence and make up such a large group that they do not deserve teaching time. Of course, learners need to keep on learning low-frequency words after they have learned the high-frequency words, but they should do this incidentally or deliberately in their own time. Teachers should focus on strategies that help learners do this 'incidental' or 'deliberate' learning. These strategies include guessing from context, learning from word cards, using word parts and dictionary use. We will look at these in more detail later in this chapter.

It is possible to increase the number of high-frequency words that teachers and learners should give attention to by looking at the needs of the learners and making special purposes vocabulary lists. The most useful of these lists is the Academic Word List (Coxhead, 2000) which is designed for learners who intend to do academic study through the medium of English. The list consists of 570 word families which account for 8.5–10% of the tokens in a wide range of academic texts. The list includes words such as *evaluate*, *invest*, *technology* and *valid*. These words are a very important learning goal for learners with academic purposes who have learned the high-frequency words of English. On average, there are 30 of these words on every page of an academic text. Some of these words have more than one largely unrelated meaning, for example *issue* ('problem'), *issue* ('produce, send out'), but almost invariably one of these meanings is much more frequent than the other.

How Should Vocabulary be Learned?

Many teachers would assume that vocabulary learning stems mainly from the direct teaching of words in the classroom. However, vocabulary learning needs to be more broadly based than this. Let us look at four strands of vocabulary learning in turn.

Learning Vocabulary from Meaning-focused Input (Listening and Reading)

Learning from meaning-focused input, that is, learning incidentally through listening and reading, accounts for most first language vocabulary learning. Although this kind of learning is less sure than deliberate study, for native speakers there are enormous opportunities for such learning (Nagy, Herman and Anderson, 1985). For such learning to occur with non-native speakers, three major conditions need to be met. First, the unknown vocabulary should make up only a very small proportion of the tokens, preferably around two per cent, which would mean one unknown word in 50 (Hu and Nation, 2000; *see* Chapter 13, *Reading*). Second, there needs to be a very large quantity of input, preferably one million tokens or more per year. Third, learning will be increased if there is more deliberate attention to the unknown vocabulary through the occurrence of the same vocabulary in the deliberate learning strand of the course and through consciousness-raising of unknown words as they occur through glossing (Watanabe, 1997), dictionary use and highlighting in the text. It is important to remember that incidental learning is cumulative and therefore vocabulary needs to be met a number of times to allow the learning of each word to become stronger and to enrich the knowledge of each word.

The core of the meaning-focused input strand of a course is a well-organized, well-monitored, substantial extensive reading programme based largely, but not exclusively, on graded readers (for substantial reviews, *see* Waring, 1997a; Day and Bamford, 1998). Graded readers are particularly helpful for learners in the beginning and intermediate stages, as they best realize the three conditions for learning outlined above. Typically, a graded reader series begins with books about 5000 words long written within a 300–500-word family vocabulary. These go up in four to six stages to books about 25,000–35,000 words long written within a 2000–2500-word family vocabulary. Nation and Wang (1999) estimate that second language learners need to be reading at least one graded reader every two weeks in order for noticeable learning to occur. In the past, graded readers have been accused of being inauthentic reduced versions of texts which do not expose learners to the full richness of the English language, and are poorly written. These criticisms all have a grain of truth in them, but they are now essentially mis-informed. There are currently some very well-written graded readers which have key advantages: even beginning and intermediate learners with limited vocabulary sizes can read simplified readers for pleasure, which is an authentic usage, even if the text itself is not purely 'authentic'. Learners find it impossible to respond authentically to texts that overburden them with unknown vocabulary.

Listening is also a source of meaning-focused input and the same conditions of low unknown vocabulary load, quantity of input and some deliberate attention to vocabulary are necessary for effective vocabulary learning. Quantity of input, which directly affects repetition, may be partly achieved through repeated listening, where learners listen to the same story several times over several days. Deliberate attention to vocabulary can be encouraged by the teacher quickly defining unknown items (Elley, 1989), noting them on the board or allowing learners the opportunity to negotiate their meaning by asking for clarification (Ellis, 1994, 1995; Ellis and Heimbach, 1997; Ellis and He, 1999). Newton (1995) found that although negotiation is a reasonably sure way of vocabulary learning, the bulk of vocabulary learning was through the less sure way of non-negotiated learning from context, simply because there are many more opportunities for this kind of learning to occur.

Learning Vocabulary from Meaning-focused Output (Speaking and Writing)

Learning from meaning-focused output, that is, learning through speaking and writing, is necessary to move receptive knowledge into productive knowledge. This enhancement of vocabulary through the productive skills can occur in several ways. First, activities can be designed, such as those involving the use of annotated pictures or definitions, which encourage the use of new vocabulary. Second, speaking activities involving group work can provide opportunities for learners to negotiate the meanings of unknown words with each other. Such negotiation is often successful and positive (Newton, 1995). Third, because the learning of a particular word is a cumulative process, the use of a partly known word in speaking or writing can help strengthen and enrich knowledge of the word.

Joe, Nation and Newton (1996) describe guidelines for the design of speaking activities that try to optimize vocabulary learning by careful design of the written input to such activities. These guidelines include predicting what parts of the written input are most likely to be used in the task, using retelling, role-play or problem-solving discussion which draws heavily on the written input, and encouraging creative use of the vocabulary through having to reshape the written input to a particular purpose.

There are no studies of the learning of particular vocabulary through writing, but written input to the writing task could play a role similar to that which it can play in speaking tasks.

Deliberate Vocabulary Learning

Studies comparing incidental vocabulary learning with direct vocabulary learning characteristically show that direct learning is more effective. This is not surprising as noticing and giving attention to language learning generally makes that learning more effective (Schmidt, 1995). Also, deliberate learning is more focused and goal-directed than incidental learning. There is a long history of research on deliberate vocabulary learning, which has resulted in a very useful set of learning guidelines (Nation, 2001). These guidelines are illustrated below through the use of word cards.

1. *Retrieve rather than recognize.* Write the word to be learned on one side of a small card and its translation on the other side. This forces retrieval of the item after the first meeting. Each retrieval strengthens the connection between the form of the word and its meaning (Baddeley, 1990). Seeing them both together does not do this.
2. *Use appropriately sized groups of cards.* At first start with small packs of cards – about 15 or 20 words. Difficult items should be learned in small

groups to allow more repetition and more thoughtful processing. As the learning gets easier increase the size of the pack – more than 50 seems to be unmanageable simply for keeping the cards together and getting through them all in one go.

3. *Space the repetitions.* The best spacing is to go through the cards a few minutes after first looking at them, and then an hour or so later, and then the next day, and then a week later, and then a couple of weeks later. This spacing is much more effective than massing the repetitions together into an hour of study. The total time taken may be the same but the result is different. Spaced repetition results in longer lasting learning.

4. *Repeat the words aloud or to yourself.* This ensures that the words have a good chance of going into long-term memory.

5. *Process the words thoughtfully.* For words which are difficult to learn, use depth of processing techniques like the keyword technique (*see below*). Think of the word in language contexts and situational contexts. Break the word into word parts if possible. The more associations you can make with an item, the better it will be remembered.

6. *Avoid interference.* Make sure that words of similar spelling or of related meaning are not together in the same pack of cards. This means days of the week should not be all learned at the same time. The same applies to months of the year, numbers, opposites, words with similar meanings, and words belonging to the same category, such as items of clothing, names of fruit, parts of the body and things in the kitchen. These items interfere with each other and make learning much more difficult (Higa, 1963; Tinkham, 1997, Waring, 1997b; Nation, 2000).

7. *Avoid a serial learning effect.* Keep changing the order of the words in the pack. This will avoid serial learning where the meaning of one word reminds you of the meaning of the next word in the pack.

8. *Use context where this helps.* Write collocates of the words on the card too where this is helpful. This particularly applies to verbs. Some words are most usefully learned in a phrase.

Deliberate vocabulary learning is a very important part of a vocabulary learning programme. It can result in a very quick (and long-lasting) expansion of vocabulary size which then needs to be consolidated and enriched through meaning-focused input and output, and fluency development. The meaning-focused and context-based exposure also complements deliberate learning in that deliberate learning by itself usually does not provide the knowledge of grammar, collocation, associations, reference and constraints on use that may be best learned through meeting items in context.

Deliberate vocabulary teaching is one way of encouraging deliberate vocabulary learning. Such teaching can have three major goals. First, it can aim to result in well-established vocabulary learning. This requires what has been called 'rich instruction' (Beck, McKeown and Omanson, 1987: 149). This involves spending a reasonable amount of time on each word and focusing on several aspects of what is involved in knowing a word such as its spelling, pronunciation, word parts, meaning, collocations, grammatical patterns and contexts of use. Such rich instruction is necessary if pre-teaching of vocabulary is intended to have the effect of improving comprehension of a following text (Stahl and Fairbanks, 1986). Because of the time involved in rich instruction, it should be directed towards high-frequency words. Second, deliberate vocabulary teaching can have the aim of simply raising learners' consciousness of particular words so that they are noticed when they are met again. Here, vocabulary teaching has the modest aim of beginning the process of cumulative learning. Third, deliberate vocabulary teaching can have the aim of helping learners gain knowledge of strategies and of systematic features of the language that will be of use in learning a large number of words. These features include sound-spelling correspondences (Wijk, 1966; Venezky, 1970; Brown and Ellis, 1994), word parts, (prefixes, stems and suffixes), underlying concepts and meaning extensions, collocational patterns and types of associations (Miller and Fellbaum, 1991).

Deliberate vocabulary teaching can take a variety of forms including:

- Pre-teaching of vocabulary before a language use activity.
- Exercises that follow a listening or reading text, such as matching words and definitions, and creating word families using word parts or semantic mapping.
- Self-contained vocabulary activities like the second-hand cloze (Laufer and Osimo, 1991).
- Word detectives where learners report on words they have found.
- Collocation activities.
- Quickly dealing with words as they occur in a lesson.

Developing Fluency with Vocabulary across the Four Skills

Knowing vocabulary is important, but to use vocabulary well it needs to be available for fluent use. Developing fluency involves learning to make the best use of what is already known. Thus, fluency development activities should not involve unknown vocabulary. The conditions needed for fluency development involve a large quantity of familiar material, focus on the message and some pressure to perform at a higher-than-normal level. Because of these conditions, fluency development activities do not usually focus specifically on vocabulary or grammar but aim at fluency in listening, speaking, reading or writing.

There are two general approaches to fluency development. The first relies primarily on repetition and could be called 'the well-beaten path approach' to fluency. This involves gaining repeated practice on the same material so that it can be performed fluently. This includes activities such as repeated reading, the 4/3/2 technique (where learners speak for four minutes, then three minutes, then two minutes on the same topic to different learners), the best recording (where the learner makes repeated attempts to record their best-spoken version of a text) and rehearsed talks. The second approach to fluency relies on making many connections and associations with a known item. Rather than following one well-beaten path, the learner can choose from many paths. This could be called 'the richness approach' to fluency. This involves using the known item in a wide variety of contexts and situations. This includes speed-reading practice, easy extensive reading, continuous writing and retelling activities. The aim and result of these approaches is to develop a well-ordered system of vocabulary. Fluency can then occur because the learner is in control of the system of the language and can use a variety of efficient, well-connected and well-practised paths to the wanted item. This is one of the major goals of language learning and is not easily achieved.

This discussion has focused on the learning of individual words, but learning MWUs can occur across the four learning strands as well. Most learning of such units should occur through extensive meaning-focused language use rather than deliberate study. Fluency development activities provide useful conditions for establishing knowledge of these units.

Strategy Development

There are four major strategies that help with finding the meaning of unknown words and making the words stay in memory (*see* Chapter 10, *Focus on the Language Learner*, for more on strategies). These strategies are guessing from context clues, deliberately studying words on word cards, using word parts and dictionary use. These are all powerful strategies and are widely applicable. Because they provide access to large numbers of words, they deserve substantial amounts of classroom time. Learners need to reach such a level of skill in the use of these strategies that it seems easier to use them than not use them. These strategies are useful for the high-frequency words of the language and they are essential for the low-frequency words. Because there are thousands of low-frequency words, and each word occurs so infrequently, teachers should not spend classroom time teaching them. Instead, teachers should provide training in the strategies so that learners can deal with these words independently.

Guessing from Context

Guessing a meaning for a word from context clues is the most useful of all the strategies. To learn the strategy and to use it effectively, learners need to know 95–98% of the tokens in a text. That is, the unknown word to be guessed has to have plenty of comprehensible supporting context. The results of using the guessing strategy have to be seen from the perspective that learning any particular word is a cumulative process. Some contexts do not provide a lot of information about a word, but most contexts provide some information that can take knowledge of the word forward. Nagy, Herman and Anderson (1985) estimated that native speakers gain measurable information for up to ten per cent of the unknown words in a text after reading it. Although this figure may seem low, if it is looked at over a year of substantial amounts of reading, the gains from such guessing could be 1000 or more words per year. For second language learners, learning from guessing is part of the meaning-focused input strand and this should be complemented by direct learning of the same words, and for the higher frequency words, opportunity to use them in meaning-focused output.

Training in the skill of guessing results in improved guessing (Fukkink and de Glopper, 1998; Kuhn and Stahl, 1998). Such training should focus on linguistic clues in the immediate context of the unknown word, clues from the wider context, including conjunction relationships, and common-sense and background knowledge. Word part analysis is not a reliable means of guessing, but it is a very useful way of checking on the accuracy of a guess based on context clues.

Successful guessing from context is also dependent on good listening and reading skills. Training learners in guessing from context needs to be a part of the general development of these skills. Training in guessing needs to be worked on over several weeks until learners can make largely successful guesses with little interruption to the reading process.

Learning from Word Cards and Using Word Parts

The strategy of learning vocabulary from small cards made by the learners has already been described in the section on the deliberate study of words. Although such rote learning is usually frowned on by teachers, the research evidence supporting its use is substantial (Nation, 2001). There are also very useful mnemonic strategies that can increase the effectiveness of such learning. The most well-researched of these is the 'keyword technique' which typically gives results about 25 per cent higher than ordinary rote learning. The keyword technique is used to help link the form of a word to its meaning and so can be brought into play once the learner has access to the meaning of the word. To explain the technique let us take the example of a Thai learner of English wanting to learn the English word *fun*. In the first step, the learner thinks of a first language word that sounds like the foreign word to be learned. This is the keyword. Thai has a word *fun* which means 'teeth'. In the second step, the meaning of the keyword is combined in an image with the meaning of the foreign word. So, for example, the learner has to think of the meaning of the English word *fun* (happiness, enjoyment) combining with the Thai keyword *fun* (teeth). The image might be a big smile showing teeth, or a tooth experiencing a lot of enjoyment.

Using word parts to help remember the meaning of a word is somewhat similar. If the learner meets the word *apposition* meaning 'occurring alongside each other', the learner needs to find familiar parts in the word, *ap-* (which is a form of *ad-* meaning 'to' or 'next to'), *pos* (meaning 'to put or to place'), and *-ition* (signalling a noun). The word parts are like keywords, and the analysis of the word into parts is like the first step of the keyword technique. The second step is to relate the meaning of the parts to the meaning of the whole word which is a simple procedure for apposition. This is done by restating the meaning of the word including the meaning of the parts in the definition –

'placed next to each other'. To make use of word parts in this way the learner needs to know the most useful word parts of English (20 or so high-frequency prefixes and suffixes are enough initially), needs to be able to recognize them in their various forms when they occur in words and needs to be able to relate the meanings of the parts to the meaning of the definition. Like all the strategies, this requires learning and practice. Because 60 per cent of the low-frequency words of English are from French, Latin or Greek and thus are likely to have word parts, this is a widely applicable strategy.

Dictionary Use

Dictionaries may be monolingual (all in the foreign language), bilingual (foreign language words–first language definitions and vice versa) or bilingualized (monolingual with first language definitions also provided). Learners show strong preferences for bilingual dictionaries and research indicates that bilingualized dictionaries are effective in that they cater for the range of preferences and styles (Laufer and Hadar, 1997; Laufer and Kimmel, 1997).

Dictionaries may be used 'receptively', to support reading and listening, or 'productively', to support writing and speaking. Studies of dictionary use indicate that many learners do not use dictionaries as effectively as they could, and so training in the strategies of dictionary use could have benefits. Dictionary use involves numerous subskills such as reading a phonemic transcription, interpreting grammatical information, generalizing from example sentences and guessing from context to help choose from alternative meanings.

Training learners in vocabulary use strategies requires assessment to see what skill and knowledge of the strategies the learners already have, planning a programme of work to develop fluent use of the strategy, helping learners value the strategy and be aware of its range of applications, and monitoring and assessing to measure progress in controlling the strategy. Each of the strategies described above are powerful strategies that can be used with thousands of words. They each deserve sustained attention from both teachers and learners.

Assessing Vocabulary Knowledge

Vocabulary tests can have a range of purposes:

- To measure vocabulary size (useful for placement purposes or as one element of a proficiency measure).
- To measure what has just been learned (a short-term achievement measure).
- To measure what has been learned in a course (a long-term achievement measure).
- To diagnose areas of strength and weakness (a diagnostic measure).

Although no standardized vocabulary test has been truly well-researched, the following four have some research evidence supporting their validity (*see* Chapter 15, *Assessment*). They include the Vocabulary Levels Test (Schmitt, 2000; Nation, 2001; Schmitt, Schmitt and Clapham, 2001), the Productive Levels Test (Laufer and Nation, 1999), the *Eurocentres Vocabulary Size Test 10KA* (EVST) (Meara and Jones, 1990) and the vocabulary dictation tests (Fountain and Nation, 2000). Each of these tests samples from a range of frequency levels and tests learners' knowledge of the words. The Vocabulary Levels Test uses a matching format where examinees write the number of their answer in the blanks.

    1   business
    2   clock   _____   part of a house
    3   horse   _____   animal with four legs
    4   pencil   _____   something used for writing
    5   shoe
    6   wall

The test has five sections, covering various frequency levels, and so the results can help teachers decide what vocabulary level learners should be working on. Because teachers should deal with high-frequency and low-frequency words in different ways, the results of this test can also help teachers decide what vocabulary work they should be doing with particular learners or groups of learners.

The Productive Levels Test requires learners to recall the form of words using a sentence cue.

They keep their valuables in a va_____ at the bank.

The first few letters of each tested word are provided to help cue the word and to prevent the learners from writing other synonymous words. This test format is useful in showing whether a learner's knowledge of a word has begun to move towards productive mastery.

The EVST uses a yes/no format where learners see a word on a computer screen and then have to decide if they could provide a meaning for the word. The test includes some imitation words that look like real words ('ploat') and learners' scores are adjusted downwards by the number of times they say that they know these non-words. The test gives an estimate of vocabulary size which can help inform placement decisions.

The vocabulary dictation tests each consist of five paragraphs, with each successive paragraph containing less-frequent vocabulary. The test is administered like a dictation but only the 20 target words at each level are actually marked. There are four versions of the test. It can be used for determining the extent of learners' listening vocabulary quickly.

As can be seen in the above examples, there is a wide variety of vocabulary test formats. Different test formats testing the same vocabulary tend to correlate with each other around 0.7, indicating that test format plays a considerable role in determining the results of a vocabulary test. This also suggests that different test formats may be tapping different aspects of vocabulary knowledge. There are a number of issues that complicate vocabulary testing and these are well covered by Read (2000) in his book devoted to assessing vocabulary.

Limitations on Generalizing Vocabulary Size Estimates and Strategies to Other Languages

It is worth pointing out that most of the research on vocabulary has been done within the broad context of English Language Teaching (ELT). This is rather unfortunate, since English is a very peculiar language in some respects, and particularly so as far as its vocabulary is concerned. This means that the findings reported in the earlier part of this chapter may not always be generalizable to other languages in a straightforward way.

The chief characteristic of English vocabulary is that it is very large. Consider, for example, the set of objects and actions that in English are labelled as: *book, write, read, desk, letter, secretary* and *scribe*. These words are all related semantically in that they refer to written language, but it is impossible to tell this simply by looking at the words. They share no physical similarities at all, and this means that learners of English have to acquire seven separate words to cover all these meanings. In other languages, this is not always the case. In Arabic, for example, all seven meanings are represented by words which contain a shared set of three consonants – in this case k–t–b. The different meanings are signalled in a systematic way by different combinations of vowels. This means that in Arabic all seven English words are clearly marked as belonging to the same semantic set, and the learning load is correspondingly reduced.

There are also some historical reasons which contributed to the complexity of English vocabulary. A substantial proportion of English vocabulary is basically Anglo-Saxon in origin, but after the Norman invasion in 1066, huge numbers of Norman French words found their way into English, and these words often co-existed side-by-side with already existing native English words. English vocabulary was again very heavily influenced in the eighteenth century when scholars deliberately expanded the vocabulary by introducing words based on Latin and Greek. This means that English vocabulary is made up of layers of words, which are heavily marked from the stylistic point of view. Some examples of this are:

cow	beef	bovine
horse	–	equine
pig	pork	porcine
sheep	mutton	ovine

The first column (Anglo-Saxon words), describes animals in the field, the second column (Norman French derivatives) describe the animals as you might find them in a feast, whereas the third column (learned words) describes the animals as you might find them in an anatomy text book. It is very easy to find examples of the same process operating in other lexical fields as well, since it is very widespread in English. Almost all the basic Anglo-Saxon words have parallel forms based on Latin or Greek, which are used in particular, specialist discourse.

English also has a tendency to use rare and unusual words where other languages often use circumlocutions based on simpler items. Thus, English uses *plagiarism* to describe stealing quotations from other people's literary works, *rustling* to describe stealing other people's cows and *hijacking* to describe stealing other people's airplanes. These terms are completely opaque in English: the words themselves contain no clues as to their meaning. In other languages, these ideas would often be described by words or expressions that literally translate as *stealing writing* or *stealing cows* or *stealing aircraft*. In these languages, the meaning of these expressions is entirely transparent, and they could easily be understood by people who knew the easy words of which these expressions are composed.

The Lexical Bar

Unfortunately for EFL learners, the opaque terms are not just an optional extra. A large part of English education is about learning this difficult vocabulary, which Corson (1995) called the 'lexical bar' or barrier, and educated English speakers are expected to know these words and to be able to use them appropriately. Trainee doctors, for example, need to master a set of familiar words for body parts (*eye*, *ear*, *back*, etc.) as well as a set of formal learned words for the same body parts (*ocular*, *auricular*, *lumbar*, etc.) They may also need to acquire a set of familiar words which refer to body parts which are regarded as taboo (*stomach/belly*, *bum*, *arse*, *bottom*, etc.). Some of these words will only occur in speech with patients, some would only be appropriately used with children, others will only appear in written reports, others might be appropriately used in a conversation with a medical colleague. Using a word in the wrong context can cause offence, make you look like an idiot or cause you to be completely misunderstood. All this represents a significant learning burden for non-native speakers, and one which is not always found to quite the same extent in other languages.

The basic problem here seems to be that English vocabulary consists of a large number of different 'items', which are layered according to the contexts in which they appear. In other languages, the number of basic items is smaller, but there is more of a 'system' for inventing new words (Ringbom, 1983). In languages with a rich morphology, for example, it is often possible to make a verb out of any noun by adding the appropriate verbal ending, or to make an adjective by adding an appropriate adjectival ending. You cannot always do this easily in English. In some other languages – German is a good example – it is possible to create new words by combining simple words into novel, compound forms. Native speakers learn these systems, and develop the ability to create new words as they need them, and to easily decode new words created by other speakers when they hear them. In these languages, having a large vocabulary may be less important than having an understanding of the process of word formation and having the ability to use these processes effectively and efficiently as the need arises.

An important consequence of this is that some of the statistical claims put forward for English will not apply straightforwardly to other languages. In English, for example, we would normally consider a vocabulary of 4000–5000 word families to be a minimum for intermediate level performance. But this may not be the case for other languages. It is possible, for example that in a language which makes extensive use of compounding, and has a highly developed morphological system, a vocabulary of 2000–3000 words might give you access to a very much larger vocabulary which could be constructed and decoded online. It is difficult to assess this idea in the absence of formal statistical evaluations, but it clearly implies that we need to evaluate the claims we make about English in the light of the particular lexical properties of other target languages.

Vocabulary Size and Language Proficiency

This means that the relationship between vocabulary size and overall linguistic ability may differ from one language to another. In English, there is a relatively close relationship between how many words you know, as measured on the standard vocabulary tests, and how well you perform on reading tests, listening tests and other formal tests of your English ability. In other languages, it is much less clear that this relationship holds up in a straightforward way. Let us imagine, for example, a language which had a relatively small core vocabulary – let's call it 'Simplish' – and let us say that Simplish has a core vocabulary of about 2000 core words but makes up for this by making very extensive use of compounding. In Simplish, anyone who had acquired the basic vocabulary and understood the rules of compounding would automatically have access to all the other words in the vocabulary as well. 'Difficult words' – in the sense of words that are infrequent – would exist in Simplish, but they would not be a problem for learners. These infrequent words would probably be long because they were made up of many components, but the components would all be familiar at some level. It might be difficult to unwrap the words at first, but in principle, even the most difficult word would be amenable to analysis. For L2 learners of Simplish, the vocabulary learning load would be tiny, and once they had mastered the core items, they would face few of the problems that L2 English speakers face. They would be able to read almost everything they encountered; they would be able to construct new vocabulary as it was needed, rather than learning it by rote in advance. For teachers of Simplish, it would be important to know how much of the core vocabulary their students could handle with ease and familiarity, but beyond that, the notion of 'vocabulary size' would be completely irrelevant. It would be useful to know whether your class had a vocabulary of 500 words or 1500 words, but once the learners had mastered the 2000 core words, it just would not make sense to ask how big their vocabulary was. It would also not make much sense to ask what words we need to teach: the obvious strategy would be to get students familiar with all the core vocabulary as quickly as possible. After that, we would need to concentrate on teaching learners how to unpack unfamiliar vocabulary and how to construct compound words in a way that was pleasing, elegant and effective.

Unfortunately, not many languages are as elegant as Simplish. However, if we think of English as being especially difficult as far as vocabulary is concerned then it seems likely that many of the languages that we commonly teach are much more like Simplish than English. This means that we would not always expect to find that vocabulary plays the same role in learning these languages as it does in English. Vocabulary size in English strongly limits the sorts of texts that you can read with ease: this might not be case in other languages, and this would make it unnecessary for teachers to invest in simplified readers. Advanced learners of English tend to exhibit richer vocabulary in their writing than less advanced learners do: in a language that makes more extensive use of a core vocabulary this relationship might not be so obvious, and this might have implications for the ways examiners evaluate texts written by learners of these languages. English has very different vocabulary registers for special areas of discourse and this makes it important for learners to acquire academic vocabulary, legal vocabulary, the vocabulary of business English and so on: in other languages, these special vocabularies may not be so obvious or necessary.

The general point here is that the sheer size of English vocabulary has a very marked effect on the way we teach English, and severely constrains the level of achievement we expect of learners. Most people agree that fluent English speakers need very large vocabularies, that it makes sense to pace the learning of this vocabulary over a long time and that we should rely principally on the learners' own motivation to get them to these very high levels of vocabulary knowledge. However, this would not be the best set of strategies to adopt if you believed that the language you were teaching was more like Simplish. In these cases, it would be worth putting a lot of effort into getting students learn the core vocabulary very quickly indeed, simply because the pay-off for this effort would be very great.

Our guess is that very many languages are much simpler than English is as far as their vocabulary structure is concerned, and that it would be wrong to assume that research findings based on English will generalize automatically to these languages. This means that teaching methods that take English vocabulary structure for granted will not always be the best way for us to approach the teaching of vocabulary in other languages.

This comparison underlines the importance of having a well-thought-out plan for helping learners with English vocabulary. The basis for this plan is an awareness of the distinction between high-frequency and low-frequency words, and of the strands and strategies which are the means of dealing with these words.

Further Reading

- Nagy, W.E., Herman, P., Anderson, R.C. (1985) Learning words from context. *Reading Research Quarterly* **20**: 233–253. The classic first language study of guessing from context.
- Nation, I.S.P. (2001) *Learning Vocabulary in Another Language*. Cambridge: Cambridge University Press. A substantial recent survey of vocabulary teaching and learning.
- Read, J. (2000) *Assessing Vocabulary*. Cambridge: Cambridge University Press. A clear, well-informed study of vocabulary testing.
- Schmitt, N. (2000) *Vocabulary in Language Teaching*. Cambridge: Cambridge University Press. An accessible introduction to vocabulary teaching and learning.
- Schmitt, N., McCarthy, M. (eds) (1997) *Vocabulary: Description, Acquisition and Pedagogy*. Cambridge: Cambridge University Press. An authoritative and accessible collection of articles on vocabulary.
- West, M. (1953) *A General Service List of English Words*. London: Longman. The classic second language 2000 word list. A model for future lists.

Hands-on Activity

Take this test (Goulden, Nation and Read, 1990) to estimate how many word families you know. You will find below a list of 50 words which is part of a sample of all the words in the language. The words are arranged more or less in order of frequency, starting with common words and going down to some very unusual ones.

Procedure

1. Read through the whole list. Put a tick next to each word you know, that is, you have seen the word before and can express at least one meaning for it. Put a question mark next to each word that you think you know but are not sure about. Do not mark the words you do not know.
2. When you have been through the whole list, go back and check the words with question marks to see whether you can change the question mark to a tick.
3. Then find the last five words you ticked (that is, the ones that are furthest down the list). Show you know the meaning of each one by giving a synonym or definition or by using it in a sentence or drawing a diagram, if appropriate.

4. Check your explanations of the five words in a dictionary. If more than one of the explanations is not correct, you need to work back through the list, beginning with the sixth to last word you ticked. Write the meaning of this word and check it in the dictionary. Continue this process until you have a sequence of four words (which may include some of the original five you checked) that you have explained correctly.

5. Calculate your score by multiplying the total number of known words by 500. Do not include the words with a question mark in your scoring.

Test

1	bag	26	regatta
2	face	27	asphyxiate
3	entire	28	curricle
4	approve	29	weta
5	tap	30	bioenvironmental
6	jersey	31	detente
7	cavalry	32	draconic
8	mortgage	33	glaucoma
9	homage	34	morph
10	colleague	35	permutate
11	avalanche	36	thingamabob
12	firmament	37	piss
13	shrew	38	brazenfaced
14	atrophy	39	loquat
15	broach	40	anthelmintic
16	con	41	gamp
17	halloo	42	paraprotein
18	marquise	43	heterophyllous
19	stationery	44	squirearch
20	woodsman	45	resorb
21	bastinado	46	goldenhair
22	countermarch	47	axbreaker
23	furbish	48	masonite
24	meerschaum	49	hematoid
25	patroon	50	polybrid

An estimate of vocabulary size is most informative if we know how much vocabulary it takes to use English in various ways. How much vocabulary do you think it takes to accomplish the following things?

- Engage in everyday conversations with your friends _____ word families
- Begin to move from graded readers to authentic texts _____ word families

- Read common authentic texts (newspapers, magazines, novels) without unknown words being a problem _____ word families
- Engage in sophisticated language use, such as studying at an English-medium university _____ word families

4   Discourse Analysis

Michael McCarthy
University of Nottingham

Christian Matthiessen
Macquarie University

Diana Slade
University of Technology, Sydney

What is Discourse Analysis?

Life is a constant flow of discourse – of language functioning in one of the many contexts that together make up a culture. Consider an ordinary day. It will, very likely, start with discourse (for example, greeting members of the household and some item of news from the radio, TV, world wide web or printed newspaper) before individuals rush off to go to work or school. The day then continues with a variety of discourse in these institutions: discussing plans at a business meeting, writing an undergraduate psychology essay in the university library, ordering lunch at a fast food outlet. (The day may, of course, include contexts that are not part of daily life, both private ones, such as a consultation with a medical specialist, and public ones, such as the inaugural speech by a newly elected official.) As the day outside the home draws to a close, the members of the household come together again, quite possibly sitting down for a joint meal with enough time to review the day and dream about the future.

If you try to document, in a 'discourse diary', the flow of discourse over a few days, you will get a good sense of the extent to which life is 'made up of' discourse, and of the extraordinary range of contexts in which you engage in communication. This will also give a good indication of the diverse demands on language faced by language learners: learning how to engage in discourse is one of the most important goals in language learning and teaching. This means that the study of discourse is absolutely central to the concerns of applied linguistics; and as a language student or language teacher it is very helpful to 'develop an ear' for discourse – to learn to attend to the different strands of patterning in discourse and to focus on those contexts and linguistic strategies that are most immediately relevant.

Because of its pervasiveness in life, discourse is studied in a number of different disciplines (*see below*). In the field of applied linguistics, the most relevant body of work is that which has come to be known as 'discourse analysis' (or 'text linguistics'). The discourse analyst studies texts, whether spoken or written, whether long or short, and is interested in the relationship between texts and the contexts in which they arise and operate. Discourse analysts always look at real texts – and in this they differ significantly from formal (as opposed to functional) grammarians and philosophers of language, since these scholars tend to work with invented (constructed) examples. In addition, discourse analysts study language independently of the notion of the sentence, typically studying longer passages of text, whereas grammarians traditionally do not work beyond the written sentence. In other words, discourse analysts work with 'utterances' (sequences of words written or spoken in specific contexts), whereas grammarians tend to work with 'sentences' (sequences of words conforming, or not, to the rules of grammar for the construction of phrases, clauses, etc.). Discourse analysts focus on the following questions when analysing texts:

- Who are the participants in the discourse, that is, the writer and reader(s), the speaker(s) and listener(s)? What is their relationship? Is it one between equals? Are there differences in power or knowledge between the participants? What are their goals? (A formal grammarian does not usually take any of these factors into account when working with out-of-context sentences.)
- How do we know what writers and speakers mean? More specifically, discourse analysts ask 'What does this piece of language *mean in this context*?' and 'What does the speaker/writer *mean by* this piece of language?' What factors enable us to interpret the text? What do we need to know about the context? What clues are there in the surrounding text which will enable us to apprehend the meaning? (In contrast, a formal grammarian can ask the question 'What does this sentence *mean*?', and a lexicologist can ask 'What does this word *mean*?', independently of context.)

The important position that discourse analysis occupies in applied linguistics has come about because it enables applied linguists to analyse and understand real language data, for example, texts written by first and second language learners, or recordings of the spoken output of second language learners, or of the interaction between teachers and learners or among learners themselves in classrooms. It also enables us to understand better the kinds of discourse that language learners are exposed to outside the classroom: the language of service encounters in shops, banks, restaurants, etc., the language of newspapers, the language of everyday informal conversation. In addition, such analyses can assist language teachers and materials writers to evaluate language course books in terms of how closely they approximate authentic language, or what needs to be modified when authentic texts are brought into the classroom. Language testing can also gain a great deal from looking at real language use as a source of criteria for the evaluation of test performances.

Speaking and Writing

Discourse analysis is the analysis of language in its social context. Discourse analysts are just as interested in the analysis of spoken discourse as they are in the analysis of written discourse. When the focus in linguistics was primarily on written language and restricted to the study of isolated sentences, spoken language was seen as formless and ungrammatical and written language as highly structured and organized. Beattie (1983) wrote: 'Spontaneous speech is unlike written text. It contains many mistakes, sentences are unusually brief and indeed the whole fabric of verbal expression is riddled with hesitations and silences' (Beattie, 1983: 33). However, recent research on the analysis of spoken discourse (Halliday, 1985; Eggins and Slade, 1997; McCarthy, 1998) shows that spoken English does have a consistent and describable structure and that in many respects the language patterning is the same as written English. Halliday (1985: 77) provides an explanation for the myth of the 'formlessness' of spoken language, arguing that it derives from the analysis of written transcriptions of conversation, with all their pauses, repetitions and false starts. He contends that an author's first draft, with its crossings-out and re-writings, would look just as ramshackle. Beneath its surface 'imperfections' (which are an essential part of its dynamic flexibility) spoken language exhibits a highly elaborate organization, and is grammatically intricate, though in a way which is quite different from the language which we read and write.

One way of approaching differences between speaking and writing is to plot individual texts along scales or dimensions. Figure 4.1 maps different kinds of spoken and written texts along such a scale. At one end of the scale, we have the most informal, concrete, interactions and, at the other, the most formal and abstract interactions.

At the most formal end of the formality continuum, there are the most dense written texts, such as academic articles, which are planned, collated and redrafted many times. At the other, are the most informal, spontaneous spoken interactions, with turn-taking, constantly shifting topics, overlapping speech

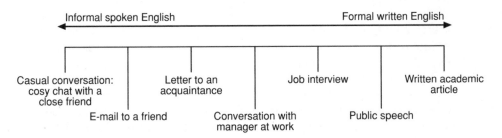

Figure 4.1 The cline between spoken and written discourse.

and frequent interruptions. It is to these informal interactions that the label 'casual conversation' is applied. In the middle of the scales are the informal, written texts (such as email and letters to friends) and the formal, spoken texts (such as service encounters, job interview or a public speech).

Academic texts are usually written in a detached and formal style (detachment or distancing oneself from the reader may be seen in the use of impersonal pronouns and passive voices, an absence of the pronoun *you* and an absence of affective/emotional vocabulary). Chatting with a friend over coffee, on the other hand, is usually a highly involved activity, with the pronouns *I* and *you* much in evidence, along with affective vocabulary. We have to hedge these statements with the word *usually*, however, as the characteristics of all types of discourse are variable to some degree. For example, chat between strangers may be much more distant and uninvolved personally, a kind of ritual where subjects such as the weather are acceptable, but where personal and intimate topics are not.

Not only is the formality of the vocabulary usually different between spoken and written discourse but the amount of content that the words carry also differs, that is, spoken and written discourse usually have different lexical densities. Lexical density in a text is the rate of occurrence of lexical items (so-called 'content words', such as, *sun, confuse, tiny*) as against grammatical items (for example, *he, was, on*). Spoken discourse typically has a far lower lexical density and it is partly because of this lexical scarcity that some people believe that spoken language 'lacks content'. In fact, much of the content is 'filled into' the grammatical words by the context. For example, the grammatical words in '*It's over there*' can be easily understood by watching the speaker gesture to a flowerpot on a shelf.

If we focus just on spoken English, it is possible to plot the differences between the most informal casual conversations, such as a dinner party conversation, and formal spoken interactions, such as doctor–patient interactions or formal job interviews. Table 4.1 illustrates that the differences between formal and informal spoken English are indicative of, but not as extreme, as the differences between spoken and written discourse. Overall, spoken interactions can be broadly categorized as interpersonally motivated or pragmatically motivated.

The significant contribution of discourse analysis is that it has demonstrated that both spoken and written discourse have consistent and describable structures, with different complexities reflecting the different functions of speech and writing in our culture. As Halliday (1985: 92) wrote, 'talking and writing, then, are different ways of saying. They are different modes for expressing linguistic meanings'.

Language teachers will be aware that most traditional grammars derive from analysis of written texts. However, recently there has been the development of grammars that deal with both spoken and written English (Halliday, 1994; Biber *et al.*, 1999; Carter, Hughes and McCarthy, 2001). Discourse analysis, provides valuable insights into the way we pattern and organize our speech. In every way possible, learners should be alerted to the special qualities

Table 4.1 Differences between informal and formal spoken discourse

Informal spoken discourse	Formal spoken discourse
Primary purpose is the achievement of interpersonal goals: to establish who we are, how we relate to others and what we think of how the world is	Primary purpose is the achievement of pragmatic goals: to talk to find out information, to pass on knowledge, to make appointments, to get jobs and to jointly participate in practical activities.
Spontaneity phenomena, such as false starts, hesitations, interruptions and overlap	Turn-taking more ordered
Constantly shifting topics as the goal is not to achieve a particular purpose	Role differentiation: there is clear role differentiation between interactants (for example, in doctor–patient interactions), which results in greater topic control
Conversations are open-ended and can continue for hours; it is in the process of talking that we explore our social relationships	Formal conversations are closed; once the task is achieved, interaction ends

of spoken language and encouraged to accord equal 'validity' to both spoken and written formulations of language.

In the next sections we will briefly describe the different approaches to discourse analysis, and then go on to discuss how discourse analysts explain semantic and lexico-grammatical features (the words and grammar of discourse).

Approaches to Discourse Analysis

Overview

Discourse analysts come from a number of different academic disciplines and the field is vast. We will not, therefore, attempt to provide a comprehensive review of approaches to discourse analysis, as this has been done elsewhere (*see* Levinson (1983), McCarthy (1991), Schiffrin (1994), Coulthard (1985), Eggins and Slade (1997)) but will, rather, focus on those approaches that have the greatest relevance to applied linguistics and language education. The different approaches that have developed since the mid-twentieth century may be classified according to different criteria. The most prominent, according to disciplinary origins, are shown in Figure 4.2.

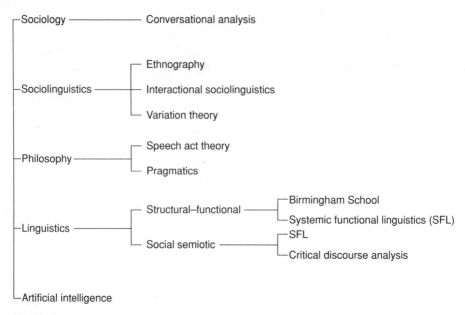

Figure 4.2 Approaches to discourse analysis according to disciplinary origins (adapted from Eggins and Slade, 1997).

The major contribution to the study of spoken discourse has come from sociology, in particular from conversational analysis. Within sociolinguistic approaches those relevant to the analysis of spoken discourse are the ethnography of speaking, interactional linguistics (Tannen 1984, 1989) and Labov and Waletzky's (1967) research on narrative within variation theory. From philosophy, speech act theory and pragmatics have shed light on how people interpret particular utterances. Within linguistics, the Birmingham School and systemic functional linguistics (SFL) have both made significant contributions to an understanding of spoken and written discourse in English. Recently, perspectives have emerged from interdisciplinary connections between linguistics and critical and cultural theory, including critical linguistics and critical discourse analysis (CDA).

Although each of the approaches listed in Figure 4.2 has made a significant contribution to our understanding of discourse, we will review only those that are currently playing a major role in the various contexts of applied linguistics and language education.

Sociology: Conversation Analysis

Conversation analysis is concerned with the detailed organization of everyday interaction; thus, it contrasts with much of the work in mainstream sociology which focuses on large-scale categories of class, gender, age groups and so on. It is concerned mainly with dialogic, spoken discourse of a fairly informal character. Conversation analysis was stimulated by Garfinkel's (1967) ethnomethodology and Goffman's (1974, 1981) frame analysis, and was developed into a distinctive field of enquiry by Sacks, Schegloff, Jefferson and others (Jefferson, 1972; Schegloff, 1972; Sacks, Schegloff and Jefferson, 1974; Schegloff, Jefferson and Sacks, 1977; Sacks, 1992). Conversation analysis focuses on conversation because it offers a particularly appropriate and accessible resource for sociological enquiry. It favours fine-grain analyses, often of quite short stretches of conversation. Key questions for conversation analysts are:

- How do people take turns in conversation?
- How do people open and close conversations?
- How do people launch new topics, close old ones, shift topic, etc.?
- How is it that conversation generally progresses satisfactorily from one utterance to the next?

Turn-taking

In conversation analysis, the basic unit of speech is the individual speaker 'turn'. A turn is each occasion that a speaker speaks and a turn ends when another speaker takes a turn. This is based on social interaction in the first place rather than on any phonological, lexico-grammatical or semantic considerations. Conversation analysts are interested in how speakers achieve smooth turn-taking, and what the 'rules' are for who speaks when.

In any ordinary, informal conversation, there is hardly any overlap or interruption, and only minimal silences between turns (on average, less than a second), if there is any silence at all. Sacks *et al.* (1974) observed that speakers are permitted to take turns when they are chosen or 'nominated' by the current speaker, or if no one is directly selected, they may speak of their own choice ('self-selection'). If neither of these conditions apply, the current speaker can simply continue. The language provides us with ways of getting the next turn. These vary in appropriateness to different contexts (*'If I may ask a question of the panel'*, *'Can I speak?'*, *'Shut up for goodness sake, I can't get a word in!'*). There are also ways of not taking the turn even when one has the chance to, for example by just saying *Mmm*. Vocalizations while another person is speaking, such as *Mmm*, *uhuh*, *yeah*, *sure*, *right*, are called 'back-channel' responses (Yngve, 1970; McCarthy, 2001) and show that the listener is still following the speaker and wishes him or her to continue. Another important aspect of turn-taking is the way interlocutors predict one another's turns and often complete the speaker's utterance for them. Also, they often overlap with the speaker as they complete the speaker's utterance even though the speaker is still talking. Neither back-channels nor completions or overlaps are normally perceived as interruptions or as rude. For conversation analysts, they represent co-operative activity by participants to facilitate communication.

Patterns in Turn-taking: Adjacency Pairs

In conversation analysis, the most basic pattern is the 'adjacency pair', which is a pair of turns that mutually affect one another. Examples of everyday adjacency pairs are *greeting–greeting*, *compliment–thanks*, *apology–acceptance*. Such pairs consist of two parts: a first pair-part and a second-pair-part:

> First pair-part   Second pair-part
> A: Good morning   →   B: Hi, good morning
> A: Congratulations on the new job   →   B: Oh, thanks

These adjacency pairs proceed smoothly and are well-formed in terms of the cultural contexts in which they typically occur in English: a greeting gets a greeting in return, and congratulations prompt a thank-you. These are examples of 'preferred sequences'. But consider this:

> A: Hi, how's it going?   →   B: Drop dead!

This would probably be perceived as a 'dispreferred sequence', a problem for the speakers. Sometimes it is necessary to produce a dispreferred second pair-part (for example, declining an invitation or offer). When this occurs, hard work is usually involved to make the sequence as little-damaging to the participants' 'face' (sense of personal worth) as possible. Apart from ritual adjacency pairs (often connected with politeness, small talk, openings and closings, etc.), other common types include 'solidary routines' (for example, A: *I have a terrible headache*, B: *Oh, I'm sorry, can I do anything?*) and 'converging pairs' (for example, A: *I just love that green sweater*, B: *Oh, so do I, isn't it great!*) (*see* Pomeranz, 1984).

Conversation analysts are also interested in conversational openings and closings (Schegloff and Sacks, 1973) and how interactants manage the topics they want to talk about (Gardner, 1987). (*See* Chapter 12, *Speaking and Pronunciation*, for more on turn-taking and topic management.)

A major contribution of conversation analysis has been to make everyday interaction a subject worthy of academic research. The strength of the observations of conversation comes, in part, from the fact that they are always based on actual recorded data of naturally occurring interactions, transcribed in meticulous detail (albeit usually giving the prosodic features of intonation and rhythm a very cursory treatment). Believing that intuition is an extremely unreliable guide for work in conversation, conversation analysis has always rejected experimental methods of collecting conversational data, such as simulating dialogues or setting up artificial interactive contexts, and has challenged discourse analysts to access the data offered by everyday life. This has implications for the language teaching classrooms: as much as possible, language learners should be given access to authentic spoken extracts, as so often the concocted examples provided in text books do not resemble real conversation at all.

Sociolinguistic Approaches: Ethnography and Variation Theory

Anthropological linguistics and sociolinguistics are concerned with studying not the isolated sentence but how language creates effective communication in the contexts of everyday life. The three sociolinguistic approaches to discourse analysis are ethnographic approaches, interactional sociolinguistics and variation theory. We will briefly outline two of these approaches, and refer readers to Schiffrin (1994), Eggins and Slade (1997), as well as to Chapter 9, *Sociolinguistics*.

Ethnography

Ethnographic approaches to conversation have been led by Hymes (Hymes, 1972a, b; Saville-Troike, 1989) and are concerned with 'the situation and uses, the patterns and functions, of speaking as an activity in its own right' (Hymes, 1974: 3). Hymes developed a schema for analysing context that has the 'speech event' in which language occurs as its prime unit of analysis:

> The speech event is to the analysis of verbal interaction what the sentence is to grammar . . . It represents an extension in the size of the basic analytical unit from the single utterance to stretches of utterances, as well as a shift in focus from . . . text to . . . interaction. (Hymes, 1972: 17)

Speech events include interactions such as a conversation at a party or ordering a meal, etc. Any speech event comprises several components and these are listed in the grid in Table 4.2. With each letter acting as an abbreviation for a different component of communication, Hymes's grid has become known as the 'SPEAKING grid'.

Table 4.2 Hymes's SPEAKING grid (Hymes, 1972b)

S	setting	temporal and physical circumstances
	scene	subjective definition of an occasion
P	participant	speaker/sender/addressor
		hearer/receiver/audience/addressee
E	ends	purposes and goals
		outcomes
A	act sequence	message form and content
K	key	tone, manner
I	instrumentalities	channel (verbal and non-verbal; physical forms of speech drawn from community repertoires)
N	norms of interaction and interpretation	specific properties attached to speaking interpretations of norms within cultural belief system
G	genre	textual categories

The SPEAKING grid provides a necessary reminder of the contextual dimensions that determine our use of language. Hymes's ethnographic framework led not only to broader notions of the 'communicative competence' language users display but also to a recognition of the close relationship between speech events and their social or cultural contexts.

A concept that is increasingly important in language teaching is the concept of 'genre'. Later, we will describe some of the different genres that occur in spoken and written English. The term 'genre' is used in many different disciplines (*see* Chapter 6, *Corpus Linguistics*, Chapter 12, *Speaking and Pronunciation* and Chapter 14, *Writing*). What each approach has in common is the recognition that there are, in both spoken and written language, different text-types or genres with their own different internal structures, which accord with different social goals. As the SPEAKING grid shows, Hymes (1972b) used the term 'genre' to refer to just one component of the speech event.

Variation Theory

Variation theory was developed by Labov (1972) and has made a major contribution to the analysis of discourse, in particular, his description of the structure of spoken narratives, which has been very influential in language teaching. Labov, with Waletsky (Labov and Waletsky, 1967), argued that the 'overall structure' of a fully formed narrative of personal experience is:

- Abstract (summary of story, with its point),
- Orientation (in respect of place, time and situation),
- Complication (temporal sequence of events, culminating in crisis),
- Evaluation (narrator's attitude towards narrative),
- Resolution (protagonist's approach to crisis),
- Coda (point about narrative as a whole).

(Labov and Waletsky, 1967: 363)

Labov did not use the word *genre*, but his analysis of text structure, in particular in relation to narratives of personal experience, has been particularly influential in work on genre in language teaching and within functional linguistics, which are described below.

Linguistic Approaches

The Birmingham School

In the early 1970s, Sinclair and Coulthard (1975) tape-recorded mother-tongue classes. The classes were traditional, teacher-fronted lessons where knowledge was typically transmitted by the pupils answering the teacher's display questions (questions where the teacher already knew the answers), engaging in some sort of activity or just listening to the teacher talking. From these recordings, Sinclair and Coulthard (1975) built a model for the analysis of classroom discourse. A typical piece of classroom discourse, from a primary school class in England is the following:

T = Teacher   P = Any pupil who speaks

T: Now then . . . I've got some things here, too. Hands up. What's that, what is it?
P: Saw.
T: It's a saw, yes this is a saw. What do we do with a saw?
P: Cut wood.
T: Yes. You're shouting out though. What do we do with a saw? Marvelette.
P: Cut wood.
T: We cut wood.

Note here:

(a)   The teacher begins this phase of the lesson with 'Now then'. This is a *discourse marker* that indicates a boundary, the start of something new.
(b)   Pupils aren't allowed just to shout their answers. The teacher nominates who speaks next.
(c)   The teacher reinforces the answer by repeating it and evaluating it as a good answer ('It's a saw, yes, this is a saw').
(d)   The discourse proceeds in units of three parts: the question, the response, and the feedback or follow-up.

(Sinclair and Coulthard, 1975: 93–94)

This extract also shows how the discourse is organized at several different levels. The top level is the lesson phases usually bounded by discourse markers such as 'Now then' and 'Right'. In the Sinclair and Coulthard (1975) model these are called 'transactions'.

The next level is illustrated in the question–answer–feedback combinations. Sinclair and Coulthard (1975) called these 'exchanges'.

The next level below is represented by the single actions of questioning, answering, feeding back, each of which is called a 'move'.

Finally, there are local, micro-actions such as nominating a pupil to speak, telling the kids to put their hands up, acknowledging, etc., which Sinclair and Coulthard (1975) called 'acts'.

These different levels form a rank-scale, in which any level is comprised of all the levels below it.

Transactions   are composed of

EXCHANGES
MOVES
ACTS

A typical exchange in the teacher-fronted classroom is the 'eliciting exchange', which has three moves, an initiating move, a responding move and a follow-up move:

T: How do we use a thermometer? Jennie.   INITIATING MOVE
P: Put it in your mouth.   RESPONDING MOVE
T: You put it in your mouth.   FOLLOW-UP MOVE

These three core moves, **I**(nitiating), **R**(esponding) and **F**(ollow-up) led to the model being referred to by the shorthand title, the 'IRF model'.

Many second language teachers will recognize in the Sinclair-Coulthard transcripts their own instinctive behaviour in front of large groups of learners, especially when institutional pressures prevent more imaginative ways of communicating in the classroom. Sinclair and Coulthard's research brought a new awareness of classroom language to a generation of language teachers in the 1970s and 1980s, and had an important informing role in boosting the move towards communicative language teaching. The model was taken into the world outside the classroom (Hoey, 1991; Francis and Hunston, 1992), and since its early days it has been immensely useful for those interested in analysing language classrooms and many other types of discourse.

Systemic Functional Linguistics

There is a family of linguistic approaches – of which systemic functional linguistics (SFL) and critical discourse analysis are members – that is socially oriented, essentially concerned with describing the relationship of language, text and social life. Within this broad band of approaches, there are functional descriptions of language which see a particular kind of relationship between language and context where one shapes the other. Functional descriptions seek to explain the nature and organization of language according to what it has to do (for example, *Excuse me, do you know the way to _____?* serves the purpose of asking for directions). Systemic functional linguistics is one variety of functional linguistics, its distinctive feature being the concern to explain the internal organization of language in terms of the functions that it has evolved to serve (Halliday, 1978, 1994).

The central concern of systemic functional linguistics is how people use language with each other to accomplish everyday social life and how social worlds are, in turn, created in and through language. This interest leads to an investigation of how language is structured to achieve socio-cultural meanings. Systemic functional linguistics therefore focuses on the analysis of texts, considered in relationship to the social context in which they occur. It has particular applicability to the analysis of spoken discourse.

The systemic functional linguistics orientation to spoken discourse is similar to that of conversation analysis, in that both are concerned to describe the relationship between language and its social context. However, the focus in systemic functional linguistics on spoken language is on the way that language is organized to enable conversation to work and to have the power it does. By contrast, conversation analysis focuses on social life, and conversation is seen as a key to that. What they share is the belief in the social nature of language: that conversation builds social contexts at the same time as these contexts guide and shape conversation.

Critical Discourse Analysis

Critical discourse analysis is concerned with the relationship between language, ideology and power (Fairclough, 1989) and the relationship between discourse and sociocultural change (Fairclough, 1992). The approach is influenced by Halliday and systemic linguistics (Fairclough, 1995: 6).

Genres in critical discourse analysis are seen as social actions occurring within particular social and historical contexts. As Miller (1984) argues, similarities in form and function are seen as deriving from the similarity in the social action undertaken. Thus, texts are looked at not only according to the textual regularities they display but also according to what class, gender and ethnic bias they incorporate, what discursive practices are constructed in the text, and, as a consequence of this, what social practices they reflect.

This new conception of genre in critical discourse analysis sees genres as both social and textual categories and no longer as fixed and immutable, but as dynamic and changing. As with the systemic accounts of genres, genres in critical discourse analysis are seen not only as a reflection of social reality but also as constructing social reality. Genres, therefore, not only arise out of the social context but, in fact, they shape the social context.

Grammar and Discourse: Spoken and Written Differences

In written discourses, writers can rely on readers to process the text in a logical and commonsense way. So, if a subject is not repeated in a co-ordinated clause, the reader simply assumes that the same subject applies:

> We stood and gazed at the sea.
> (Understood: We stood and **we** gazed at the sea.)

But because spoken discourse is usually so tied to its immediate context (unlike written texts which are often produced at one time and place to be read at another), speakers usually have even less need to refer to everything that is in the context and can take for granted that listeners will know what is being referred to. This is often reflected in very short, reduced turns in informal conversation, where items normally required by the grammar of writing are simply absent. For instance, it is a general rule of English, that verbs in interrogative clauses must have a subject, and yet subjects and auxiliary verbs are often absent in questions directly referring to the listener(s):

> Hi, Nigel, been working?
> (Understood: '**Have you** been working?')

> A: Anybody want soup?
> B: No thank you.
> (Understood: '**Does** anyone want soup?)

Statements, too, often occur without a subject where the subject is obvious or may be assumed to be known:

> Turned out well in the end.
> (Understood: '**It** turned out well in the end.')

Countable nouns sometimes occur without articles of any kind:

> A: Nice restaurant.
> B: Yes, it is, isn't it.
> (Understood: '**It's a** nice restaurant.')

These common features of spoken discourse mean that a grammar written solely on the basis of written texts, where such phenomena might be rare or completely absent, is incomplete. Equally, some structures which are common in writing may be very rare indeed in everyday conversation, for example non-finite *-ing* clauses in English. At the beginning of this chapter we used this sentence to introduce types of discourse:

> As the day outside the home draws to a close, the members of the household will again come together, **quite possibly sitting down** for a joint meal with enough time to review the day and dream about the future.

This type of *-ing* clause is very rare indeed in informal conversation. So, once again, we can say that a grammar that fails to make the spoken–written distinction may be incomplete or even misleading, giving the impression that structures are equally common in speech and writing. A discourse grammar, since it derives its description from real contexts of use rather than from isolated or invented sentences, will necessarily be interested in the spoken–written divide wherever it is relevant. Carter and McCarthy (1995) give further examples of typically spoken grammatical phenomena, and argue that language teaching should take note of the differences, especially where skills are separated into speaking or listening skills and writing or reading skills, in syllabuses, materials and language testing. At least one major new descriptive grammar now offers wide-ranging information on spoken and written differences (Biber *et al.*, 1999).

Lexical Patterns in Spoken Language

Discourse analysts are interested in how speakers' and writers' use of lexis creates patterns over longer stretches of text beyond the sentence (*see* Chapter 2, *Grammar*, and Chapter 6, *Corpus Linguistics*). Here, we shall focus on spoken texts. Speakers make their lexical choices, and listeners receive and interpret them. It is clear from actual discourse contexts that the fixedness of meanings that we associate with dictionary definitions is open to negotiation, and that lexical meaning emerges from context, rather than being entirely pre-ordained. For example, agreed meanings can be signalled and confirmed by repetition, where the listener repeats the speaker's lexis:

> Speaker 1: And then we went down to San Diego. Santa Barbara.
> Speaker 2: California. Lovely.
> Speaker 1: Yeah. Oh.
> Speaker 2: Yeah.
> Speaker 1: It was really **beautiful**.
> Speaker 2: It's a **beautiful** place.

However, a notable feature of conversation is the way speakers often trade approximate synonyms, rather than repeating one another, especially when exchanging subjective meanings, in an attempt to converge on agreed interpretations. In the next extract, *lovely* and *so nice* are matched:

> Speaker 1: Alice where did you get that skirt? Cos I want one like that.
> Speaker 2: Isn't it **lovely**?
> Speaker 1: It's **so nice**.
> Speaker 3: In Top Shop.

This phenomenon is known as 'relexicalization' (McCarthy 1988). Repetition and relexicalization enable conversational participants to converge on meanings, to negotiate them in particular contexts. Sometimes, more than one pair of lexical items is involved, and complex chains of lexical interaction may be observed, involving both repetition and relexicalization in the same stretch of talk:

> Speaker 1: Ooh. Look at the sky.
> Speaker 2: Oh that's **lovely**.
> Speaker 1: **Gorgeous**. The sky is **absolutely beautiful**.
> Speaker 2: **Beautiful**.

Another feature related to the negotiation of meaning is the display of opposites in the same utterance, which enables speakers to focus lexical meaning:

> Speaker 1: I can take a bit of the burden off Jim. Sometimes it's **hard** but I sometimes really feel as though I'm bashing my head against a wall though.
> Speaker 2: Well it is it is it is **hard** isn't it. It's **not easy** to go forward.

McCarthy (1988) refers to 'instantial' lexical meanings in describing synonyms and antonyms used in this way in context, to distinguish them from out-of-context semantic meanings, such as are found in dictionary entries for single words. What is very clear is that the native speaker or expert user's mental lexicon of any language is organized in terms of meaning connections such as similarity and opposition, and that this is not a mere abstract convenience (*see* Schmitt, 2000). Synonyms and antonyms are speedily accessed and used fluently by speakers in conversation as part of their basic strategy for creating meaning. The implications of this are that the abstract domains of lexical semantics and the pedagogical issues of learning and using vocabulary should by no means be divorced from what happens in ordinary communication. Repetition and relexicalization are part of the speaking skill, and in the case of relexicalization (that is, the ability to retrieve synonyms and antonyms quickly), present a considerable challenge to second language learners.

Corpus Linguistics and Variation in Discourse

In recent years, discourse analysts have been able to greatly expand the scope of their work thanks to computer software that can analyse large corpora (*see* Chapter 6, *Corpus Linguistics*). Corpus linguistics sprang from a desire to be more objective about language and to free description from subjective intuition (*see* Halliday (1966) and Sinclair (1966) for early arguments in favour of using corpora). Corpus linguists believe that external evidence, looking at language use, is a better source for description than internal evidence, or native speaker intuition (for a good introduction, *see* Biber, Conrad and Reppen, 1998). Broadly, corpus linguistics may be performed in two ways: quantitative and qualitative. The quantitative approach usually looks for the largest corpus possible (up to 100–400 million words at the time of writing), from as wide a range of sources as possible. These data are then analysed computationally and the output comprises sets of figures that tell the discourse analyst about the frequency of occurrence of words, phrases, collocations or structures. These statistics are then used to produce dictionaries, grammars and so on. But for the discourse analyst, statistical facts raise the question '*Why?*', and answers can only be found by looking at the contexts of the texts in the corpus. Discourse analysts, therefore, work with corpora in a qualitative way. For example, a spoken corpus frequency list might show an unexpectedly high frequency for words such as *absolutely*, *exactly* and *brilliant* compared with a written corpus frequency list. Here are some frequency figures for *absolutely*:

	CIC* written: five million word sample	CANCODE* spoken: five million words
absolutely	276	1234

*CIC = Cambridge International Corpus; CANCODE = Cambridge and Nottingham Corpus of Discourse in English.
© Both corpora are copyright Cambridge University Press.

The discourse analyst then seeks an explanation for this, and finds that in the spoken corpus, these high-frequency words often occur as single-word responses to incoming talk, for example:

> Speaker 1: I thought it was wonderful, you know.
> Speaker 2: Yeah, **absolutely**.

In this way, spoken discourse analysts use corpus statistics to get at notions such as listener feedback, turn-taking distributions, the distribution of items such as hedges and intensifiers (which often reveal much about politeness and communicative strategies) and the frequency and distribution of discourse markers such as *you know, I mean, you see, well, right, anyway, okay*, etc. Written text analysts can gain similar information from statistical procedures, as well as the frequency and distribution of cohesive devices, how academic writers hedge or how they cite others' work, and so on. Such information is immensely useful to those designing language teaching materials, since a corpus offers direct evidence of language use on a wide scale. McCarthy (1998) is one example of using a corpus to pursue answers to questions that interest discourse analysts and language teachers alike. There is no doubt that corpus linguistics will continue to influence discourse analysis as corpora become more available and software easier to manipulate, and that the results of corpus-based discourse analysis will feed through to the teaching of speaking and writing in language pedagogy.

Implications for Pedagogy

The ideas outlined in this chapter have the following direct implications for language pedagogy:

- Discourse analysts describe and analyse how language is structured in different contexts of use. This enables language practitioners to more precisely delineate in syllabuses and materials the different genres of language with which learners will need to engage, and to select and evaluate discourses that are relevant to particular learners' needs.
- When modelling different types of writing (for example, academic paper, business letter), discourse analysis can help teachers to explain the underlying features of the text types associated with those types of writing.
- In both teacher training programmes and for the teacher already in the classroom, models of analysis, such as the IRF, may serve to raise awareness of the nature of teacher–learner interaction. For example, traditional teacher-fronted classrooms may offer an impoverished context for learners to engage in the genuine interaction which seems to facilitate language acquisition. Insights from the analysis of discourse can help teachers consider their own interaction practices in a more systematic manner.
- Teachers can use insights from discourse analysis to better evaluate their own learners' performance in classroom tasks, such as pair work and

group work, in terms of its proximity to or distance from real-world discourse. The results of such evaluation may also lead to better classroom task design.

- Conversation analysis shows that everyday talk is not as disorganized as it may seem, and this offers the possibility of systematic teaching of features, such as the language of openings and closings, discourse markers and common adjacency pairs.
- Discourse analysis provides the descriptive information which pedagogical grammarians and lexicographers require to produce more true-to-life descriptions and guidelines for the use of language. The products of these descriptions (especially corpus-based ones) come in the form of pedagogical grammars and learners dictionaries which are more sensitive to context and the different demands that speech and writing place on the learner.

Further Reading

- Cook, G. (1989). *Discourse*. Oxford: Oxford University Press.
  A good first introduction to the field, which gives a helpful and accessible summary of the IRF model.
- Hughes, R. (1996). *English in Speech and Writing*. London: Routledge.
  An activity-based book, which provides the most comprehensive account of the differences between spoken and written discourse.
- McCarthy, M.J. (1991). *Discourse Analysis for Language Teachers*. Cambridge: Cambridge University Press.
  In addition to giving a more detailed treatment of the various approaches to spoken and written discourse analysis covered in the present chapter, this book also has chapters on grammar and lexis at the discourse level.
- Eggins, S. and Slade, D. (1997). *Analysing Casual Conversation*. London: Cassell.
  Based on a large body of authentic conversational data, this book develops a functionally oriented model for the systematic analysis and critical interpretation of casual conversation in English.
- McCarthy, M.J. (1998). *Spoken Language and Applied Linguistics*. Cambridge: Cambridge University Press.
  This book contains a detailed treatment of spoken genres and integrates discourse analysis with corpus-based analyses of spoken language.
- Schiffrin, D. (1994). *Approaches to Discourse*. Cambridge, MA: Basil Blackwell.
  An advanced exposition of all of the issues in discourse analysis which are of interest to language teachers and applied linguists.

Hands-on Activity

Read the two texts below and consider their similarities and differences. In particular, consider:

- How dependent each text is on context.
- The nature of the vocabulary in each text.
- The grammatical complexity of each text.
- The lexical density of the beginning of each text where the lexical words have been underlined for you.

Text 1: Cockroaches

<u>Cockroaches</u> are <u>eminently</u> <u>tropical</u>, but certain <u>species</u> have become <u>widely</u> <u>disseminated</u> through <u>commerce</u> and are now <u>cosmopolitan</u>. <u>Cockroaches</u> are <u>nocturnal</u> in <u>habit</u>, <u>hiding</u> themselves during the <u>day</u>; the <u>domestic</u> <u>species</u> are <u>omnivorous</u> but are especially <u>addicted</u> to <u>starchy</u> or <u>sweetened</u> <u>matter</u> of various <u>kinds</u>, as a <u>rule</u> they <u>injure</u> and <u>soil</u> far more than <u>consume</u>, and most <u>species</u> <u>emit</u> a <u>disagreeable</u> <u>odour</u>.

Text 2: Cockroaches

Turn	Speaker	
1	Pat	I <u>remember</u> we were <u>sitting</u> for our <u>analytical</u> <u>chemistry</u> <u>exam</u> and it was the <u>final</u> <u>exams</u> and they have sort of like <u>bench</u> <u>desks</u> where there's three to a <u>bench</u> normally and they had the <u>middle seat</u> <u>empty</u> and two <u>sat</u> either side and I was <u>sitting</u> there and I <u>thought</u> 'Geez I can <u>feel</u> something on my <u>foot</u>.'
2	Pauline	uuhh
3	Pat	And I thought 'No, no, don't worry about it,' you know 'what on earth is this chemical equation?' and I am trying to think 'but there's something on my foot!' and I looked down and there was this cockroach like this [gesture] – and I just screamed and jumped up on the chair and as I did that I knocked the bench and it went up and all Geoff's exam stuff went into the bin next to him, and I was standing on this chair screaming and the exam supervisor came running over, 'what's going on there?' [laughs] And I said 'there's a cockroach down there' [laughs] 'cause you're not allowed to speak, sneeze, cough, anything in those final exams, and um, there's me screaming on the chair.
Non-verbal		[Pat and Pauline both laugh]

5 Pragmatics

Helen Spencer-Oatey and Vladimir Žegarac
University of Luton

Introduction

> An operational definition of an insecure science is: a science whose
> leaders say they are in quest of a paradigm, or have just found a
> paradigm. (Hacking, 1995: 352)

Over the past 30 years or so, pragmatics has grown into a well-established,
'secure', discipline in institutional terms. There are a number of specialist
journals (*Journal of Pragmatics*, *Pragmatics*, *Pragmatics and Cognition*,
Multilingua as well as others), there is at least one major professional organization (The International Pragmatics Association) whose membership goes
into thousands, and regular international conferences are held the world over.
Yet despite these achievements, pragmatics remains a good example of an
insecure science in terms of Hacking's (1995) definition. None of the many
pragmatic theories and frameworks comes close to being a generally accepted
paradigm, and in fact, there is no consensus as to the domain of pragmatics.
Nevertheless, most people working in the field would probably not disagree
with some interpretation or other of the suggestion, put forward by Charles
Morris (1938: 30), that pragmatics is 'the science of the relation of signs to
their interpreters'. In other words, pragmatics is concerned not with language
as a system or product *per se*, but rather with the interrelationship between
language form, (communicated) messages and language users. It explores
questions such as the following:

- How do people communicate more than what the words or phrases of
  their utterances might mean by themselves, and how do people make these
  interpretations?
- Why do people choose to say and/or interpret something in one way rather
  than another?
- How do people's perceptions of contextual factors (for example, who the
  interlocutors are, what their relationship is, and what circumstances they

are communicating in) influence the process of producing and interpreting language?

Pragmatics thus questions the validity of the 'code-model' of communication that was developed within the discipline of semiotics. In the code-model, communication is seen as an encoding–decoding process, where a code is a system that enables the automatic pairing of messages (that is, meanings internal to senders and receivers) and signals (that is, what is physically transmitted (sound, smoke signals, writing) between the sender and the receiver). According to this view, communication is successful to the extent that the sender and the receiver pair signals and messages in the same way, so that the message broadcast in the form of a given signal is identical to the one received when that signal is decoded. The code-model has the merit of describing one way in which communication can be achieved (for example, between machines, or bees), but it is wholly inadequate as an account of how people actually communicate (*see* Sperber and Wilson, 1986/95: Chapter 1). Modern approaches to pragmatics recognize that human communication largely exploits a code (a natural language such as English, German or Japanese), but they also try to do justice to the fact, illustrated in the next section, that human communicative behaviour relies heavily on people's capacity to engage in reasoning about each other's intentions, exploiting not only the evidence presented by the signals in the language code but also evidence from other sources, including perception and general world knowledge.

In a brief chapter like this, it is impossible to explain properly the many topics that are usually studied within pragmatics, and the various different approaches that are taken within the field. So our goal is to provide a taster to these topics and issues and the methods used to study them, to show how pragmatic concerns have relevance to areas of applied study, such as foreign language teaching, and to suggest references for follow-up reading.

Pragmatic Perspectives on Language Use

This section uses a brief (authentic) dialogue in order to introduce some important terms and concepts in modern pragmatics and to illustrate briefly the sorts of phenomena that pragmatics needs to account for.

A Sample Dialogue

> Situation: Kiki and Sharon are students at a British University. They have been flatmates for a short time and do not know each other very well. Kiki is Greek and Sharon is English. Sharon is getting ready to go out.

[1] Kiki: Where are you going tonight?
[2] Sharon: Ministry.
[3] Kiki: Ministry?

[4] Sharon: Ministry of Sound. A club in London. Heard of it?
[5] Kiki: I've been clubbing in London before.
[6] Sharon: Where to?
[7] Kiki: Why do you want to know?
[8] Sharon: Well, I may have been there.
[9] Kiki: It was called 'The End'.
[10] Sharon: Nice one!
[11] Kiki: I hope you have a good time at the Ministry.

(Contributed by Kelly-Jay Marshall)

Pragmatic Meaning

It is often (though not universally) assumed that the task of 'semantics' is to describe and explain linguistic meaning (that is, what a given utterance means by virtue of the words used and the ways in which they are put together), whereas 'pragmatics' is concerned with the study of the meaning that linguistic expressions receive in use. So one task of pragmatics is to explain how participants in a dialogue such as the one above move from the decontextualized (that is, linguistically encoded) meanings of the words and phrases to a grasp of their meaning in context. This process can involve several aspects:

- The assignment of reference in context; for example, what does *Ministry* [line 2] refer to?
- The assignment of sense in context; for example, what does *Nice one* [line 10] mean in this context?
- The interpretation of illocutionary force; for example, what was Kiki's communicative purpose in asking *Where are you going tonight?* [line 1]?
- The interpretation of implicated meaning; for example, what does Sharon imply when she asks *Heard of it?* [line 4]?

In our sample dialogue, the process of handling these pragmatic issues sometimes goes smoothly, but sometimes it does not (as is typical of real life). Let us consider each of them in turn.

Assigning Reference in Context

Kiki starts by asking Sharon where she is going, but Sharon's one-word answer is not informative enough for Kiki to be able to figure out what Sharon is actually referring to. Sharon's utterance takes it for granted that the name 'Ministry' has a referent (in other words, it presupposes the existence of a referent), but Kiki's general world knowledge is insufficient for her to identify the specific referent that Sharon intended for 'Ministry' in this context. Only upon further clarification (requested in [3] and given in [4]), is Kiki able to work out that, by saying '*Ministry*' ([2]), Sharon intends to convey something like: I am going to a London club called 'Ministry of Sound'. So, there is a gap between the decontextualized meaning of the utterance (roughly, what the word *Ministry* means according to the dictionary) and the thought expressed by that word (roughly: a London club called 'Ministry of Sound'). Kiki needs to bridge this gap, and initially fails to do so. In other words, a listener needs to assign reference to the words that a speaker uses, and since there is no direct relationship between entities and words, the listener typically has to make inferences as to what the speaker intends to identify. If this inferencing process is too difficult, communication will falter, and so to be co-operative, a speaker needs to anticipate how much information the listener will need. As Yule (1996) points out:

> . . . [reference] is not simply a relationship between the meaning of a word or phrase and an object or person in the world. It is a social act, in which the speaker assumes that the word or phrase chosen to identify an object or person will be interpreted as the speaker intended.
>
> (Yule, 1996: 22)

The process of assigning reference also involves the interpretation of 'deictic expressions'. These are linguistic items that point to contextually salient referents without naming them explicitly. There are several types of deictic expressions in the dialogue: person deictics (such as the personal pronouns *you* ([1], [7]), *it* ([4], [9]), *I* ([5], [8], [11]); place deictics (*there* ([8]) and time deictics (such as the tensed forms of the verbs). In context, they refer to particular people or things, places and moments in time, respectively, but on different occasions they pick out different referents. For example, when Sharon says *I may have been there* [8], the deictic *there* refers to the particular club in London which Kiki has visited. But, when used on another occasion, the same word will refer to some other place.

Assigning Sense in Context

Sometimes the process of identifying pragmatic meaning (that is, contextually determined aspects of utterance meaning) involves interpreting ambiguous and vague linguistic expressions in order to assign them sense in context. For example, in line [10] Sharon says *Nice one*. This could be taken to mean that a particular previously mentioned thing is nice (in this context, the London club called 'The End'), but this expression also has another conventionalized (and somewhat vague) meaning, roughly: 'Good idea', or 'Well done'. In this dialogue, it is unclear whether Kiki has interpreted the phrase in one way rather than another, or whether she treats both interpretations as possible.

These observations show that contextual meaning (reference and sense) is not fully determined by the words that are used: there is a gap between the meaning of the words used by the speaker and the thought that the speaker intends to express by using those words on a particular occasion. More technically, the linguistic meaning of an utterance underdetermines the communicator's intended meaning. This gap is filled by the addressee's reasoning about what the communicator (may have) intended to communicate by his or her utterance. Hence, pragmatics plays a role in explaining how the thought expressed by a given utterance on a given occasion is recovered by the addressee.

Inferring Illocutionary Force

Yet another element to the working out of pragmatic meaning involves interpreting the illocutionary force of utterances. Let us consider Kiki's first question [1] *Where are you going tonight?* Why did she ask that question? Was she requesting factual information? Was she hinting that she wanted to be invited out with Sharon? Or was she perhaps criticising Sharon for going out too much? In other words, what was her intention in asking such a question, or more technically, what was its illocutionary force?

These are the kinds of questions that speech act theory deals with. This theory, which was generated by the philosopher John Austin (1975) and developed by another philosopher John Searle (1969), views language as a form of action – that when we speak, we 'do' things like make requests, make statements, offer apologies and so on. Austin's (1975) initial insight was that people do not simply make statements that can be judged as 'true' or 'false'; rather, they use language to perform actions that have an impact in some way on the world. Both he and Searle (1969) tried to classify speech acts into different categories, and to identify the 'felicity conditions' that enable a speech act to be performed 'successfully'.

Working Out Implicated Meaning

The main import of an utterance may, in fact, easily lie not with the thought expressed by the utterance (that is, with what is communicated directly) but rather with the thought(s) that the hearer assumes the speaker intends to suggest or hint at. More technically, it lies with what is implicated, or communicated indirectly. For example, in line [4] Sharon asks *Heard of it?*, indicating that information about whether Kiki has heard of the club in question is desirable to her. However, Kiki interprets Sharon's question as evidence that Sharon considers her incompetent or inadequate in the social sphere. Therefore, she responds to (what she takes to be) the implicit import of Sharon's utterance ([5]), rather than giving the information explicitly requested. So, pragmatics needs to explain how implicitly communicated ideas (in this case: Sharon thinks Kiki is socially incompetent and/or inadequate) are recovered.

By far the most influential solution to this problem was developed in the mid-1960s by the Oxford philosopher Paul Grice (1967, 1989). He argued that people are disposed to presume that communicative behaviour is guided by a set of principles and norms, which he called the 'Co-operative Principle' and maxims of conversation.

The Co-operative Principle

Make your conversational contribution such as is required, at the stage at which it occurs, by the accepted purpose or direction of the talk exchange in which you are engaged.

(Grice, 1989: 26)

Deriving an interpretation that satisfies the Co-operative Principle is effected through four maxims which the communicator is presumed to abide by:

- **Truthfulness** (communicators should do their best to make contributions which are true).
- **Informativeness** (communicators should do their best to be adequately informative).
- **Relevance** (communicators should do their best to make contributions which are relevant).
- **Style** (communicators should do their best to make contributions which are appropriately short and clearly expressed).

Grice (1989) labelled the maxims using terms which are, perhaps, less intuitive: 'quality', 'quantity', 'relation' and 'manner', respectively. Grice's fundamental point was not that people always observe these maxims, but rather that they are unstated assumptions that underlie communication. So, if a speaker clearly flouts one or more of the maxims (for example, by giving a very brief answer when a more informative one is expected), the speaker may be prompting the listener to look for a meaning that is different from (or additional to) the meaning that is expressed verbally; in other words, to work out the 'conversational implicature'.

Grice's approach provides a reasonably neat account of implicated meaning. For example, what might Kiki mean by saying *I've been clubbing in London before* ([5])? Superficially, it might seem that her answer is not relevant. However, given the context set by the exchange up to that point, and assuming that Kiki is trying to be co-operative, informative, relevant and concise, it seems clear why Sharon would be justified in concluding that Kiki implicates (that is, intends to imply) that she is familiar with the London club scene, that she is generally socially competent and the like. Nevertheless, Grice's theory has a number of limitations; for example, it does not incorporate the impact of social or interpersonal factors (*see below*), and yet they seem to be important in explaining why Kiki interprets Sharon's question *Heard of it?* [4] as questioning her social competence; nor does it explain the fact that context plays an extremely important role in determining the thought expressed by an utterance.

The challenge of describing and explaining the reasoning processes involved in communication has also been taken up by cognitive approaches to pragmatics, such as Sperber and Wilson's (1986/1995) 'relevance theory', which maintains that the reasoning processes involved in communication are constrained by a single principle: the principle of relevance, making the Co-operative Principle and the maxims of quality, quantity and manner redundant.

Explaining the Impact of Social Factors

Grice's (1989) theory of conversation, and in particular his view that conversation is governed by a set of norms, pointed to the importance of investigating the social regularities which arise through and are reflected in communicative interaction. In contrast to the cognitive framework of relevance theory, work within social pragmatics has sometimes led to the introduction of additional communicative norms. For example, Leech (1983) maintains that the 'Politeness Principle' is a necessary supplement to Grice's Co-operative Principle, arguing that people often break the Co-operative Principle for 'politeness' reasons; in other words, 'to maintain the social equilibrium and the friendly relations which enable us to assume that our interlocutors are being cooperative in the first place' (Leech, 1983: 82). Leech proposes a set of 'politeness maxims', such as the 'modesty maxim' and the 'agreement maxim', which operate in conjunction with the co-operative maxims. They are worded as 'rules' (for example, minimize praise of self, maximize dispraise of self; minimize disagreement between self and other, maximize agreement between self and other), but in fact, they aim to describe the interactional principles that underlie language use. Leech (1983) also suggests that language use involves a 'pragmalinguistic' perspective and a 'sociopragmatic' perspective. This distinction is a useful one that has been widely adopted, although it can be fuzzy at times.

The pragmalinguistic perspective focuses on the linguistic strategies that are used to convey a given pragmatic meaning, whereas the sociopragmatic perspective focuses on the socially based assessments, beliefs and interactional principles that underlie people's choice of strategies. For example, suppose I am a dinner guest and want to reach the salt which is placed at the other side of the table. I have various options available: I could stand up and reach for it, I could say *'Pass the salt, will you'*, or *'Can you pass the salt, please'*, or even *'I like my food quite salty'*.

A sociopragmatic perspective focuses on the social judgements associated with such a scenario; for example, what the relationship between the participants is (for example, close or distant, equal or unequal) and the social acceptability of reaching for food in such a context. A pragmalinguistic perspective, on the other hand, focuses on the linguistic strategies used to operationalize the request: for example, whether it is a direct request (*'Pass the salt, will you'*), a conventionally indirect request (*'Can you pass the salt please?'*) or a non-conventionally indirect request (*'I like my food quite salty'*). Thomas (1983) suggests that when there is a mis-match in people's sociopragmatic conventions (as when one person thinks it is acceptable to say *'sorry'* and stand up and reach for the salt, whereas someone else does not), sociopragmatic failure can occur, and that when there is a mis-match in people's pragmalinguistic conventions (for example, one person typically uses a direct request in this context, whereas another person typically uses a conventionally indirect request), pragmalinguistic failure can occur.

One of the most influential models that tries to explain the impact of social factors on people's use of language is Brown and Levinson's (1978/1987) 'face' model of politeness. Brown and Levinson (1987: 61) define 'face' as 'the public self-image that every member wants to claim for himself' and they draw a distinction between positive face and negative face. Positive face reflects every person's need that his or her self-image is appreciated and approved of, and negative face reflects every person's 'basic claim to territories, personal preserves, rights to non-distraction – that is, to freedom of action and freedom from imposition' (Brown and Levinson, 1987: 61). So, for example, Kiki's question [1] *Where are you going?* could be interpreted by Sharon as an infringement of her personal preserves, or in other words, as a threat to her negative face. This threat may well have been aggravated by the fact that Sharon was getting ready to go out and was too busy or preoccupied to engage in small talk with Kiki. But, in a more general sense, every utterance is an imposition on the hearer, because, by producing the utterance, the speaker indicates that he or she requests the hearer's attention. Clearly, the request for attention may be justified if the information communicated by the utterance is desirable to the hearer. But when the speaker requests information from the hearer, as Kiki did in line [1], her request for Sharon's attention may easily be taken as an imposition, because the information requested is seen as desirable to Kiki, rather than to Sharon, who is asked to supply it. Various forms of 'polite' linguistic behaviour have developed precisely to show that the speaker acknowledges the imposition (and, possibly, that she would consider herself in the hearer's debt, if the latter decided to accept the imposition). Examples in English include expressions such as: *I know I'm interrupting you, but . . .*, *Could you . . ., I'd be grateful if . . .*, and many others.

A face interpretation may also be given to Sharon's question [4] *Heard of it?* Kiki interprets this question as a challenge to her social competence, or in other words, as a threat to her positive face. In fact, Sharon may not have meant it in this way, but Kiki may be particularly sensitive to positive face threats of this kind since she is a foreigner (a Greek student in Britain) and may be insecure as to whether she has been accepted as a member of the local youth culture.

The fact that the two interlocutors are from different cultural backgrounds raises further possibilities. It could be that they have slightly different conventions for initiating small talk. In some languages (Chinese, for example), a question like *Where are you going?* is a phatic remark which is not really meant to be treated as a request for information, but rather is meant simply as a superficial friendly remark, similar to the way in which we routinely say *How are you?* in English without expecting a detailed or particularly truthful response. However, this 'cultural difference' explanation is unlikely to be satisfactory in Kiki's case, as this type of question is not commonly used as a phatic remark in Greek. So, perhaps the rather 'clumsy' start to the conversation is a reflection of Kiki's uncertainty as to how to start a conversation appropriately in English with someone she does not know very well.

Brown and Levinson (1987) argue that speakers take three main variables into account when deciding how to word a face-threatening utterance such as a request or a challenge:

- The power differential between hearer and the speaker (that is, amount of equality or inequality, labelled **P**).
- The distance–closeness between them (labelled **D**).
- The degree of imposition of the content of the utterance (confusingly labelled **R** for rank).

They maintain that, other things being equal, the greater the power differential, the greater the distance and the greater the imposition, the more careful and more indirect the speaker will be. In our sample conversation, the interlocutors are equal, and the content of Kiki's initial request [1] *Where are you going tonight?* is not particularly imposing. So, in many respects we would not expect her to phrase it particularly diplomatically. On the other hand, the two of them do not know each other very well, so we might have expected a slightly more tentative remark, such as *Going anywhere special tonight?* Perhaps Kiki's direct question *Where are you going tonight?* reflected the Greek tendency to use positive politeness strategies (to use 'approach-oriented' strategies that assume a certain level of closeness) in contrast to the British tendency to use negative politeness strategies (to use 'imposition-acknowledgement' strategies) to people they do not know well (cf. Sifianou, 1992). Or perhaps she was doing this strategically to try and build up her friendship with Sharon.

Conversational Patterns and Structure

Conversational patterns such as those in lines [6]–[9] have been studied extensively within the framework of conversation analysis (*see* Chapter 4, *Discourse Analysis*). This is an approach that starts from the commonsense observation that people take turns in conversation, and that relies on descriptions of naturally occurring data to discover the rules involved in the patterning of conversational exchanges. In this view, conversation proceeds through ordered pairs of utterances, called 'adjacency pairs'. The utterances in a pair are ordered, in that the first member of a pair requires a second member. For example, a question requires an answer. Within the framework of conversation analysis, one would say that the adjacency pair consisting of the question in line [6] and the answer in line [9] is interrupted by another adjacency pair ([7] and [8]), thus forming an 'insertion sequence'. Conversation analysis is really an approach to discourse analysis; however, patterns such as insertion sequences may also be analysed from a pragmatic perspective, in which case factors such as 'face' are included to try and explain why such patterns occur. On the other hand, pragmatists working within other frameworks, such as Sperber and Wilson's (1986/95) cognitive–psychological approach, would argue that the patterns observed by conversation analysts follow from general principles of human cognition and communication. They would, therefore, dispute the need for and the plausibility of turn-taking rules and most of the apparatus of conversation analysis.

The Role of Context

Context plays a major role in the communication process, and so an important task for pragmatic theory is to elucidate this process (Verschueren, 1999). In social pragmatics, it is widely accepted that the following features of the situational context have a particularly crucial influence on people's use of language:

- The participants: their roles, the amount of power differential (if any) between them, the degree of distance–closeness between them, the number of people present.
- The message content: how 'costly' or 'beneficial' the message is to the hearer and/or speaker, how face-threatening it is, whether it exceeds or stays within the rights and obligations of the relationship.
- The communicative activity (such as a job interview, a lecture or a medical consultation): how the norms of the activity influence language behaviour such as right to talk or ask questions, discourse structure, and level of formality.

Brown and Levinson's (1987) three variables, **P**, **D** and **R** have been particularly widely used in social pragmatic studies, and have been manipulated in various ways to try and find out how they influence language use. Unfortunately, context is sometimes taken to be the concrete aspects of the environment in which an exchange takes place and that have a bearing on the communication process. But in pragmatics, a more psychological notion of context is crucial. The physical environment (the time, the place, and the objects and people present) does not impinge directly on utterance production and interpretation; it does so only indirectly via people's representations of it. For example, if you do not want your colleague in the next office to hear what you are about to say, you may speak in a low voice. However, your decision to speak in this way depends not so much on whether your colleague is actually in the next office or not as on your beliefs about his or her possible presence and ability to overhear your conversation. So, in pragmatics, context can be defined as the set of assumptions (that is, mental representations capable of being true or false) that have a bearing on the production and interpretation of particular communicative acts.

One of the main problems of pragmatics is to explain the constant updating of contextual assumptions in the course of a communicative exchange. For instance, in the conversation between Kiki and Sharon, Kiki probably begins the conversation with the belief that Sharon considers her to be socially competent. Following her request for clarification in line [3], she abandons this background contextual assumption, because she thinks that she has displayed her lack of essential social knowledge about the London club scene. The continuation of the conversation is influenced by Kiki's newly formed contextual assumption that Sharon considers her socially inadequate. In fact, the role of some linguistic items is precisely to help the addressee – they point to the type of contextual assumptions that the communicator intends the addressee(s) to exploit in the interpretation. For example, in the conversation, Kiki says that she has been clubbing in London before ([5]); Sharon asks her which London club(s) she has been clubbing in ([6]) and Kiki (who assumes that Sharon's question implicates that she does not believe her statement in line [5]), asks ([7]) *Why do you want to know?* Sharon's answer ([8]) begins with the word *well*, whose function is, roughly, to indicate that the answer that follows should not be interpreted in the context which Sharon presumes is most salient to Kiki; in this case, a set of assumptions about Sharon's doubts as to whether Kiki has really been clubbing in London. So, the word *well* does not contribute to what Sharon intends to say, but rather helps Kiki access the context for the interpretation of the utterance which follows. Linguistic elements, such as *well, anyway, however, but, so, after all*, which help the addressee to contextualize what is said by the utterance, are called 'semantic constraints' on implicatures (*see* Blakemore, 1987). Other authors (Mey, 1993) consider them to be similar to adverbials, such as *obviously, unfortunately* and the like, which do not contribute to the thought expressed by the utterance, but rather provide a comment on the speaker's attitude towards that thought. For example, imagine an Arsenal football club supporter saying: *Unfortunately, Manchester United will win the Premiership League again.* This utterance expresses a proposition that describes a state of affairs in the future, and at the same time it includes the speaker's attitude towards that state of affairs. Hence, a comment like: *That's not true*, would be taken as challenging the claim: *Manchester United will win the Premiership League*, not as disputing the Arsenal supporter's attitude towards that statement.

Pragmatics Research: Paradigms and Methods

As the section above implies, there are two broad approaches to pragmatics, a cognitive–psychological approach and a social–psychological approach. Cognitive pragmaticists are primarily interested in exploring the relation between the decontextualized, linguistic meaning of utterances, what speakers mean by their utterances on given occasions, and how listeners interpret those utterances on those given occasions. Social pragmaticists, on the other hand, tend to focus on the ways in which particular communicative exchanges between individuals are embedded in and constrained by social, cultural and other contextual factors. These two approaches tend to use different research paradigms and methods. Generally speaking, work within social pragmatics tends to take an empirical approach, and emphasizes the collection of pragmatic data, partly for descriptive purposes, and partly so that existing theories (for example, Brown and Levinson's (1987) face model of politeness) can be tested and if necessary modified. Work within the cognitive–psychological tradition, on the other hand, is less concerned with large-scale data collection, and instead tends to theorize from specific examples of communicative utterances. In fact, many key pragmatic insights were developed within philosophy; Austin, Searle and Grice, for example, were all philosophers.

In terms of data collection, pragmatics borrows from other sciences such as psychology, sociology and anthropology, and thus uses a variety of methods. For example, it uses video/audio-recording and detailed field notes to collect on-line discourse, such as authentic conversations, elicited conversations and role-played interactions; and it uses questionnaires, diaries and interviews to obtain offline pragmatic data in which participants report, discuss and/or comment on their use of language. Some methods are more suitable than others for exploring given research questions, so it should not be thought that one method is necessarily always better than another. Moreover, the different methods can provide useful complementary information and perspectives and thus help to ensure 'triangulation' (the use of two or more different methods focusing on the same research question so that complementary and converging data may be obtained and that the conclusions can be more robust). For instance, discourse data (obtained by recording an authentic interaction) may usefully be supplemented by post-event interview data in that participants can often provide rich and illuminating insights into their use of language in the recorded interchange. They may describe a sociocultural principle that is important to them, for example, or they may comment how they felt when someone said a particular thing.

The collection of online data brings into focus the problem of the 'Observer's Paradox': the concern that the interactants' awareness of being observed and recorded for research purposes may actually affect their communicative behaviour and thus distort the primary research data. Many researchers have found that any such effect tends to be temporary, but as Kasper (2000: 320) points out, 'since initial observer effects are quite possible, researchers should refrain from the get-your-data-and-run type of data collection'.

Despite their thematic and methodological differences, the cognitive–psychological and the social approaches to communication should be seen as complementary. For example, the realization of communicative directness–indirectness in different cultures is an important topic in social pragmatics, yet sociopragmatic descriptions can benefit from a characterization of the reasoning processes involved in direct and indirect communication. Roughly, the stronger the evidence the communicator presents for intending to communicate a particular assumption, the more directly communicated that assumption will be, and vice versa. For example, when Kiki asks *Where are you going tonight?*, her utterance, by virtue of its linguistic form, presents Sharon with conclusive evidence that some information about Sharon's plans for the evening is relevant to Kiki. In other words, it communicates strongly a request for information. The same question presents far less compelling evidence as to Kiki's purpose in asking the question: Kiki is genuinely interested in Sharon, Kiki is trying to avoid the embarrassment of silence, Kiki wants to show that she considers Sharon a friend, Kiki is lonely and is hoping that Sharon will invite her to come along with her, and so on. These [intentions] are less well-evidenced linguistically, and so are communicated indirectly, if at all. Cognitive pragmatics needs to spell out how the contextual evidence available to interactants combines with the linguistic evidence to help them work out what is communicated on any given occasion. If the account is sufficiently explicit and detailed, it could help with the description and classification of cultural constraints on how people select context for the interpretation of language and how they choose linguistic expressions to convey messages indirectly.

Implications for Language Teaching, Learning and Use

The Importance of Context

As explained above, context is a crucial factor in pragmatic analysis – it influences what people say, how they say it, and how others interpret what they say. So, when designing language teaching materials and language learning activities, it is vital to clearly identify relevant contextual information such as the following:

- The roles (for example, teacher–student, waiter–customer) and relationships (for example, equal–unequal, distant–close) of the interlocutors.
- The number of people present.
- The communicative setting of the interaction (at a bus stop or in a lecture theatre).
- What the communicative event is (lecture or job interview) and what the goals are.

By identifying this 'starting point' contextual information, students can learn (explicitly or implicitly) about the influence of context on language use. In fact, this has long been recognized in foreign language teaching, so in lessons following the standard 'Presentation, Practice, Production' (PPP) structure, for example, it is standard practice to present and practise the target teaching point(s) in as authentic a context as possible. Similarly, in EFL examinations such as CAE and PET, it is now rare for writing tasks such as 'Write an essay about friendship' to be set, where the writing purpose and target audience are unclear. Instead, writing tasks are normally contextualized, with quite detailed information such as 'You are . . ., you want . . ., here are the facts . . ., do this'. Candidates are thereby told what role they should assume, what their writing purpose is, and who their target audience is.

All this is essential from a pragmatic perspective. However, while it is vital to make clear this 'starting point' contextual information, it is also important to remember that context is created dynamically as an interaction proceeds. From a teaching point of view, it is probably not necessary to focus particularly on this, but when there are clear developments that have an impact on language use (such as when two people get annoyed with each other and start speaking in a different manner, for instance), it could be useful and interesting to discuss this change.

The Complexity of Meaning Construction

Communication is a collaborative process in which both speakers or writers and listeners or readers construct meaning. This process of constructing meaning involves the use of all kinds of background knowledge (for example, physical characteristics of objects and sociocultural conventions), and so this means that the less background knowledge people have in common, the more difficult the process of communicating will be. This has major implications for foreign language teachers, both in terms of how they appraise the level of difficulty of texts and also in terms of their own use of language. Teachers need to consider not only how familiar their students are with the subject matter and cultural content of reading/listening texts but also need to monitor their own speech. For example, different conventions for the use of direct or indirect conversational styles can give rise to difficulties, as one of our British colleagues working in China experienced. He frequently told his class of in-service teacher trainees that they 'might like to do' a certain exercise by the next lesson. He meant it as an 'order', but by keeping to the fairly common British convention of avoiding explicit directives, he confused his students. Nearly all of them interpreted it as an optional possibility, and were surprised and embarrassed when they discovered the next day that they were supposed to have done the work.

The Impact of Speech Act Theory

Speech act theory has had a crucial impact on foreign language teaching, as it played a major role in the emergence of the functional perspective on language learning and teaching in the 1970s, and in the subsequent development of communicative language teaching (*see* Chapter 1, *An Overview of Applied Linguistics*). Wilkins (1976), for example, in his analysis of the communicative meanings that language learners need to understand and express, described two types of meanings: notional categories (such as quantity, location, frequency) and functional categories (such as requests, apologies, complaints). And Munby (1978), in his processing model of communicative competence, specified an inventory of micro-functions. Such work had a very major impact on the development of communicative language teaching, and for a time, many syllabuses and foreign language textbooks were organized almost exclusively from a functional perspective. Nowadays, a more complex organizational network (which includes other concerns, such as structures, topics and task types) is usually used, but the functional use of language is still an extremely important component.

The Possibility (or Likelihood) of Pragmatic Transfer

It is widely acknowledged that people's use of a second (or subsequently learned) language can be influenced by the characteristics of their first (or earlier learned) language (it is particularly noticeable, for instance, in people's accents). It is important, therefore, for teachers to consider the possibility of pragmatic transfer occurring (Kasper, 1992; Žegarac and Pennington, 2000).

Naturally, there can be pragmatic differences between languages, just as there can be phonological or syntactic differences. Some of these differences can be relatively 'grammatical'; for example, in phrases like 'In the light of this' or 'Having said that', which refer to what has been said previously, a singular deictic (*this*, *that*) is used in English, whereas a plural is used in Greek. Other differences are more socially based; for example, in China if you thank a close friend after they have done you a favour, this would be inappropriate because it would be 'distancing' behaviour; in England, on the other hand, <u>failure</u> to thank would be inappropriate because it implies taking the friend for granted. During the last 20 years or so, pragmaticians have carried out contrastive research into many different pragmatic features in a very wide range of languages. This area of research is known as 'cross-cultural pragmatics'. The majority of studies have focused on speech acts across cultures; for example, many have explored the following questions:

- What cultural differences (if any) are there in the effect of context on the performance of speech acts? (For example, if two strangers slightly bump into each other, do British and Greek people evaluate this similarly in terms of degree of seriousness, and thus have similar conceptions as to whether a verbal apology is required?)
- What cultural differences (if any) are there in the impact of sociopragmatic principles on people's performance of speech acts? (For example, when responding to a compliment, is it more important to express verbal modesty in Chinese than in English?)
- What language differences (if any) are there in the influence of pragmalinguistic conventions on the performance of speech acts? (For example, when expressing disagreement, is it common to soften the impact by using an 'I agree with you but . . .' structure, or by asking for further information?)

Both similarities and differences have been found across many languages and cultural groups, so this raises another question: what are the implications of the findings for foreign language teaching and learning? Researchers who are interested in this question typically work within 'interlanguage pragmatics', and explore how foreign language learners' performance compares with that of native speakers. Up to now, nearly all of the studies have been cross-sectional rather than longitudinal, so unfortunately there is little information available as yet on the process or stages that learners move through in developing pragmatic competence.

The implications for foreign language teaching and learning of the occurrence of positive and/or negative pragmatic transfer are very similar in many respects to those for other types of transfer. Yet it is important to realize that the ways in which pragmatic differences are handled may need to vary according to whether they are primarily pragmalinguistic differences (that is, differences in the linguistic strategies typically used to convey a given illocutionary force) or primarily sociopragmatic differences (that is, differences in the social assessments, beliefs and principles that underlie language use). As Thomas (1983:104) points out, learners are often more sensitive about having their sociopragmatic judgements called into question than their pragmalinguistic judgements, because of their strong social basis. So, teachers need to consider, for example, whether it is appropriate to train students to say 'Bless you' when someone sneezes, whether they should ask students to address them by their first name when the students' sociocultural norm is to show respect by using the title plus last name or whether they should encourage students to say 'thank you' in response to a compliment when the students' sociopragmatic convention is to ritualistically reject the compliment out of modesty. Are such matters legitimate teaching points in that they help students interact more naturally with native speakers, or are they a form of language imperialism? There are no easy answers to such questions, and teachers need to think them through very carefully, perhaps in conjunction with their students.

People's Sensitivities to Face

Teachers and students need to have a good rapport between them if they are to feel comfortable with each other and if the students are to make satisfactory progress. So pragmatic insights from face and politeness theory can be of great practical relevance to teachers, especially in terms of classroom management and social interaction. For example, face considerations are extremely important when teachers are giving feedback, making suggestions, criticizing a student in some way, or even just nominating someone to answer a question. They can also arise among the students themselves when they are taking part in pair or group activities. Needless to say, some individuals (and maybe some cultural groups) are more sensitive to face issues than others, but nevertheless they are extremely important considerations to which teachers always need to be very sensitive.

Acknowledgement

The authors would like to thank Kelly-Jay Marshall for providing us with the dialogue that we discuss, and Theo Maniski for his comments on the chapter.

Further Reading

Introductions to Pragmatics

- Thomas, J. (1995) *Meaning in Interaction. An Introduction to Pragmatics.* London: Longman.
- Yule, G. (1996) *Pragmatics.* Oxford: Oxford University Press.

  Both of these books provide concise and extremely accessible introductions to pragmatics. Thomas (1995) is particularly rich in interesting examples.

- Mey, J. (2000) *Pragmatics. An Introduction* (second edition). Oxford: Blackwell. This book takes a strong social perspective, and explores pragmatics in much greater depth than either Thomas (1995) or Yule (1996) but is very accessible.

Pragmatics and Culture

- Kasper, G., Blum-Kulka, S. (eds) (1993) *Interlanguage Pragmatics*. Oxford: Oxford University Press. This book comprises empirical studies of interlanguage pragmatics, with a focus on speech acts.
- Spencer-Oatey, H. (ed.) (2000) *Culturally Speaking. Managing Rapport through Talk across Cultures*. London: Continuum. This book comprises both theoretical and empirical chapters. There are particularly useful chapters on pragmatic transfer and pragmatic data collection, as well as cross-cultural (comparative) and intercultural (discourse) studies.
- Thomas, J. (1983) Cross-cultural pragmatic failure. *Applied Linguistics* 4: 91–112. This widely quoted journal article discusses different types of pragmatic failure and the difficulties faced by non-native speakers.

Hands-on Activity

Read the following authentic interchange, and then carry out a pragmatic analysis of it, paying particular attention to the following features:

- Reference.
- Illocutionary force.
- Agreement/disagreement.
- Face-threatening behaviour.
- Context.
- Conversational patterns/structure.

The Rice Episode

Brian, an American student spending a year in Germany, has cooked a meal for Andi, a German friend, who has recently helped him with his German seminar paper. Andi has just arrived.

01	Brian:	hallo Andi how are you?
02	Andi:	yeah fine oh fine really yeah;
03	Brian:	so (.) everything's ready now (.) I hope you like it (0.3) I have cooked it myself [so because]
04	Andi:	[yeah fine]
05	Brian:	that's what we eat in the South
06	Andi:	{in a loud voice} but that's so much that is FAR TOO MUCH rice

07 Brian: that doesn't MATTER (0.1) I have paid for it (.) and I have
INVITED you (.) [you have]

08 Andi: [no it] DOES matter it DOES it DOES think
of the many poor people who go hungry and would like to eat
something like that [well I]

09 Brian: [I   I] believe I (0.1) I [find]

10 Andi: [I find] one should in
this common world in which we do all live (0.2) the world in
which we are all endowed with material goods so UNequally
we should at least on a small scale try to produce no waste no
useless [waste]

11 Brian [well Andi] I am not I (0.2) [don't believe]

12 Andi: produce [no waste] and always in
our consciousness think that we in the rich western world ...
{monologue continues for 1–1/2 minutes}

(House, 2000: 154–155)

Transcription Conventions

Meaning	Symbol	Example
Overlapping text	word [word] word [word] word	Andi: no useless [waste] Brian: [well Andi] I
Micropause	(.)	Andi: I have paid for it (.) and I
Pause of indicated length (in seconds)	(0.5)	Andi: I (0.1) I find
Emphasized word	CAPITAL LETTERS	Andi: no it DOES matter
Relevant additional information	{descriptive comment}	{in a loud voice}

6   Corpus Linguistics

Randi Reppen
Northern Arizona University

Rita Simpson
University of Michigan

What is Corpus Linguistics?

Recently, the area of study known as 'corpus linguistics' has enjoyed much greater popularity, both as a means to explore actual patterns of language use and as a tool for developing materials for classroom language instruction. Corpus linguistics uses large collections of both spoken and written natural texts (*corpora* or *corpuses*, singular *corpus*) that are stored on computers. By using a variety of computer-based tools, corpus linguists can explore different questions about language use. One of the major contributions of corpus linguistics is in the area of exploring patterns of language use. Corpus linguistics provides an extremely powerful tool for the analysis of natural language and can provide tremendous insights as to how language use varies in different situations, such as spoken versus written, or formal interactions versus casual conversation.

Although corpus linguistics and the term 'corpus' in its present-day sense are pretty much synonymous with computerized corpora and methods, this was not always the case, and earlier corpora, of course, were often not computerized. Before the advent of computers, or at least before the proliferation of personal computers, many empirical linguistics who were interested in function and use did essentially what we now call corpus linguistics. An empirical approach to linguistic analysis is one based on naturally occurring spoken or written data as opposed to an approach that gives priority to introspection. Although empirical approaches to issues in linguistics are not new, they may be experiencing some degree of renewed acceptance over the past decade or so, partly as computer tools and resources have become more sophisticated and widespread. Advances in technology have led to a number of advantages for corpus linguists, including the collection of ever larger language samples, the ability for much faster and more efficient text processing and access, and the availability of easy to learn computer resources for linguistic analysis. As a result of these advances, there are typically four features that are seen as characteristic of corpus-based analyses of language:

- It is empirical, analysing the actual patterns of use in natural texts.
- It utilizes a large and principled collection of natural texts, known as a 'corpus', as the basis for analysis.
- It makes extensive use of computers for analysis, using both automatic and interactive techniques.
- It depends on both quantitative and qualitative analytical techniques.

(From Biber, Conrad and Reppen, 1998: 4.)

As mentioned above, a corpus refers to a large principled collection of natural texts. The use of natural texts means that language has been collected from naturally occurring sources rather than from surveys or questionnaires. In the case of spoken language, this means first recording and then transcribing the speech. The process of creating written transcripts of spoken language can be quite time-consuming, involving a series of choices based on the research interests of the corpus compilers. Even with the collection of written texts there are questions that must be addressed. For example, when creating a corpus of personal letters, the researcher must decide what to do about spelling conventions and errors. There are a number of existing corpora that are valuable resources for investigating some types of language questions. Some of the more well-known available corpora include the British National Corpus (BNC), the Brown Corpus, the Lancaster/Oslo–Bergen (LOB) Corpus and the Helsinki Corpus of English Texts.

However, researchers interested in exploring aspects of language use that are not represented by readily available corpora (for example, research issues relating to a particular register or time period) will need to compile a new corpus.

The text collection process for building a corpus needs to be principled, so as to ensure representativeness and balance. The linguistic features or research questions being investigated will shape the collection of texts used in creating the corpus. For example, if the research focus is to characterize the language used in business letters, the researcher would need to collect a representative sample of business letters. After considering the task of representing all of the various types of businesses and the various kinds of correspondence that are included in the category of 'business letters', the researcher might decide to focus on how small businesses communicate with each other. Now, the researcher can set about the task of contacting small businesses and collecting inter-office communication. These and other issues related to the compilation and analysis of corpora will be described in greater detail in the next section of this chapter.

Because corpus linguistics uses large collections of naturally occurring language, the use of computers for analysis is imperative. Computers are tireless tools that can store large amounts of information and allow us to look at that information in various configurations. Imagine that you are interested in exploring the use of relative clauses in academic written language. Now, imagine that you needed to carry out this task by hand. As a simple example of how overwhelming such a task can be, turn to a random page in this book and note all the relative clauses that occur on that page – imagine doing this for the entire book! Just the thought of completing this task is daunting. Next, imagine that you were interested in looking at different types of relative clauses and the different contexts in which they occur. You can easily see that this is a task that is better given to a computer that can store information and sort that information in various ways. Just how the computer can accomplish such a task is described in the 'What can a Corpus Tell Us?' section of this chapter.

The final characteristic of corpus-based methods stated above is an important and often overlooked one (that is, that this approach involves both quantitative and qualitative methods of analysis). Although computers make possible a wide range of sophisticated statistical techniques and accomplish tedious, mechanical tasks rapidly and accurately, human analysts are still needed to decide what information is worth searching for, to extract that information from the corpus and to interpret the findings. Thus, perhaps the greatest contribution of corpus linguistics lies in its potential to bring together aspects of quantitative and qualitative techniques. The quantitative analyses provide an accurate view of more macro-level characteristics, whereas the qualitative analyses provide the complementary micro-level perspective.

Corpus Design and Compilation

A corpus, as defined above, is a large and principled collection of texts stored in electronic format. Although there is no minimum size for a text collection to be considered a corpus, an early standard size set by the creators of the Brown Corpus was one million words. A number of well-known specialized corpora are much smaller than that, but there is a general assumption that for most tasks within corpus linguistics, larger corpora are more valuable, up to a certain point. Another feature of modern-day corpora is that they are usually made available to other researchers,* most commonly for a modest fee and occasionally free of charge. This is a significant development, as it enables researchers all over the world to access the same sets of data, which not only encourages a higher degree of accountability in data analysis, but also permits collaborative work and follow-up studies by different researchers. This section presents a summary of corpus types and some of the issues involved in designing and compiling a corpus. Because such a wide range of corpora is accessible to individual teachers and researchers, it is not necessary – or even desirable – for those interested in corpus linguistics and its applications to build their own corpus, and this section should not be taken as encouragement to do so. However, as noted above, it is possible that at some point you will be interested

---

*In some cases, the compilation of a corpus is funded by a publishing (or testing) company, which has a financial interest in restricting access to the corpus to a select group of key researchers.

in research questions that cannot be properly investigated using existing corpora, and this section offers an introduction to the kinds of issues that need to be considered should you decide to compile your own corpus. Aside from that, it is important to know something about how corpora are designed and compiled in order to evaluate existing corpora and understand what sorts of analyses they are best suited for.

Types of Corpora

It could be said that there are as many types of corpora as there are research topics in linguistics. The following section gives a brief overview of the most common types of corpora being used by language researchers today. General corpora, such as the Brown Corpus, the LOB Corpus or the BNC, aim to represent language in its broadest sense and to serve as a widely available resource for baseline or comparative studies of general linguistic features. Increasingly, general corpora are designed to be quite large. For example, the BNC, compiled in the 1990s, contains 100 million words, and the American National Corpus, which is in the planning stages, is attempting to replicate the BNC's model. The early general corpora like Brown and LOB, at a mere one million words, seem tiny by today's standards, but they continue to be used by both applied and computational linguists, and research has shown that one million words is sufficient to obtain reliable, generalizable results for many, though not all, research questions. A general corpus is designed to be balanced and include language samples from a wide range of registers or genres, including both fiction and nonfiction in all their diversity (Biber, 1993a, 1993b). Most of the early general corpora were limited to written language, but because of advances in technology and increasing interest in spoken language among linguists, many of the modern general corpora include a spoken component, which similarly encompasses a wide variety of speech types, from casual conversations among friends and family to academic lectures and national radio broadcasts. However, because written texts are vastly easier and cheaper to compile than transcripts of speech, very few of the large corpora are balanced in terms of speech and writing. The compilers of the BNC had originally planned to include equal amounts of speech and writing, and eventually settled for a spoken component of ten million words, or ten per cent of the total. A few corpora exclusively dedicated to spoken discourse have been developed, but they are inevitably much smaller than modern general corpora like the BNC, for example the Cambridge and Nottingham Corpus of Discourse in English (CANCODE) (*see* Carter and McCarthy, 1997).

Although the general corpora have fostered important research over the years, specialized corpora – those designed with more specific research goals in mind – may be the most crucial 'growth area' for corpus linguistics, as researchers increasingly recognize the importance of register-specific descriptions and investigations of language. Specialized corpora may include both spoken and written components, as do the International Corpus of English (ICE), a corpus designed for the study of national varieties of English, and the

TOEFL-2000 Spoken and Written Academic Language Corpus. More commonly, a specialized corpus focuses on a particular spoken or written variety of language. Specialized written corpora include historical corpora (for example, the Helsinki Corpus (1.5 million words dating from AD850 to 1710) and the Archer Corpus (two million words of British and American English dating from 1650 to 1990) and corpora of newspaper writing, fiction or academic prose, to name a few. Registers of speech that have been the focus of specialized spoken corpora include academic speech (the Michigan Corpus of Academic Spoken English; MICASE), teenage language (COLT) and child language (the CHILDES database). Another type of specialized corpus that is becoming increasingly important for language teachers is the so-called 'learner's corpus'. This is a corpus that includes spoken or written language samples produced by non-native speakers, the most well-known example being the International Corpus of Learner English (ICLE).

Issues in Corpus Design

One of the most important factors in corpus linguistics is the design of the corpus (Biber, 1990). This factor impacts all of the analysis that can be carried out with the corpus and has serious implications for the reliability of the results. The composition of the corpus should reflect the anticipated research goals. A corpus that is intended to be used for exploring lexical questions needs to be very large to allow for accurate representation of a large number of words and of the different senses, or meanings, that a word might have. A corpus of one million words will not be large enough to provide reliable information about less frequent lexical items. For grammatical explorations, however, the size constraints are not as great, since there are far fewer different grammatical constructions than lexical items, and therefore they tend to recur much more frequently in comparison. So, for grammatical analysis, the first generation corpora of one million words have withstood the test of time. However, it is essential that the overall design of the corpus reflects the issues being explored. For example, if a researcher is interested in comparing patterns of language found in spoken and written discourse, the corpus has to encompass a range of possible spoken and written texts, so that the information derived from the corpus accurately reflects the variation possible in the patterns being compared across the two registers.

A well-designed corpus should aim to be representative of the types of language included in it, but there are many different ways to conceive of and justify representativeness. First, you can try to be representative primarily of different registers (for example, fiction, non-fiction, casual conversation, service encounters, broadcast speech) as well as discourse modes (monologic, dialogic, multi-party interactive) and topics (national versus local news, arts versus sciences). Another category of representativeness involves the demographics of the speakers or writers (nationality, gender, age, education level, social class, native language/dialect). A third issue to consider in devising a representative sample is whether or not it should be based on production or reception. For example, e-mail messages constitute a type of writing produced by many people, whereas bestsellers and major newspapers are produced by relatively few people, but read, or consumed, by many. All these issues must be weighed when deciding how much of each category (genre, topic, speaker type, etc.) to include. It is possible that certain aspects of all of these categories will be important in creating a balanced, representative corpus. However, striving for representativeness in too many categories would necessitate an enormous corpus in order for each category to be meaningful. Once the categories and target number of texts and words from each category have been decided upon, it is important to incorporate a method of randomizing the texts or speakers and speech situations in order to avoid sampling bias on the part of the compilers.

In thinking about the research goals of a corpus, compilers must bear in mind the intended distribution of the corpus. If access to the corpus is to be limited to a relatively small group of researchers, their own research agenda would be the only factor influencing corpus design decisions. If the corpus is to be freely or widely available, decisions might be made to include more categories of information, in anticipation of the goals of other researchers who might use the corpus (*see below* for more details on encoding). Of course, no corpus can be everything to everyone; the point is that in creating more widely distributed resources, it is worthwhile to think about potential future users during the design phase. Many of the decisions made about the design of a corpus have to do with practical considerations of funding and time. Some of the questions that need to be addressed are: How much time can be allotted to the project? Is there a dedicated staff of corpus compilers or are they full-time academics? How much funding is available to support the collection and compilation of the corpus? In the case of a spoken corpus, budget is especially critical because of the tremendous amount of time and skilled labour involved in transcribing speech accurately and consistently.

Corpus Compilation

When creating a corpus, data collection involves obtaining or creating electronic versions of the target texts, and storing and organizing them. Written corpora are far less labour intensive to collect than spoken corpora. Data collection for a written corpus most commonly means using a scanner and optical character recognition (OCR) software to scan paper documents into electronic text files. Occasionally, materials for a written corpus may be keyboarded manually (for example, in the case of some historical corpora, corpora of handwritten letters, etc.). Optical character recognition is not error-free, however, so even when documents are scanned, some degree of manual proofreading and error-correction is necessary. The tremendous wealth of resources now available on the world wide web provides an additional option for the collection of some types of written corpora or some categories of documents. For example, most newspapers and many popular periodicals are now produced in both print versions and electronic versions, making it much easier to collect a corpus of newspaper or other journalistic types of writing. Other types of documents readily available on the web that may comprise small specialized corpora or sub-sections of larger corpora include, for example, scholarly journals, government documents, business publications and consumer information, to say nothing of more informal (formerly private) kinds of writing, such as travel diaries, or the abundant archives of written-cum-spoken genres found in e-mail discussion or news groups and the like. There is a danger, of course, in relying exclusively on electronically produced texts, since it is possible that the format itself engenders particular linguistic characteristics that differentiate the language of electronic texts from that of texts produced for print. However, many texts available online are produced primarily for print publication and then posted on the web.

The data collection phase of building a spoken corpus is lengthy and expensive, as mentioned above. The first step is to decide on a transcription system (Edwards and Lampert, 1993). Most spoken corpora use an ortho-graphic transcription system that does not attempt to capture prosodic details or phonetic variation. Some spoken corpora, however, (for example, CSAE, London–Lund) include a great deal of prosodic detail in the tran-scripts, since they were designed to be used at least partly, if not primarily, for research on phonetics or discourse-level prosodics. Another important issue in choosing a transcription system is deciding how the interactional characteristics of the speech will be represented in the transcripts; over-lapping speech, backchannels, pauses and non-verbal contextual events are all features of interactive speech that may be represented to varying degrees of detail in a spoken corpus. For either spoken or written corpora, an important issue during data collection is obtaining permission to use the data for the corpus. This usually involves informing speakers or copyright owners about the purposes of the corpus, how and to whom it will be available, and in the case of spoken corpora, what measures will be taken to ensure anonymity. For these reasons, it is usually impractical to use existing record-ings or transcripts as part of a new spoken corpus, unless the speakers can still be contacted.

Markup and Annotation

A simple corpus could consist of raw text, with no additional information provided about the origins, authors, speakers, structure or contents of the texts themselves. However, encoding some of this information in the form of markup makes the corpus much richer and more useful, especially to researchers who were not involved in its compilation. Structural markup refers to the use of codes in the texts to identify structural features of the text. For example, in a written corpus, it may be desirable to identify and code structural entities such as titles, authors, paragraphs, subheadings, chapters, etc. In a spoken corpus, turns (*see* Chapter 4, *Discourse Analysis*, and Chapter 12, *Speaking and Pronunciation*) and speakers are almost always identified and coded, but there are a number of other features that may be encoded as well, including, for example, contextual events or paralinguistic features. In addition to structural markup, many corpora provide information about the contents and creation of each text in what is called a header attached to the beginning of the text, or else stored in a separate database. Information that may be encoded in the header includes, for spoken corpora, demographic information about the speakers (such as gender, social class, occupation, age, native language or dialect), when and where the speech event or conversation took place, relationships among the participants and so forth. For written corpora, demographic information about the author(s), as well as title and publication details may be encoded in a header. For both spoken and written corpora, headers sometimes include classifications of the text into categories, such as register, genre, topic domain, discourse mode or formality.

In addition to headers, which provide information about the text (for example, production circumstances, participants, etc.), some corpora are also encoded with certain types of linguistic annotation. There are a number of different kinds of linguistic processing or annotation that can be carried out to make the corpus a more powerful resource. Part-of-speech tagging is the most common kind of linguistic annotation. This involves assigning a grammatical category tag to each word in the corpus. For example, the sentence: 'A goat can eat shoes' could be coded as follows: A (indefinite article) goat (noun, singular) can (modal) eat (main verb) shoes (noun, plural). Different levels of specificity can be coded, such as functional information or case, for example. Other kinds of tagging include prosodic and phonetic annotation, which are not uncommon, and syntactic parsing, which is much less common, and used especially, though not exclusively, by computational linguists. A tagged corpus allows researchers to explore and answer different types of questions. In addition to frequency of lexical items, a tagged corpus allows researchers to see what grammatical structures co-occur. A tagged corpus also addresses the problem of words that have multiple meanings or functions. For example, the word *like* can be a verb, preposition, discourse marker or adverb, depending on its use. The word *can* is a modal or a noun, but the tag in the example above identifies it as a modal in that particular sentence. With an untagged corpus, it is impossible to retrieve automatically specific uses of words with multiple meanings or functions.

What Can a Corpus tell Us?

Word Counts and Basic Corpus Tools

There are many levels of information that can be gathered from a corpus. These levels range from simple word lists to catalogues of complex grammatical structures and interactive analyses that can reveal both linguistic and non-linguistic association patterns. Analyses can explore individual lexical or linguistic features across texts or identify clusters of features that characterize particular registers (Biber, 1988).* The tools that are used for these analyses range from basic concordancing packages to complex interactive computer programs.

The first, or most basic information that we can get from a corpus, is frequency of occurrence information. There are several reasonably priced concordancing tools (for example, MonoConc, WordSmith Tools, etc.) that can easily be used to provide word frequency information. A word list is simply a list of all the words that occur in the corpus. These lists can be arranged in alphabetic or frequency order (from most frequent to least frequent). Frequency lists from different corpora or from different parts of the same corpus (for example, spoken versus written texts or personal letters versus editorials) can be compared to discover some basic lexical differences across registers. Tables 6.1 and 6.2 show two excerpts from the MICASE word list; Table 6.1 shows the 50 most frequent words and Table 6.2 shows the 38 words with a frequency of 50 in the whole corpus (out of a total of 1.5 million words).

Table 6.1 The 50 Most frequent words in the Michigan Corpus of Academic Spoken English (MICASE)

N	Word	Frequency	N	Word	Frequency
1	THE	68,036	16	HAVE	11,590
2	AND	41,091	17	IT'S	11,560
3	OF	35,053	18	WE	11,383
4	YOU	34,986	19	WHAT	11,236
5	THAT	34,085	20	LIKE	11,037
6	TO	33,029	21	BUT	10,402
7	A	32,236	22	KNOW	10,000
8	I	31,483	23	FOR	9282
9	IS	23,535	24	ONE	9267
10	IN	23,255	25	OKAY	9250
11	IT	21,883	26	BE	8874
12	SO	17,669	27	THEY	8799
13	THIS	17,110	28	ON	8650
14	UM	15,346	29	ARE	8596
15	UH	14,859	30	IF	8440

*'Register' is the term we are using to describe varieties of texts that are defined by situational characteristics (for example, spoken versus written, edited versus online production). Registers can be described at various levels of specificity. For example, spoken language versus written language constitute two broadly defined registers. A subcategory of the register of written language is the register of academic textbooks. It is also possible to further divide the category of academic textbooks according to discipline (such as biology, business, education, art history, etc.) or by level (undergraduate, graduate, freshman, sophomore, etc.).

Table 6.1 – *continued*

N	Word	Frequency		N	Word	Frequency
31	YEAH	8292		41	CAN	6350
32	WAS	8179		42	AT	6312
33	JUST	7970		43	AS	6229
34	DO	7675		44	THERE	5991
35	NOT	7638		45	THINK	5796
36	OR	7488		46	DON'T	5650
37	THAT'S	7042		47	XX*	5646
38	ABOUT	7014		48	THEN	5443
39	RIGHT	6980		49	ALL	5289
40	WITH	6726		50	TWO	4937

*Note: (xx) is the convention used to indicate unintelligible speech.

Table 6.2 Words with a frequency of 50 in MICASE

N	Word	Frequency
2039	ABSOLUTE	50
2040	BECOMING	50
2041	CAUSED	50
2042	CHARACTERISTIC	50
2043	CLASSROOM	50
2044	CONSISTENT	50
2045	CORE	50
2046	CURVES	50
2047	DAILY	50
2048	DESCRIPTION	50
2049	DETECT	50
2050	DISSERTATION	50
2051	EXECUTION	50
2052	EXPOSED	50
2053	FIGURED	50
2054	GARDEN	50
2055	GRAVITY	50
2056	HABITAT	50
2057	OPENING	50
2058	PAGES	50
2059	PHRASE	50
2060	PRESENTED	50
2061	RAISED	50

Table 6.2 – *continued*

N	Word	Frequency
2062	RANDOMLY	50
2063	REGIONS	50
2064	REVELATION	50
2065	SELECTION	50
2066	SHORTER	50
2067	SHUTTLE	50
2068	SPLIT	50
2069	SURVEY	50
2070	TAIL	50
2071	THEORETICAL	50
2072	TRAITS	50
2073	TUMOR	50
2074	WHOA	50

Word lists derived from corpora can be useful for vocabulary instruction and test development. For example, a word list from an appropriate corpus could be used to select vocabulary words occurring within a specified target frequency range – say words occurring five to ten times per million words – to be included in a course syllabus or pool of test items. Similarly, a teacher trying to decide what modal verbs to teach and what sequence to teach them in could consult a wordlist from one or more corpora to find the relative frequencies of the modals.

In addition to frequency lists, concordancing packages can provide additional information about lexical co-occurrence patterns. To generate a concordance listing showing these patterns, a target word or phrase needs to be selected. Once the search word/phrase is selected, the program can search the texts in the corpus and provide a list of each occurrence of the target word in context. This display, referred to as a 'key word in context' (KWIC) may then be used to explore various uses or various senses of the target word. Figure 6.1 shows a screen shot of a KWIC for the target word *like* from a small corpus of spoken children's language.

The top portion of the screen display provides context for the occurrence of *like* that is highlighted in the lower portion of the screen. The size of the windows and the amount of context can be adjusted, allowing users to adjust settings according to their needs. This small KWIC display of *like* shows that the students (fifth-graders) engaged in informal conversations were primarily using *like* as a verb and that it was often preceded by a personal pronoun and followed by an infinitive (for example, we like to talk, we like to walk, I don't like to listen). Of course, this small display does not show all of the occurrences of *like*; other uses do occur in the corpus.

A concordance program can also provide information about words that tend to occur together in the corpus. For example, we could discover which

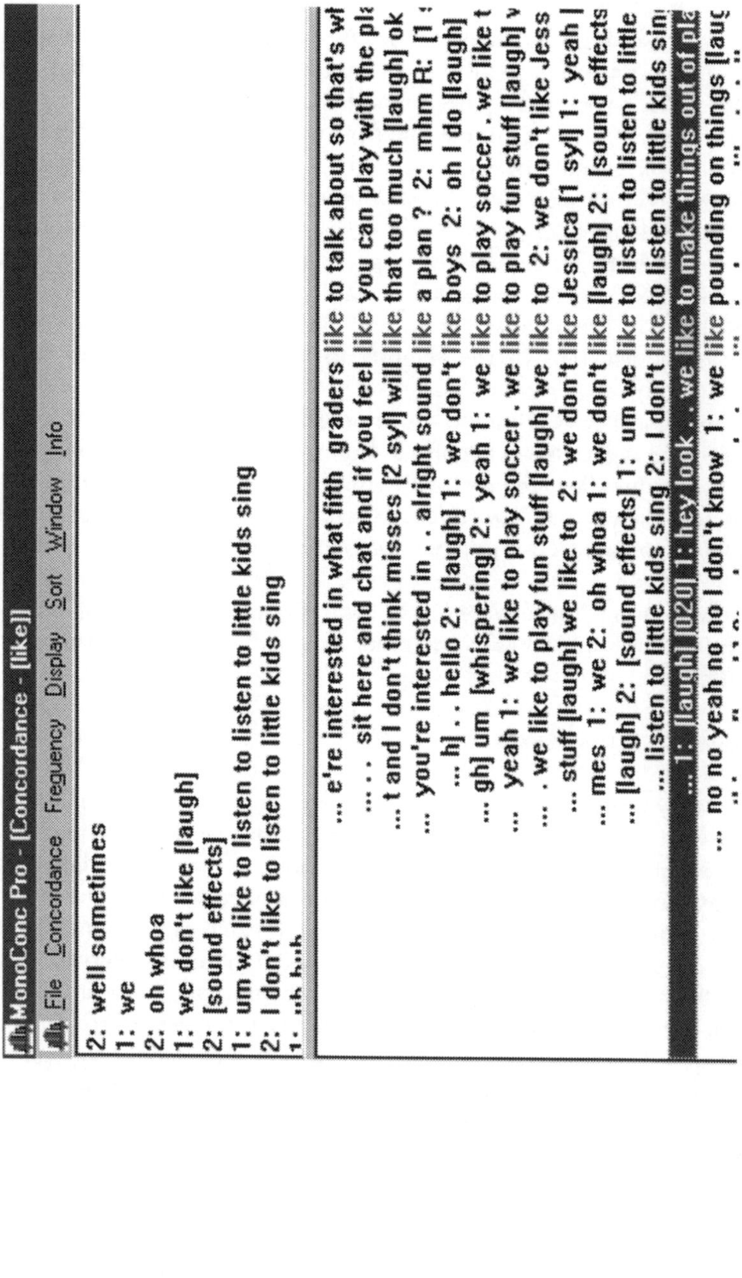

MonoConc Pro - [Concordance - [like]]

File Concordance Frequency Display Sort Window Info

2: well sometimes
1: we
2: oh whoa
1: we don't like [laugh]
2: [sound effects]
1: um we like to listen to listen to little kids sing
2: I don't like to listen to little kids sing
1: uh huh

... e're interested in what fifth graders like to talk about so that's wh
... . sit here and chat and if you feel like you can play with the pl
... t and I don't think misses [2 syl] will like that too much [laugh] ok
... you're interested in . . alright sound like a plan ? 2: mhm R: [1
... h] . . hello 2: [laugh] 1: we don't like boys 2: oh I do [laugh]
... gh] um [whispering] 2: yeah 1: we like to play soccer . we like t
... yeah 1: we like to play soccer . we like to play fun stuff [laugh] v
... . we like to play fun stuff [laugh] we like to 2: we don't like Jess
... stuff [laugh] we like to 2: we don't like Jessica [1 syl] 1: yeah
... mes 1: we 2: oh whoa 1: we don't like [laugh] 2: [sound effects
... [laugh] 2: [sound effects] 1: um we like to listen to listen to little
... listen to little kids sing 2: I don't like to listen to little kids sin
... 1: [laugh] [020] 1: hey look . . we like to make things out of pl
... no no yeah no no I don't know 1: we like pounding on things [laug

Figure 6.1 MonoConc concordance display of KWIC for the target word *like*.

words most frequently occur just to the right or just to the left of a particular target word, or even within two or three words to the left or right of the target word. Words that commonly occur with or in the vicinity of a target word (that is, with greater probability than random chance) are called 'collocates', and the resulting sequences or sets of words are called 'collocations'. An analysis of collocations provides important information about grammatical and semantic patterns of use for individual lexical items (*see* Sinclair, 1991 for more information on collocations).

Through the use of corpus analyses we can discover patterns of use that previously were unnoticed. Words and grammatical structures that seem synonymous often have strong patterns of association or preferences for use with certain structures. For example, the nearly synonymous verbs *begin* and *start* have the same grammatical potential. That is, they can be used with the same variety of clause elements (for example, transitive, intransitive). Yet from corpus-based investigations we have learned that *start* has a strong preference for an intransitive pattern, in particular in academic prose (Biber, Conrad and Reppen, 1998). A detailed example of nearly synonymous words is provided later in this chapter in section on 'Examples of Corpus-based Classroom Activities' and in the 'Hands-on Activity' at the end of this chapter.

Lexical phrases or lexical bundles is another area of collocational studies that has come to light through corpus linguistics. Like collocations, these lexical phrases or bundles are patterns that occur with a greater than random frequency (*see* Chapter 1, *An Overview of Applied Linguistics*, for an example). *The Longman Grammar of Spoken and Written English* (Biber *et al.*, 1999) provides a good discussion of these extended collocations and lists frequent three-, four- and five-word lexical bundle patterns by register. Without the use of sophisticated computer programs, these patterns would remain undetected.

Working with Tagged Texts

In order to carry out more sophisticated types of corpus analyses, it is often necessary to have a tagged corpus. As mentioned in the previous section, when a corpus is tagged, each word in the corpus is given a grammatical label. The process of assigning grammatical labels to words is complex. For example, even a simple word such as *can* falls into two grammatical categories. It can be a modal – 'I *can* reach the book'. Or, it can be used as a noun – 'Put the paper in the *can*'. By writing computer programs that include rules and probability information, computers can quite accurately identify the grammatical labels for many words. However, there are certain features that remain elusive. For these features, programs that work interactively with a user can result in accurate identification. These programs are similar to spellcheckers and bring problematic or ambiguous words to the screen for the user to select the correct classification. Biber, Conrad and Reppen (1998) provide a fuller description of tagged texts and interactive tagging.

Once texts have been tagged it is possible to explore a variety of complex linguistic issues. Clusters of features can be counted, thus providing a fuller picture of the texts in a register. Rather than information from a single linguistic feature, the researcher can explore how features work together in texts. For example, studies have shown that interactive spoken texts produced under time constraints have particular linguistic features associated with them which are different from informational texts. Interactive texts typically have more contractions and a greater use of first and second pronouns (for example, *I, we, you, my*), whereas informational texts have an absence of these features.

Overview of Different Types of Corpus Studies

Over the years, corpora have been used to address a number of interesting issues. The question of language change is one that intrigues many researchers, teachers and language students. The area of historical linguistics has been well established in Europe, with numerous scholars carrying out extensive projects to see how language has changed over the centuries.

In addition to exploring changes across the centuries, scholars have used specialized corpora to gain insights into changes related to language development, both in first and second language situations. These types of studies can provide valuable insights as to the linguistic developmental changes that take place as individuals acquire their first language and also can provide important insights as to patterns of developmental changes that apply to different first language groups as they acquire a second language.

Corpora have also been used to explore similarities or differences across different national or regional varieties of English. Several collections of corpora that represent different varieties of English (Australian English, American English, British English, Indian English) have yielded interesting information about the systematic linguistic differences that occur in these different regional varieties of English.

There have been large-scale studies to explore the differences between spoken and written language. In addition to large-scale comparisons, there have been descriptions of subregisters, such as newspaper language, or even comparisons focusing on different sections of newspapers (for example, news reportage, letters to the editor, feature articles, etc.). Many of the patterns of language use discovered through corpus studies could not have been uncovered through traditional techniques. Prior to corpus linguistics it was difficult to note patterns of use, since observing and tracking use patterns was a monumental task. In addition, many of these findings run counter to our intuitions of how we use language (for example, use of progressive aspect in conversation). For instance, a quick look at most ESL/EFL conversation textbooks will show an emphasis on the use of the progressive aspect. Although the progressive is more common in spoken language than in written, its use is relatively small when compared with simple aspect (Biber *et al.*, 1999).

Describing the characteristics of a particular register can often provide valuable resources for teachers and students. For example, MICASE, a specialized corpus of spoken academic language, may be used to better prepare students to meet the demands of spoken language that they will encounter at university. Teachers can use this corpus evidence to develop materials for students that more accurately reflect the spoken language tasks they will face in a university setting. In the final section of this chapter, we focus on the potential pedagogical applications of corpora and corpus linguistics.

How can Corpora inform Language Teaching?

The impact of corpus linguistic studies on classroom language teaching practices is already taking shape. The availability of corpus findings, along with the increased availability of tools for exploring corpora (for example, MonoConc, WordSmith Tools, Paul Nation's vocabulary programs*) is a considerable benefit to the language classroom. Corpus-based studies of particular language features and comprehensive works such as *The Longman Grammar of Spoken and Written English* (Biber *et al.*, 1999) will also serve language teachers well by providing a basis for deciding which language features and structures are important and also how various features and structures are used. For the first time, teachers and materials writers can have a basis for selecting the material that is being presented and for the claims that are being made about linguistic features. Rather than basing pedagogical decisions on intuitions and/or sequences that have appeared in textbooks over the years, these decisions can now be grounded on actual patterns of language use in various situations (such as spoken or written, formal or casual situations).

There are several works that encourage teachers to explore the use of corpora in the language classroom (Flowerdew and Tong, 1994; Johns, 1994; Barnbrook, 1996; Wichmann *et al.*, 1997; Simpson and Swales, 2001). *Exploring Spoken Language*, by Carter and McCarthy (1997), is the first widely available textbook to combine the use of corpus material with language instruction. The challenge now is how best to translate frequency information and knowledge about patterns of language use into classroom materials.

Bringing Corpora into the Language Classroom

Corpus-based information can be brought to bear on language teaching in two ways. First, teachers can shape instruction based on corpus-based information. They can consult corpus studies to gain information about the features that they are teaching. For example, if the focus of instruction is conversational English, teachers could read corpus investigations on spoken language to determine which features and grammatical structures are characteristic of

---

*MonoConc Pro available at www.athel.com; WordSmith Tools available from Oxford University Press http://www.oup.com/elt/global/isbn/6890; Vocabulary analysis programs by Paul Nation (RANGE and WORD) available at http://www.vuw.ac.nz/lals/software.htm. See also Tom Cobb's webpage at http://132.208.224.131/.

conversational English. Instruction could then be shaped by the features that students are most likely to encounter. If the focus of instruction is a particular grammatical structure, corpus-based studies can provide a picture of the range of use of that particular structure, identifying lexical and pragmatic co-occurrence patterns associated with it. If teachers have a corpus available, they can make their own enquiries into the use of language features that they are teaching.

A second way that corpus information can be brought into the language classroom is by having learners interact with corpora. This can take place in one of two ways. If computer facilities are adequate, learners can be actively involved in exploring corpora; if adequate facilities do not exist, teachers can bring in printouts or results from corpus searches for use in the classroom. An example of this type of activity is provided in the Hands-on Activity at the end of this chapter.

It is worth noting here that the use of concordancing tasks in the classroom is a matter of some controversy – strongly advocated by those who favour an inductive or data-driven approach to learning ((Johns, 1994), but criticized by others who argue that it is difficult to guide students appropriately and efficiently in the analysis of vast numbers of linguistic examples (Cook, 1998). Clearly, there is a need for classroom-based research and experimentation on the effectiveness of exposing language students to corpora and concordance tools. Concrete evidence about how effective these methods are will only become apparent over time, once enough teachers have experimented with the use of corpora as reference sources and learning tools.

Examples of Corpus-based Classroom Activities

The creation of appropriate, worthwhile corpus-based teaching materials takes time, careful planning and access to a few basic tools and resources. All the activities described in this section assume access to a computer, texts and to a concordancing package, but the activities do not require a sophisticated skills or computer programming ability. Several vocabulary activities can be generated through simple frequency lists and concordance output (Donley and Reppen, 2001). If the teacher has the ability to scan or obtain an electronic version of the texts that are being read by the students, frequency lists generated from these texts may be used to identify and prioritize vocabulary words that need to be taught. If too many words are unknown, then the teacher might decide to wait and introduce the text later, when students are more prepared to cope with the vocabulary demands of the text. Frequency lists can also be a starting point for students to group words by grammatical category (for example, verb, nouns, etc.) or semantic categories. In addition, students could do activities that explore how to change words with various suffixes (for example, *nation* to *national* to *nationalize*).

Concordances of target words can be used to better understand those words' meaning and usage. Initially, concordances can be utilized to discover what a word 'means'. However, the use of a word and its patterning characteristics also contribute to its meaning senses. For example, words often are seen as synonymous when actually, their use is not synonymous. Dictionaries often list the 'resulting copulas' (copulas which indicate a change of state due to some force or action) *become, turn, go* and *come* as synonyms, with meanings like 'to become', 'to get to be', 'to result', 'to turn out'. However, most dictionaries provide no clues to how these four words might differ in meaning. In contrast, corpus research shows that these words differ dramatically in their typical contexts of use. In particular, *turn* almost always refers to a change of colour or physical appearance (for example, The water turned grey); *go* almost always describes a change to a negative state (as in go crazy, go bad, go wrong) and *come* is almost always used to describe a change to a more active state (as in come awake or come alive) (Biber *et al.*, 1999). Thus, corpus activities, coupled with dictionary activities, can provide a much richer language-learning environment and one which engages the student in the process of fine-tuning word senses.

Understanding a word's patterns of use is crucial for language learners, and native speaker intuitions often do not prove helpful in predicting the patterns. Thus, in the above example, unexpected combinations would be judged as wrong by native speakers who would have trouble understanding combinations such as go awake or come wrong, but may be at a loss to explain why or think of additional examples of the correct patterns. Although traditional dictionaries are of little help here, students and teachers can easily discover such patterns through corpus analyses. Collocational activities can be used to help advanced language learners refine the context of use and move toward native-like use.

The patterns of language use that can be discovered through corpus linguistics will continue to reshape the way we think of language. Detailed descriptions and models of this use are now being published for teachers' benefit. Evidence from corpus research is also beginning to have a positive impact on the materials that we use to teach language. Perhaps the most exciting possibility is that corpus linguistics now gives students and teachers the ability to explore for themselves the way that various aspects of language are used, helping to guide them toward their language goals.

Further Reading

- Barnbrook, G. (1996). *Language and Computers: A Practical Introduction to the Computer Analysis of Language*. Edinburgh: Edinburgh University Press. A comprehensive introduction to corpus-based language research that focuses on the computer side of the field. Discusses the rationale for using computers, how to collect a corpus, and various ways of using a computer to analyse and annotate texts for linguistic research and natural language processing. Includes appendices with programming examples.
- Biber, D., Conrad, S., Reppen, R. (1998). *Corpus Linguistics: Investigating Language Structure and Use*. Cambridge: Cambridge University Press. An introduction to the range of linguistic analyses that lend themselves to a

corpus-based approach, including studies focusing on lexicography, grammar, discourse, register variation, language acquisition, and historical linguistics. Includes detailed explanations of the methodologies involved in investigating different linguistic features.

- Simpson, R., Swales, J. (eds) (2001). *Corpus Linguistics in North America: Selections from the 1999 Symposium.* Ann Arbor, MI: University of Michigan Press. A collection of selected and revised papers from the first corpus linguistics symposium in North America, sponsored by the University of Michigan's English Language Institute in 1999. The book contains 12 chapters divided into two parts – the first on corpus building and tools, and the second on corpus-based analyses.
- Wichmann, A., Fligelstone, S., McEnery, T., Knowles, G. (eds) (1997) *Teaching and Language Corpora.* London: Longman. A selection of 21 papers presented at the first conference on Teaching and Language Corpora at Lancaster University in 1994. The papers deal with various aspects of teaching languages and linguistics that utilize corpus-bases analyses and materials.

Useful Websites for Corpus Linguistics

The pages listed below provide a useful and friendly sampler of some of the corpora and useful corpus resources that are available through the web. Of course, web address and links change over time, so please be understanding if some of these have changed.

- web.bham.ac.uk/johnstf/timconc.htm
  Tim Johns' Data Driven Learning Page with numerous links to corpus-based data-driven learning and teaching materials, as well as more general links related to corpora and language teaching.
- www.liv.ac.uk/~ms2928/homepage.html
  Homepage of Mike Scott, author/developer of Wordsmith Tools, a concordancing and text analysis program.
- visl.hum.ou.dk/visl/en
  Site of the 'Visual Interactive Syntax Learning' project at the University of Southern Denmark; a set of online text databases and automatic text analysis tools for classroom teaching and scholarly research.
- www.hti.umich.edu/m/micase
  Online access to transcripts of the Michigan Corpus of Academic Spoken English (MICASE), including search facility for browsing specified transcripts and key-word-in-context concordance search function.
- info.ox.ac.uk/bnc
  Homepage of the British National Corpus, with links to the BNC online service, a simple search function, and order forms for purchasing the full 100-million-word corpus or the sampler.
- www.ruf.rice.edu/~barlow/corpus.html
  Michael Barlow's corpus linguistics page; an extensive listing of various

corpus collections and resources, including a list of corpora organized by language, links to text analysis and annotation tools, bibliographies and course syllabuses.

- americannationalcorpus.org
  Home page for the American National Corpus provides information on the design and construction (in progress) of a 100 million-word corpus of American English with a similar design to the BNC.

Hands-on Activity

Imagine that you have been asked to explain the difference in use between *think of* and *think about*. First, try to decide if through experience and intuition you can come up with a pattern for when one form is preferred over the other. Next, look at the concordance lines provided below for *think of* and *think about*, taken from a corpus of informal spoken conversation. Pay special attention to what comes before and after the target words (for example, *think of/about* what?). Are there any generalizations that can be made that would help a learner know when to use *think of* and when to use *think about*? To help you, the target expressions, *think of* and *think about*, have been bolded in the concordance lines presented below.

THINK OF

```
                  stank. Then, as he was trying to think of something to say to her (all
              yes, wedding presents. We must think of something. You probably don't
  racking my brains for three hours to think of something, I simply cannot last
              a second catastrophe. I tried to think of something to say myself, but my
                    offered frills. Nicandra tried to think of something pleasing to say:
          only you were here, then we could think of something to do. 'Christopher
          groaning quietly, perhaps trying to think of something that summed up what
                let said nothing. He had tried to think of something to say, but the only
                  lunch?' 'Ah me, the young! You think of nothing but your stomachs.
        sympathy and collusion. But I can think of nothing to say. Perdie says,
              she tried to speak, but she could think of nothing, and her mother, shifting
        anything so familiar, and he could think of nothing on earth to say. It
              man in the world.' 'As he could think of nothing else, Martin repeated
            But try as she might, she could think of nothing to say like that, fierce
                    listening. 'Can we ourselves think of nothing that needs to be done?

              'what an idiot I was not to think of it before! You all right Elfie?
        . . . no, wait a minute, come to think of it you 're finding. hmm.
    or him, on other occasions, come to think of it. We've been aware of each
    happened to those kids. And come to think of it, Hamelin's rats and children
              like that five years ago, come to think of it, or even ten. It 's the
        wash his feet, he had seen, come to think of it, the moon not too remote from
    probably cheaper than Selina, come to think of it, what with the hotel mark
              could have. I didn't happen to think of it then. 'And when did you
          her pregnant. Better not even to think of it. Just go on hating him,
        and done with. Don't let us ever think of it again. My family always
                  'How nice. What did you think of it?' Patrice held her breath,
```

THINK ABOUT

<pre>
                    You wouldn't just think about it it 's just gone isn't it
        Well that 's a good way, if you think about it he's got, he's got four
    more, I mean they can wear, if you think about it they were suits in the
                    When you think about it, yeah he was So what '
    it seems easier that way when you think about it dunnit? Mm it's a lot be
  does that come from? Oh when you think about it Pledge, why do they call
  wasn't the money really when you think about it because at end of day,
      more. I mean they can wear if you think about it they wear suits in the
  week! And why, they don't need to think about it, they can talk you out of
</pre>

<pre>
        penetrating as lasers. 'We might think about that, 'I say at last.
              I'll have to start and think about that train, Dwight.
          see it. That's the way I like to think about that sort of place. It's
    another way, but I don't want to think about that for a while. 'Timothy
      get eight to twenty-five. Now think about that. The district attorney
</pre>

II ESSENTIAL AREAS OF ENQUIRY IN APPLIED LINGUISTICS

7 Second Language Acquisition

Nina Spada
OISE/University of Toronto

Patsy M. Lightbown
Concordia University

What is Second Language Acquisition?

Second language acquisition research focuses on the developing knowledge and use of a language by children and adults who already know at least one other language. This field of research has both theoretical and practical importance. The theoretical importance is related to our understanding of how language is represented in the mind and whether there is a difference between the way language is acquired and processed and the way other kinds of information are acquired and processed. The practical importance arises from the assumption that an understanding of how languages are learned will lead to more effective teaching practices. In a broader context, a knowledge of second language acquisition may help educational policy makers set more realistic goals for programmes for both foreign language courses and the learning of the majority language by minority language children and adults.

This chapter begins with a discussion of some of the linguistic and psychological theories which have informed second language acquisition research. This is followed by a review of research findings on learners' developing knowledge and use of their second language (L2), including a discussion of how previously learned languages affect that development. The final section examines the role of instruction in L2 development.

Theories of L2 Learning

Both linguistic and psychological theories have influenced research and theory in second language acquisition. One of the fundamental differences between theories developed in these two disciplines is the role they hypothesize for internal and external factors in the learning process. Some linguistics have suggested that language acquisition is based on the presence of a specialized module of the human mind containing innate knowledge of principles common to all languages. In contrast, most psychologists have argued that language is processed by general cognitive mechanisms that are responsible for a wide range of human learning and information processing and requires no specialized module.

Linguistic Perspectives

Universal Grammar

The idea that there exists a universal grammar (UG) of human languages originated with Chomsky's (1968) view on first language (L1) acquisition. He was looking for an explanation of the fact that virtually all children learn language at a time in their cognitive development when they experience difficulty grasping other kinds of knowledge which appear to be far less complex than language. Furthermore, it was observed that even children with impaired intellectual ability were usually successful in acquiring the language they heard around them. Chomsky (1968) argued, furthermore, that the kind of information which mature speakers of a language eventually have of their L1 could not have been learned from the language they hear around them. This problem came to be called the 'logical problem of language acquisition'. Chomsky pointed out that children were exposed to samples of language that were incomplete and sometimes 'degenerate' (for example, slips of the tongue, false starts, etc.). In addition, some L1 researchers noted that parents did not provide systematic feedback when young children produced speech that did not match the adult language, and yet children would eventually leave behind their childish errors and acquire full competence in the language they were exposed to. Thus, Chomsky inferred that children must have an innate language faculty. This faculty, originally referred to as the language acquisition device (LAD) and later as UG, was described as a specialized module of the brain, pre-programmed to process language. UG was said to contain general principles underlying all languages. The child's task would be to discover how the language of his or her environment made use of those principles.

Chomsky's theory of UG was offered as an explanation for L1 acquisition and, although it has been questioned in that context (Elman *et al.*, 1996), it is widely accepted as at least a plausible explanation for L1 acquisition. The question of whether UG can also explain L2 learning is controversial. One of the reasons for this controversy is the claim that there is a critical period for language acquisition. That is, it is suggested that while UG permits a young child to acquire language during a particular developmental period, referred to as the 'critical period' for language acquisition, UG is no longer available to older learners. Even some theorists who accept UG as the basis for L1 acquisition argue that UG is no longer available after puberty and that older L2 learners must make use of more general learning processes (Bley-Vroman, 1989). Because these are not specific to language, second language acquisition by older learners is more difficult than for younger learners and it is never complete. Other researchers have suggested that language acquisition continues to be based on UG but that, once a first language has been learned, UG is no longer neutral and open to the acquisition of any language. That is, although L2 grammars are still consistent with universal principles of all human languages, learners tend to perceive the L2 in a way that is shaped by the way their L1 realizes these principles (White, 1989).

Researchers who study second language acquisition from a UG perspective seek to discover a language user's underlying linguistic 'competence' (what a language user knows) instead of focusing on his or her linguistic 'performance' (what a language user actually says or writes). Therefore, researchers have usually used indirect means of investigating that competence. For example, rather than record spontaneous conversation, the researcher may ask a language user to judge whether a sentence is grammatical or not. In this way, it is possible to determine whether the linguistic feature of interest is part of an individual's linguistic competence, even if it is rarely or never used. Alternatively, a child might be asked to use toy animals to demonstrate a sentence such as 'The tiger is chased by the lion.' If the child's linguisitc competence does not yet include passive sentences, it is likely that the toy tiger will chase the lion.*

Monitor Theory

This theory shares a number of the assumptions of the UG approach but its scope is specifically second language acquisition. As with UG, the assumption is that human beings acquire language without instruction or feedback on error. Krashen developed this theory in the 1970s and presented it in terms of five 'hypotheses' (Krashen, 1982). The fundamental hypothesis of Monitor Theory is that there is a difference between 'acquisition' and 'learning'. Acquisition is hypothesized to occur in a manner similar to L1 acquisition, that is, with the learner's focus on communicating messages and meanings; learning is described as a conscious process, one in which the learner's attention is directed to the rules and forms of the language. The 'monitor hypothesis' suggests that, although spontaneous speech originates in the 'acquired system', what has been learned may be used as a monitor to edit speech if the L2 learner has the time and the inclination to focus on the accuracy of the message. In light of research showing that L2 learners, like L1 learners, go through a series of predictable stages in their acquisition of linguistic features, Krashen (1982) proposed the 'natural order hypothesis'. The 'comprehensible input hypothesis' reflects his view that L2 learning, like L1 learning, occurs as a result of

---

*Note that the distinction between competence and performance is not the same as the distinction between comprehension and production. In communicative contexts, learners are often able to understand language that is, in the purely linguistic sense, well beyond their linguistic competence. For example, if there is an accompanying picture, a sentence such as 'The boy was hit by the ball' may be interpreted correctly. However, when such a sentence is encountered outside an illustrative context, a young child or a second language learner may be uncertain about whether the boy or the ball was hit. That is, they can guess the meaning with contextual help, but their linguistic competence does not yet include the passive construction.

exposure to meaningful and varied linguistic input. Linguistic input will be effective in changing the learner's developing competence if it is comprehensible (with the help of contextual information) and also offers exposure to language which is slightly more complex than that which the learner has already acquired. The 'affective filter hypothesis' suggests, however, that a condition for successful acquisition is that the learner be motivated to learn the L2 and thus receptive to the comprehensible input.

Krashen (1982) has been criticized for the vagueness of the hypotheses and for the fact that some of them are difficult to investigate in empirical studies. Nonetheless, Monitor Theory has had a significant impact on the field of L2 teaching. Many teachers and students intuitively accept the distinction between 'learning' and 'acquisition', recalling experiences of being unable to spontaneously use their L2 even though they had studied it in a classroom. This may be especially true in classrooms where the emphasis is on meta-linguistic knowledge, or the ability to talk about the language, rather than on practice in using it communicatively. *good print!*

We teach about the lg not the lg!

Psychological Perspectives

Learn not acquire.

Behaviourism

For much of the first half of the twentieth century, behaviourism dominated psychology and education and, consequently, theories of L2 learning and teaching. Behaviourism was based on the view that all learning – including language learning – occurs through a process of imitation, practice, reinforcement and habit formation. According to behaviourism, the environment is crucial not only because it is the source of the linguistic stimuli that learners need in order to form associations between the words they hear and the objects and events they represent but also because it provides feedback on learners' performance. Behaviourists claimed that when learners correctly produce language that approximates what they are exposed to in the input, and these efforts receive positive reinforcement, habits are formed (Skinner, 1957).

Behaviourism came under attack when Chomsky (1968) questioned the notion that children learn their first language by repeating what they hear in the surrounding environment. He argued that children produce novel and creative utterances – ones that they would never have heard in their environment. Researchers asserted that children's creative use of language showed that they were not simply mimicking what they heard in the speech of others, but rather, applying rules and developing an underlying grammar. Following Chomsky's critique of behaviourist explanations for language acquisition and a number of studies of L1 acquisition, behaviourist interpretations of language acquisition fell into disfavour. It has taken almost 30 years for some of the principles of behaviourism to re-surface and gain recognition in a different framework.

One of the ideas associated with behaviourism was the notion that the L1 habits which learners had already established would interfere with the formation of new habits in the L2. The contrastive analysis hypothesis (CAH) was proposed to account for the role of the L1 in L2 learning. CAH predicted that where similarities existed between L1 and L2 structures, there would be no difficulty for L2 learning. Where there were differences, however, the L2 learner would experience problems (Lado, 1964). When put to the test, CAH was not fully supported. It failed to predict errors that L2 learners were observed to make, and it predicted some errors that did not occur. Researchers found that L2 learners from different backgrounds made some of the same errors and that some of these errors would not have been predicted by a contrastive analysis between learners' L1 and L2. These findings, together with the rejection of behaviourist learning theories which CAH had been associated with, led a number of second language acquisition researchers in the 1970s and 1980s to argue that there was, in fact, very little L1 influence in second language acquisition (Dulay, Burt and Krashen, 1982). Later research has tended to re-establish the importance of L1 influence, but it has also shown that the influence is complex and that it changes as the learner's competence in the second language develops (Kellerman and Sharwood Smith, 1986; Odlin, 1989).

Cognitive Psychology

Since the late 1980s, there has been a revival of interest in psychological theories of language learning. McLaughlin (1987) and others argued that, contrary to the hypotheses of linguistic theories, there is no reason to assume that language acquisition requires specific brain structures used uniquely for language acquisition. Cognitive psychologists hypothesized that second language acquisition, like other learning, requires the learner's attention and effort – whether or not the learner is fully aware of what was being attended to. Some information processing theories suggested that language, like other skilled activity, is first acquired through intentional learning of what is called 'declarative knowledge' and that, through practice, the declarative knowledge can become 'procedural knowledge'. Other theorists make a similar contrast between 'controlled' and 'automatic' processing. The difference is that controlled processing is not necessarily intentional. Controlled processing occurs when a learner is accessing information that is new or rare or complex. Controlled processing requires mental effort and takes attention away from other controlled processes. For example, a language learner who appears relatively proficient in a social conversation may struggle to understand complex information because the controlled processing involved in interpreting the language itself interferes with the controlled processing that would be needed to interpret the content. Automatic processing, on the other hand, occurs quickly and with minimal attention and effort. Indeed, it is argued that we cannot prevent automatic processing and have little awareness or memory of its occurrence. Thus, once language itself is largely automatic, attention can be focused on the content. The information processing model offers a useful explanation as to why learners in the initial phases of learning seem to put so much effort into understanding and producing language.

For teachers: how can they help learners make controlled processes → automatic

According to the information processing model, learning occurs when, through repeated practice, controlled knowlege becomes automatic. In addition to practice, it is also hypothesized that a process referred to as 'restructuring' may result in learners appearing to have made quite sudden changes in their interlanguage systems rather than gradually increasing the speed with which they use constructions that were already present. Restructuring is a cognitive process in which previously acquired information that has been somehow stored in separate categories is integrated and this integration expands the learner's competence (McLaughlin and Heredia, 1996). Sometimes the restructuring can lead learners to make errors that had not previously been present. For example, when a learner comes to understand that English question forms require inversion, there might be a period in which embedded questions (Do you know what the children are doing?) would be produced with inversion as well (*Do you know what are the children doing?).

Some researchers working within information processing models of second language acquisition have argued that nothing is learned without 'noticing'. That is, in order for some feature of language to be acquired, it is not enough for the learner to be exposed to it through comprehensible input. The learner must actually notice what it is in that input that makes the meaning. This idea has raised a considerable amount of interest in the context of instructed second language learning (Schmidt, 1990).

Connectionism

Another psychological approach to understanding language learning is that taken in connectionist, emergentist and parallel distributed processing models (Ellis, 1999; Rumelhart and McClelland, 1986). These approaches are like the behaviourist approach in the sense that they hypothesize the development of strong associations between items that are frequently encountered together. According to these views, the brain creates networks which connect words or phrases to other words or phrases (as well as to events and objects) which occur at the same time. It is suggested that these links (or connections) are strengthened when learners are repeatedly exposed to linguistic stimuli in specific contexts. For example, when L2 learners produce *I go* and *she goes*, the latter does not reflect an underlying knowledge of a rule for the placement of 's' with the third person singular. Rather, the connection between *she* and *goes* is thought to be established through high-frequency exposure to these co-occurring structures in the linguistic input. The pronoun *she* activates *goes* and the pronoun *I* triggers *go* because the learner has heard these forms in combination many many times.

Research which has investigated connectionist explanations for first and second language learning has typically involved computer simulations of the learning of either artificial languages or small units of real language. Many of these studies provide evidence to support associative accounts of learning (Ellis and Schmidt, 1997). There is growing interest in this explanation for second language acquisition. Related to this approach is the observation that much of the language that even highly proficient speakers produce consists of chunks or strings of language that have a high probability of occurring together (Wray, 1999; *see also* Chapter 2, *Grammar*, and Chapter 3, *Vocabulary*). Researchers working within these frameworks are proposing that language is represented in the mind as a very large number of linguistic units with varying degrees of likelihood of co-occurrence, rather than as a set of linguistic rules for creating novel sentences.

Multidimensional Model

One of the central questions within psychological accounts of second language acquisition is why it is that L1 and L2 learners go through a series of predictable stages in their acquisition of grammatical features. Slobin (1973) proposed 'operating principles' to help explain what L1 learners found easier or harder to process and learn. Within second language acquisition, the 'Multidimensional Model' represents a way to relate underlying cognitive processes to stages in the L2 learner's development.

The Multidimensional Model was originally developed as a result of studies of the acquisition of German word order and later, on the basis of research with L2 learners of English (Pienemann, 1989). In this research, L2 learners were observed to acquire certain syntactic and morphological features of the L2 in predictable stages. These features were referred to as 'developmental'. Other features, referred to as 'variational', appeared to be learned by some but not all learners and, in any case, did not appear to be learned in a fixed sequence. With respect to the developmental features, it was suggested that each stage represented a further degree of complexity in processing strings of words and grammatical markers. For example, it seemed that learners would begin by picking out the most typical word order pattern of a language and using it in all contexts. Later, they would notice words at the beginning or end of sentences or phrases and would begin to be able to move these. Only later could they manipulate elements which were less salient because they were embedded in the middle of a string of words. Because each stage reflected an increase in complexity, a learner had to grasp one stage before moving to the next, and it was not possible to 'skip a stage'. One of the pedagogical implications drawn from the research related to the Multidimensional Model is the 'Teachability Hypothesis' that learners can only be taught what they are psycholinguistically ready to learn.

Interactionist Perspectives

Some theorists who work primarily within a second language acquisition framework assume that a great deal of language learning takes place through social interaction, at least in part because interlocutors adjust their speech to make it more accessible to learners. Some of the L2 research in this framework is based on L1 research into children's interaction with their caregivers and peers. L1 studies showed that children are often exposed to a specialized variety of speech which is tailored to their linguistic and cognitive abilities (that is, child-directed speech). When native speakers engage in conversation with L2 learners, they may also adjust their language in ways intended to make it more comprehensible to the learner. Furthermore, when L2 learners interact with each other or with native speakers they use a variety of interaction techniques and adjustments in their efforts to negotiate meaning. These adjustments include modifications and simplifications in all aspects of language, including phonology, vocabulary, syntax and discourse. In an early formulation of this position for second language acquisition, Long (1985) hypothesized that, as Krashen suggests, comprehensible input probably is the essential ingredient for interlanguage development. However, in his view, it was not in simplifying the linguistic elements of speech that interlocutors helped learners acquire language. Rather, it was in modifying the interaction patterns, by paraphrasing, repeating, slowing or otherwise working with the L2 speaker to ensure that meaning is communicated. Thus, he hypothesized, interactional adjustments improve comprehension, and comprehension allows acquisition.

Although considerable research has been done to document the negotiation of meaning in native/non-native interaction, we do not know how (or whether) interaction contributes to L2 grammatical development. In a recent formulation of the interaction hypothesis, Long (1996) acknowledges that negotiation of meaning may not be enough for the successful development of L2 vocabulary, morphology and syntax and that implicit negative feedback provided during interaction may be required to bring L2 learners to higher levels of performance.

Sociocultural Perspectives

Theorists working within a sociocultural perspective of L2 learning operate from the assumption that there is an intimate relationship between culture and mind, and that all learning is first social then individual. It is argued that through dialogic communication, learners jointly construct knowledge and this knowledge is later internalized by the individual. Like cognitive psychologists, sociocultural theorists assume that the same general learning mechanisms apply to language learning as with other forms of knowledge. However, sociocultural theorists emphasize the integration of the social, cultural and biological elements. This theory, initially proposed by Vygotsky (1987), has been brought to the field of second language acquisition by researchers including Lantolf (2000), Swain (2000) and Ohta (2000). (*See also* Chapter 1, *An Overview of Applied Linguistics*.)

Summary

All theories of language acquisition are meant to account for the working of the human mind, and all use metaphors to represent this invisible reality. Theorists can draw some of their evidence from neurological research that taps language processing more directly. In general, however, second language acquisition theories must be based on other kinds of evidence – primarily the language which L2 learners produce, understand and judge to be appropriate or grammatical. In the next section, we will look at some of the findings of research on learner language.

Learner Language

In the 1970s, a number of researchers began to call attention to the fact that, although the language produced by L2 learners did not conform to the target language, the 'errors' that learners made were not random, but reflected a systematic, if incomplete, knowledge of the L2 (Corder, 1967). The term 'interlanguage' (Selinker, 1972) was coined to characterize this developing linguistic system of the L2 learner.

Several error analysis studies in the 1970s classified L2 learners' errors and found that many errors could not be attributed to L1 influence (Richards, 1974). For example, both L1 and L2 learners of English make similar over-generalization errors such as *two mouses* and *she goed*. The finding that not all L2 errors could be traced to the L1 led some researchers not only to reject traditional contrastive analysis, but to claim that L2 learners did not rely on L1 as a source of hypotheses about the L2 (Dulay and Burt, 1976). Furthermore, because of the association between contrastive analysis and behaviourist explanations of language learning, the influence of the L1 in L2 learning was either minimized or completely ignored by some researchers. The focus was instead on the similarities among all L2 learners of a particular language, regardless of L1.

Developmental Sequences

In the late 1960s and especially in the 1970s, a number of researchers studied second language acquisition in ways that were based on previous work in L1 acquisition. This was reflected in the methods which were used to investigate interlanguage, the specific linguistic features under investigation, and as we saw earlier in this chapter, the theories proposed to explain language development.

One of the most influential studies of the acquisition of L1 English was Brown's (1973) longitudinal research on the language development of three children. One part of that study focused on how the children acquired grammatical morphemes such as possessive *'s* and past tense *-ed*. Brown and colleagues (1973) found that the children acquired these forms in a similar order. Other L1 studies showed that children acquire syntactic patterns such as interrogative and negative sentences of the L1, in a series of stages that are common to all children learning the same L1. L1 learners also make errors which show that they are not simply repeating words or phrases exactly as they have heard others produce them. For example, a typical L1 error in English is putting an 's' on *foot* to express the plural. This kind of error is based on a logical generalization since the pattern of adding 's' to express plurality works with regular nouns in English. The finding that children go through a series of predictable stages in the acquisition of their first language and that their errors are systematic and similar among learners is used as evidence to support the hypothesis that language learning is based at least in part on internal processes, not just on simple imitation of speech or environmental factors such as frequency of occurrence and feedback on error.

One of the important questions for early second language acquisition researchers was whether L2 learning was similiar to L1 acquisition. A number of early studies focused on learners' use of the English morphemes such as the plural, past tense and progressive *-ing* that Brown and colleagues studied in L1 (Dulay and Burt, 1974; Hakuta, 1976; Larsen-Freeman, 1976). Researchers looked at the speech of L2 learners whose ages and L1 backgrounds differed and calculated the accuracy with which they produced the morphemes. They found an accuracy order that was similar regardless of the age or L1 background of the L2 learners. Even though it was not the same as the L1 acquisition order, the similarity across L2 learners suggested that L2 learning, like L1 learning, is governed partly by internal mechanisms. This does not mean that there was no evidence of L1 influence in the L2 morpheme studies, but the overall patterns were more similar than different.

L2 learners were also observed to acquire other grammatical features of the language in a predictable order. These acquisition sequences have been observed in the language of L2 learners learning a variety of target languages. For example, L2 learners of French and English acquire features such as negatives and interrogatives in a similar sequence – a sequence which is also similar to that observed in L1 learners of these languages. L2 learners of German from a variety of L1 backgrounds have been observed to acquire word order features in predictable stages. Figure 7.1 shows an example of a developmental sequence for interrogatives in the acquisition of L2 English. As can be seen, at each stage, some of the questions learners produce may be grammatical within a particular context. Indeed, at Stage 1, chunk-learned whole questions may appear quite advanced. But this does not mean that the learner has mastered all aspects of question formation. As they progress to higher stages, they are able to manipulate more linguistic elements. Thus a Stage 3 question such as 'What the dog are playing?' may be more advanced than an apparently correct question such as 'What's your name?'

The existence of developmental patterns is widely acknowledged. Within this framework, it is possible to look at L1 influence in a different light.

L1 Influence

In spite of the rejection of contrastive analysis by some second language acquisition researchers, most teachers and researchers have remained convinced that learners draw on their knowledge of other languages as they try to learn a new one. Current research shows that L1 influence is a subtle and evolving aspect of L2 development. Learners do not simply transfer all patterns from the L1 to

Stage 1	**Single words, formulae or sentence fragments**	Children?
		What's your name?
		A spot on the dog?
Stage 2	**Declarative word order**	
	no inversion, no fronting:	It's a monster in the right corner?
		The boys throw the shoes?
Stage 3	**Fronting**	
	wh-fronting, no inversion:	Where the little children are?
		What the dog are playing?
	do-fronting:	Do you have a shoes on your picture?
		Does in this picture there is four astronauts?
	other-fronting:	Is the picture has two planets on top?
Stage 4	**Inversion in *wh*- and yes/no questions**	
	copula in *wh*- questions:	Where is the sun?
	auxiliary other than do in yes/no questions:	Is there a fish in the water?
Stage 5	**Inversion in *wh*- questions**	
	inverted *wh*- questions with do:	How do you say [proche]?
	inverted *wh*- questions with auxiliaries other than do:	What's the boy doing?
Stage 6	**Complex questions**	
	question tag:	It's better, isn't it?
	negative question:	Why can't you go?
	embedded question:	Can you tell me what the date is today?

Figure 7.1 Developmental stages for question formation (adapted from Lightbown and Spada, 1999.

the L2, and there are changes over time, as learners come to know more about the L2 and thus to recognize similarities between L1 and L2 that were not evident in earlier stages of L2 acquisition.

It has been observed that some aspects of language are more susceptible to L1 influence than others. For example, pronunciation and word order are more likely to show L1 influence than grammatical morphemes. Learners seem intuitively to know that it is not possible to simply add a grammatical inflection such as -*ing* to a verb in another language, although some very young second language learners are heard to produce such hybrid forms. In addition, learners seem to be sensitive to the fact that some patterns in the L1 are idiomatic or unusual in some way and are therefore not transferable (Kellerman, 1986). Also, there is evidence that when learning a language which is very different from the L1, learners are less likely to attempt transfer (Ringbom, 1986).

One important aspect of L1 influence is the way in which it appears to interact with developmental sequences (Wode, 1981; Zobl, 1980). Although developmental sequences are common among learners from different L1 backgrounds, learners may be slowed down when they reach a developmental level at which a particular interlanguage pattern is similar to a pattern in their L1. For example, although all learners seem to pass through a stage of pre-verbal negation (*I no like that*), Spanish L1 learners tend to use this form longer than learners whose L1 does not have pre-verbal negation. L1 influence can also lead learners to create sub-stages which are not observed in learners from different L1 backgrounds. For example, when German learners of English reach the stage of placing the negative marker after the modal or auxiliary verb (*He can not play baseball.*), they may, for a time, use post-verbal negation with lexical verbs (*He plays not baseball.*) in a way that matches German negation patterns. This sub-stage would not be expected in the L2 speech of learners whose L1 does not have post-verbal negation.

Another way in which the L1 interacts with developmental sequences is in the constraints which L1 influence may place on the use of L2 patterns within a particular stage. For example, French speaking learners of English L2 who had reached an advanced stage in the use of subject–verb inversion in questions, nevertheless failed to use (and rejected as ungrammatical) questions in which the subject was a noun. That is, they used and accepted questions such as 'Can he play baseball?' but rejected sentences such as 'Can John play baseball?' This is consistent with French in that full noun subjects cannot be inverted with the verb to form questions while pronoun subjects can (Spada and Lightbown, 1999).

Instruction and Second Language Acquisition

Research shows that instruction can have a significant effect on L2 acquisition, at least in terms of the rate of learning and the long-term success that learners achieve in using the language accurately. That is, instruction does not prevent learners from going through developmental stages which are similar to those of learners whose exposure to the L2 is primarily outside a classroom, but it may permit learners to move through the stages faster, and to replace some learner language characteristics with more target-like use of the L2 (Larsen-Freeman and Long, 1991).

In light of the evidence that learners pass through developmental stages and that much of second language acquisition is based on processes internal to the learner, teachers and researchers have raised questions about the role of instruction in second language acquisition. Krashen (1982) argued that instruction tended to lead only to what he called 'learning' and that instruction could potentially interfere with language 'acquisition'. He concluded that exposure to 'comprehensible input' would be sufficient to allow learners to progress through developmental stages on the grounds that the language that learners needed to make further progress would always be available if there were enough natural language exposure. Pienemann (1989) recommended a more precise matching of instructional input and developmental stages. Some research confirms that input and instruction targeted to the next stage beyond the learner's current developmental level is most effective (Pienemann, 1989; Mackey and Philp, 1998). Some other research has shown, however, that teaching features which are typical of more advanced stages may hasten learners' progress through the lower stages (*see* Hamilton, 1994). Note that all the research is consistent with the view that instruction does not permit learners to skip stages.

Certain kinds of instruction may appear to alter the developmental path of L2 acquisition. This has been observed when learners are exposed to a kind of classroom input which is restricted to discrete point presentation of one grammatical form after another. In these classrooms, learners do sometimes develop unusual learner language characteristics and hypotheses about the L2, based on the fact that the input they have received is itself a distortion of the target language (Lightbown, 1985).

One way to provide learners with more natural input is through communicative and content-based language teaching. In such classes, the emphasis is on meaning, and learners are exposed to language which is not presented according to a sequence of grammatical forms but rather according to a theme or a lesson in a school subject such as history or science. Such instructional environments allow learners to develop more effective comprehension and communication skills than are typical in more traditional language teaching approaches. Even in such richly communicative environments, however, there are limitations on the L2 input available for acquisition. These limitations arise from the fact that some language features are simply not very frequent in 'natural' language and from the absence of certain types of situational contexts in the classroom. Swain (1988) has reported that, even in history lessons in French immersion classes, learners may not hear the past tense used regularly. Teachers often use the historical present tense typical of narratives to make the events more engaging to the learners. In particular, classroom language is likely to have a restricted range of sociolinguistic and discoursal features. Lyster (1994) found that students who had had several years of French immersion were still uncertain about the use of formal and informal address forms *vous* and *tu*. In classrooms where the only proficient speaker is the teacher, Tarone and Swain (1995) comment that speech and discourse characteristics which are typical of adolescent interaction are rare or absent. Thus, learners whose only or primary exposure to the L2 is in the classroom will inevitably have gaps in their knowledge of the language and the way it is used outside the classroom setting.

Another limitation of second language acquisition that takes place in an environment which does not include form-focused instruction is that learners may not develop high levels of accuracy. For example, research has shown that while L2 learners in communicative and content-based classrooms develop comprehension and fluency abilities, they continue to experience problems with grammatical accuracy and lexical precision (Harley and Swain, 1984; Lightbown and Spada, 1990). In classrooms when learners are able to understand the meaning, they may overlook details of the forms required to express those meanings. When they are able to make themselves understood with inaccurate language and when there are no L2 peers to serve as models, there may be no motivation to move beyond their current level of language use.

Certain types of errors may be easier for L2 learners to overcome than others. In the context of communicative interaction, learners seem to be able to benefit more from instruction and error feedback which focus on semantic or lexical errors than from that which targets syntactic errors. Semantic and lexical errors often result in a breakdown of communication and the reaction of the teacher or fellow student is often based on a genuine need for clarification. This is likely to make the information more memorable to the learners but it is also the case that such errors usually involve a change in a single word or phrase rather than of a more systematic pattern in the learner's interlanguage. As we have seen, errors of the latter type may reflect a developmental stage which learners are not yet ready to move away from. However, instruction and feedback on those developmental features may provide learners with information that they can store as chunk-learned examples, and these may contribute to their progress when the time is right (Sharwood Smith, 1981; Lightbown, 1998).

Errors that are influenced by the L1 and do not interfere with meaning may be particularly difficult. For example, when a French-speaking learner of English says, 'She is wearing a skirt red', the word order error does not lead to confusion. If there is no breakdown in communication, learners may never notice that more proficient speakers of English do not use this word order. Or, if they do notice that others place the adjective before the noun, they may simply assume that this is another way to say the same thing. In these cases, instruction which includes explicit information about how L1 and L2 differ may be the only way for learners to eliminate these features from their L2 (White, 1991; Kupferberg and Olshtain, 1996). Both observational and experimental studies have shown that learners in communicative and content-based classrooms benefit from opportunities to focus on language form (Spada, 1997; Norris and Ortega, 2000).

Over the past 10–15 years, many observational and experimental studies have been carried out to examine the contributions of form-focused instruction and corrective feedback to classroom second language acquisition. This work has been carried out with primarily school-age learners receiving communicative and content-based instruction in a second language. In these studies, efforts were made to draw the L2 learners' attention to different language forms under different instructional conditions. This included instructional activities and strategies which varied along an explicit/implicit continuum – for example, the provision of meta-linguistic rules and overt signalling and correction of errors (that is, more explicit techniques) contrasted with high-frequency exposure and the enhancement of specific language features (that is, more implicit techniques). The overall findings of this work have shown that learners in communicative and content-based classrooms benefit from opportunities to focus on language form, in particular when the instructional input is more explicit in nature (Spada, 1997; Norris and Ortega, 2000).

Conclusion

Since the 1960s, second language acquisition research has, in some ways, become a field in its own right, with numerous conferences and journals devoted entirely to studies of L2 learning. In 1980 it was possible to read almost everything that had been written about second language acquisition theory and research and to keep up to date on new studies. Today, the field of second language acquisition has enormous scope and depth both in terms of the variety of topics under investigation and the research approaches used to investigate them. In a 1994 survey of second language acquisition research, Ellis included over 1500 references to research in this area and there has been a continued increase in the rate of publications since then. In this chapter, we have touched on some of the principal topics in second language acquisition. Several other chapters in this volume refer to other areas of work in second language acquisition, including Chapter 3, *Grammar*, on grammatical acquisition and Chapter 8, *Psycholinguistics*, on lexical acquisition.

Further Reading

- Ellis, R. (1994). *The Study of Second Language Acquisition*. Oxford: Oxford University Press. This book provides a comprehensive treatment of research and theory in second language acquisition and serves as a useful reference for students and applied linguists.
- Gass, S., Selinker, L. (2000). *Second Language Acquisition: An Introductory Course* (second edition). Hillsdale NJ: Lawrence Erlbaum Associates. This coursebook on second language acquisition is directed at graduate and undergraduate students in linguistics and applied linguistics.
- Larsen-Freeman, D., Long, M. (1991). *An Introduction to Second Language Acquisition Research*. London: Longman. This survey provides comprehensive coverage of the major topics in second language acquisition through 1990. It was written for students of applied linguistics and second language teachers.
- Lightbown, P.M., Spada, N. (1999) *How Languages are Learned*. Oxford: Oxford University Press. This is a basic introduction to second language learning and its relevance to second language teaching written for teachers.
- Mitchell, R., Miles, F. (1998). *Second Language Learning Theories*. London: Edward Arnold. A review and critical commentary of the major

theories influencing second language acquisition research is provided for students of linguistics and applied linguistics.

- Towell, R., Hawkins, R. (1994) *Approaches to Second Language Acquisition.* Clevedon: Multilingual Matters. This book reviews 'linguistic, sociolinguistic, and psychological' approaches to second language acquisition research. It gives particular attention to the Universal Grammar perspective.

Hands-on Activity

This picture of a busy airport (Figure 7.2) was used to elicit examples of questions from a group of young learners of L2 English. Each student was given a sheet with the picture and 11 blank numbered lines corresponding to the bubbles in the cartoon picture. The instructions were to imagine what people were saying and to write the question on the lines provided. The students who wrote the questions below were grade six (11- and 12-year-old) native speakers of French who began learning English in grade four (about age nine). The total amount of classroom instruction they had received was about 350 hours – 60 hours per year in regular ESL classes in grades four and five and an intensive ESL course in grade six in which they had English classes for most

Figure 7.2 Airport cartoon used to elicit examples of questions from a group of young learners of L2 English.

of every school day for a period of five months. These questions were written when they were near the end of the five-month intensive class. The instructional approach in both the regular and intensive classes was communicative, with minimal attention to form. Teachers provided some corrective feedback, but the emphasis was always on the exchange of meaning rather than on the accuracy of English usage. Most students had little exposure to English outside of school although English television and pop music were certainly available to them.

- Using the information in Figure 7.1, determine what stage each question represents. Remember that you are not asked to determine whether the question is grammatically correct, but which stage it corresponds to.
- In your opinion, which student appears to be the most advanced? Why? Which student is the least advanced? Why?
- Some of the questions produced on this task appear to be more advanced than the questions which the same students produced in an oral interaction task. How would you explain this?
- If you know French, look for examples of interlanguage features that you think may be influenced by the students' L1.

Asking Questions at the Airport

An airport is a very busy place. People ask for directions. They ask for help with their baggage. Some people need information about renting cars or taking taxis. Sometimes children get lost.

In the picture (*see* Figure 7.2), people are asking <u>questions</u>. For example, Number 4 seems to be asking, 'What time is it?'

On the lines below, write the <u>question</u> that you think each person is asking.

1   ?
•
•
•
11   ?

		Stage
Student A		
1	Do you need something?	1
2	Why did you bring this bomb?	2
3	Where do I put the money, boss.	3
4	Hey, short stuff. What time is it?	4
5	Why are you crying little boy?	5
6	Hey mom! It looks like your ugly skirt!	6
7	What did you find on this terrorist, agent 007?	7
8	Can I have a coke please?	8

9	Do you [have] a big uncomfeterble car, Mrs?	9
10	Where's gate number 5?	10
11	Dad, are you sure you can bring this alone?	11

Student B

1	Everting is okay?	1
2	It's normal to have guns in your countries?	2
3	What's the mission for today boss?	3
4	When do you go to Quebec City?	4
5	Are you loss litle baby?	5
6	It's that your socks?	6
7	It's you on this passports?	7
8	It's that good?	8
9	Do you pay cash or on the credit card?	9
10	Where's the gate 5?	10
11	Do you pass a go [good?] time at the logan airport?	11

Student C

1	Do you want something to drink?	1
2	What do you have in your trunk?	2
3	Where do I have to go?	3
4	Do you have the hour?	4
5	Do you want milk?	5
6	Do you like my new shoes?	6
7	Do you have your passport?	7
8	Do you have beer?	8
9	Do you like this car?	9
10	Mister, do you know where is the gate 5?	10
11	Can I know witch one is my trunk?	11

8 Psycholinguistics

Kees de Bot
University of Nijmegen

Judith F. Kroll
Pennsylvania State University

What is Psycholinguistics?

Psycholinguistics is the study of the cognitive processes that support the acquisition and use of language. The scope of psycholinguistics includes language performance under normal circumstances and when it breaks down, for example, following brain damage. Historically, the focus of most psycholinguistics has been on the first language (L1), in studies of acquisition in children and in research on adult comprehension and production. The questions that have been the focus of investigation include:

- What is the nature of the input that is critical for language to develop?
- To what extent is this developmental process biologically constrained?
- How are words recognized when listening to speech or reading text?
- How do we understand sentences and texts?
- By what means are lexical and syntactic ambiguities resolved?
- How are abstract thoughts mapped onto utterances prior to speaking?

More recently, psycholinguists have recognized the importance of extending the study of language processing to individuals who are acquiring or actively using more than one language. (In this chapter, the term 'bilinguals' is used to refer to such individuals, even though their additional languages may not be as strong as their L1.) Because bilinguals outnumber monolinguals in the world's population, bilinguals more than monolinguals provide a geninuely universal account of the cognitive mechanisms that underlie language performance. Furthermore, the use of two or more languages provides a powerful tool for investigating issues of cognitive representation and processing that are otherwise hidden from view. Specific questions with respect to bilinguals are:

- Is L2 acquisition different from L1 acquisition?
- To what extent does the L1 play a role in using the L2?
- Are there rules governing code-switching (the use of more than one language in an utterance)?
- How do speakers of more than one language keep the two languages apart?
- How are languages acquired at some point in time lost or maintained over time?

In this chapter we provide a selective review of some recent illustrative psycholinguistic research on second language (L2) acquisition and competent bilingual performance. This work is framed by an important set of assumptions about language and cognition. First, it is assumed that the cognitive processes that are revealed as individuals acquire proficiency in a second language share a common basis with the processes that are in place for competent bilinguals. Although we do not intend to downplay aspects of development that may differentially influence performance over the course of acquisition, the basic assumption is that L2 learners and proficient bilinguals rely on similar cognitive mechanisms. Second, it is assumed that these mechanisms are generally universal across languages, although the relative importance of some factors may differ depending on the structural properties of the languages involved. For example, whether the L2 shares the same alphabet with the L1 can have profound consequences for the nature of cross-language interactions (*see* Chapter 13, *Reading*). Yet we assume that fundamentally the same cognitive resources are drawn upon when a native Chinese speaker learns English or a native English speaker learns French. Third, it is assumed that the same cognitive resources are universally available to all learners although individuals will differ in some respects that may have specific implications for success in L2 learning. For example, the degree to which individuals can devote memory and attentional resources to processing and storage may play an important role in their ability to develop automaticity in the L2, to resolve ambiguities during sentence comprehension, and to inhibit the L1 when required to do so.

The chapter is outlined as follows. First, we focus on the way in which psycholinguists construct cognitive models to characterize the representations and processes that underlie language performance. Because our review will necessarily be brief, our illustration is restricted to a model of language production that has been extended to bilingual speakers. The model captures many of the core problems that need to be resolved when speakers have more than one language available:

- To what extent are the two languages kept separate?
- How is control effected so that words only from the intended language are spoken?

The model may also be used to illustrate the way in which psycholinguists formulate hypotheses and conduct experiments to test theoretically based predictions.

Second, we illustrate the contribution of psycholinguistic research by considering a set of selected questions that have been the focus of empirical work on second language learning and bilingualism. These include the non-selective nature of lexical access in word recognition, the development of lexical proficiency in L2, and aspects of language retention and attrition. One of our goals in this section is to illuminate the general logic and method of psychological approaches to research.

Finally, in the Hands-on Activity, we ask you to apply these ideas to the results of a recent study on the development of L2 lexical fluency.

Cognitive Models: Language Production in Bilinguals

Modelling Language Production of the Competent Bilingual

In psycholinguistics, researchers try to develop models to describe and prefer-ably predict specific linguistic behaviour. The aim is to capture all aspects of language use. Ultimately, the goal is to have a model that describes how language is processed in our brains, but the link between functional models, that is, models that describe adequately how language functions in communi-cation, and structures in the brain (neural substrates) is still underdeveloped. The creator of the model to be described below, the Dutch psycholinguist William Levelt, used the term 'blueprint', by which he means that this is probably the structure of the system as it really works in the brain, but where and how it is located in the brain is still unclear. Levelt's 'Speaking' model (1989, 1999) aims at describing the process of language production from the development of communicative intentions to the articulation of the sounds. For this incredibly complex process a number of sub-components, each performing specific tasks, are proposed. The first component is the 'conceptualizer' in which communicative intentions are turned into something that can be expressed in human language. This is more or less the level of our thinking. Though there has been considerable discussion about this, it is now generally accepted that most of our thinking does not take place in a form that is linguistic in nature, at any rate not in the linguistic forms we use while speaking. At this level utterances are planned on the basis of the meanings to be expressed. The second component is the 'formulator'. Here, isolated words and meanings are turned into sentences that are translated accordingly into sounds by the third component, the articulator.

Let us look at the Levelt model in terms of lexis, expecially as language production is largely lexically based. This means that we first select words, or to be more precise: lexical items, on the basis of the meanings we want to express. Then through the activation of 'lexical items', syntactic procedures are triggered that lead to sentence formation. Lexical items consist of two parts, the 'lemma' and the morpho-phonological form or 'lexeme'. In the lemma the lexical entry's meaning and syntax are represented, whereas morphological and phonological properties are represented in the lexeme. In production, lexical items are activated by matching the meaning part of the lemma with the semantic information in the pre-verbal message. The selection of the lemmas with their meaning and syntactic information leads to the formation of the 'surface structure' (an ordered string of lemmas grouped in phrases and sub-phrases of various kinds (Levelt 1989: 11)) . While the surface structure is being formed, the morpho-phonological information belonging to the lemma is activated and encoded. The phonological encoding provides the input for the articulator in the form of a phonetic plan, which leads to the spoken utterance.

As mentioned above, three levels are particularly relevant. At the conceptual level all information about a concept is stored. This includes for instance that a *horse* has four legs, that it can jump and pull carts, but also how it smells and how it sounds. The lemma level holds the semantic information required to match the conceptual and syntactic information necessary to arrive at a surface structure. Thus the lemma can be said to be the link between meaning and form. The distinction between three levels: conceptual, lemma and lexeme, is crucial to the model used here. Moreover, there is compelling evidence that the mind actually works in this manner, although the underlying mechanics of the process are not yet very clear. For example, concepts have a conceptual speci-fication in which all the meaning components necessary to represent a communicative intention are represented. This conceptual specification serves to match a concept with a lemma. However, we are still not quite sure how this matching takes place and how a specific match is evaluated (that is, is there enough overlap between the specification in the concept and in the lemma).

The lemma/lexeme distinction figures in most theories in language. Evidence for this distinction comes from research on naturally occurring and elicited speech errors, aphasia, 'tip-of-the-tongue' phenomena and various experimen-tal paradigms, such as word/picture naming.* There is no perfect one-to-one match between lemmas and lexemes, however. The activation of a lemma through the matching on the basis of the conceptual specification does not always lead to retrieval of the (right) lexeme, and the lexeme is not always retrieved as a whole. Evidence from speech errors such as 'heft-lemisphere' for 'left-hemisphere' show that the lexeme is not a ready-made template, but that it consists of a phonological frame in which phonological segments are inserted. The imperfect match between lemma and lexeme is very obvious in tip-of-the-tongue phenomena: in studies like those of Brown and McNeill (1966) and Jones and Langford (1987) subjects in a tip-of-the-tongue state appear to know the number of letters, the initial letter, the number of syllables and the syllable which carries primary stress well above chance level.

Levelt's Speaking model is primarily a model of the fully compenent mono-lingual speaker. In her discussion of learners of a foreign language as bilingual speakers, Poulisse (1997) mentions the following factors that have to be taken into account if we want to turn a monolingual model into a bilingual model:

---

*Aphasia is the condition where language centres of the brain have been physically damaged through illness or accident. In a 'tip-of-the-tongue' state, a person is trying to remember a word, but cannot quite recall the complete word form. The individual is likely to remember some elements of the form, however, such as the number of syllables in the word.

- L2 knowledge is typically incomplete. L2 speakers generally have fewer words and rules at their disposal than L1 speakers. This may keep them from expressing messages they had originally intended to convey, lead them to use compensatory strategies, or to avoid words or structures about which they feel uncertain.
- L2 speech is more hesitant, and contains more errors and slips, depending on the level of proficiency of the learners. Cognitive skill theories such as Schneider and Shiffrin's (1977) or Anderson's ACT* (1983) stress the importance of the development of automatic processes that are difficult to acquire and hard to unlearn. Less automaticity means that more attention has to be paid to the execution of specific lower-level tasks (such as pronouncing difficult phonemes clearly), which leads to a slowing down of the production process and to a greater number of slips because limited attentional resources have to be spent on lower-level processing.
- L2 speech often carries traces of the L1. L2 speakers have a fully developed L1 system at their disposal, and may switch to their L1 either deliberately ('motivated' switches) or unintentionally ('performance' switches). Switches to the L1 may, for example, be motivated by a desire to express group membership in conversations in which other bilinguals with the same L1 background participate, or they may occur unintentionally, for example when an L1 word is accidentally accessed instead of an intended L2 word. Poulisse and Bongaerts (1994) argue that such accidental switches to the L1 are very similar to substitutions and slips in monolingual speech. In addition to such code switches, L2 speech also contains traces of the L1 which are due to transfer or cross-linguistic influence.

Poulisse (1997) argues that the incomplete L2 knowledge base and the lack of automaticity of L2 speakers can be handled adequately by existing monolingual production models, but that the occurrence of L1 traces in L2 speech poses problems for such models. Paradis (1981), on the other hand, claims that neither switches to the L1 nor cross-linguistic influence phenomena call for adaptations of existing models. Paradis (1981) claims that a phenomenon which is very similar to cross-linguistic influence is operating in monolingual speech production, for example, when monolinguals use words from another style in an incorrect way (informal words in formal speech). In terms of processing, Paradis (1981) argues, cross-linguistic influence phenomena cannot be distinguished clearly from code-switching phenomena: both result from the working of the production system in an individual speaker, and the fact that cross-linguistic influence may sometimes be undesirable in terms of an external model of the target language is not relevant here.

Keeping Languages Apart

Psycholinguistically, code-switching and keeping languages apart are different aspects of the same phenomenon. In the literature, a number of proposals have been made on how bilingual speakers keep their languages apart. Earlier proposals suggested that there were 'switches' controlling the input and output of different languages, but these have been abandoned for models based on activation spreading. On the basis of research on bilingual aphasia, Paradis (1981) has proposed the 'sub-set hypothesis', which, it is claimed, can account for most of the data found. According to Paradis (1981), words (or syntactic rules or phonemes) from a given language form a sub-set of the total inventory. Each sub-set can be activated independently. Some sub-sets (for example, from typologically related languages) may show considerable overlap in the form of cognate words. The sub-sets are formed and maintained by the use of words in specific settings: words from a given language will be used together in most settings, but in settings in which code-switching is the norm, speakers may develop a sub-set in which words from more than one language can be used together. A major advantage of the sub-set hypothesis is that the set of lexical elements from which a selection has to be made is reduced dramatically as a result of the fact that a particular language or sub-set has been chosen. Our claim is that the sub-set hypothesis may explain how languages in bilinguals may be kept apart, but not how the choice for a given language is made.

According to the sub-set hypothesis, bilingual speakers have stores for lemmas, lexemes, syntactic rules, morpho-phonological rules and elements, and articulatory elements that are not fundamentally different from those of monolingual speakers. Within each of these stores there will be sub-sets for different languages, but also for different varieties, styles and registers. There are probably relations between sub-sets in different stores, that is, lemmas forming a sub-set in a given language will be related to both lexemes and syntactical rules from that same language, and phonological rules from that language will be connected with articulatory elements accordingly.

Language Choice

Returning to the model, we will now discuss how language choice is implemented. In speaking, the step which is probably most crucial is the matching of chunks from the pre-verbal message with the meaning part of lemmas, because here the transition from (language-independent) conceptual-ization to language-specific coding takes place. In Levelt's description, the lemma consists basically of three parts: a semantic specification, syntactic information and a pointer to a particular lexeme.

The semantic specification is 'the set of conceptual conditions under which the lemma can be appropriately used' (Levelt, 1993: 4), which is matched with a chunk from a pre-verbal message. It is likely that in lexical retrieval a single concept can temporarily activate more than one semantically related lemma, which suggests that the lemma store is organized according to semantic principles.

The syntactic information refers to the syntactic category of a lemma and its grammatical functions. When a lemma is activated, its particular syntactic environment is defined as well: for example, the verb *sell* will involve a subject, an object and a prepositional phrase. Other lemmas will be labelled as 'recipient' or 'agent'. The lemmas that have been activated will 'search' for other lemmas that fit, that is, the verb will 'search' for a subject (and sometimes an direct object/indirect object). 'Grammatical encoding is like solving a set of simultaneous equations: the surface structure must be such that for all lemmas the required syntactic environments are realized' (Levelt, 1993: 4).

The third type of information in the lemma is a pointer to a lexeme. Lexemes contain the phonological specifications of a lemma and the morphological makeup, although the exact relation between the lemma and the lexeme is not entirely clear.

Thus there are a number of steps in the process of lexical access where choices have to be made. When choosing lemmas, Poulisse and Bongaerts (1994) argue that 'language' is one of the features used in the selection process. So, for the selection of the lemma 'boy', not only do the semantic features 'male' and 'young' have to match relevant conceptual information in the pre-verbal message, but, for a bilingual speaker who has English as one of his languages, the lemma 'boy', will also need to contain information about which language it belongs to (English) and this information will have to match the language cue in the pre-verbal message. Translation equivalents such as 'boy' and 'jongen' (Dutch) show considerable overlap in their semantic specifications, but differ mainly with respect to the 'language' feature.

In the preceding sections we gave a short description of the production model that represents the state of the art at the moment. However, many aspects of bilingual processing are still unclear. One has to do with 'timing': to what extent is the precise timing of the sub-processes in our production system (as measured in milliseconds) based on characteristics of our L1? Do languages that are structurally different require different internal timing between the sub-processes? If so, might there be a mis-match between the timing in place due to the L1 and and the timing required to use an L2 effectively? Many questions such as these remain which will keep this sub-field very lively for the near future.

Experimental Studies of Language Production in L1 and L2

Compared to research on language comprehension, there is as yet not that much experimental research on language production. One important reason is, no doubt, that the kind of careful manipulations of the stimuli that may be made in comprehension studies, as described later on, cannot be done in a similar way in language production. In studies of comprehension, a word, sentence or text can be presented and we can examine the way in which processing reflects its structure and meaning. However, it is much more difficult to elicit speech with particular characteristics, even in response to a simple picture or scene.

Recent studies have used a set of experimental tasks to constrain the words that speakers produce in order to investigate the planning of utterances in real time. For example, in a simple picture-naming task, participants are shown a picture of a drawing and asked to speak the name of the picture aloud as quickly and as accurately as possible. By measuring the time to begin to speak the picture's name in L1 or L2 it is possible to infer the bilingual's relative proficiency in the two languages. Typically, even proficient bilinguals are faster to name pictures in L1 than L2. However, the time difference alone does not reveal the source of the language difference. One possibility is simply that bilingual speakers are slower to access the phonology of L2 than L1 and therefore they are slower on any production task in L2. Evidence from single-word translation and word- naming (Kroll and Stewart, 1994) is consistent with this view, although the delay in L2 naming relative to L1 appears to be greatest in production tasks which require lexicalization, that is, the selection of a single word on the basis of initial conceptual activation. Thus, an alternative account is that L2 is not only slower to speak but also harder to select for output. L2 lemmas may be more weakly activated than the corresponding L1 lemmas or they be more vulnerable to competition from the more active L1 alternatives. Green (1998) has recently proposed an 'inhibitory control model' in which L1 lemmas are suppressed to allow bilinguals to speak words in L2. A focal issue in this area of research is to understand the source of this control. Does it arise from within the processing dynamics of the lexicon itself? Or is it externally imposed by general cognitive mechanisms that modulate the allocation of attentional resources as a function of the task and context in which it is placed?

The main empirical approach to language production in monolinguals has been to examine the pattern and timecourse of interference effects in a variant of the picture-naming task known as picture–word interference. A picture is presented to be named, just as in the simple picture-naming task, but now a word distractor is also presented, either visually or auditorily, and the participant is instructed to ignore the word and name the picture. By varying the time at which the word is presented relative to the picture (before, during or after the picture) and the relation of the word to the picture's name (whether the word is identical to the picture's name, phonologically or semantically related to the name, or completely unrelated), it is possible to infer the nature of the processes that must have been operating at different moments in time prior to speaking. The results of studies taking this approach have shown that semantically related distractors appear to produce the greatest effects early in the process of planning the picture's name, whereas phonological effects are largest later in planning, although they are sometimes observed at earlier points as well (Schriefers, Meyer and Levelt, 1990; Levelt *et al.*, 1991; Starreveld and La Heij, 1995; Levelt, Roelofs and Meyer, 1999; Starreveld, 2000). At a general level, the empirical results of these time course studies support the claims of production models such as the one outlined above in suggesting that first the meaning of intended utterance needs to be established, and only later can the form of the utterance be planned. However, there has been a great deal of debate about the fine tuning of this process. Some recent studies (Jescheniak and Schriefers, 1998; Peterson and Savoy, 1998) have shown that concepts that can be named in two alternative ways (for example, close synonyms such as *couch* versus *sofa* in English) compete with each other for quite a long time during speech planning, to the point where the phonology of both alternatives appears to be active.

Although close synonyms may be the exception rather than the rule for monolingual speakers, for individuals who speak more than one language, the situation may be more complicated because translation equivalents may actively compete for selection. A set of recent experiments has examined this issue in bilingual speakers using the picture–word interference task described above (Hermans, Bongaerts, de Bot and Schreuder, 1998; Costa, Miozzo and Caramazza, 1999; Hermans, 2000). Although they come from differnt theoretical positions, the empirical results that they report converge closely. Perhaps most significant is that they find evidence for cross-language semantic interference. That is, picture-naming in either of the bilingual's two languages is slowed when a semantically related word is presented, regardless of whether or not the word is in the language they are about to speak. This observation suggests that lemmas in both languages are active during speaking. However, unlike the monolingual case for close synonyms, there is little evidence in this work to suggest that the phonology of the translation is active. There appears to be initial competition among cross-language candidates but it appears to be resolved before the alternative is on the tip of the speaker's tongue. We might tentatively conclude that language selection occurs at the level of the lemma (*see also* Green, 1998), but work in this area is too new to reach such firm conclusions.

Illustrative Research on Second Language Acquisition and Bilingualism

The Non-selective Nature of Lexical Access

The topic of selectivity of lexical access mentioned above in the discussion of language production research is also a key issue in understanding how knowledge of the bilingual's two languages is organized and accessed, in particular for understanding the role of the L1 during L2 acquisition. Early research on this issue suggested that lexical access was indeed selective by language. One approach to this problem was to ask bilinguals to make lexical decisions about letter strings that might be words in one or both of their languages. In the lexical decision task, letter strings are presented and the participant must decide whether they are real words or not. On some trials the letter strings form real words but on others they are non-words that are possible but not actual words. The participant must make the decision as quickly as possible and indicate his or her response by pressing a 'Yes' or 'No' button. Gerard and Scarborough (1989) used the lexical decision to test the selectivity of lexical access by having English–Spanish bilinguals judge whether letter strings were real words in their L2. The condition of interest consisted of interlingual homographs or false friends – words that exist in both of the bilingual's languages, but that have different meanings in the two languages.

For example, in Spanish the word *red* means 'net', whereas in English the same letter string refers to a colour. If lexical access is selective then it should be possible for a bilingual to retrieve only the language-appropriate reading of the homograph. Gerard and Scarborough (1989) found support for the selective hypothesis because bilinguals were able to accept an interlingual homograph as a real word as quickly as a control word that was exclusively a word in one language only. That is, it appeared that the non-intended reading of the word did not affect processing, suggesting that it was unavailable.

More recently, the conclusion that lexical access is selective by language has been challenged by a series of studies that used a slightly modified version of the above procedure. Instead of including only L1 words that were homographs, L1 words (Dutch) that were not similar to English words were also included. It is assumed that this required the L1 to be active to reject these L1 words (Dijkstra, Van Jaarsveld and Ten Brinke, 1998). In these studies, there was significant interference for the interlingual homographs relative to their control 'words'. The result suggests that when the non-target language was sufficiently active, the alternative reading of the L1 word was also active. In the same series of studies, when the task was changed from English lexical decision to generalized lexical decision, with a 'Yes' decision indicating that the letter string is a real word in either English or Dutch, there was facilitation for the interlingual homographs relative to control 'words', suggesting again that both readings of the word were active.

Subsequent research has supported the claim that lexical access is language non-selective in comprehension (Dijkstra and Van Heuven, 1998; Dijkstra, Van Heuven and Grainger, 1998; Dijkstra, Grainger and Van Heuven, 1999; Dijkstra, de Bruijn, Schriefers and Ten Brinke, 2000; de Groot, Delmaar and Lupker, 2000; Jared and Kroll, 2001). One aspect of these results that may seem a bit surprising from the perspective of L2 acquisition, is that these studies have almost all examined the performance of highly proficient bilinguals. Even skilled bilinguals appear to be unable to control the consequences of activating information in the unintended language, at least in these out-of-context word recognition tasks. One implication is that learners may be even more vulnerable to the consequences of the effects of L1 lexical form on processing in L2. Furthermore, we might ask whether these findings are confined to bilinguals for whom the two language share orthographic properties. Will Hebrew–English or Chinese–English bilinguals also show evidence for non-selective access? The few studies that have examined these effects across languages that do not share the same alphabet or script suggest that there are still persistent interactions attributable to shared phonology (Gollan, Forster and Frost, 1997; Jiang, 1999).

Developing Lexical Proficiency in a Second Language

If competent bilinguals activate lexical forms in both languages when presented with information in one language alone then what about learners? Relatively few studies have taken a developmental approach to this issue to ask how the nature of activated lexical information changes with increasing proficiency in L2. The few that have compared performance across proficiency groups have observed differences consistent with the view that initially the high degree of activation of L1 influences processing in L2 but that effects of L2 on L1 that can be obtained with competent bilinguals are less likely to be seen (Bijeljac-Babic, Biardeau and Grainger, 1997; Jared and Kroll, 2001).

The main focus in psycholinguistic research on the development of L2 expertise has instead been on the availability of the L1 translation equivalent during L2 processing. An important paper by Potter, So, van Eckardt and Feldman (1984) used the comparison between picture naming and single word translation as a means of determining whether bilinguals were able to access concepts directly for L2 or whether access proceeded through the L1 first. Potter *et al.* (1984) observed similar picture naming and translation performance and concluded that bilinguals conceptually mediate L2 without L1 influence. However, a subsequent series of studies (Kroll and Curley, 1988; Chen and Leung, 1989) showed that the pattern of results depended on the level of L2 proficiency. The results for skilled bilinguals replicated the findings of Potter *et al.* (1984), suggesting that at this level of proficiency concepts can be accessed directly for L2. However, the results for L2 learners suggested that at earlier stages of L2 development there was indeed lexical mediation whereby L1 translation equivalents were activated to facilitate access to concepts.

More recent research has considered the implications of this developmental course, for example, is the early reliance on L1 something that one outgrows when one gains sufficient knowledge and automaticity in L2? Kroll and Stewart (1994) reported a set of results which suggest not. They showed that the performance of even a group of highly proficient Dutch–English bilinguals revealed the use of direct lexical-to-lexical connections to perform translation from L2 to L1. When bilinguals translated words from L1 to L2, there were strong effects of a semantic variable, whether the words appeared in lists that were organized by semantic category or randomly mixed. However, when they translated from L2 to L1, there were no apparent effects of the semantics of the list, suggesting that they were able to bypass conceptual processing in this direction of translation. These findings have been a focus of debate because other studies suggest that conceptual processing is directly available for L2 for both proficient bilinguals and learners (La Heij, Kerling and Van der Velden, 1996; Altarriba and Mathis, 1997). It will remain for future research to map out a complete account of lexical development that traces the role of the L1 translation equivalent (*see also* the Hands-on Activity at the end of this chapter for an opportunity to consider these issues in more detail).

Forgetting and Relearning

In this chapter, we have looked at the storage and retrieval of L2 knowledge. A growing field of research now deals with the opposite of language acquisition: language attrition and language loss (*see* de Bot (1996) and Hansen (2001) for overviews). As discussed above, level of acquisition of linguistic knowledge is crucial in production and perception. Through non-use of a language, the level of activation of knowledge in that language decreases, even to the point that that knowledge is considered lost. An important point for foreign language teaching is how such knowledge can be reactivated again using our knowledge of the mechanics of language production and perception. Unfortunately, very little has been done on this so far.

Many people assume that words can be lost completely, but is this true? de Bot and Stoessel (2000) report on a number of experiments on reactivation of language skills. In those studies, they made use of the 'Savings' method for establishing low levels of activation of items in memory. This method is based on the assumption that words, once learned, are never really lost and that even for words that cannot be recognized using traditional test procedures there are residues of knowledge that possibly can be used in reactivating these words. The procedure is fairly simple: subjects are presented with a list of words: some of these have been learned at some point in the past but cannot be remembered ('old'), whereas others have never been seen before ('new'). The task is to translate the words from the second language into the first language. Then, the subjects are presented with the words and their translations and are asked to learn the translations. Finally, they are tested on those same words again. In a number of experiments with Dutch as a second language, and German and French as a foreign language, de Bot and Stoessel (2000) showed significant savings effects for the old words. Relearning the old words was easier than learning completely new words, which indicates that there was indeed residual knowledge of the old words, which helped to activate them. These findings can be used to help language learners who learned a second language at some point in the past reactivate the language they feel they have forgotten. The data show that very short relearning activities (presenting words in L1 and their translation in L2 for six seconds per pair) lead to high retention scores for such once-learned words.

In terms of language maintenance, Harley (1994) discusses a number of case studies of Anglophone Canadians who successfully retained their French skills learned at school. Among the people interviewed there was unanimity on the role of high initial proficiency and continuing contact with the foreign language. Motivation is also important, as it leads to learners actively seeking opportunities to use the foreign language in different settings.

Implications

Probably the one main implication of this, largely theoretical chapter is that for both language production and language perception two factors determine accessibility of linguistic elements, in particular in non-balanced bilinguals and language learners: the information must have been acquired and stored, and it must be accessible in time. Both production and perception are incredibly fast processes, and information that is not readily available will hamper processing of input and output. So far, little attention has been paid to the crucial role of speed of processing. An exception to this is the work by Jan Hulstijn and his colleagues who are now actually training early learners of a second language to access linguistic elements as quickly as possible, and their preliminary results show that there is a direct and probably causal relation between speed of processing and reading skills. No research has been done so far on productive skills, but it is quite likely that specific training of speeded processes will have a positive effect on those skills as well. The use of computers in language teaching will allow for the use of programs that can train and evaluate such processing. In addition, insights from psycholinguistic research should be applied more frequently in the area of language testing. Although the language production system in particular has been treated as a 'black box' whose hidden mechanisms are difficult to discern, psycholinguists have been successful in explaining many of its workings. This information should inspire language testers to design more sophisticated and valid measures of language proficiency in which the input and output subprocesses are measured along with the global outcome of the system as a whole (cf. de Bot, 2000).

Another, maybe less welcome implication is that much of our linguistic knowledge is by definition unstable: words and rules are not always equally available, availability depends on similarity to the L1 or other languages acquired earlier in life, recency and frequency of use and many other factors. Having learned a word through translation lists does not mean that such a word is then available with all its nuances; rather, only a first connection between a form and a meaning are established. It is only through extensive contact with that word in a variety of contexts that it will gradually develop a full, close to native, set of links.

Psycholinguistic insights also can inform some of the discussions and controversies on bilingual education and bilingual upbringing. The most important one is that there is no support for the hypothesis that bilingualism or learning an additional language at any age will have negative consequences on cognitive processing. It is remarkable that there is a long history of negative attitudes towards bilingualism but basically no empirical evidence to support the assumptions that being or becoming bilingual has negative effects. As Hakuta (1986) has argued convincingly, the debate on bilingual education in the USA (and similar discussions on bilingual upbringing in educational circles) is based much more on attitudes and beliefs than on facts. Apparently, the evidence for positive effects of bilingualism at an early age have little effect on such beliefs. It is quite likely that the growing internationalization in many parts of the world will show the need for multilingualism on all levels. In Canada, the requirement of bilingualism for a good work position lead to changes in attitudes towards learning French. Similarly, the need for proficiency in more languages in the global market may change attitudes in other places as well.

Further Reading

- Carroll, D.W. (1999). *Psychology of Language* (third edition). Belmont, CA: Wadsworth Publishing. Carroll's book is a popular introductory psycholinguistics text. It covers basic topics on acquisition, comprehension, and production and also the biological bases of language and the cultural context in which language is used. It is an excellent starting point for a reader without background in psycholinguistics or cognitive psychology.

- De Groot, A.M.B., Kroll, J.F. (eds) (1997). *Tutorials in Bilingualism: Psycholinguistic Perspectives*. Mahwah, NJ: Lawrence Erlbaum. This volume consists of 12 tutorial chapters on the psycholinguistics of bilingualism and second language acquisition. The chapters cover acquisition, the debate about critical periods for L2, individual differences, lexical and semantic memory, language production and reading, the neuropsychology of bilingualism, and the consequences of bilingualism for cognition.
- Levelt, W.J.M. (1989). *Speaking. From Intention to Articulation*. Cambridge, MA: MIT Press. This is probably the most influential book in psycholinguistics in the last decade. It contains a full description of the work on (monolingual) language production and a blueprint of the speaker based on that research. Although a lot of new research has been done since, the basic model still stands.
- Nicol, J.L. (ed.) (2001). *One Mind, Two Languages: Bilingual Language Processing*. Cambridge, MA: Blackwell Publishers. This recently edited volume contains chapters on topics ranging from the control of the bilingual's two languages, to the lexicon, language production and code switching, sentence parsing in two languages, and sign language.
- Poulisse, N. (1999). *Slips of the Tongue: Speech Errors in First and Second Language Production*. Amsterdam/Philadelphia: John Benjamins. In this book, slips of the tongue of foreign language learners are described and analysed using the model presented in Levelt (1989) and various adaptations that have been suggested in the literature to apply the model to bilinguals. The transcripts and analyses are a rich source of data for research and teaching
- Schreuder, R., Weltens, B. (eds) (1993). *The Bilingual Lexicon*. Amsterdam/Philadelphia: John Benjamins. This edited volume contains a number of contributions that have been the basis of present theoretical models of bilingual processing. The papers cover a wide range of issues that are still relevant.

Hands-on Activity

We illustrate the psycholinguistic approach to second language acquisition by asking you to interpret data from a study by Talamas, Kroll and Dufour (1999). We will walk you through the logic, experimental design and methodology. Then we will present some results for you to interpret. The starting point for the study was the observation that high school learners of Spanish at early stages of acquisition often make errors of lexical form. For example, the word *mujer* which means 'woman' in Spanish, might be confused with the word *mejor* which means 'best'. If the meaning of L2 words is not readily available to learners then words that look or sound alike will be difficult to distinguish. Talamas et al. (1999) were interested in bringing this observation into the laboratory to see whether it could be replicated experimentally and to then investigate its developmental course. At what point do learners become able to access meaning for L2 words? (*See* the discussion in the chapter on the development of lexical proficiency in L2.)

To capture this classroom observation in the laboratory, Talamas *et al.* (1999) compared the performance of less and more proficient English–Spanish learners on a translation recognition task (De Groot, 1992). In translation recognition, individuals are presented with two words, one in each language. Their task is to decide whether the second of the two words is the correct translation of the first. For example, if you were shown the word *man* and then the word *hombre* you would respond 'Yes' because *hombre* is the correct translation of *man*. The experiment was performed on a computer and participants were tested individually. A word in one language appeared briefly on the screen and was followed by a word in the other language. The participant had to decide as quickly as possible whether the second word was the correct translation of the first and respond 'Yes' if it was and 'No' otherwise by pressing one of two designated buttons. Talamas et al. (1999) measured both the amount of time it took participants to make their decision and their accuracy.

The critical conditions of the experiment involved word pairs which were not the correct translation of one another. Some of these pairs were simply unrelated words (for example, *man* followed by *casa* which means 'house' in Spanish). But others were form distractors, like the errors that students had been observed to produce spontaneously (for example, *man* followed by *hambre* which means 'hunger' but looks like the correct translation, *hombre*). A final condition consisted of semantic distractors which were semantically related words but not translation equivalents (for example, *man* followed by *mujer* which means 'woman').

A summary of the conditions is shown in Table 8.1.

Table 8.1 Summary of conditions in the translation recognition task (after Talamas, Kroll and Dufour, 1999)

Translation recognition task: Is the second word the correct translation of the first word?		
Condition	**Example**	**Correct response**
Correct translation	*man–hombre*	Yes
Incorrect translations		
form-related	*man–hambre*	No
semantically related	*man–mujer*	No
unrelated control	*man–casa*	No

Talamas *et al.* (1999) hypothesized that less proficient learners would be tricked by the similarity of the form distractors. If so, they should take longer to reject incorrect translation pairs, such as *man–hambre* than unrelated controls and also be more likely to make the error of incorrectly responding 'Yes' to the incorrect translation. Furthermore, Talamas *et al.* (1999) predicted that the performance of less proficient learners would suffer more from form interference than the performance of more proficient learners, who can more readily access the meaning of the words. Similarly, they hypothesized that the performance of the more proficient learners would be more sensitive to the semantic distractors than the performance of the less proficient learners.

The results of this experiment are shown in Table 8.2 for the critical 'No' pairs.**

Table 8.2 Results of the critical 'No' pairs experiment*

Condition	Example (correct response)	Learner groups	
		Less proficient	More proficient
Form-related	*man–hambre* (No)	972 ms (58%)	903 ms (82%)
Semantically related	*man–mujer* (No)	898 ms (72%)	967 ms (85%)
Unrelated control	*man–casa* (No)	868 ms (88%)	852 ms (99%)

*Mean response latencies (time in milliseconds to make the 'No' decision) and per cent accuracy.

For the purpose of the activity, we will ignore statistical considerations and simply focus on overall differences between conditions. Assume that any difference in the response latency data larger than 50 milliseconds is statistical reliable and that any difference greater than 10 percentage points in accuracy is also significant.

Questions:

- Is there any evidence in the data to support the hypothesis based on the observation of classroom errors that less proficient learners are more likely to be fooled by similarity in the lexical form of L2 words?
- Do the data provide support for the prediction that more but not less proficient learners are sensitive to the meaning of L2 words? Is there any evidence that the less skilled learners were influenced by the semantically related distractors?

**Note that for the purpose of this activity, the data from the Talamas, Kroll and Dufour (1999) study have been averaged over conditions. The interested reader is encouraged to consult the original report of this work for a more complete discussion of the experiment and results

- Using these results, how would you characterize L2 lexical development, that is, the difference between high and low proficiency groups?
- What are the implications of the observed form interference in the more proficient group for claims about the selectivity of lexical access discussed in the chapter?

9 Sociolinguistics

Carmen Llamas
University of Aberdeen

Peter Stockwell
University of Nottingham

What is Sociolinguistics?

The most obvious definition of 'sociolinguistics' is that it is the study of language in society. However, if it was as easy as that, then almost every language event would form part of the field of sociolinguistics. After all, there is a social and contextual dimension to every naturally occurring use of language, and it is always these social factors that determine the choice and form of what is written or said or understood. If sociolinguistics is not to encompass all linguistics, psychology and social theory, then we need a more precise and complex definition.

So, sociolinguistics is the study of the linguistic indicators of culture and power. This is much more specific. This allows us to focus on language but also allows us to emphasize the social force of language events in the world. It allows us to use the tools of linguistics as outlined in the first part of this book (grammar, vocabulary, corpus linguistics, discourse analysis and pragmatics), as well as phonology, but it also encourages us to see the influences of ethnicity, gender, ideology and social rank on language events. Above all, this definition allows sociolinguists to be descriptive of pieces of language in the world, whilst encouraging us to recognize that we are all included in that world too. It could even be argued that sociolinguists have a special responsibility to use their privileged knowledge to influence the direction of, for example, government language policies, educational practices, media representations and so on.

Many sociolinguists have argued strongly for this ethically-involved position. However, we must recognize that the majority of sociolinguistic studies are primarily descriptive and aim towards a scientific objectivity, even when dealing with very complex social influences on language. That is, most studies focus on giving an account of social aspects of language in the real world that is as precise and systematic an account as possible within the current state of knowledge. Sociolinguistics is thus progressive as a discipline in the sense that new studies and new thinking are continually testing and developing our understanding of the way language and society work in relation to each other. This means we need a definition of sociolinguistics that covers the central concerns of the majority of the discipline.

So, finally and centrally, sociolinguistics is the study of language variation and language change. This definition foregrounds the essential features of language: societies differ from each other and change over time, and language is bound up with these processes. The two dimensions can be seen as complementary axes: an historical or 'diachronic' axis which is concerned with the ways in which language use has changed over time; and a snapshot of a moment in time, usually contemporary, on the 'synchronic' axis. All the tools of linguistics may be deployed to focus in on particular features along these two dimensions, as we will outline in the rest of this chapter.

Issues in Sociolinguistics

Sociolinguistics is a fieldwork-based discipline. Researchers collect examples of language usage in their naturally occurring environments and study them in relation to the findings of other sociolinguists' research work. In this sense it is truly an example of applied linguistics: there is no introspection, nor intuitive conclusions nor impressionistic evaluation involved. This means it is relatively easy for researchers new to the discipline to engage in genuine and valuable sociolinguistic research at an early stage in their study. Indeed, this sort of practical investigation would be the best way to develop your own thinking and knowledge of sociolinguistics.

In order to demonstrate this fact, we introduce the key ideas in the field by illustration, using the current sociolinguistic fieldwork data of Carmen Llamas. This research concentrates on the area of Teesside in the north-east of England, although the techniques Llamas uses and several of her findings are connected to many published sociolinguistic studies (Wolfram and Schilling-Estes, 1998; Foulkes and Docherty, 1999; Kerswill, Llamas and Upton, 1999; Llamas, 2000, 2001).

Categorizing the Ways People Speak

Idiolect and Sociolect

Individuals speak in characteristic ways that might be peculiar to them in certain circumstances: we call this pattern their 'idiolect'. However, people often use language in ways that they share with many other people: most generally we can call these patterns 'sociolects'. In part, the sociolects that individuals use help us to define them as a coherent social group.

Sociolinguistics is mainly interested in the different forms of sociolect, in suggesting patterns and frameworks by which such sociolects seem to operate. It is a process of generalization away from the detail of specific data. In doing this, sociolinguistics does not deny the value of individual experience; indeed, the fact that social patterns are made explicit can be of immense value in understanding the place of individuals in society.

Standard, Non-Standard and Codification

An example of the potential conflict that might result from these patterns can be seen in the tension – felt in almost all languages around the world – between the 'standard' form and 'non-standard' varieties. Standardization is a process that is apparent in almost all modern nations, in which one variety of a particular language is taken up (by government, the education system, newspapers and other media) and promoted as the 'standard' form. This often involves prescribing its use in the classroom and public examinations, reporting the workings of government in this form, printing national publications and any formal or prestigious material through its medium, and treating it as the 'correct' and 'proper' form of the language (when, technically, there is no such thing). 'Codification' is a prominent feature of standard forms: grammar books and dictionaries are written promoting the form; texts of religious or cultural significance and canonical literature in the form are valued; and the variety is taught to children in schools (*see* Pennycook, 1994; Bex and Watts, 1999; Milroy and Milroy, 1999).

Prestige, Stigmatization and Language Loyalty

By contrast, other non-standard forms of the language can be treated as 'poor' or 'incorrect' varieties: they are 'stigmatized'. Standard forms receive 'prestige'. It is easy to measure the relative prestige or stigma of a variety by asking the following questions:

- Has the variety been 'standardized' and codified institutionally?
- Is the variety spoken by a 'living community' of speakers?
- Do the speakers have a sense of the long 'history' of their variety?
- Do the speakers consider their variety to be independent of other forms and 'autonomous'?
- Do the speakers use the variety for all social functions and in all contexts or does it have a 'reduced scope' of usage?
- Do the speakers consider their variety 'pure' or a 'mixture' of other forms?
- Are there 'unofficial' rules of the variety, even where there is no codified grammar book; is there a sense of a 'good' and 'bad' form?

(List adapted from Bell, 1976.)

You will notice that these factors of prestige and stigmatization depend very much on speakers' attitudes to their own variety. This is an important feature of sociolinguistic enquiry. People's attitude to their own language often affects the form of that language. For example, stigmatized varieties of language often survive even under institutional pressure because groups have a 'language loyalty' that preserves the varieties in the face of the standardized form.

Dialect, Accent and Language Planning

A standardized variety is usually a regional 'dialect', which has been elevated in prestige and often loses its regional associations as a result. A dialect refers to the characteristic patterns of words and word-order (lexico-grammar) which are used by a group of speakers. The standard form of a language is an institutionally-valued dialect, which has been selected by historical accident or by deliberate 'language planning' by governments to be held up as the standard language. Dialect usually refers just to the form of the lexico-grammar of the variety as it could be written down, rather than its pattern of pronunciation. The latter is called 'accent'.

An accent can also be standardized and stigmatized. It is important to realize that accent and dialect are separate concepts. In principle, any dialect can be spoken in any accent, for example, the dialect known as Standard UK English can be heard in all of the regional accents of Britain. In practice, non-standard dialects tend to be spoken in specific local accents: it would be very strange (though possible) to hear a Liverpool dialect spoken in a New York accent, for instance. However, we often hear regional dialects spoken in foreign accents when they are being learned by non-native speakers. It is also important to realize that every form of spoken language is uttered as a dialect and in an accent. When people say they have no accent, they usually mean that they are speaking in a standardized and prestigious accent.

Speech Communities

The way people speak often serves to define them as a group. We can talk of the 'speech community', which might correspond with the group as defined by other non-linguistic means: nationality, age range, gender, town or city population, political allegiance and so on. As we will see in this chapter, the coherence generated by all these factors – including the linguistic factor – can operate as a self-serving reinforcement of all sorts of social values to do with local or community or ethnic identity. Language variants may also be maintained and reinforced, even against standardization pressure, in this way.

Descriptive Tools of Language Variation

Any single piece of language is an integrated whole, but in order to investigate its different aspects we must explore it in convenient categories. Traditionally, linguistics has categorized the different dimensions of language as a 'rank scale' from the smallest units of individual sounds or letters up to the largest scale of whole texts and discourses. Each of these levels often corresponds with a linguistic sub-discipline, as follows:

Language element		Linguistic sub-discipline
discourse		discourse analysis
text		text linguistics
utterance		pragmatics
sentence	meaning →	semantics
clause		&
phrase	structure →	syntax
word/lexeme		lexicology
morpheme		morphology
sound/phoneme		phonology
letter/grapheme		graphology

(For an overview of all these dimensions, *see* Jackson and Stockwell, 1996). You will have noticed that some of the chapters in the first part of this book cover several of these sub-disciplines. Like second language acquisition and psycholinguistics in this part of the book, the sub-discipline of sociolinguistics is not confined to one of these levels; instead, it investigates different levels from a sociolinguistic perspective.

Although sociolinguistic variation occurs throughout the language system, sociolinguistic studies have focused on particular types of patterns, especially at the phonological level. Phonological variation is a useful level to study since it is easier to find an occurrence of a particular sound rather than a word, phrase or grammatical structure; also, phonological variation is often below the level of awareness of speakers and so is less affected by self-conscious alteration. However, sociolinguistic exploration has also been undertaken at the grammatical, lexical, discoursal and whole-language levels.

The Linguistic Variable

The main tool in sociolinguistics has been the concept of the 'linguistic variable'. This is any single feature of language which could be realized by different choices. In the word *farm*, for example, some people do not pronounce the /r/ and some do, and there are also variations in the ways the /r/ can be pronounced. This is a linguistic variable which is strongly determined by geographical location: non-/r/-pronouncers are likely to be from England, Wales, Australia, Massachusetts or the southern states of the USA. Furthermore, you could pronounce the /r/ as a sort of 'tap' against the back of the teeth (almost like a /d/), in which case you are likely to be from the Scottish Highlands or the west of Ireland.

The linguistic variable feature could be a sound, or a word, or a phrase, or a pattern of discourse and so on. For example, common words for round bread products include the lexical variants: *bun, roll, cob, bap, barm, fadgie, stotty, cake, batch, loaf* and no doubt many others. You might not even recognize some of these, but their use is determined by the social factor of geographical location. Do you *park your car, rank it* or *file it*? Do you buy sugar in a *bag*, or a *sack*, or a *poke*? Do you *call someone* or *phone them up* or *ring them* or *give them a phone* or *give them a bell* or *give them a buzz*? All of these will vary depending on where you live, and who you are talking to.

Phonological Variation

Although the linguistic variable can be from any level of the linguistic rank structure, it is variation in 'accent' that has provided the major focus of sociolinguistic studies so far. This is partly because observing and recording occurrences of individual sounds is very much easier than waiting around all day for a particular word, structure or discourse pattern to appear, or setting up a complicated and artificial test situation. Phonological variables also have the advantage that they are usually below the level of conscious awareness, so the recorded data can be relied on to be naturalistic.

People ordinarily talk of 'broad' or 'strong' accents and describe sounds as 'precise' or 'clipped' or a 'drawl'. However, in order to be able to describe accents systematically and precisely, sociolinguists use the International Phonetic Alphabet (IPA). This is a system of special letters, each one of which corresponds with a very particular sound. The full IPA covers every speech sound it is possible to make with the human mouth and throat (*see* Ball and Rahilly, 1999). Table 9.1 lists a selection of some symbols which you might find useful in sociolinguistics.

Grammatical Variation

Linguistic variables operating at a grammatical level have also been studied in sociolinguistics. For example, variations in the morphology of subject–verb agreement have been observed among the speech of British schoolchildren. The third person morpheme '-s' (*he goes, she knows*) was used by some children for all verb agreements (*I goes, I knows*). It was noted that this non-standard pattern tended to be used with a greater frequency by boys than girls, and seemed to be a marker of group solidarity among the boys.

Centrality in the social group and speech community is often marked by the frequent use of certain realizations of linguistic variables. A major feature of African–American vernacular English (AAVE) is the non-use of the verb 'to be' in some contexts: *he a big man, you the teacher*. This is known as 'copula deletion', and is the grammatical form to use when the verb could be contracted in general American English or standard British English: *he's a big man, you're the teacher*. By contrast, African–American vernacular has developed an invariant 'be' to signal habitual states: *he be busy, she be running all day*.

A common grammatical variable that AAVE shares with many other non-standard grammars is the requirement for 'negative concord': that is, in a negated sentence, every element must be negated (*Ain't nobody going to help you, don't nobody know me*). This can be used for heavy emphasis (*Ain't no cat can't get in no coop*), where standard Englishes would need to use a few more phrases to achieve the same effect (*There isn't a single cat that can get into any coop at all*) (*see* Labov, 1972; Kochman, 1981).

Table 9.1 Selected International Phonetic Alphabet (IPA) symbols

Consonants

p	–	pip	tʃ	–	church
b	–	bib	dʒ	–	judge
t	–	ten	m	–	man
d	–	den	n	–	man
k	–	cat	ŋ	–	sing
g	–	get	l	–	let
f	–	fish	r	–	ride, parrot ('trilled r')
v	–	van	ɾ	–	rubbish (Scots) ('tapped r')
θ	–	thigh	ɹ	–	farm (US) ('approximant r')
ð	–	thy	ʋ	–	'very' as 'vewy'
s	–	set	w	–	wet
z	–	zen	j	–	yet
ʃ	–	ship	ʔ	–	bu'er, 'butter pronounced without
ʒ	–	leisure			the /t/' (glottal stop)
h	–	hen	x	–	loch (Scots)

Vowels
(Monophthongs)

ɪ	–	pit		aɪ	–	bite, night
ɛ	–	pet		əɪ	–	night (Scots, Canadian)
æ	–	pat		ɛɪ	–	bait
ɒ	–	pot (British accent)		ɔɪ	–	boy
ʌ	–	putt (British), color (US)		əʊ	–	roe
ʊ	–	put		aʊ	–	house
ə	–	patter (British)		ʊə	–	sewer, poor (British)
o	–	eau (French), low (N England)		ɪə	–	ear (British)
a	–	calm (Scouse), farm (Teesside)		ɛə	–	air (British)
y	–	tu (French), school (Scouse)				
ø	–	peu (French), boat (Geordie)				
i:	–	bean				
ɜ:	–	burn				
ɑ:	–	barn				
ɔ:	–	born				
u:	–	boon				
e:	–	bait (Northern England)				

Lexical Variation

Dialectal variation depends largely on different lexical items being used from region to region. Traditionally, 'dialectologists' were able to draw lines across maps in order to delineate the boundaries where different words or phrases were used. When making tea, you might *stew*, *mash*, *brew* or *draw* the tea in boiling water. Most local areas have specific lexical items that serve to identify their speakers: your nose is a *neb* in Yorkshire; a *square* is to Philadelphians what a *block* is to a New Yorker; an American *resume* is a British *CV*, which is South African *biodata*; South African *robots* are British *traffic lights*; American police *batons* are British *truncheons* which are Indian *lathis* and so on.

Phrasal variations include the Irish and Scottish *Is that you?* when an English person would say *Are you finished?* and an American would say *Are you done?* or *Are you through?* Prepositional variation is very difficult to explain: why do Americans *talk with* and *meet with* when British people *talk to* and just *meet*? Something *in back of* the house in America is *behind* or *at the back of* it in Britain. There are dozens of others, usually consequences of historical divergence or interference from other languages.

Discoursal Variation

Variability in discourse organization is a very fruitful area of investigation at the moment. Strategies of conversational structure can be observed and analysed, for example, and it is easy to see how politicians can be trained to exploit techniques for 'keeping their turn' (*see* Chapter 12, *Speaking and Pronunciation*) and dominating the discussion. Alternatively, the different ways that men and women organize narratives or conduct conversations or arguments have been investigated to show up apparently different objectives in speech.

Aspects of politeness and social solidarity represent another dimension of discourse organisation that can be explored (*see* Chapter 5, *Pragmatics*). Again, gender studies have led the way here, and insights into how politeness (and impoliteness) works have been generalized cross-culturally in comparative studies.

Linguistic Variation

Lastly, the entire language can be treated as a variable. Bilingual or multilingual individuals can often move from one language to another within a single utterance and sometimes even within a sentence. This is called 'code-switching', and the shift into another language can be used to indicate that a different 'domain' of experience is being signalled.

Sometimes entire speech communities share two or more languages, as in Switzerland (German, French, Italian) or Canada (French, English). Where there is a functional division between the languages' usage, for example when one is used for formal or printed contexts and the other just in speech, then a situation of 'diglossia' is said to exist. One variety becomes the H (as in High German) and the other the L (Low German) variety. For example, classical Arabic, the language of the Koran, is the H variety that can be read by all Arabic speakers, but in different Arab countries a range of different L varieties of Arabic is spoken.

Sociolinguistics explores aspects of such situations, as well as deliberate attempts by governments and authorities to engage in language planning: the promotion and standardization of one variety of language, and attempted interventions in linguistic usage (such as Noah Webster's dictionary with its new spellings of 'American English' words, or prohibitions by the Academie Française of Anglicisms such as *le weekend* or *le hot-dog* in French).

Lastly, sociolinguists explore the birth and death of languages, for example in the development of 'pidgin' languages. These are new languages, often based on two or more languages in contact, with their own systematic grammatical rules. When some pidgins become the first languages of a new generation, they are called 'creoles' (such as South African Afrikaans, Jamaican Patwa, West African Krio, Louisiana Crioule and many others). Creolists have provided insights into the processes of development of all languages, by investigating new and emerging creoles (*see* Holm 1988, 1989; Romaine, 1988; Sebba, 1997).

Social Factors that Correlate with Language Variation

In the section above, it was very difficult for us to talk about linguistic variables without mentioning the social factors with which they may correlate. This is the whole point of sociolinguistics. In investigation, a linguistic variable is set against the social variable in order to work out the influence of that social aspect on language. A range of social variables have been focused upon in sociolinguistic studies (*see* Milroy and Milroy, 1993).

Geographical and Social Mobility

Dialects within a language are often localized geographically. We can speak of 'dialect chains' where the shift from one dialect to the next is not sudden between one town or county or state and the next. Instead, dialects merge and overlap across distances. Even at national boundaries, speakers on either side of the border can sometimes understand each others' dialects (such as neighbouring Dutch and Germans) better than speakers within their own 'language' community (northern Germans and Bavarian Germans, for example).

If dialect chains complicate the dialect map, towns and cities complicate matters further. The migration of people into urban areas disrupted neat dialect divisions, and the study of 'urban dialectology' was only achieved by the realization that there is social stratification in urban areas on the basis of class. Increasing geographical mobility has been matched over the last century in the western world by increasing social mobility. The self-consciousness that this brings can be observed in people of certain social groups aiming for a more prestigious form of language than they would naturally use, for example, 'overdoing' an upper-middle class accent in formal situations. This is called 'hypercorrection'.

The counterpart of hypercorrection is the phenomenon observed when some people use stigmatized forms of language (as a sort of 'streetwise' accent signal): this is known as 'covert prestige'. Factors such as these are major influences on language loyalty and language change.

Gender and Power

The influence of gender and asymmetries in power relations have been a major aspect of sociolinguistic discussion in recent years. The notion of a 'genderlect' has been proposed to account for some of the apparently systematic differences in the ways men and women use language. These differences can be observed across the whole range of linguistic variables, from plans of narrative and discourse organization, to the different accents that men and women have even from the same area (*see* Coates and Cameron, 1986; Coates, 1993; Cameron, 1995; Crawford, 1995; Mills, 1995).

Age

Older people and younger people use language differently. When corresponding features of these speakers are compared, such differences can reveal evidence of changes in the language over time. In other words, the 'snapshot' of current usage across the age ranges can suggest historical language changes. This is the 'apparent time hypothesis'; it gives us the ability to observe potential change in progress, which was not thought possible in the past.

Audience

Taking into account the audience and reception of language use provides insights into the ways speakers behave. Most conversations have a 'recipient design', that is, speakers plan their utterances with the addressee in mind. This factor often results in speakers adjusting their accent, style or language towards their addressees. This phenomenon is called 'accommodation' and it seems that such convergence of accents is an important cause of language change over time.

Identity

This is an important social factor. Not only do linguistic patterns signal social and individual identity, but people's conscious awareness of their personal, ethnic, geographical, political and family identities is often a factor in their language use. Allegiance and membership of different social groups can be expressed by language patterns, and sometimes those groups are even defined by these patterns, whether this is a language or style or jargon.

Social Network Relations

It has been recognized that the relative strength of relations between individuals within a social group (their 'social network') is also important in understanding how linguistic features are maintained, reinforced and spread. Whether individuals have strong or weak ties to the group can be used as a measure of their sociolinguistic influence (*see* Milroy, 1987; Milroy and Milroy, 1999).

Working with Sociolinguistic Data

Collecting and Analysing Sociolinguistic Data

When collecting data, the fieldworker must be aware of a range of issues involved in 'sampling' and the 'representativeness' of the population surveyed. A variety of techniques have been developed by sociolinguists to gain access to the least monitored forms of speech, below the level of common self-awareness.

Among the 'experimental' forms of elicitation that can be used are interviews, questionnaires (spoken or written), 'thinking-out-loud protocols/ think-aloud protocols' (TOL/TAP) given with a passage to read, role-play and storytelling. Linguists have also investigated speech styles by use of a series of elicitation techniques that have increasing degrees of informant self-awareness, for example, starting with an informal conversation, then giving a reading passage, then a list of words to read, and finally a list of potential minimal pairs (such as *moon/moan, which/witch* or *cot/caught*). Another example of an innovative technique was used by Llamas in her fieldwork: 'a sense relation network' sheet (also know as a 'semantic map') intended to elicit local speech variants.

It is a fact of sociolinguistic research that if people are aware they are being observed, they often alter their linguistic behaviour. This is the 'observer's paradox', and several of the methods above were developed in order to minimize its impact on the data collected. The 'ethical' consequences of data collection must also be considered, in relation to the informants' rights of privacy.

Interpreting Sociolinguistic Data

Now that we have introduced some of the key concepts involved in socio-linguistics and we have considered factors to bear in mind when collecting sociolinguistic data, we must think about how we interpret the data we collect. As well as discovering variation, we must attempt to explain what motivates this variation. Some questions we must think about include:

- Why does language variation exist (particularly variation between speakers from the same speech community)?
- What function does the variation serve?
- How do languages change?
- What processes are involved?
- Does the data we collect from one speech community have wider implications?

In this section we shall use aspects of Llamas's research on Teesside English to consider what linguistic data can tell us about the nature and function of language variation and change. Before looking at data from the Teesside study, however, we shall consider some models and frameworks we work within when interpreting language variation and change. This will allow us insight into decisions made in the design of the Teesside study and research questions it addresses.

Models and Frameworks

The axiom underlying our initial definition of sociolinguistics is that language is variable at all times. Variation means there is the potential for change, and the causes and effects of language change are, therefore, central concerns of sociolinguistics. In seeking the motivation for language change, we must consider whether the changes are internal or external to the linguistic system. Internal changes are 'system-based', brought about by pressures internal to the linguistic system. For example, vowel changes affecting a number of northern cities in the USA are often explained from the perspective of a 'chain shift model'. In this framework, changes in vowel sounds are co-ordinated, that is, movement of one vowel triggers movement of another and another and so on down the chain. Within sociolinguistics, external changes are 'speaker-based', brought about by speakers adopting forms from other varieties. The Teesside study focuses on variation in the realisation of certain consonants and considers the variation to be speaker-based. The motivation for the variation is thus seen as social and external to the linguistic system.

Unprecedented changes have been witnessed in spoken British English in recent years, most of which appear to be best accounted for by factors external to the linguistic system. A 'dialect levelling model' of change has been used to account for data in a number of studies. 'Dialect' or 'accent levelling' involves the eradication of locally marked forms in a variety. Large-scale homogenization appears to be taking place in spoken British English: differences between accents are becoming less marked. A 'gravity model' of 'diffusion', which involves the spreading of variants from an identifiable local base into other geographical localities, also appears to be underway. Many of the spreading features in British English are thought to be moving northwards from a south-eastern epicentre. Forms associated with London English are now found in urban centres far from the capital.

Both levelling and diffusion come about through the 'dialect contact' caused by geographical and social mobility. As people increasingly travel and move across society, speakers often experience considerable face-to-face contact with speakers of other varieties. In these contact situations, speakers tend to avoid very locally marked forms of speech (this is called 'accommodation', where speakers move towards their interlocutor's speech patterns). If this happens sufficiently frequently and in sufficiently large numbers, the accommodation can become permanent. Contact-based changes have often been thought to be changes towards the standard variety. However, non-standard varieties are exercising more and more influence in British English and many of the current changes in progress involve the spread of non-standard forms.

Let us look at some evidence from the Teesside study to see whether our linguistic data can be interpreted by the models of change we have been considering.

The Teesside Study

The study set out to investigate whether localized forms were coming under pressure from other vernacular forms spreading from outside the area. A previously unresearched urban variety of British English was chosen as the locality for the research: Middlesbrough, the major urban centre of the conurbation around the River Tees, lies some 260 miles north of London, and offered a good case study situation. Llamas wanted to discover whether local forms were being eradicated and whether spreading vernacular forms had made inroads into Middlesbrough English (MbE).

Combined with analysing variation within MbE, evidence for linguistic change in progress was sought in the study. For this reason the two social variables of age and gender were included in the design of the fieldwork sample. Data were taken from a sample of 32 speakers from Middlesbrough who formed a socially homogeneous group, all being 'working-class' by their own self-assessment. In order to detect potential linguistic changes in progress using the 'apparent time hypothesis', four age groups of speakers were included in the sample (Table 9.2).

Table 9.2 Design of the fieldwork sample

Old (60–80)		Middle-aged (32–45)		Young adult (19–22)		Adolescent (16–17)	
Male	Female	Male	Female	Male	Female	Male	Female
4	4	4	4	4	4	4	4

Llamas conducted interviews with informants in self-selected pairs, using a new method of data elicitation. The method was designed to elicit data which are analysable on five levels of the rank scale we looked at earlier: phonology, morphology, syntax, lexicology and discoursal variation (although only the first four were analysed in the study). The principal research tool used in the interview was a Sense Relation Network sheet, where subjects were given prompts, such as *tired, throw away* or *tell to be quiet,* and then asked to write in alternative words or phrases from their own vernacular.

So, let us look at some data from the study to see whether we can detect any systematic variation in the sample or any evidence for possible change in progress in MbE.

One of the linguistic variables included in the study was intervocalic /r/ (as in *carry, area, a real* and *to reach*). Three variants of /r/ were analysed in the data:

- The alveolar tap [ɾ].
- The alveolar approximant [ɹ].
- The labio-dental approximant [ʋ].

(Note: Whereas phonemes are represented in slashes, for example /r/, the various slightly different ways of pronouncing a phoneme are represented by square brackets, for example [ɾ], these are called 'allophones' (*see* Celce-Murcia, Brinton and Goodwin, 1996, for a description of phonemes and allophones and how they are produced in the vocal tract).

- [ɾ] This tap may be considered the 'localized variant' which is found in northern England and Scotland.
- [ɹ] This alveolar approximant is the non-localized, or 'standard variant'.
- [ʋ] This labio-dental is the 'spreading variant' which is currently spreading rapidly from the south of England.

Figure 9.1 reveals whether use of the localized variant, the standard variant and the spreading variant can be correlated with any of the social groups of speakers.

What Figure 9.1 reveals is that there is a great deal of variation in the use of variants of /r/ among the speakers of the sample. This variation is both gender-correlated and age-correlated.

If we consider the age variation first, the data suggest that use of the localized variant [ɾ] is in steady and dramatic decline (it is used by the old

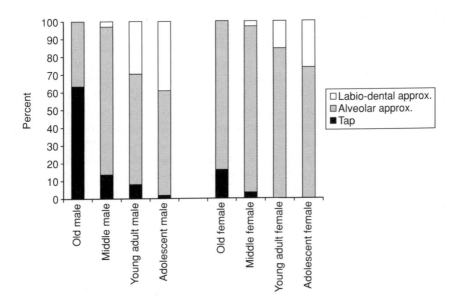

Figure 9.1 Distribution of variants of /r/ in Middlesbrough English.

speakers, but almost rejected categorically by the young speakers). The age-correlated variation also suggests that [ʊ] is a new variant which has appeared in MbE very recently (it is used to a considerable extent by the young speakers, but not found at all in the speech of the old). What we have, then, is evidence suggesting change in progress in MbE. This change appears to involve the processes of both levelling and diffusion.

There also seems to be a gender difference between the initiators of these processes of change. The findings indicate that the females lead in the levelling out of variants, with males following (note the much lower female use of [ɾ]). Males, on the other hand, lead in the diffusion of new variants into the vernacular, with females following (note the higher use of [ʊ] among young males).

It seems, then, from the data for /r/ that MbE is indeed undergoing a process of levelling and features which are spreading from the south-east of England are appearing in the speech of the young in Middlesbrough. Does this mean that MbE is becoming like accents of the south-east of England? Let's look at another variable.

Intervocalic, word-medial /p/ was also taken as a variable in the study (as in 'paper'). Three allophones of /p/ were under investigation:

- The standard variant is the released bilabial stop [p].
- Another possible variant is the glottal stop [ʔ].
- The variant local to the north-east of England is a glottalized [ʔp] (this represents a simultaneous glottal stop and 'p' sound).

Given the dialect levelling in evidence in the variable /r/, we may expect the same to be true of /p/ with a marked decline revealed in the use of [ʔp]. Let us see.

The most immediately striking thing we see in Figure 9.2 is the marked gender difference. The women show a clear preference for the standard variant [p], whereas the men favour the localized [ʔp]. This type of gender-correlated variation has been found repeatedly in sociolinguistic studies. If we look closely at the data, however, we notice that the young women are acting quite differently from the old and middle-aged women. The young women demonstrate a much higher use of the localized north-eastern [ʔp]. Such is the increase in usage that [ʔp] is the preferred variant of the adolescent women compared with a 4.6 per cent use among the old female speakers. Far from being levelled out then, use of the localized variant of /p/ appears to be on the increase. Also, an increase is revealed in use of the glottal stop, in particular among the young female speakers. Again, we have evidence which suggests change in progress in MbE as well as the existence of sharply differentiated genderlects.

It is clear, then, from looking at just two linguistic variables and co-varying them with two social variables that socially meaningful language variation can be detected, and from the evidence of variation we can infer patterns of change. Evidence from /r/ and /p/ both suggest that change is in progress in MbE. In both variables we also see that men speak differently from women of

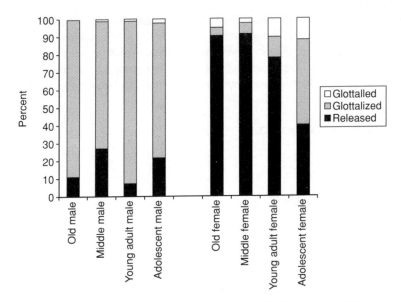

Figure 9.2 Distribution of variants of /p/ in Middlesbrough English.

the same speech community, indeed, in many cases of the same family. The variation in language is clearly not random or free. Rather, it appears to be systematic and to be constrained by social factors.

Although the groups we are working with are made up of individuals (a fact we should not forget), the individual speakers appear to systematically prefer or disprefer variants that are available to them depending on whether they are male or female, young or old. In this way speakers realize their sociolinguistic identity and are able to project the linguistic identity they choose to the outside world. Gaining insight into the motivation for these choices is also part of our job as sociolinguists. The different variants must carry symbolic meaning to the speakers whether or not the speakers would be able to explain what that meaning is. By analysing other factors – how mobile the speakers are, how they evaluate the variants under consideration – we may find answers to some of the questions posed by our findings:

- Why are some variants adopted from other varieties and others are not?
- Why are some variants in decline and others are increasing?
- Why are some variants preferred by females speakers and others by males?

The data we have looked at have revealed another important fact to us. Although the increasing variants we have seen, [ʋ] and [ʔp], are different – one is new to MbE and the other is local to MbE – one thing they have in common is that they are both non-standard forms. The changes in progress that are suggested by the evident variation in the data, then, do not represent a movement of MbE towards the standard variety. This is true of many other localities and many other variables. The 'covert prestige' carried by non-standard forms seems to be exercising more and more influence on language variation and change. This suggests we should re-evaluate the influence of the standard variety, for example Received Pronunciation (RP) in British English, and to question its status as a model to be imitated in language teaching.

Applications of Sociolinguistics

Many sociolinguistic studies have a practical application as their main objective. Sociolinguistics has informed the thinking of government policy on education and language planning across the world, with insights from the field finding their way directly into teacher-training courses and educational programmes, especially in the UK and USA. Teachers who are aware of the sociolinguistic context have insights at their disposal which can make them better teachers. For example, what was once regarded as 'bad' grammar can be seen as a systematic non-standard dialect, and corrective teaching can be replaced by an awareness of multi-dialectalism. This can give students a greater repertoire in their performance, including access to the prestigious standard forms, and a greater confidence in their own language abilities. It encourages us to recognize diversity as richness. Lippi-Green (1997), for example, contains a wealth of information on how language prejudice and ideological planning have operated in the USA.

There are many other uses of sociolinguistics. Film actors imitating accents will have been trained using insights from sociolinguistics. Criminals have been caught by pinpointing their accent origins. Politicians, advertisers and assertiveness trainers all learn discourse patterns that convey their message most effectively. In addition, sociolinguistic studies have contributed greatly to our understanding of how languages change. For example, Labov (1994, 2001) and Milroy (1992) demonstrate a sociolinguistic view of the historical development of English. This not only helps us to 'read' the past but also offers us guidance on the likely social implications in the future.

Finally, the methods developed in sociolinguistics have led the way in the consideration of research ethics and in the use of naturalistic data in linguistic study. Sociolinguistics reveals the complexity of context when language is studied in its real, applied setting, and it also suggests ways of understanding this context and the richness of language uses.

Further Reading

There are some very good book-length introductions to sociolinguistics, such as the following:

- Holmes, J. (2001) *An Introduction to Sociolinguistics* (second edition). London: Longman. This is a good survey of the field with some excellent illustrations and case-studies.

- Stockwell, P. (2002) *Sociolinguistics: A Resource Book for Students*. London: Routledge. This is a very readable 'flexi-text' which takes students from key concepts rapidly to their own explorations, and also contains some key readings by leading sociolinguists.
- Wardhaugh, R. (1998) *An Introduction to Sociolinguistics* (third edition). Oxford: Blackwell. This is probably the standard textbook in the area: comprehensive and authoritative.

For other good introductions, *see also* Downes (1994) and Trudgill (1983).

The following are more advanced books or collections:

- Chambers, J.K. (1995) *Sociolinguistic Theory: Linguistic Variation and Its Social Significance*. Oxford: Blackwell. This is an advanced reference work which focuses on the consequences of sociolinguistic studies on linguistic theory.
- Coulmas, F. (1997) *The Handbook of Sociolinguistics*. Oxford: Blackwell. This has become the definitive manual of the field.
- Coupland, N. and Jaworski, A. (1997) *Sociolinguistics: A Reader and Coursebook*. Basingstoke: Macmillan. This is an excellent resource for key texts in sociolinguistics; its range of articles covers the broad range of approaches and it provides a good orientation in the field.

For other good collections and comprehensive surveys, *see also* Hudson, 1996; Chambers and Trudgill, 1998; Wolfram and Schilling-Estes, 1998; Labov, 2001.

Hands-on Activity

The passage below is a humorous attempt to imitate the spoken vernacular of Middlesbrough in written form (and also pokes some gentle fun at socio-linguists). We have chosen this passage as it is likely to be unfamiliar to most of the readers of this book. However, you do not need to understand the passage at first to be able to use it as sociolinguistic data. First, draw a large table divided as follows:

	Middlesbrough English	Standard English

Phonological examples
(Any novel spellings that seem to be used to represent the accent)
Lexical examples
(Any words you do not recognize, or which seem to be used in an unusual way)

Grammatical examples
(Including strange idioms, as well
as unusual phrases and syntactic
ordering that you find odd)
Discoursal examples
(Anything which seems to be trying
to capture spoken discourse)

Then go through the passage, systematically trying to identify as many representations of the Middlesbrough accent and dialect as you can, in these four categories. At this stage you do not need to know exactly what the non-standard forms mean. Here is the passage:

NOW YOU'RE TALKIN'

EE, well us Teessiders have finally been recognised by the posh Cockneys coz of the class way what we talk, eh?
It was on the telly news and everything. Did yer see it, eh?
What it is, right, there's this new dictionary out this week – which is good news like coz I've finished reading the other one now, like, and – get this – we only get a mention!

Honest. They reckon more new words and phrases are made up on Teesside than anywhere else . . . well me and the lads in the Streetfighters Arms do anyway, like.
Hey, this dictionary, it's huge! Its been genetically modified I reckon. It's not like them rubbishy efforts at school with all the mucky words underlined in red and that.
This one's got 18,000 smart official new words in it. I didn't know there were that many words in the world, me – mind, to be fair I reckon Our Lass gets through at least that many when she's got a right cob on with us, like!

I swear down dead, it's got all these top Teessidisms in it like 'ee', 'gadgie' and 'parmo' – words what we're learning the rest of the country, like.
Not that they're new words or owt like, just ones what all the eggheads down Oxford have finally figured out what we've been saying all along, eh? The boffins reckon it shows Teesside has 'a dynamic and vibrant regional vernacular'. That's rubbish, that is.
Mind, if you want to hear some choice new words for next year's book yer wanna get yerselves round Our House when Boro lose!
So anyroad like, I was just gobsmacked when Our Tony walked into the Streetfighters and plonked his show-off copy of *The Guardian* on the bar.

He said he'd got something to show us like and that it was the new 'lingua gadgia' but like I said, I don't give a hoot about no Italian cars.

Anyroad, it turns out it was this thing about all these new words and that.
And there we were on page eight like: 'ee', a North-eastern alternative to 'oh'; 'gadgie', a Teesside version of 'bloke' derived from ancient romany; and 'parmo', a late night breaded pork and cheese dish claimed to be of Italian origin but actually peculiar to Middlesbrough.
That's right, that is, like. When we went down to Wembley the fest time we all went down the West End and had a right chew on in this little Italian when they wouldn't serve us a parmo.
I mean, they said they'd never heard of it! Said we were making it up. Cheeky nowts.

Mind, to be fair, they haven't even heard of it in Stockton, although that is Durham and over there they can't even tell a 'croggie' from a 'tan'! (*Evening Gazette*, 12 June, 1999)

You should now have a list of words and phrases that cause you problems in understanding. Some of your difficulties, of course, will also be a result of not having enough contextual local knowledge. So, for example:

- Teessiders – people mainly from the Teesside towns of Middlesbrough and Stockton.
- Cockneys – people from east London, but used here to mean anyone from England south of Teesside.
- Streetfighters Arms – an invented pub name.
- Boro – nickname for the local football team.
- *The Guardian* – a quality broadsheet national newspaper with a reputation for being read by educated liberals.
- Wembley – the national football stadium where cup finals are played.
- West End – the main entertainment district in London.
- little Italian – here meaning an Italian restaurant.
- Durham – a cathedral city north of the river Tees; Stockton used to be in County Durham and Middlesbrough in Yorkshire.

You can now try to fill in the second column in your table, by guessing, from context, the equivalent expressions in standard English. Our interpretations are presented in the Suggested Solutions section.

Can you imagine a similar passage written in your own local dialect? You could analyse your dialect in a similar way, breaking it down into its different categories, and deciding where and when it would be most appropriate to use certain features.

Focus on the Language Learner: Motivation, Styles and Strategies

10

Andrew D. Cohen
University of Minnesota

Zoltán Dörnyei
University of Nottingham

Introduction: Learner Characteristics

Success in learning a foreign or second language (L2) depends on a variety of factors such as the duration and intensity of the language course, the characteristics and abilities of the teacher, the appropriateness of the teaching methodology, the quality of the textbook, the size and composition of the learner group, the amount of natural L2 practice opportunities, and last but not least, the characteristics of the language learner. This chapter will focus on the last factor, that is, on the impact of the most important learner features on language learning achievement.

The importance of learner characteristics cannot be overestimated. When students embark on the study of an L2, they are not merely 'empty vessels' that will need to be filled by the wise words of the teacher; instead, they carry a considerable 'personal baggage' to the language course that will have a significant bearing on how learning proceeds. Past research in applied linguistics has identified a number of key components of this learner 'baggage' and has also provided clear evidence that these components determine how fast and how well we are likely to master the L2. In this chapter we will first briefly look at three learner characteristics which are largely beyond the teacher's control, and then concentrate on three factors that teachers can actively address to increase the effectiveness of instruction: motivation, learning styles and learner strategies.

Characteristics Outside the Teacher's Control

Age and Gender

What are the chief learner characteristics – or as researchers like to call them, 'individual differences' – that influence language learning success? It is appropriate to start with the two main demographic variables, the learner's age and gender. The former has been the subject of a great deal of research over the last 40 years. The traditional view has been that the younger we start to learn a second language, the better chance for success we have. Previously, this advantage was explained in terms of a 'critical period', where a person needed to learn the L2 in the period roughly before puberty, or lose the ability to become native-like altogether. However, recent research shows that 'the younger the better' principle is only valid in environments where there is a constant and natural exposure to the L2 (for example, learning French in France); in typical classroom environments where the amount of exposure is relatively small, older learners seem to have the advantage over their younger peers, that is, here, older is better. Also, age seems to have a much greater effect on pronunciation than on other linguistic abilities, such as grammar or vocabulary. Even here, it seems that some late-starting learners have been able to develop native-like pronunciation. Thus, although the 'age factor' may have some physiological basis in the way the brain handles language, there are also likely to be several other age-related factors at work, including the amount and pattern of L2 input, the amount of verbal analytical ability and the motivation to learn the L2 (*see* Singleton, 2001, for a recent overview).

The second factor, the learner's gender, is important because research has consistently found girls to outdo their male peers when it comes to language learning. However, because this factor is beyond the teacher's control, we will not dwell on it here.

Language Aptitude

Let us now turn to what is probably the best-known individual difference variable in language learning: 'language aptitude'. This factor has been referred to under different names, for example, a special 'ability', 'gift', 'knack', 'feel' or 'flair' for languages, and everybody – learners, teachers and researchers alike – will agree that it is a very important attribute of learning effectiveness (*see* Dörnyei and Skehan, in press, for a recent review). It is best seen as the language-related aspect of intelligence, and it determines the rate of learning and the amount of energy the progress is likely to require of the learner. Someone with a high aptitude will pick up the L2 relatively easily, whereas for another person the same level of proficiency can only be achieved by means of hard work and persistence. Having said this, it is important to note that language aptitude does *not* determine whether or not someone can learn a language. If a learner is not a natural language learner, this can be compensated for by various other factors such as high motivation or the use of effective language learning strategies. Indeed, the majority of people *are* able to achieve at least a working knowledge of an L2 regardless of their aptitude – so where there is a will, there is most likely a way. Speaking of the learner's 'will' brings us to the first characteristic on which teachers can have a significant impact and on which we will therefore elaborate – motivation.

Motivation

Motivation is often seen as the key learner variable because without it, nothing much happens. Indeed, most other learner variables presuppose the existence of at least some degree of motivation. Motivation can be promoted consciously, which is good news for L2 teachers: it means that by employing certain methods it is possible to change learners' motivation in a positive direction. For this reason, skills in motivating learners are an important aspect of any teacher's methodological repertoire.

The Social Nature of L2 Motivation

Motivation to learn a second language is very different from the motivation to learn any other school subject. This is because an L2 is not only a communication code, but also a representative of the L2 culture where it is spoken. Learning a second language therefore always entails learning a second culture to some degree. As Williams (1994: 77) argues:

> The learning of a foreign language involves far more than simply learning skills, or a system of rules, or a grammar; it involves an alteration in self-image, the adoption of new social and cultural behaviours and ways of being, and therefore has a significant impact on the social nature of the learner.

As a consequence, L2 motivation will always have a strong sociocultural component. Learners may well be reluctant to set about learning the language of a cultural group towards which they have truly negative feelings, and similarly, having favourable attitudes towards a language community may well increase the motivation to learn their language. In fact, recognition of this reality inspired the initiation of L2 motivation research at the end of the 1950s in Canada by Robert Gardner and Wallace Lambert. The social psychological approach they adopted (*see below*) is still one of the most influential directions in the study of L2 motivation (for an overview, *see* Gardner, 1985; Clément and Gardner, 2001).

Motivation as a Dynamic Process

A second important aspect of L2 motivation is that it is not stable and static but is rather in a continuous process of change. Dörnyei (2001a) argues that motivation undergoes a cycle that has at least three distinct phases.

- First, motivation needs to be *generated*. The motivational dimension related to this initial phase can be referred to as 'choice motivation' because the motivation that is generated then leads to the selection of the goal or task to be pursued.
- Second, the generated motivation needs to be actively *maintained* and *protected* while the particular action lasts. This motivational dimension has been referred to as 'executive motivation' (or 'volition'), and it is particularly relevant to learning in classroom settings, where students are exposed to a great number of distracting influences, such as off-task thoughts, irrelevant distractions from others, anxiety about the tasks or physical conditions that make it difficult to complete the task.
- Finally, there is a third phase following the completion of the action – termed 'motivational retrospection' – which concerns learners' *retrospective evaluation* of how things went. The way students process their past experiences in this retrospective phase will determine the kind of activities they will be motivated to pursue in the future.

These three phases are associated with largely different motives. That is, people will be influenced by different factors while they are still contemplating an action from those that influence them once they have embarked on some action. And similarly, when we look back at something and evaluate it, again a new set of motivational components may well become relevant. Bearing this in mind, let us look at the most important motives discussed in psychology.

The Most Important Motives to Learn an L2

With regard to 'choice motivation', the most important components are the values and attitudes related to the L2, the L2 speakers and language learning in general. These were the focal issues in Gardner's (1985) influential motivation theory, which placed the emphasis on understanding the broad sociocultural nature of L2 motivation. Within this theory, three concepts in particular have become well-known.

- 'Integrative orientation', which reflects a positive disposition toward the L2 group and the desire to interact with and even become similar to valued members of that community.
- 'Instrumental orientation', where language learning is primarily associated with the potential pragmatic gains of L2 proficiency, such as getting a better job or a higher salary.
- The 'integrative motive', which is a complex construct made up of three main components: (a) *integrativeness* (subsuming integrative orientation, interest in foreign languages, and attitudes toward the L2 community); (b) *attitudes toward the learning situation* (comprising attitudes toward the teacher and the course); and (c) *motivation* (made up of motivational intensity, desire and attitudes towards learning the language).

Another important aspect of choice motivation, the 'expectancy of success and perceived coping potential', refers to learners' confidence in being able to carry out the tasks associated with L2 learning. A key element of this aspect, 'linguistic self-confidence', has been identified as a significant motivational subsystem in L2 acquisition (Clément, 1980; Clément, Dörnyei and Noels, 1994); a plausible explanation for this is that what matters in foreign languages learning is not really the objective level of one's language abilities but rather the subjective perceptions of assurance and trust in oneself. (This is partly why some people will be able to communicate with 100 words while others will not be able to even with thousands of words).

It is also easy to see that the learners' initial beliefs about L2 learning will affect motivation, since unrealistic beliefs about the amount of time it will take to attain a certain level of language functioning will inevitably lead to disappointment. Similarly, whether or not the learner receives positive or negative messages from the larger environment (for example, media, friends) plays an important role in reinforcing or blocking one's initial commitment.

The most important aspect of 'executive motivation' is related to the perceived quality of the learning experience. This quality dimension can be described satisfactorily using Schumann's (1997) framework. Drawing on research in neurobiology, Schumann (1997) argues that humans appraise the stimuli they receive from their environment along five dimensions:

- 'Novelty' (degree of unexpectedness/familiarity).
- 'Pleasantness' (attractiveness).
- 'Goal or need significance' (whether the stimulus is instrumental in satisfying needs or achieving goals).
- 'Coping potential' (whether the individual expects to be able to cope with the event).
- 'Self and social image' (whether the event is compatible with social norms and the individual's self-concept).

These appraisals, then, constitute the person's overall evaluation of the quality of a particular experience. Although the 'quality of the learning experience' factor provides a broad coverage of a range of classroom-specific issues, it is useful to look at the motivational role of the participants in any given learning experience separately. First and foremost come the teachers, whose motivational influence is crucial in every aspect of learning. In their position of officially designated leaders they are the most visible figures in the classroom, embody group conscience, and serve as a reference and a standard. Their personal characteristics, their rapport with the students and the specific ways they model motivational values (for example, how they present tasks or give feedback and praise) are all likely to have an impact on the students' commitment to learning. In addition, we need to consider the role of the parents since educational psychologists have long recognized that various family characteristics and practices are linked with school achievement. Finally, in situations where learning takes place within groups of learners, the motivational influence of the whole 'learner group' is also considerable – as can be evidenced by every student whose initial enthusiasm for a subject was quickly killed by being called a 'brain', a 'nerd', a 'creep' or a 'swot' (or something even worse) by his/her peers (*see* Dörnyei, 2001a).

A second important constituent of executive motivation, 'autonomy' (or as it is often called in psychology, 'self determination'), has also generated a lot of research recently (for a review, *see* Benson, 2001) because there is a consensus that autonomy and motivation go hand in hand, that is, 'Autonomous language learners are by definition motivated learners' (Ushioda, 1996: 2). In addition, research by Noels and colleagues (Noels, Clément and Pelletier, 1999; Noels, 2001) indicates that the teachers' orientation towards autonomy, namely whether they are 'autonomy-supporting' or 'controlling', also plays an important role in shaping their students' motivation, with the former leading to increased student involvement and commitment.

The last main phase of the motivational process, 'motivational retrospection', involves the process whereby learners look back and evaluate how things went. Various characteristics will strongly influence learners' overall impressions about the past – some learners will gain a positive impetus even from less-than-positive experiences, whereas others may not be completely satisfied even with outstanding performance. From a practical point of view, however, the feedback, the praise and the grades that learners receive are the most significant determinants of their final self-evaluation. The nature of such rewards are too complex to cover in detail here, but we might note that they can function as double-edged swords – grades in particular. If there is too much emphasis on them, getting good grades can become more important than learning; as Covington (1999: 127) concludes, 'many students are grade driven, not to say, "grade grubbing", and this preoccupation begins surprisingly early in life'.

Finally, knowledge of and skills in using various 'learner strategies' also have an impact on learners' motivation in all three phases of the motivational process. Being aware of certain 'made-to-measure' strategies (for example, a computer devotee is told about an effective method of learning an L2 through the use of computer games and tasks) might give the necessary incentive to initiate learning. Then, while learning, well-used strategies increase one's self-confidence and lead to increased success, and – as the saying goes – success breeds further success. Finally, one very important function of the retrospective stage is for learners to consolidate and extend the repertoire of personally useful strategies, which will in turn function as a source of inspiration for future learning. Indeed, strategies and motivation are very closely linked.

Motivating Learners

How can motivation research help classroom practitioners? The most obvious way is by providing a list of practical motivational techniques that teachers can apply. For such lists to be comprehensive and valid, they need to be based on a solid underlying theoretical framework. Motivational recommendations have been offered by a number of scholars in the L2 field (Alison, 1993; Brown, 1994; Oxford and Shearin, 1994; Williams and Burden, 1997; Dörnyei and Csizeér, 1998), with Dörnyei (2001b) providing a comprehensive summary of the topic. Dörnyei (in press) uses the model described above (choice motivation/executive motivation/motivational retrospection) as an organizing framework and identifies four principal aspects of motivational teaching practice:

- 'Creating the basic motivational conditions' (establishing rapport with the students; fostering a pleasant and supportive classroom atmosphere; developing a cohesive learner group with appropriate group norms).
- 'Generating initial student motivation' (enhancing the learners' L2-related values and attitudes; increasing the learners' expectancy of success; increasing the learners' goal-orientedness; making teaching materials relevant to the learners; creating realistic learner beliefs).
- 'Maintaining and protecting motivation' (making learning stimulating; setting specific learner goals; presenting tasks in a motivating way; protecting the learners' self-esteem and increasing their self-confidence; allowing learners to maintain a positive social image; creating learner autonomy; promoting co-operation among the learners; promoting self-motivating strategies).
- 'Encouraging positive retrospective self-evaluation' (providing motivational feedback; promoting motivational attributions; increasing learner satisfaction; offering rewards and grades in a motivating manner).

Learning Styles

Researchers both in educational psychology and the L2 field have observed that various learners approach learning in a significantly different manner, and the concept of 'learning styles' has been used to refer to these differences. Indeed, we learn in different ways and what suits one learner may be inadequate for another. Learning styles seem to be relatively stable, and so teachers may not have such a direct influence on this learner variable as with motivation. However, they can modify the learning tasks they use in their classes in a way that may bring the best out of particular learners with particular learning style preferences. It is also possible that learners over time can be encouraged to engage in 'style-stretching' so as to incorporate approaches to learning they were resisting in the past. For example, let us say that a given reader may have been so global in her approach to reading academic texts that she was missing specific details that could have assisted her in deriving meaning from the texts. With proper encouragement from the teacher, she can become more versed at maintaining her global perspective, whilst paying more attention to particulars as well.

Learning style researchers have attempted to develop a framework that can usefully describe learners' style preferences, so that instruction can match these. Although numerous distinctions are emerging from the literature, the following style preferences are considered particularly relevant and useful to understanding the process of language learning (Reid, 1995; Ehrman, 1996):

- Being visual, auditory or hands-on.
- Being more extroverted versus introverted.
- Being more abstract and intuitive versus more concrete and thinking in step-by-step sequence.
- Preferring to keep all options open versus being closure-oriented.
- Being more global versus more particular.
- Being more synthesizing versus being more analytic.

The Hands-on Activity at the end of this chapter includes a self-assessment instrument and detailed explanations to illustrate what these style dimensions involve in actual learning. Let us look at an example to illustrate how styles may play a role in language learning and language use. Suppose an instructor assigns a task of reading a 500-word text about a new 'dot.com' organization on the market and then completing three activities that accompany the text. The learners are to write out the main point of the passage in one or two sentences, respond to an inference item ('From what is reported about the dot.com's weaknesses, what can be inferred about the rival dot.com's strengths?') and summarize the key points of the passage. In this example, we would suppose that certain style variables are going to be activated more than others – let us say, for the sake of illustration, that they are the following style contrasts: concrete–sequential versus abstract–intuiting, analytic versus synthesizing and particular versus global. In this instance, we might expect that those learners who are more concrete–sequential are the ones who will check the headings and sub-headings in the text to get a sense of its organization, whereas the more abstract–intuitive learners will skip around the text, looking for key words here and there but without a sequential pattern motivating their search. Both types of learners arrive at the main idea, but possibly using different strategic approaches.

With regard to the sub-task calling for inference, learners with a more abstract–intuitive preference may take some clues from the text, but they may be most comfortable relying on their background knowledge and opinions to infer what is *not* stated in the text about the strengths of the rival dot.com. The more concrete–sequential learners, on the other hand, may focus more exclusively on the clues in the text and remain somewhat frustrated that the answer to the question is illusive for them since it cannot be found in the text itself. Finally, the more global and synthesizing learners may enjoy a summarization task because they are predisposed to using strategies for integrating material into a summary, whilst analytic learners may find it more difficult because they are predisposed to focus on details. The style preferences are presented as dichotomies in the discussion above, but clearly many learners do not favour one learning style to the exclusion of all others. This means that many learners operate somewhere in the middle ground between the extreme positions, for example, usually being a global learner, but at times focusing on details depending on the task.

Learner Strategies

Strategy Definitions

When learning and using an L2, learners may employ a number of strategies which are usually aimed at improving their performance. Second-language researchers first noticed the importance of various learning strategies when they were examining the 'good language learner' in the 1970s (*see* Rubin, 1975). The results indicated that it was not merely a high degree of language aptitude and motivation that caused some learners to excel but also the students' own active and creative participation in the learning process through the application of individualized learning techniques (for a review, *see* Cohen, 1998). Research has found that the 'good language learner' is in command of a rich and sufficiently personalized repertoire of such strategies.

Although learner strategies have been categorized in numerous ways, one helpful distinction is between language learning and language use strategies.

'Language learning strategies' – referring to the conscious and semi-conscious thoughts and behaviours used by learners with the explicit goal of improving their knowledge and understanding of a target language.

'Language use strategies' – referring to strategies for using the language that has been learned, however incompletely, including four sub-sets of strategies:

- 'Retrieval strategies' (strategies used to call up language material from storage, for example, calling up the correct verb in its appropriate tense or retrieving the meaning of a word when it is heard or read).
- 'Rehearsal strategies' (strategies for practising target language structures, for example, rehearsing the subjunctive form for several Spanish verbs in preparation for using them communicatively in a request in Spanish to a teacher or boss to be excused for the day).
- 'Communication strategies' (strategies used to convey a message that is both meaningful and informative for the listener or reader, for example, when we want to explain technical information for which we do not have the specialized vocabulary).
- 'Cover strategies' (strategies for creating an appearance of language ability so as not to look unprepared, foolish or even stupid, for example, using a memorized and partially understood phrase in a classroom drill in order to keep the action going, or laughing at a joke that you did not understand at all).

Along with the two general strategy types described above, language learning and language use strategies, we would like to add a third one, 'self-motivating strategies', which learners can use to increase or protect their existing motivation. This is a rather new area in educational psychology, but research during the past decade has shown that learners' self-motivating capacity is a major factor contributing to success.

Communication Strategies

Communication strategies have unquestionably received the most focus in the research literature (Faerch and Kasper, 1983; Tarone and Yule, 1989; Poulisse, 1990; Dörnyei and Scott, 1997; Kasper and Kellerman, 1997). Communication strategies have primarily been viewed as the verbal (or non-verbal) first aid devices which may be used to deal with problems or break-downs in communication. These devices enable learners to stay active partners in communication even when things do not go well. They may, for example, use communication strategies to steer the conversation away from problematic areas, to express their meaning in creative ways (for example, by paraphrasing a word or concept), to create more time for them to think and to negotiate the difficult parts of their communication with their conversation partner until everything is clear. Thus, these strategies extend the learners' communicative means beyond the constraints of target-language proficiency and consequently help to increase their linguistic confidence as well. Moreover, communication strategies also include conversational interaction strategies and strategies for maintaining the floor which learners who are not experiencing gaps in their knowledge may use.

Researchers have adopted several different taxonomies to classify the relevant problem-solving strategies (Dörnyei and Scott, 1997; Cohen, 1998). Table 10.1 summarizes the most well-known categories and strategy types.

Table 10.1 Some commonly used communication strategies

Avoidance or reduction strategies

Message abandonment: leaving a message unfinished because of some language difficulty
Topic avoidance: avoiding topic areas or concepts which pose language difficulties
Message replacement: substituting the original message with a new one because of not feeling capable of executing it

Achievement or compensatory strategies

Circumlocution: describing or exemplifying the target word you cannot remember (for example, 'the thing you open bottles with' for *corkscrew*)
Approximation: using an alternative term which expresses the meaning of the word you cannot remember as closely as possible (for example, *ship* for 'sailing boat')
Use of all-purpose words: extending a general, 'empty' lexical item to contexts where specific words are lacking (for example, the overuse of *thing, stuff, make, do* as well as using words like 'thingie', 'what-do-you-call-it', 'what's-his-name', etc.)
Word-coinage: creating a non-existing L2 word based on a supposed rule (for example, 'vegetarianist' for *vegetarian*)

Table 10.1 – *continued*

Use of non-linguistic means: mime, gesture, facial expression or sound imitation
Literal translation: translating literally a lexical item, an idiom, a compound word or structure from L1 to L2
Foreignizing: using an L1 word by adjusting it towards the L2 phonologically (that is, with a L2 pronunciation) and/or morphologically (for example, adding a L2 suffix to it)
Code switching: including an L1 word with L1 pronunciation or an L3 word with L3 pronunciation in L2 speech

Stalling or time-gaining strategies

Use of fillers and other hesitation devices: using filling words or gambits to fill pauses and to gain time to think (for example, *well, now let me see, as a matter of fact*, etc.)
Repetition: repeating a word or a string of words immediately after they were said (either by the speaker or the conversation partner)

Interactional strategies

Appeal for help: turning to the conversation partner for help either directly (for example, 'What do you call . . .?') or indirectly (e.g., rising intonation, pause, eye contact, puzzled expression)
Asking for repetition: requesting repetition when not hearing or understanding something properly (e.g. 'Sorry?', 'Pardon?')
Asking for clarification: requesting explanation of an unfamiliar meaning structure (e.g. 'What do you mean?', 'The what?')
Asking for confirmation: requesting confirmation that one heard or understood something correctly (e.g. 'You mean?', 'Do you mean?')
Expressing non-understanding: expressing that one did not understand something properly either verbally or nonverbally (e.g. 'Sorry, I don't understand', 'I think I've lost the thread')
Interpretive summary: extended paraphrase of the interlocutor's message to check that the speaker has understood correctly (e.g. 'So what you are saying is . . .', 'Let me get this right; you are saying that . . .')

It is important to note that communication strategies may or may not have any impact on learning. For example, learners may use a vocabulary item encountered for the first time in a given lesson to communicate a thought, without any intention of trying to learn the word. In contrast, they may insert the new vocabulary item into their communication expressly in order to promote their learning of it.

Cognitive, Meta-cognitive, Affective and Social Strategies

Aside from classifying strategies as focusing on the learning or the use of language, there are two other notable approaches to categorizing strategies. One is to categorize them into one of four groups according to whether they are cognitive, meta-cognitive, affective or social (Chamot, 1987; Oxford, 1990). Another is to group them according to the skill area to which they relate

(Cohen, 1990). Let us first describe the four-way grouping, and then provide an illustrative classification of strategies according to skill area.

'Cognitive strategies' encompass the language learning strategies of identification, grouping, retention and storage of language material, as well as the language use strategies of retrieval, rehearsal and comprehension or production of words, phrases and other elements of the L2. In short, they cover many of the processes or mental manipulations that learners go through in both learning and using the target language. 'Meta-cognitive strategies' are those processes which learners consciously use in order to supervise or manage their language learning. Such strategies allow learners to control their own cognition by planning what they will do, checking how it is going and then evaluating how it went.

Affective strategies serve to regulate emotions, motivation and attitudes (for example, strategies for reduction of anxiety and for self-encouragement). So, for example, before a job interview in the L2, a learner may engage in positive self-talk about focusing on the message rather than on the inevitable grammatical errors that will emerge. Finally, 'social strategies' include the actions which learners choose to take in order to interact with other learners and with native speakers (for example, asking questions to clarify social roles and relationships or co-operating with others in order to complete tasks). Such strategies are usually directed at increasing the learners' exposure to L2 communication and to interactive practice. For example, an American learner of Japanese in Hawaii may develop and then consciously select a series of strategies for starting conversations with Japanese tourists in Waikiki, a daunting challenge since rules for starting conversations with strangers differ across the two cultures.

There is one obvious problem relating to this kind of classification of strategies. A learner's use of what is ostensibly a single strategy may actually represent a continual shifting or 'dance' from one of these categories to another. For example, let us say that a given learner, Herbert, practises a gracious self-introduction for a job interview. On one level, Herbert's strategy is a cognitive one since he is rehearsing pragmatic behaviour in order that it be done gracefully, appropriately and without too many grammatical errors. If Herbert is doing it as a conscious planning strategy, it may also represent a meta-cognitive strategy, especially during the moments when he thinks to himself that this is what he wants to do. The strategy may also serve as an affective strategy since Herbert could be choosing it as a means of reducing anxiety regarding the imminent interview. Finally, the rehearsal of self-introductions can serve as a social strategy in that the better Herbert is at self-introductions, the easier it may be for him to introduce himself to others, the more motivated he may feel to do so, and consequently the more encounters he may be motivated to have with speakers of the L2.

Classifying Strategies According to Skill Areas

The next type of classification of strategies is by skill area. The receptive skills, listening and reading, and the productive skills, speaking and writing, are the four basic skill categories. There are, however, other skill areas as well. For example, there are strategies associated with vocabulary learning which cross-cut the four basic skills. Then, there is also the strategic use of translation, perhaps less conspicuous a skill area for strategizing, but undoubtedly an area that learners draw on. By translation, we are not referring to figurative or polished translation, but rather to the kind of literal or rough translation that most learners engage in from time to time or even extensively in order to function in all four of the basic skill areas. Table 10.2 shows the skill-related strategy categories, along with representative examples of specific strategies.

Table 10.2 A brief sampling of strategies associated with different skill areas

---

Listening strategies

Strategies to increase exposure to the new language:
  Listening to a talk show on the radio, watching a TV show, going to see a movie in the new language, or attending some out-of-class event conducted in the target language

Strategies to become more familiar with the sounds in the new language:
  Looking for associations between the sound of a word or phrase in the new language and the sound of a familiar word
  Imitating the way native speakers talk

Strategies for better understanding the new language in conversation
Before listening to the language:
  Deciding to pay special attention to specific language aspects, for example, the way the speaker pronounces certain sounds

When listening in the language:
  Listening for word and sentence stress to see what natives emphasize when they speak
  Practising 'skim listening' by paying attention to some parts and ignoring others

If some or most of what someone says in the language is not understood:
  Making educated guesses and inferences about the topic based on what has already been said
  Looking to the speaker's gestures and general body language as a clue to meaning

Reading strategy use

With regard to reading habits in the target language:
  Making a real effort to find reading material that is at or near one's level

As basic reading strategies:
  Planning how to read a text, monitor to see how the reading is going, and then check to see how much of it was understood
  Making ongoing summaries either in one's mind or in the margins of the text

When encountering unknown words and structures:
  Guessing the approximate meaning by using clues from the surrounding context
  Using a dictionary so as to get a detailed sense of what individual words mean

Speaking strategy use

In order to practise for speaking:
> Practising new grammatical structures in different situations to check out one's confidence level with the structures
> Asking oneself how a native speaker might say something and then attempting to practice saying it that way

In order to engage in conversations:
> Initiating conversations in the new language as often as possible
> Asking questions as a way to be sure to be involved in the conversation

When not able to think of a word or expression:
> Looking for a different way to express the idea; for example, using a synonym or describing the idea or object being talked about
> Using words from one's native language, perhaps adding vowels or consonants so that they seem like words in the target language

Writing strategy use

As basic writing strategies:
> Planning how to write an academic essay, monitoring to see how the writing is going, and then checking to see how well the product fits the intentions
> Making an effort to write different kinds of texts in the target language (for example, personal notes, messages, letters and course papers)

While writing an essay:
> Reviewing what one has already written before continuing to write new material in an essay
> Postponing editing of the writing until all the ideas are written down

Once a draft essay has been written:
> Revising the essay once or twice to improve the language and content
> Looking for ways to get feedback from others, such as having a native writer put the text in his or her own words and then comparing it to one's original version

Vocabulary strategies

To memorize new words:
> Analysing words to identify the structure and/or meaning of a part or several parts of them
> Making a mental image of new words whose meaning can be depicted.

In order to review vocabulary:
> Going over new words often at first to make sure they are learned
> Going back periodically to refresh one's memory about words previously learned.

In order to recall vocabulary:
> Making an effort to remember the situation where the word was heard or seen in writing, and if written, trying to remember the page or sign it was written on

As a way of making use of new vocabulary:
> Using words just learned in order to see if they work
> Using familiar words in different combinations to make new sentences

Table 10.2 – *continued*

Strategic use of translation

In order to enhance language learning and use:
  Planning out what one wants to say or write in the L1 and then translating it into the target language
  While listening to others, translating parts of what they have said into one's own L1 to help store the concepts

To work directly in the target language as much as possible:
  Making an effort to put one's native language out of mind and to think only in the target language
  Being cautious about transferring words or concepts directly from the L1 to the target language.

Self-motivating Strategies

As indicated above, there is yet another set of learner strategies which may play a role in empowering learners to be more committed and enthusiastic language learners, namely, 'self-motivating strategies'. Even under adverse conditions in certain classrooms and without any teacher assistance, some learners are more successful at staying committed to the goals they have set for themselves than others are. How do they do it? The answer is that they apply certain self-management skills to overcome environmental distractions or distracting emotional or physical needs/states; in short, they motivate themselves. And if they can do so, surely others can do so as well, particularly if teachers and other language educators provide some coaching. This assumption about students' self-motivating capacity has received confirmation during the past decade and scholars have come up with a number of useful techniques that learners can apply to keep progressing when their initial motivation is flagging.

A recent book concentrating on motivational strategies (Dörnyei, 2001b) draws on Kuhl's (1987) and Corno and Kanfer's (1993) research to suggest that self-motivating strategies are made up of five main classes, which are listed below with two typical example strategies for each:

1. Commitment control strategies for helping to preserve or increase the learners' original goal commitment:
    - *Keeping in mind favourable expectations or positive incentives and rewards* (for example, a film director fantasizing about receiving an Oscar).
    - *Focusing on what would happen if the original intention failed.*
2. 'Meta-cognitive control strategies' for monitoring and controlling concentration, and for curtailing unnecessary procrastination:
    - *Identifying recurring distractions and developing defensive routines.*
    - *Focusing on the first steps to take.*

3. 'Satiation control strategies' for eliminating boredom and adding extra attraction or interest to the task:
   • *Add a twist to the task* (for example, reordering certain sequences or setting artificial records and trying to break them).
   • *Use your fantasy to liven up the task* (for example, treating the task as a game, creating imaginary scenarios).
4. 'Emotion control strategies' for managing disruptive emotional states or moods, and for generating emotions that will be conducive to implementing one's intentions (note that these strategies are often similar to 'affective learning strategies' discussed earlier):
   • Self-encouragement.
   • Using relaxation and meditation techniques.
5. 'Environmental control strategies' for eliminating negative environmental influences and exploiting positive environmental influences by making the environment an ally in the pursuit of a difficult goal:
   • *Eliminating negative environmental influences* (such as sources of interference: for example, noise, friends; and environmental temptations: for example, a packet of cigarettes).
   • *Creating positive environmental influences* (for example, making a promise or a public commitment to do or not to do something, asking friends to help you or not to allow you to do something).

We believe that raising learners' awareness of self-motivation strategies, in particular drawing attention to specific strategies that are especially useful in a given situation, may have a significant 'empowering effect' on the students.

Pedagogical Implications: the Intersection of Motivation, Styles and Strategies

Steps for Style- and Strategies-based Instruction

Research has found that it is possible to teach learners to enhance their strategy use, that is, to help them to be more conscious and systematic about the strategies that they already use and to add new strategies to their repertoire (Dörnyei, 1995; Weaver and Cohen, 1997; Cohen, 1998). The earlier discussion of learning styles underscored the importance of having learners determine their style preferences and be more cognizant of the fit between their style preferences and the strategies that they select for language learning and language use tasks. The following are steps that teachers can take to make their instruction style- and strategies-based, along with motivating learners to engage themselves in this type of awareness-raising:

• Raise learner awareness about learning style preferences and language learner strategies at the outset in order to generate motivation to be more conscious about style preferences and more proactive about the use of language strategies.

- Find out which styles the learners favour, and which strategies the students may already use or may wish to add to their repertoire.
- Suggest and model what 'style-stretching' might look like, as well as modelling new strategies.
- Provide a rationale for strategy use, since learners are likely to apply strategies or develop new ones only if they become convinced about their usefulness.
- Provide guided exercises or experiences to help students put the strategies into practice.
- Encourage students to enhance their current strategy repertoire.
- Encourage students to be willing to use such strategies even when it may mean taking risks.
- Highlight cross-cultural differences in how strategies (especially communicative strategies) might be employed (for example, when it is appropriate to use filled pauses in a language, such as the use of *eto* and *ano* in Japanese or *este* in Spanish, since their usage is somewhat different from that of *uh* in English).
- Organize 'sharing sessions': from time to time ask students to share information about their learning style preferences and about the strategies they have generated or found particularly useful. Because of their direct involvement in the learning process, students often have fresh insights they can share with their peers. In addition, personalized learning strategies are sometimes amusing to hear about and students may enjoy sharing them, especially when they see that their peers are doing some of the same things.

The Use of Style and Strategy Surveys

We would recommend actively involving learners in diagnosing for themselves their style and strategy preferences, as well as their 'motivational temperature'. There are various published learning style surveys, with the 'Style Analysis Survey' (Oxford, 1995: 208–215) being more focused on language learning than some of the other instruments (cf. also the short self-assessment tool at the end of this chapter). In addition, teachers can administer self-report questionnaires that cover strategy use by skill area such as in Table 10.2, communication strategies such as those listed in Table 10.1, or strategies classified in some other manner (for example, cognitive, meta-cognitive, affective and social as in Oxford's 'Strategy Inventory for Language Learning' (Oxford, 1990: 283–291). With regard to student motivation, the main strategies a teacher can apply are listed in detail in Dörnyei (2001b), but even in this domain the self-motivating strategies listed on pages 184–185 would allow active learner participation.

A key factor is to make the interrelationship of motivation, styles and strategies a matter of explicit discussion early on, rather than to assume that 'things will come automatically' or that learners know what to do in each instance. If learners are made aware of the importance of these individual difference variables, and are given tools for dealing with them, they are likely to take more responsibility of their own learning and will adopt those attitudes and techniques that characterize the good language learner.

Conclusion

The individual difference variables of motivation, style and strategies are inter-related in numerous ways. If students with certain style preferences succeed in finding learning strategies that particularly suit them (for example, an auditory learner taking the initiative to tape-record portions of a class session and then playing them back in order to review vocabulary and fix the words more solidly in memory), such actions may also enhance their interest in the task and expectancy of success, which will in turn increase their motivation with this task and ideally with others. Similarly, effective and well-personalized communication strategies (such as when the extroverted learner keeps a conversation going with a well-placed paraphrase when the target-language word for *insight* escapes her) can increase the learners' linguistic self-confidence and generate increased satisfaction in their L2 use. Finally, a teacher who keeps learner self-motivating strategies firmly in mind can check periodically to make sure that they are in the learners' repertoire and that they are doing everything to assist learners in keeping their motivational level high. Given the numerous other pedagogical issues to consider in the classroom, teachers may not feel that there is time to engage in this kind of top-down motivation, style and strategy planning for a given course. In reality, it may be just such planning which makes the teaching of a language course more productive for both the teacher and the students, as well as more enjoyable.

Further Reading

- Cohen, A.D. (1990). *Language Learning: Insights for Learners, Teachers, and Researchers*. Boston, MA: Heinle & Heinle. The first set of chapters provides examples for the reader to practice the strategies presented (for vocabulary, speaking, reading, and writing) and the rest of the book consists of a survey of the language learning strategy research.
- Cohen, A.D. (1998). *Strategies in Learning and Using a Second Language*. Harlow: Longman. This volume distinguishes language learning from language use strategies, describes research methods for investigating these strategies, and then presents research which links the use of strategies on specific tasks with language performance on those tasks.
- Dörnyei, Z. (2001). *Teaching and Researching Motivation*. Harlow: Longman. This is an accessible overview of L2 motivation research, with a balanced treatment of both theoretical and practical issues. It also provides research guidelines and over 150 questionnaire items for those who would like to conduct their own investigations.

- Dörnyei, Z. (2001). *Motivational Strategies in the Language Classroom*. Cambridge: Cambridge University Press. Written for practicing teachers, this book is the first publication that is entirely devoted to discussing L2 motivational strategies, that is, practical techniques to generate and maintain student motivation in the language classroom.
- Reid, J.M. (Ed.) (1995). *Learning Styles In the ESL/EFL Classroom*. Boston, MA: Heinle & Heinle. This book provides an edited collection of essays on learning styles and a number of sample learning style surveys.
- Weaver, S.J., Cohen, A.D. (1997). *Strategies-based Instruction: A Teacher-training Manual* (CARLA Working Paper Series #7). Minneapolis: Center for Advanced Research on Language Acquisition. This teacher-training manual provides a broad range of activities and materials to demonstrate how strategies-based instruction can be used in the language classroom. The manual outlines a 30-hour training course, ideas for three-, six- and 15-hour versions of the course, as well as optional activities.

Hands-on Activity

The following is a shortened version of the 'Learning Style Survey' (adapted by Julie Chi and Andrew Cohen from Rebecca L. Oxford's (1993, in Reid, 1995) 'Style Analysis Survey'), designed to assess language learners' general approach to learning. Your task is to fill in the survey, then total your points, and based on your scores, consider your overall learning preferences. In the Suggested Solutions section we will provide specific guidelines on how to interpret your scores.

For each item, circle your immediate response:

- 0 = Never
- 1 = Rarely
- 2 = Sometimes
- 3 = Often
- 4 = Always

Part 1: How I Use My Physical Senses

I remember something better if I write it down	0 1 2 3 4
I understand lectures better when they write on the board	0 1 2 3 4
Charts, diagrams and maps help me understand what someone says	0 1 2 3 4
	Visual – Total
I remember things better if I discuss them with someone	0 1 2 3 4
I prefer to learn by listening to a lecture rather than reading	0 1 2 3 4
I like to listen to music when I study or work	0 1 2 3 4
	Auditory – Total

I need frequent breaks when I work or study 0 1 2 3 4
If I have a choice between sitting and standing, I'd rather stand 0 1 2 3 4
I think better when I move around (for example, pacing or
  tapping my feet) 0 1 2 3 4

Tactile – Total

Part 2: How I Expose Myself to Learning Situations

I learn better when I work or study with others than by myself 0 1 2 3 4
I meet new people easily by jumping into the conversation 0 1 2 3 4
It is easy for me to approach strangers 0 1 2 3 4

Extroverted – Total

I am energized by the inner world (what I'm thinking inside) 0 1 2 3 4
I prefer individual or one-on-one games and activities 0 1 2 3 4
When I am in a large group, I tend to keep silent and just listen 0 1 2 3 4

Introverted – Total

Part 3: How I Handle Possibilities

I have a creative imagination 0 1 2 3 4
I add many original ideas during class discussions 0 1 2 3 4
I am open-minded to new suggestions from my peers 0 1 2 3 4

Random–Intuitive – Total

I read instruction manuals (for example, for VCRs) before using
  the device 0 1 2 3 4
I trust concrete facts instead of new, untested ideas 0 1 2 3 4
I prefer things presented in a step-by-step way 0 1 2 3 4

Concrete–Sequential – Total

Part 4: How I Approach Tasks

My notes and other school materials are carefully organized 0 1 2 3 4
I write lists of everything I need to do each day 0 1 2 3 4
I enjoy a sense of structure in the classroom 0 1 2 3 4

Closure-oriented – Total

I gather lots of information, and then I make last-minute decisions 0 1 2 3 4
I prefer fun or open activities rather than structured activities 0 1 2 3 4
My schedule is flexible for changes 0 1 2 3 4

Open – Total

Part 5: How I Deal with Ideas

I can summarize information easily	0 1 2 3 4
I enjoy tasks where I have to pull together ideas to form one large idea	0 1 2 3 4
By looking at the whole situation, I can easily understand someone	0 1 2 3 4

Synthesizing – Total

I prefer to focus on grammar rules	0 1 2 3 4
I enjoy activities where I have to compare or contrast two things	0 1 2 3 4
I'm good at solving complicated mysteries and puzzles	0 1 2 3 4

Analytic – Total

Part 6: How I Deal with Input

It is easy for me to see the overall plan or big picture	0 1 2 3 4
I get the main idea, and that's enough for me	0 1 2 3 4
When I tell an old story, I tend to forget lots of specific details	0 1 2 3 4

Global – Total

I need very specific examples in order to understand fully	0 1 2 3 4
I can easily break down big ideas into their smaller parts	0 1 2 3 4
I pay attention to specific facts or information	0 1 2 3 4

Particular – Total

III LANGUAGE SKILLS AND ASSESSMENT

11

Listening

Tony Lynch
University of Edinburgh

David Mendelsohn
York University

What is Listening?

Listening involves making sense of spoken language, normally accompanied by other sounds and visual input, with the help of our relevant prior knowledge and the context in which we are listening. However, rather than thinking of listening as a single process, it is more accurate to conceive of it as a bundle of related processes – recognition of the sounds uttered by the speaker, perception of intonation patterns showing information focus, interpretation of the relevance of what is being said to the current topic and so on.

Usually we are unaware of these processes in our own language; achieving comprehension seems relatively effortless unless we encounter unhelpful conditions, such as poor acoustics or an unfamiliar accent. Under more demanding conditions, we become more conscious of listening processes, and the same thing applies in trying to understand a second or foreign language (L2). Not the least of the problems we face as listeners is the fact that we generally get only one chance to process the (linguistic and other) input, and have to do so in real time. Only sometimes do we get the chance to ask the speaker to repeat or rephrase.

Traditionally, listening was viewed as a passive process, in which our ears were receivers into which information was poured, and all the listener had to do was passively register the message. Today we recognize that listening is an 'active' process, and that good listeners are just as active when listening as speakers are when speaking.

Active listening is also an interpretive process. Listening used to be thought of as the exact decoding of the message. In fact, listening involves subtle interpretation. This interpretive notion has long been recognized in reading, but it has taken a long time for it to be accepted in terms of listening. Its acceptance directly affects our notions of 'correctness' – it requires an acknowledgement of the inherent variation in listeners' comprehension of what they hear, and of the importance of context and non-linguistic variables in this interpretation.

Finally, it is important to note that listening is not merely an auditory version of reading, just as speech is not simply a spoken version of writing. Among the unique features of listening are the following:

- Its usually ephemeral, one-shot nature.
- The presence of a rich prosody (stress, intonation, rhythm, loudness and more), which is absent from the written language.
- The presence of characteristics of natural fast speech, such as assimilation, making it markedly different from written language, for example /gəmmt/ for *government*.
- The frequent need to process and respond almost immediately.

Issues in Listening

Models of Listening

We have come a long way in our understanding of how people manage to make sense of what they hear. The last half-century has seen the development of successive theories or models of comprehension, reflecting current knowledge, concerns and technology. We will summarize four of the most important.

Communication Theory Model

'Communication Theory' or, more precisely, 'the mathematical theory of communication' (Shannon and Weaver, 1949), was intended to make telecommunications systems more efficient. Communication theory has given us terms such as 'transmission', 'signal', 'reception' and 'noise'. Since it was developed to solve an engineering problem, human participation in the process of communication was peripheral: '[T]he concern was with intelligibility rather than perception, and the results were used to evaluate equipment rather than listeners' (Licklider and Miller, 1951: 1040). Communication theory researchers themselves had warned against assuming that their work reflect human comprehension; nevertheless, communication theory stimulated thinking about the ways in which comprehension could not be characterized in terms of straightforward 'reception' of a message.

Information Processing Model

The second type of comprehension model is 'Information Processing', strongly influenced by research in computing and artificial intelligence. Central to information processing are the concepts of input, processing and output, with the human being seen as a limited processor, so that when doing complex tasks, we have to devote more attention to one aspect of the task and less to another. Typical information processing models are 'Perception, Parsing and

Utilization' (Anderson, 1985) and 'Identify, Search, File and Use' (Brown, 1995a). Although both imply 'stages' of understanding, it is now recognized that listeners are only able to achieve real-time processing by resorting to parallel distributed processing. This entails integrating information from multiple sources simultaneously, and working 'bottom-up' (looking for clues in linguistic input) and 'top-down' (activating background knowledge and exploiting context).

Social/Contextual Model

A third type of listening model is the 'Social/Contextual', in which human beings are considered much more than (relatively limited) processors, and comprehension is seen as 'a cognitive process ... that unites the social and the individual' (Ohta, 2000: 54). In the social/contextual model, in contrast to communication theory and information processing, we are seen as participants in and creators of meaning, and meanings are achieved in the interactional space between us and not just inside our individual heads. Even in highly constrained contexts, such as those investigated in controlled experiments, conversational partners negotiate meanings and work towards a 'mutual cognitive environment' (Sperber and Wilson, 1995: 61). Context is assigned a primary role by writers adopting the social-constructive view of language, such as van Lier (1996, 2000), who has argued that the current tendency to use computing metaphors such as 'input' is misleading, since they belie the active participation of the successful listener in interaction.

Situated Action Model

Finally, a more speculative alternative to information processing models comes from work on the evolution of language and society. Evolutionary psychologists argue that people spend much of their time trying to understand in order to do things ('situated action'), rather than to store information in memory. Barsalou (1999) claims that language evolved from the need to control the actions of others in activities such as hunting, gathering and simple industry: '[T]he foundational properties of human language today reflect those evolutionary pressures then. Formal education and science have occurred much too recently to have had such impact' (Barsalou, 1999: 66). Supporters of the situated action model do not entirely rule out an archival function for comprehension, but emphasize that our daily interactions are more often oriented towards future action, for example, where to shop for fresh food or how best to treat a child with a sinus infection.

These four comprehension models are complementary rather than mutually exclusive. Even the most limited, the communication theory model, adequately describes restricted comprehension tasks, such as taking down someone's telephone number. As we investigate the full range of listening tasks, we find that the different elements required for successful listening are best explained by a combination of the comprehension models available.

Types of Listening

There are two main types of listening: one-way listening and two-way ('reciprocal' or 'interactional') listening. These derive directly from the identification of two major functions of language: 'transaction' and 'interaction' (Brown and Yule, 1983). Transaction has as its main purpose the transferral of information, whereas the primary function of interaction is the maintenance of social relations. Although it is true, in speech in particular, that virtually all communication involves elements of both, in most cases one of the two purposes is dominant.

One-way Listening

Popular opinion has traditionally linked listening to the transactional function of language and this has strongly influenced the teaching of listening to L2 learners. Until recently it also resulted in an almost exclusive use of monologue for listening practice.

It is certainly true that one-way, transactional listening is important, first and foremost in academic settings, such as lectures and school lessons. This could be termed 'listening in order to learn'. Pedagogic discourse has certain well-defined characteristics: density of cognitive content; often decontextualized; rather formal language (more like writing); and the need to do something with what has been heard, such as take notes on the content.

Other situations in which one-way listening takes place are watching a film or television or listening to the radio, but here the language being listened to is likely to be of the 'spoken' variety, and the purpose of the listening is different.

Two-way Listening

People usually think of listening as one-way, despite the fact that most everyday listening involves two-way interaction (reciprocal, interactive). Again, this assumption has been reflected in the teaching of L2 listening comprehension – although it is encouraging that recently this has begun to change, under the influence, in particular, of work done at the University of Edinburgh (Brown and Yule, 1983; Brown, 1986; Anderson and Lynch, 1988; Lynch, 1995).

Two-way listening might be more accurately termed 'listening-and-speaking', because it involves dialogue or discussion, where all sorts of differences come into play, some making it easier than one-way listening, others making it more difficult. Among the factors making two-way listening easier are the lower density of cognitive content and the opportunity to request clarification or repetition. Conversely, factors that make it harder include the need to produce a response while listening to one's interlocutor, the intensity of time pressure in the processing of what is being heard and the risk of misinterpreting the interlocutor's intent – often leading to hurt feelings.

Resources for Listening

The main resources available to the listener can be grouped under bottom-up and top-down processes. A competent listener uses both of these kinds of processes in order to fully comprehend spoken language, and a key factor in successful listening is the individual's ability to integrate information gathered from the two.

Bottom-up Processing

Bottom-up processing involves piecing together the parts of what is being heard in a linear fashion, one by one, in sequence. For a long time, this was seen as a complete and accurate description of successful listening. Anderson and Lynch (1988: 9) described this view as 'listener as tape recorder'. Even if, as we will argue, top-down processing is important, bottom-up processing is indispensable; listeners always have to do some bottom-up processing of what they hear at the acoustic level, for example, discriminating between different but similar sounds (Byrnes, 1984; Brown, 1990), in order to facilitate subsequent top-down processing.

Top-down Processing

Top-down processing is in some ways the converse of bottom-up: holistic, going from whole to part, and focused on interpretation of meaning rather than recognition of sounds, words and sentences – listeners actively formulate hypotheses as to speaker's meaning, and confirm or modify them where necessary. Top-down processing has been called 'listener as active model-builder' (Anderson and Lynch, 1988: 11).

In top-down processing we rely on what we already know to help make sense of what we hear. The term 'schema' (plural 'schemata') is used to refer to a 'package' of prior knowledge and experience that we have in memory and can call on in the process of comprehension (and perception in general). Schemata are of two types: 'content schemata' and 'rhetorical schemata'.

Content schemata are networks of knowledge on different topics, for example, 'earthquakes', comprising knowledge gained from a range of sources and also personal experience. When we hear someone talking about a topic that we are able to link to an existing content schema, then we find comprehension very much easier.

Rhetorical schemata (also known as 'organizational' or 'textual' schemata) are based on our knowledge of the structure and organization of discourse genres, for example an academic lecture, a sermon. An awareness of what sort of discourse is being listened to makes it easier to engage in top-down processing strategies, such as predicting and inferencing. Predicting is defined as guessing at the rest of a message based on only part of the information – the information might be only partial because either only part of the discourse has been heard so far, or only part has been comprehended. Inferencing is more subtle and in a sense operates at a higher level: 'everything is comprehensible, but there is meaning to the discourse that exceeds the understanding of each of the utterances or part of it. Adding these together, only by inferencing will the whole be comprehended' (Mendelsohn, 1994: 105). Inferencing may be thought of as 'listening between the lines'.

Listening Skills

The convention is to refer to 'the four language skills', but it is clear that each of these comprises a large number of sub-skills, whose value and relevance vary from one situation to another. Richards (1983) was one of the first to consider the nature of the sub-skills required in different listening situations; he came up with 33 micro-skills for conversational listening and a further 18 for academic listening to lectures. Richards' (1983) analysis raises a number of interesting questions, of which we will briefly mention two.

The first question is: What is the relationship between conversational and academic micro-skills? Richards (1983) implied it was incremental, that all conversational listening micro-skills are required for academic listening, but that certain more specialized academic listening micro-skills (such as 'coping with different styles of lecturing') are required only in the lecture hall – making a possible academic listening total of 51 micro-skills. On the other hand, some micro-skills listed in both sets, such as 'identifying and reconstructing topics' (in the conversational listing list) and 'identifying the lecture topic and following its development' (in the academic listening list), appear to rely on the same comprehension processes.

Second, there is the question of the internal ordering of the micro-skills. Richards (1983) used the term 'taxonomies' of listening skill, which implied that the relationship within each set was hierarchical. That leads us to ask whether the successful use of some micro-skills depends on prior success in using others. Presumably it does; for example, one can hardly deduce the meaning of a word (conversational listening micro-skill 12) until you have distinguished its boundaries, for example recognized its phonological form from the rest of the speech stream (conversational listening micro-skill 8).

Richards' (1983) analysis has been extremely influential in helping language teachers to distinguish and prioritize the components of different types of listening, and his article is still widely cited in discussion of materials design. His micro-skill taxonomies were later reshaped and developed by Rost (1990), who emphasized the importance of identifying 'clusters' of listening micro-skills. As Rost (1990) pointed out, his proposal for clustered practice reflected wider doubts as to whether learning a complex skill can be effectively helped by step-by-step practice of its components, and whether learners can re-synthesize them in actual use.

Rost's (1990) clusters of micro-skills are shown in the box below, which makes clear his key distinction between 'enabling skills' (those employed in order to perceive what the speaker is saying and to interpret what they intend to mean) and 'enacting skills' (those employed to respond appropriately to the message).

ENABLING SKILLS

Perception
Recognizing prominence within utterances, including:

- Discriminating sounds in words, especially phonemic contrasts
- Discriminating strong and weak forms, phonetic change at word boundaries
- Identifying use of stress and pitch (information units, emphasis, etc.)

Interpretation
Formulating content sense of an utterance, including:

- Deducing the meaning of unfamiliar words
- Inferring implicit information
- Inferring links between propositions

Formulating a conceptual framework linking utterances, including:

- Recognizing discourse markers (clarifying, contrasting)
- Constructing a theme over a stretch of discourse
- Predicting content
- Identifying elements that help you to form an overall schema
- Maintaining and updating the context

Interpreting (possible) speaker intentions, including:

- Identifying an 'interpersonal frame' speaker-to-hearer
- Monitoring changes in prosody and establishing (in)consistencies
- Noting contradictions, inadequate information, ambiguities
- Differentiating between fact and opinion

ENACTING SKILLS

Making an appropriate response (based on the above), including:

- Selecting key points for the current task
- Transcoding information into written form (for example, notes)
- Identifying which points need clarification
- Integrating information with that from other sources
- Providing appropriate feedback to the speaker

(Adapted from Rost, 1990: 152–153.)

Rost's (1990) division of listening into perception, interpretation and response shows parallels with the information processing models we mentioned earlier: 'Perception, Parsing and Utilization' (Anderson, 1985) and 'Identify, Search, File and Use' (Brown, 1995a). It helps us to distinguish between the levels of comprehension success and to pinpoint failure.

In the Hands-on Activity at the end of this chapter we will be using Rost's (1990) micro-skills clusters (*see* above) to help us to categorize areas of success and failure in an individual L2 learner's understanding of a listening text.

Listening Strategies

Interest in strategy use and strategy instruction derives from research over the past quarter of a century into ways of facilitating language learning (Rubin, 1975; Wenden and Rubin, 1987; O'Malley and Chamot, 1990; Oxford, 1990; *see also* Chapter 10, *Focus on the Language Learner: Motivation, Styles and Strategies*). Chamot (1987: 71) provides a good basic definition of learning strategies: 'techniques, approaches, or deliberate actions that students take in order to facilitate the learning and recall of both linguistic and content area information'. Research into strategy use has led to the development of what Mendelsohn (1994) terms a 'strategy-based approach' to teaching listening comprehension. As we stated earlier, people are usually not conscious of how they listen in their first language unless they encounter difficulty. So, what second or foreign language learners need to do when listening is to make conscious use of the strategies they use unconsciously in their first language.

Learning strategies are usually divided into meta-cognitive, cognitive and social/affective – a tripartite classification developed by O'Malley, Chamot, Stewner-Manzanares, Kupper and Russo (1985). Skilful listeners use them in combination, varying their use according to the needs of the specific situation. A meta-cognitive strategy of particular value for listening is developing a conscious awareness of the strategies we find ourselves using as we listen. An example of a cognitive listening strategy would be listening to the way people address each other (*Darling*, or *Dr Rose*, or *Jamie*) as a clue to the inter-personal relationship between them. An example of a social/affective strategy of particular importance in interactive listening is asking for assistance from the interlocutor.

How do we Gain Insights into Listening?

Settings

Experiments

Experimental investigation has concentrated on aspects such the effects of prosodic patterns on speech recognition. We know that the characteristic patterning of speech in our L1 provides a metrical template that influences the way we process L2 speech. Speakers of French, for example, rely on syllable patterns to segment the stream of spoken French, whereas speakers of English use stress patterns rather than syllable patterns to parse L1 speech (Cutler, 1997). Delabatie and Bradley (1995) found that maintaining these unconscious L1 metrical habits caused listeners problems up to relatively advanced levels of L2 proficiency.

Experimental approaches are well-suited to assessing the effects of other quantitative features on L2 comprehension. In the case of speed of speaking, for example, the absolute rate of speaking seems to matter less than the position and frequency of pauses. However, since real-life listening occurs in a specific social and cognitive context, other approaches are necessary to study the processes of making sense of 'meaning', as opposed to recognizing form.

Pedagogic Tasks

As we mentioned earlier, the literature on L2 listening has tended to focus on pedagogic settings, such as the lecture theatre (Wesche and Ready, 1985; Chaudron and Richards, 1986; Flowerdew, 1994). Among the main findings have been the beneficial effects on L2 comprehension of content redundancy, pausing, macro-level signposting and visual support. Foreign language class-room studies that have explored listening within an interactive setting (Yule and Powers, 1994; Lynch, 1997) have emphasized the additional complexities for the listener of having, in Rost's (1990) terms, to 'enact' a response, by con-tributing relevantly and coherently at an appropriate point in the discourse.

Test Performances

Researchers with access to candidates' performances in listening in world-wide tests, such as IELTS and TOEFL, have been able to investigate listening skills on a very large scale. One recent study sampled 150,000 item performances by Chinese learners of English to investigate whether skill in bottom-up process-ing (rather than top-down) makes some listeners more successful than others (Tsui and Fullilove, 1998). Tsui and Fullilove (1998) compared performances on questions where the correct answer matched the likely content schema with items where the answer conflicted with the schema. Candidates who got the correct answer for non-matching schema items tended to be more skilled listeners; presumably, the less skilled could rely on guessing for the matching items, but not for non-matching ones. Bottom-up processing seemed therefore to be more important than top-down processing in discriminating between candidates' listening performance.

Real-life Communication

Although test-based studies have the advantage of scale, what they gain in terms of statistical robustness has to be weighed against what they may lose in life-likeness. An important source of insight into listening is our own first-hand experience of communicative encounters and the listening problems to which they give rise. In academic discussion, such evidence tends to be dismissed as 'anecdotal'. This is particularly unfortunate in the case of everyday conversa-tion, since our privileged access to our own listening processes is what makes anecdotal evidence so rich, especially evidence from occasions when you realize you have misconstrued what a speaker has said, or where you notice that other participants in a conversation have missed the point. Examples from real life testify to the multi-layered complexity of conversational listening, which may be heightened in cases where the speakers are from different cultures – a point underlined by research such as that of Bremer, Roberts, Vasseur, Simonot and Broeder (1996) and Kasper (1997). We will be analysing an example of intercultural misunderstanding in the second Hands-on Acitivity for this chapter.

Methods

The fact that listening comprehension occurs largely unobserved means that it can be very difficult to establish the 'process' by which listeners reach their interpretations, even if we have evidence of the 'product' (what they understood). However, to the listening researcher or language teacher it is vital to establish the source of listening problems: 'Until the teacher is provided with some sort of method of investigating the student's problems, the teacher is really not in a position of being able to help the student "do better"' (Brown, 1986: 286). Investigations of the routes by which listeners achieve understanding have adopted three main methods: 'observation', 'introspection' and 'retrospection'.

Observation

Observation takes many forms, from informal noticing of real-life examples of misunderstandings (Bond and Garnes, 1980) to experiments designed to create ambiguities and referential conflicts (Brown, 1986). Numerous studies have investigated communication on map-based tasks (Brown, Anderson, Shillcock and Yule, 1984; Brown, 1986; Yule and Powers, 1994). By adjusting the degree of difficulty built in to the tasks at specific 'trouble spots', the researcher can adjust the amount of negotiation required to resolve the problems. However, even in the most controlled of experiments the researcher cannot be certain of the cause of the listener's doubts, or the current state of the listener's mental model.

Introspection

One way of supplementing the information available from observation is to use introspection (comments by the listener at, or immediately after, the time of listening). This form of inquiry is also known as the 'think-aloud protocol'. A particularly enlightening study was carried out by Ross (1997), who tested the view that listeners at different levels of L2 proficiency adopt different processing strategies. The task Ross (1997) set his Japanese students was to listen to a recorded message in English and match it with one of a number of icons. He then asked them to introspect about the reasons behind their selection of icon. He found that weaker listeners tended to focus on a key word, produce an initial mental model and stick to it, without searching for confirming clues; the more proficient listeners also identified the key word but continued to search for further clues in the rest of the message.

Introspection studies are open to three main criticisms. First, the demands of online reporting may lead listeners to listen differently from normal. Second, the data obtained can be greatly influenced by the listeners' skill in verbalizing mental processes, especially if the self-reporting is done in the L2. Third, listeners' reports may reflect prior knowledge, rather their listening. These last two problems can be reduced, for example, by allowing subjects to report in L1, or by selecting unfamiliar topics, but researchers using introspective approaches have had greater difficulty in addressing the problem of inter-ference in normal comprehension processes.

Retrospection

An alternative method of throwing light on listening is 'retrospection', in which the listener is asked to recall the experience of comprehending some time later, usually prompted by memory support such as reviewing a recording of the original conversation. One recent retrospective study investigated the relationship between linguistic processing and listeners' use of background knowledge (Wu, 1998). Chinese learners of English heard a three-minute text twice – once all the way through as they completed multiple-choice questions on content and then in sections. After each section, they were asked to recall their route to comprehension and their strategies for dealing with problems. Wu (1998) concluded that linguistic (bottom-up) processing was basic to successful comprehension; failure or partial success at the linguistic level can lead listeners to allow schematic knowledge to dominate their interpretation – as in other studies we have mentioned (Ross, 1997; Tsui and Fullilove, 1998).

As with introspection tasks, there is a risk of 'contamination' in retrospec-tion: subjects asked to recall how they understood a text may elaborate what they actually understood first time, adding later rationalizations. However, as with the listening models we discussed earlier, the three methods summarized in this section – observation, introspection and retrospection – need not be mutually exclusive. Applying them in judicious combination is probably the best approach to finding out how individuals listen and how they deal with comprehension problems.

From Theory to Practice: Issues in Teaching L2 Listening

The point of contact between theory and application is to be found in the work on learning strategies. We have already mentioned Mendelsohn's (1994) strategy-based approach. Field (1998: 12) suggests what he calls a 'diagnostic approach', in which a listening lesson would involve pre-listening, listening and then an extended post-listening session 'in which gaps in the learners' listening skills could be examined and redressed through short micro-listening exercises'. Despite minor differences, Mendelsohn (1994) and Field (1998) are both advocating teaching learners how to listen.

Berne (1996, 1998) examined the relationship between the theory and the practice of acquiring listening competence, and other than the mutual interest in listening strategies mentioned above, there is a disturbing mis-match between researchers' and classroom practitioners' interests. Better communication between the two sides is essential to help close this gap (*see* Mendelsohn, 1998, forthcoming, for more on this).

Difficulty Factors in Listening

An examination of traditional listening comprehension materials for L2 learners shows that the selection of texts was not systematically based on criteria of difficulty. This resulted in a situation in which the materials used to teach listening were often unsuitable, and the tasks assigned after listening were inappropriate for the text or for the particular needs of the learners in question. Attention was usually given primarily to the appropriacy of the 'topic' rather than to other aspects.

Research over the past number of years has attempted to define which factors contribute to making a particular listening passage difficult or easy to comprehend. Among the most notable work is that of Brown (1986, 1995b) and Rubin (1994). Rubin's excellent review of listening identified five characteristics that affect listening:

- Text characteristics.
- Interlocutor characteristics.
- Task characteristics.
- Listener characteristics.
- Process characteristics.

By way of illustration, here is a brief synopsis of Brown's characterization of the first of those characteristics, those related to the text itself. It has been shown that a listening text will be easier:

- If there are few speakers and objects.
- If the speakers and objects are distinct and different from one another.
- If the spatial relations are clear (for example, when describing a motor accident).
- If the order of telling the events matches the order in which the event occurred.
- If the inferences called for are those that one would have predicted.
- If the content of the text fits with what the listener already knows (exploiting an existing schema).

Teaching versus Testing of Listening

In the past, if listening was taught at all, then what was done under the heading of teaching listening comprehension tended not to be teaching, but rather 'testing'. The teacher would play a tape to the learners and then ask them to answer a set of comprehension questions. But the learners were not taught how to go about understanding the text. Other weaknesses, too, made this approach more testing than teaching:

- The students were seldom given any pre-listening activities to activate their schematic knowledge, so they had little idea what they would be listening to – a highly unnatural situation, which did not reflect the reality of actual communication.
- The students were rarely told what sort of questions they would be asked after listening, so they had no choice but to listen for every detail, just in case – something that encouraged practices that conflict with what is advocated today.
- The students were expected to listen to all texts in the same way, for the same kind of small detail traditionally asked about in comprehension questions.
- The listening material was usually audiotaped, depriving the learners of any visual clues, and, what is more, the texts featured were scripted in a 'written' style, dense in cognitive content and lacking the natural redundancy of real spoken language.

Authenticity of Text and Task

Authenticity of Text

The debate over the use of authentic materials to teach listening has been going on for at least two decades (Geddes and White, 1979; Porter and Roberts, 1981). 'Authentic' in this context is generally defined as 'not designed or recorded for non-native speakers, or for language learning purposes'. Although current opinion is that authenticity is highly desirable (Rings, 1986; Field, 1998; Mendelsohn, forthcoming), it is necessary to sound a word of caution, and to suggest that we may have gone too far in our demand for authenticity. Authentic materials are not automatically 'good' materials, or necessarily appropriate for learners and their specific goals. It is tempting, under pressure of work, for teachers to choose to use materials because they are available rather than because they provide pedagogically helpful content.

Moreover, if we accept the need to 'teach' our students how to listen and not simply test how much they have understood, then we have to ensure that they get plenty of practice in what they are learning to do; and this is not always possible using only authentic materials. For example, if we are teaching students to deduce interpersonal relations between speakers by listening for the ways in which they address each other, it is unlikely that we will find in 'naturally occurring' texts sufficient occurrences of the use of names, nick-names and titles to provide adequate practice. For this reason we advocate the inclusion of training activities which are not authentic, but which abound in the feature being taught, before using authentic material.

Authenticity of Task

Ever since the advent of Communicative Language Teaching, efforts have been made by materials developers and teachers to make learning tasks as realistic as possible. One example of this is the 'information gap' task which cannot be completed unless the learners share the relevant different bits of information in their possession. However, the same caveats are observed as were stated when discussing authenticity of text above; that is, it may be necessary to help learners approach fully authentic tasks gradually, rather than trying to make tasks lifelike from the beginning.

Strategy Instruction

Strategy instruction is not revolutionary or 'faddish'. Neither is it something that should be viewed as an 'add-on' to what happens in the listening lesson. Strategy instruction is at the root of teaching learners how to tackle a listening text. It involves showing learners clues as to how to get at meaning when there are gaps in their competence making this difficult. Moreover, strategy instruction can contribute significantly to learner autonomy.

Mendelsohn (1994), as part of his strategy-based approach, offers examples of strategies to determine setting (S), interpersonal relationships (I), mood (M) and topic (T) (SIMT) arguing that this facilitates comprehension. Setting relates to 'where' and 'when', interpersonal relations relate to 'who', mood and atmosphere relate to 'how' things are being said (the tone), and topic relates to 'what' is being said and 'why'. One example of a strategy to determine mood and atmosphere is training students to listen for changes in voice quality. They might hear the following dialogue twice: the first time with normal voice, the second, with 'whispery voice':

> A: Jane, have you met the new office secretary?
> B: No, not yet. Why?
> A: She's really nice. Did you know that she's pregnant?

> (Mendelsohn, 1994: 90)

They would then discuss the difference in meaning between the two dialogues and hopefully come to the conclusion that when the last line is whispered, it implies secrecy and not merely a statement of fact.

Two notes of caution should be sounded about strategy instruction. First, if strategy instruction is to be effective, it requires thorough preparation of teacher and students, and it needs to be provided over an extended period with plenty of practice. There have been a number of research projects testing the effectiveness of strategy instruction that have found it made no significant difference, which may well have been due to insufficient training. On the other hand, in a long-term study designed to meet the conditions described above, Thompson and Rubin (1996) found that strategy instruction was very effective, and they helpfully discuss in detail the conditions that support listening improvement. Our second caveat on strategy instruction is that it should not be regarded as the answer to 'everything'. A successful listener is not simply someone that is good at compensating for their weaknesses by skilful use of top-down strategies, but someone who also possesses and uses form-oriented L2 listening skills effectively for bottom-up processing. Some of the most important features of listening are discussed in the following section.

Skills Training

As we said earlier, a certain level of linguistic proficiency is required in order to handle listening comprehension. This includes a minimum level of mastery of the features of the sound system, but also of the grammatical system (at sentence level) and of discourse. As Brown (1990: 11–12) states, despite the current emphasis on top-down processing, 'you still need to be able to monitor the incoming acoustic signals so that you know which of your predictions is being confirmed and which is not'.

This mastery of basic linguistic competence as it relates to listening to spoken English should be assessed through diagnostic testing and if necessary, taught early on in a listening course, and prior to the detailed strategy instruction. (For more detail, *see* Mendelsohn, 1994: Chapter 5.) Some of the features that need to be practised are:

- Discriminating between similar sounds.
- Coping with and processing 'fast speech'.
- Processing stress and intonational differences.
- Processing the meaning of different discourse markers.
- Understanding communicative functions and the non-one-to-one equivalence between form and function.

Conclusion

As we have shown in this chapter, listening processes are complex, and therefore listening comprehension is difficult in a second or foreign language. Until relatively recently, teachers either did not teach listening at all, or attempted to teach it, but did so rather poorly; learners learned to comprehend the spoken language 'in spite of the teaching', not because of it. We have made substantial progress in the past 30 or so years in our understanding of the listening process, and how we should go about teaching it. Much of this has been thanks to the work on learning strategies. It now remains for textbook writers not only to 'endorse' the importance of listening strategy instruction, but also to strike a balance between practice-focused listening skills work and strategy instruction in their listening textbooks.

Further Reading

- Bremer, K., Roberts, C., Vasseur, M., Simonot, M., Broeder, P. (1996) *Achieving Understanding: Discourse in International Encounters*. London:

Longman. A collection of studies of listening from an ethnographic perspective, focusing on the lives of immigrants in five European countries. A major strength of the book its detailed analysis of the multiple layers of misunderstandings and non-understandings in two-way listening.

- Brown, G. (1995) *Speakers, Listeners and Communication*. Cambridge: Cambridge University Press. Gillian Brown discusses the characteristics of effective listening in transactional face-to-face communication, using data from experiments with secondary and tertiary students in L1. Among her principal themes are the nature and power of context, and ways in which collaborative 'effort after meaning' may be made or withheld by partners in a conversation.
- Lynch, T. (1996) *Communication in the Language Classroom*. Oxford: Oxford University Press. This book focuses on face-to-face interaction, and suggests ways of incorporating interactive strategies and the negotiation of meaning into lessons in all four traditional language skills.
- Mendelsohn, D., Rubin, J. (eds) (1995) *A Guide to the Teaching of Second Language Listening*. San Diego, CA: Dominie Press. A book offering language teachers practical advice on appropriate methods for teaching listening. Part One explores the principles underlying good practice, including strategies in both L1 and L2 listening, and the cognitive dimensions of difficulty in understanding. Part Two addresses practical pedagogy.
- Rost, M. (1990) *Listening in Language Learning*. London: Longman. This remains probably the most-quoted book on listening comprehension, providing a thorough survey of the role of listening in the development of the L2. A key feature of the book is the overall balance between 'social' and 'psychological' aspects of listening, and its detailed analysis of listening test materials.
- White, G. (1998) *Listening*. Oxford: Oxford University Press. A practical guide to classroom listening activities informed by current research. In particular she advocates an increase in time-on-task in listening classes and focussed analysis of comprehension problems experienced by the learners.

Hands-on Activity

There are obvious problems in trying to represent the 'process' of listening on the printed page. We have chosen two different sorts of listening data for you to analyse: the first comes from a dictation exercise done by an L2 learner of English; the second is an example of misunderstanding observed in real life.

A Classroom Example

For our purposes here, the advantage of using a dictation example is that it shows precisely what the learner understood and allows us to speculate as to how he reached that interpretation.

On the left-hand side below are the 10 sentences of an English for Academic Purposes dictation about the problems of talking to native speakers. The text was recorded onto a cassette at slightly less than conversational speed but with natural pronunciation and assimilation. The learners were told the topic of the text, which they would hear as separate sentences, and were asked to write down what they heard, in 30-second pauses between the sentences. On the right-hand side is the version of the text produced by an intermediate-level Japanese learner of English.

Original version	Learner version
1. Conversing with native speakers can cause a range of difficulties.	Convergent is very difficult.
2. However, many of them have practical solutions.	However, many be made practical solution.
3. One thing you have to get used to is uncertainty.	One thing you have to get on seventy.
4. For instance, you may not be able to decipher every word.	Whatever may be you're able to decide everywhere.
5. But then you can use the context to guess.	But then you can get contact the guest.
6. Another problem is the cultural assumptions in what is said.	Another problem is consumption in what he said.
7. You may catch the words but fail to grasp their meaning.	You might catch the dog while wandering.
8. In either case, you want to get your doubts cleared up.	You may want to be done clear-up.
9. Requesting repetition and clarification is natural in our mother tongue.	Repetition and indication is natural in another tongue.
10. In the foreign language it is more demanding but beneficial.	In the language, there is more demand than benefit.

Question 1: Listening Sub-skills

Look back to the micro-skills list on p. 199. Compare the two versions of the dictation text, and look for points where the learner had problems in applying the following sub-skills:

- Discriminating sounds in words.
- Recognizing word boundaries.
- Deducing the meaning of unfamiliar words.

Question 2: Overall Comprehension

What did the learner appear to think the text was about? Does his text give you any clue about his own professional field?

The Real-life Example

Tony Lynch heard this during an interview on BBC television in 1999. The setting was a mosque in Glasgow, where Muslims were celebrating the end of the Ramadhan fast. A BBC Scotland TV reporter was sitting at a table with two Pakistani men (father and son) and had just taken his first mouthful of their celebration meal.

Reporter: Wow, this is hot!
Interviewee: Well, when we break the fast, we like to eat something tasty.
Reporter: This is certainly . . . tasty (*laughs awkwardly; looks briefly towards the camera*). I don't suppose you have a carry-out, do you?
Interviewee: (*laughs*) No, I'm a doctor, a general practitioner.

(Note: In Scotland, 'carry-out' is used to refer either to a take-away meal or to the premises where the meal is made and sold.

Question 3: Intercultural Misunderstanding

What was the misunderstanding, and how can you explain it?

12   Speaking and Pronunciation

Anne Burns
Macquarie University, Sydney

Barbara Seidlhofer
University of Vienna

What are Speaking and Pronunciation?

We take as our starting point the notion of spoken language in use, drawing on insights from discourse analysis which make it clear that language is used to negotiate and achieve meaning in social contexts and so cannot be divorced from those contexts (*see* Chapter 4, *Discourse Analysis*). This perspective takes us beyond a purely psycholinguistic model of speech, where underlying mental processes are highlighted (Levelt, 1989). The perspective also takes us beyond the focus on the sentence, which has traditionally been the unit of analysis in much grammatical analysis and language teaching. In our discussion here, 'sentences' as formal grammatical units are irrelevant; rather, we are concerned with spoken 'utterances', which could be anything from *'yeah'* to an extended monologue. We would argue that this more contextualized perspective represents a shift from what has been a prevailing model of spoken language in second language teaching – one that is essentially sentence- and form-based – to one that takes text and function as a starting point (*see* McCarthy and Carter, 1994).

'Speaking' is so much part of daily life that we tend to take it for granted. However, learning speaking, whether in a first or other language, involves developing subtle and detailed knowledge about why, how and when to communicate, and complex skills for producing and managing interaction, such as asking a question or obtaining a turn. One of the most important aspects of everyday talk is that it always takes place in cultural and social contexts. We speak in order to carry out various social activities and, although we may not always be consciously aware of doing so, we attune our language and the meanings we wish to exchange to our specific purposes for speaking in that context.

Zooming in on speaking more closely, we can make further intriguing discoveries about other things we are usually unaware of when talking to somebody. Every time we open our mouths to say anything at all, even a short utterance such as *'Thank you!'*, several things happen all at once that fall within the scope of pronunciation: we can say *'Thank you'* loudly or softly, quickly or slowly, with a certain voice quality, with a certain speech melody; we can stress either the first or the second syllable, and there are different ways of pronouncing the individual sounds which make up the utterance. All these elements together make up the way we sound to our interlocutors, and so are crucial factors in conveying meaning when we talk. For language teaching this means that every lesson involving the spoken language is (also) a pronunciation lesson.

The way we sound to our interlocutors is not a trivial or unimportant matter; it is how we project our identity as individuals and how we indicate our membership of particular communities as social beings – like the way we look, the way we sound influences how we get judged by fellow humans. At the same time, and sometimes even in conflict with this 'identity' function, our pronunciation is also responsible for 'intelligibility' – whether or not we can get our message across. The issue of intelligibility is one that second or foreign language learners are keenly aware of. In pronunciation learning and teaching, matters are complicated by the fact that many of these things normally happen subconsciously and so are not really accessible to conscious analysis and intervention. Overall, then, the significance of understanding what makes up 'pronunciation' is far-reaching, and a basic knowledge in this area can be a valuable and powerful resource for language teachers and learners alike (*see also* Seidlhofer, 2001).

Issues in Speaking

Spoken interaction involves producing and negotiating language rather differently from the way it is used in writing. Speakers and listeners ('interlocutors') are involved simultaneously in both producing and processing spoken interactions. They are under time constraints which mean that they must process language as they go, with no opportunities to go back and make changes. Speakers must also take account of relationships with others, adjusting their language according to the meanings they wish to get across, and responding to verbal or non-verbal signals from their listeners that they are being understood. Many spoken interactions consist of commenting on immediate actions or events, or casually moving from one topic to another. However, it is also true that some types of speech may be more planned in advance (such as meetings) or written to be spoken (such as news broadcasts). Differences between spoken and written language are probably best thought about as a 'cline' or 'continuum', rather than a sharp division (*see* Cook, 1989; Halliday, 1989).

We can see some of the features that result from 'online' processing of speech in the following text. Here, two female Australian friends, Anne and Jane, talk about a time when Anne's neighbour, Stan, was bitten by a poisonous insect, a funnel web spider. We will use this text throughout the chapter for illustration.

A funnel web spider jumped out . . .

A = Anne, J = Jane

A1: years ago when I was married, about I don't know how long ago about 10 or 12 years ago I lived in Mosman and I had a really nice neighbour called Stan . . . sometimes he used to cut the grass outside our place and sometimes we'd cut the grass outside his place . . . and one weekend, I was away when this happened, but he told me about it much later, this weekend Stan cut the grass outside the front and was clipping along the edges of our garden with a little axe.

J1: mmm . . .

A2: and a funnel web spider jumped out and . . .

J2: a funnel web!

A3: yeah, and bit him on the fleshy part of his thumb . . . and unbelievably he banged the spider with the axe or something, took off his belt, wrapped his belt around his arm, went in and got a jar, put the spider in the jar and walked to the corner . . . you . . . do you remember Rosebery Street almost went up to Military Road?

J3: yes, yes

A4: on that corner was a doctor's surgery – he walked up to the doctor's surgery

J4: good heavens

A5: and um . . .

J5: did the doctor have an antivenene? [American spelling: antivenin]

A6: no, the doctor called an ambulance and they put him in, took him straight to North Shore [hospital] and . . .

J6: aaah

A7: and that's . . . he said the pain was excruciating, it was like someone had turned a blowtorch on his hand

J7: what the poison goes straight up the arm into their . . .

A8: I don't know if it was the poison or the fangs of the spider or whatever it was that caused the pain but he said it was just like a blowtorch

J8: ahh

A9: and then he had antivenene in hospital but two weeks later his hand was still numb

J9: good heavens!

A10: he was terribly lucky

J10: ohhh

> A11: I mean I would never have reacted that way would you?
> J11: my God, doesn't it give you the creeps?
> A12: yes, absolutely dreadful
> > (From de Silva Joyce and Burns, 1999: 98–99.)

Anne produces her first turn (A1) fluently, mainly by using a series of clauses linked by the co-ordinating conjunction *and* (*but* is also a common spoken conjunction). Informal spoken language tends to contain many clauses that are independent of each other, in contrast to written language, which typically contains more dependent clauses. We can also notice diversions and back-tracking as Anne processes the information she wants to deliver, '*I was away when this happened*'. Anne's utterance also contains 'formulaic expressions', wordings that commonly go together and are used as a kind of shorthand in familiar situations, for example, '*I don't know how long ago*'. 'Ellipsis', the omission of parts of structures that would usually be expected, also eases the pressure in speaking production. Anne refers to '*outside the front*', in the expectation that Jane will understand from the context and her previous reference to '*our place*' that she means the front of the house.

Genres of Speaking

One way we can think about spoken discourse at a macro-level is to consider the concept of discourse types, or 'genres'. In daily life, we use this concept repeatedly to identify the kinds of interactions in which we are involved, for example speeches, jokes, doctor's consultations (*see* Chapter 4, *Discourse Analysis*, for more on genres). Martin and Rothery (1980–1981) define genre as a 'staged, goal-oriented, social process', indicating that:

1. a genre evolves within a culture and its social institutions (hence social)
2. social processes are purposeful (hence goal-oriented)
3. it usually takes a number of steps to achieve one's purpose (hence staged)

> (Painter, 2001: 168)

Within particular social contexts, having identified genres with their different purposes, speakers also anticipate the various kinds of interactions and language they might use in relation to a genre. Purposeful language variation will involve recognizing the overall shape or structure of the text, but also selecting from the vast repertoire of language resources available to us, the language features and patterns appropriate to a particular spoken 'transaction or interaction'.

Transactional communication is primarily motivated by an exchange of goods and service, for example, booking a flight at a travel agent or phoning a careers' centre for information, whereas the motivation for interactional communication is primarily to create and maintain social relationships, for example, casual conversations between friends (*see also* Dalton and Seidlhofer,

1994: 9–12, 53). We say 'primarily' because in reality talk in daily life is often a mixture of the two.

Recent work by Slade (1997) on casual conversation distinguishes between 'chat', highly interactive multiple speaker sequences of conversation, and 'chunks', sequences where primarily one speaker holds the floor. Chunks are more readily analysable for their generic structures as they tend to follow predictable patterns (*see* Eggins and Slade, 1997; Burns, 2001, for further discussion). The spider text is an example of a complete chunk where Anne is the speaker who has gained an extended series of turns. The text she and Jane produce is an example of 'story telling' (Slade, 1997), a genre that is very commonly found in casual conversations. To sum up, the text is i) more chunk than chat; ii) interactional.

Generic Structure

Generic or schematic structure (Martin, 2001) refers to the overall way in which a text unfolds. The spider text is a personal 'narrative' (an entertaining story involving the resolution of a crisis), which typically shows the structure (Labov and Waletkzy, 1967: 39):

(Abstract)^Orientation^Complication^Evaluation^Resolution^(Coda)
[( ) = optional elements; ^ = followed by]

Genres contain both obligatory and optional elements; Abstract and Coda will not be present in all instances of narrative. However, the obligatory elements are the key elements and must be present for a text to be defined and recognized as reflective of a particular genre.

The Abstract, which summarizes or encapsulates the main point, usually signals the start of a story – a classic example might be *'Did I ever tell you about* ... [my neighbour's encounter with a funnel web spider?]. This is followed by the Orientation – the who, what, where, when – that orients the listener to the situation, place and time. In the text Anne begins the story at the Orientation stage, indicating the main player, Stan, and the time and place, but towards the end of her first long utterance (A1) she shifts towards the Complication. The Complication, the main part of the narrative, presents events in time sequence which lead up to a problem or crisis. *'And one weekend, I was away when this happened...'* begins Anne's move towards the Complication, which culminates in the crisis, *'And a funnel web spider jumped out...'* (A2) and the surrounding events (A3).

The Evaluation shows the speakers' reactions to the story and we can see this in Anne's (A7, A8, A10) and Jane's (J6, J7, J8, J9, J10) utterances. The Resolution stage reveals how the story's main players resolve the crisis (A4–A6). In this text, as with other narratives, the Evaluation may appear at any stage, running through the text, sustaining the story and reflecting its personal and social significance to the speakers. We can see that Resolution and Evaluation are interspersed. In the concluding stage of Coda the story is brought full circle; Coda makes a point about the text as a whole and reorients the speakers to the present (A11, J10, A12).

We can go further than providing an analysis of the overall generic structure. Different stages of a genre are characterized by typical lexical (vocabulary) and grammatical (grammatical structures) patterns. Table 12.1 illustrates some of the linguistic choices that characterize a narrative.

Table 12.1 Characteristic choices that characterize a narrative

Stage	Lexico-grammatical features
Abstract Signals the story and the reason for telling it	(No abstract stage in the text)
Orientation (A1) Orients the listener to the story by giving details of time, location, characters, etc.	Expressions of time/place – who, what, where, when: *in Mosman, one weekend, outside his place* Past tense verbs (*was, had*) Use of nouns and pronouns for participants (*I, Stan, he, our*)
Complication (A2–A3) Introduces the problem	Events sequenced in time Past tense action verbs (*bit, banged, took off*) Expressions of place (*on the fleshy part of his thumb*) and manner (*with the axe*)
Evaluation (J6–J8) Establishes the significance of the story and builds suspense	Action suspended through evaluation of events and suspense-building Repetition (*it was just like a blowtorch*) Intensifiers (*excruciating, terribly*) Confirmation check (*what, the poison goes . . .?*)
Resolution (A4–J6, A9–J10) Explains resolution of problem	Events are time-sequenced Past tense action verbs Normality restored (*he was terribly lucky*)
Coda (A11–A12) Comments on the overall story and brings it back to present	Evaluation of story through Vocabulary expressing speakers' attitude (*absolutely dreadful*) Return to present (*doesn't it give you the creeps?*)

The information above is valuable in language teaching and learning because language learners who wish to speak fluently and coherently must have an understanding, at least implicitly, of the organization of the genres in which they will be interacting, and of the linguistic features which realize the generic structure.

Exchange

Texts do not, of course, emerge intact as finished products; Anne and Jane must negotiate their narrative together dynamically at a micro-level, turn by turn. Exchange structure analysis (*see* Chapter 4, *Discourse Analysis*) provides a way of showing 'how speakers can keep taking turns' (Eggins and Slade, 1997: 44). The 'classic' Initiation (I)–Response (R)–Follow-up (F) exchange (Sinclair and Coulthard, 1975) is illustrated in the following:

> J7: What the poison goes straight up the arm into their . . .
> (Initiation)
> A8: I don't know if it was the poison . . . just like a blowtorch
> (Response)
> J7: Aah (Follow-up)

The function of follow ups is to acknowledge information supplied in the response, show our social and emotional reactions to the topic and indicate 'convergence' (Widdowson, 1979) or shared understanding. Formulaic expressions ('*Isn't that great, terrible . . .*', etc.) are common in follow-ups:

> J11: My God, doesn't it give you the creeps?
> A11: Yes, absolutely dreadful

However, in many interactions, follow-ups are delayed by a more protracted series of responses when, for example, further clarifications or checks are sought.

Learner exchanges in classrooms may omit the follow-up, making them sound stilted and interview-like, and so learners should be helped to produce more natural exchange patterns. One way of doing this is to explore similar expressions in other languages. By giving learners opportunities to observe and use this core aspect of spoken interaction, their repertoire of discourse skills should be usefully extended.

Turn-taking and Turn Types

Jointly constructing the interaction means that speakers must also judge when to take a turn (Sacks, Schegloff and Jefferson, 1974). One possibility for obtaining a turn is to self-select. Jane does this in J5, taking advantage of a slight break in the flow of Anne's story (A5) (*see also* comments below on pitch and volume). Turns can be difficult to get when there is high competition, urgency or disagreement and speakers must attune to local transition points in the conversation such as pauses, or signals that turns are ending (for example, laughter, fillers such as *'so'* or *'anyway'*). Another turn-taking opportunity comes when the current speaker nominates the next. This may be done directly – *'What do you think, Jane?'* – or through the type of turn the speaker selects. In A11, Anne poses a question, thereby offering Jane the opportunity to respond. 'Adjacency pairs' are major types of turns occurring together that enable speakers to allocate or give up turns. Question/answer is one of the most common, although there are many others, for instance, *'Hello/Hi'* (greeting/greeting); *'Close the window/OK'* (request/grant). Not all responses are preferred (or positive); some are dispreferred, and in English typically accompanied by some kind of justification or explanation, as in this invented example:

> Anne: Did I ever tell you about my neighbour's encounter with a funnel web?
>
> Jane: No . . . I'd love to hear about it, but I have to rush to catch my train

In a narrative, it is the storyteller (here Anne) who has more turns than the other speakers. However, the listener's role is also important. Although their turn-taking rights are limited, it would seem very odd if listeners remained passive and silent; Jane's contributions play an important part in showing she is on track (J1) (backchannelling), predicting what will come up (J5) – *'Did the doctor have any antivenene?'* – and assisting Anne to evaluate the significance of the events (J8), without which the entertainment value (the 'so what?') of the story would be absent.

Topic Management

Closely related to turn-taking is the way speakers manage and negotiate topics. Speakers must ensure mutual understanding, selecting appropriate levels of explicitness (cf. Grice, 1975) and using discourse stategies, such as clarifying, checking, summarizing and adapting to points made by other speakers. Observe how Anne:

- Checks mutual knowledge with Jane (A3).
- Assumes it elsewhere with the reference to North Shore [Hospital] (A6).
- Provides further information (A4) on the basis of her response (J3).

Jane's 'backchannels' (J1, J8) provide Anne with feedback that she is negotiating the topic successfully.

Repetition (McCarthy, 1998) is another discourse device used to manage topic negotiation. Speakers repeat each other's words to move the topic forward. Too much exact repetition tends to reflect non-co-operative situations where the interaction gets held up. Socially co-operative interaction, such as in the spider text, is typified by repetition as in A2/J2 (*'a funnel web spider'*), J5/A9 (*'antivenene'*), A7/A8 (*'the pain was excruciating, like a blowtorch'*), J7/A8 (*'the poison'*).

Knowledge about turn-taking and topic management can help learners understand the changing roles that speakers take up in conversation and the way meaning is negotiated at the micro-level of each turn.

Issues in Pronunciation

In addition to what we have observed about the workings of spoken discourse so far, there is another level at which we can analyse speaking: 'pronunciation' and the role it plays in getting our meaning across, both transactionally and interactionally. Pronunciation is a term used to capture all aspects of how we employ speech sounds for communicating.

Revisiting some of the aspects of speaking we described above, then, we can fine-tune our analysis to a consideration of how the actual sounds we produce contribute to communication. In so doing, we shall move from larger to smaller units, attempting to explain and illustrate some of the most important concepts and terms as we go along. We shall consider elements of pronunciation that extend over entire utterances (whether these are long texts or just one word) and thus go beyond individual sound segments – which is why they are called 'suprasegmental' (or 'prosodic') features. Also, acts of speech are physical acts which often involve the whole body, so pronunciation does not work in isolation from other factors: in addition to employing our voice, we also use eye movement, mime and gesture. As Abercrombie (1972: 64) puts it, 'we speak with our vocal organs, but we converse with our entire bodies'.

Tone Units/Chunking

To start with, there are certain patterns to how speakers use their voices to structure what they say, thus providing important signposts for listeners as how to process what they hear. A good example is the way we usually say telephone numbers in certain groups, and the variation in these patterns we can observe in different linguacultures. These patterns are achieved by chunking utterances into what is called 'sense or tone groups' or 'tone units', which indicate what, from the speaker's point of view, 'belongs together'. Observe how Anne's first long sentence (A1) can be chunked into:

> //Years ago // when I was married // about I don't know how long ago // about 10 or 12 years ago // I lived in Mosman // and I had a really nice neighbour called Stan //.

Tone groups are characterized by 'pitch movement' (also called 'tone'), that is, the voice going up and down, and sometimes set off by pauses. Some of the chunking is very obvious, but in other cases there is more than one possibility, so that if readers were to read this utterance out loud, some would say:

> // I lived in Mosman // and I had a really nice neighbour called Stan //

as two units, whereas others would divide it up into three:

> // I lived in Mosman // and I had a really nice neighbour // called Stan //

Prominence

Staying with the same utterance for a moment, Anne makes certain syllables more salient than others, that is to say, she gives them 'prominence'. To do this, she uses pitch movement on the syllables highlighted by small capitals: MOSMAN, NEIGHbour, STAN; she also pronounces these syllables slightly more loudly. In any tone unit, the syllable on which the major pitch movement takes place, or begins, is called 'tonic syllable' – the syllable with the greatest prominence. Analysing her 'intonation', or speech melody, thus helps us recognize how she uses the prosodic feature of 'pitch' (perceptual label for 'high'/'low'), sometimes in combination with slightly increased loudness and vowel length, to foreground what is important. Signalling prominence clearly is an extremely important factor in getting our message across.

Turn-taking

Next, it always seems to be very clear to both interlocutors in our example when they should speak, when they should be silent, and when and how (not) to yield the floor to the other person. For the precise timing of this turn-taking, 'pitch' and 'loudness' are particularly important. Thus Jane's back-channel signal *'Mmm'* (J1) is fairly low in pitch and volume, indicating that she is listening, not bidding for a turn or interrupting. Her next utterance, however, *'A funnel web!'* is spoken much more loudly and with considerable pitch movement, reaching fairly high pitch on the first syllable of *funnel*. Anne's subsequent *'Yeah'* may be seen as her acknowledgement of this much more noticeable interjection by Jane before she continues her story. A little later, Anne's *'And um'* (A5) is again at relatively low pitch and volume, giving the impression that she is hesitating, trying to think of what she wants to say next. This offers Jane an 'opening' for putting her question in (J5). In this sense, then, Anne's low pitch functions as a turn-yielding device, whereas the higher pitch of Jane's *'Did'* signals a bid for a turn.

Introducing and Ending Topics

We can also look at pitch level from the point of view of speakers' topic management, which is closely bound up with turn-taking mechanisms. It is easy to imagine Anne's initial *'And'* (A5) being pronounced quite differently: emphatically, dramatically, to heighten Jane's anticipation of what happened next, with higher pitch and higher volume, and even some pitch movement on this one syllable. In that case Jane would have been very unlikely to come in with her question (J5). Consider, for instance, how Anne introduces the topic of the spider (A2):

// And a FUNnel web spider jumped out and //

where she jumps to 'high pitch' on the first prominent syllable of the tone unit. 'High pitch' (and 'low' pitch) are, of course, not absolute values but mean high (or low) in comparison to the immediately preceding tone unit, in this case higher than the concluding tone unit in A1, where '... *with a little* AXE' finishes on a relatively low pitch to end that topical segment. Pitch level, then, can be used to indicate relationships between successive tone units in terms of the informational value speakers attribute to them. A particularly useful example of this is the function of intonation in conveying 'contrastive stress'. Notice, for instance, how in A1, Anne stresses pronouns, which would normally be unstressed, to convey this contrast:

// Sometimes HE used to cut the grass outside OUR place // and sometimes WE'D cut the grass outside HIS place //.

Thus, contrastive stress is a very important signpost for listeners.

Social Meanings and Roles/Degrees of Involvement

Dramatic pitch movement is often a sign of strong emotional involvement: in our text, for instance, Jane's // Good HEAVens // (J4 and J9) and her // doesn't it give you the CREEPS // as well as Anne's *'unbeLIEVably'* and //absolutely DREADful // display such pitch movement. But emotional involvement and attitudinal meaning are notoriously difficult to generalize in any helpful way, as they are so highly dependent on context, situation and relationships. This is why descriptions of 'intonational meaning' can hardly go beyond ad hoc observations (O'Connor and Arnold, 1973).

In contrast, Brazil's (1997) model of the communicative role of intonation is a powerful one, as it works with a limited set of possible choices to capture the state of play in discourse as it is negotiated moment by moment by the interlocutors. A central concept for Brazil is that of 'common ground', 'what knowledge speakers [think they] share about the world, about each other's experiences, attitudes and emotions' (Brazil, Coulthard and Johns,

1980: 15). According to Brazil (1997), it is this assessment as to what is shared and what is not that determines the speaker's choice of tone. The basic options are: tones ending in a fall (that is, a 'fall' or 'rise–fall') for a part of the message which the speaker regards as part of the existing common ground, and tones ending in a rise ('fall–rise' and 'rise') for what they see as adding to the common ground. Anne's first utterance illustrates this distinction: in // Years ago when I was married //, *'married'* will end in a rise if she assumes that Jane knows about this, and in a fall if she thinks this is new to Jane. // called Stan // , on the other hand, is clearly new, and therefore ends in a fall. The distinction between end-rising and end-falling tones is thus a distinction between invoking 'the togetherness aspect of the conversational relationship' as opposed to expressing 'unassimilated viewpoints' (Brazil, 1997: Chapter 4).

In this sense, then, intonation is the most important means by which interlocutors negotiate their mutual relationship and indicate how they view the topic under discussion. During the interaction, intonation enables participants to constantly check and establish common ground in order to achieve convergence and conversational solidarity or, alternatively, to assert conversational dominance.

Stress and Unstress

We have seen that the way we signal prominence in tone units by stressing important words is a crucial prosodic device for getting our meaning across. So 'which' words get stressed is to a great extent a matter of speaker choice in the constantly evolving state of play in the participants' conversation. However, speakers are not entirely free in their stress-placement: there are also certain grammatical and lexical constraints. Generally speaking, socalled 'content words' (nouns, verbs, adjectives, etc.) tend to be the main carriers of meaning and so often get selected for prominence. In contrast, socalled 'function words' (articles, prepositions, pronouns and conjunctions) mainly serve to indicate grammatical relationships and are usually unstressed in utterances (except when they carry contrastive stress). In A9, for example, the stressed words include *antivenene, numb* and *later*, and the unstressed ones *And, he, in, but* and *was*. It is important to realize, however, that for natural conversation these are general tendencies, not invariable rules, and that within any particular word, the syllable(s) to be stressed is relatively fixed.

Sound Segments

Having moved from the larger units of intonation to the smaller ones of stress in words, we can now consider the smallest units we can isolate intuitively, the individual sounds which make up utterances. However, it has to be emphasized that speech is a continuous stream without clear-cut borderlines between individual sounds, and when we speak, rather than producing carefully enunciated 'citation forms' of individual words, we tend to minimize our articulatory effort by making sounds more like each other ('assimilation'), sometimes leaving sounds out altogether ('elision') and sometimes inserting a sound to make for a smoother transition ('linking'). The strangely persistent notion that pronunciation only has to do with individual sounds and how they are articulated is probably due to a human tendency to simplify and idealize in our effort to understand complex processes.

Individual sounds, then, are just one part of the story, but an important one. As all foreign language learners know, we find some sounds easy and others difficult when we study a new language. This is so because different languages select different parts of the sound spectrum ('vowels and consonants') for linguistic use. During first language acquisition, we come to regard the sounds of our mother tongue as 'normal', thus acquiring a kind of mental 'filter' which predisposes us to regard certain sounds as significant and others as not. To many learners of English, for instance, the so-called 'th-sounds' seem rather peculiar, whereas for English speakers, the 'tones' of, say, Mandarin Chinese and the 'clicks' of certain African languages are equally unfamiliar. On the other hand, most languages have o-like, i-like and e-like sounds. How exactly speech sounds get produced and received as physiological and acoustic events is explored in the field of 'phonetics'. How they are utilized, how they are organized into a system of sounds in a particular language is the domain of 'phonology'. Each distinctive sound within the system, for example /p/ or /b/, is called a 'phoneme' (*see* Chapter 9, *Sociolinguistics*, for a listing of the IPA representations of most of the phonemes of English).

What is not represented in the phoneme system is the actual phonetic realization of these distinctive sounds, which are called 'allophones'. As in our handwriting, where the actual letters we write vary and are often quite different from the 'ideal' shape, no two realizations of a phoneme, even by the same person, are ever exactly the same. In addition, there are individual and dialectal differences between the 'accents' of different speakers of the same language, that is, users of the same phoneme inventory. Also, certain sounds are pronounced differently depending on the position they occur in, such as the three occurrences of /l/ in A9: many English speakers would use a so-called 'clear l' in *later* and a 'dark l' in *hospital* and *still* – however, the way this phoneme is realized does not make any difference to the meaning. We can thus say that we 'think in phonemes' but 'speak in allophones' (Dalton and Seidlhofer, 1994: Chapter 2).

Implications for Pedagogy

In this section we raise a series of questions typically asked, in our experience, about teaching speaking and pronunciation, and offer some practical suggestions. These suggestions assume ideas related to general learning theory that need to be taken into account, such as the tenet that perception needs to precede production and achievability, that is, success in little steps is important to counter the insecurity of learning another language. This factor also highlights the teacher's role in 'scaffolding' manageable learning opportunities by providing more explicit support and input in initial learning through activities that giving guided practice and strategically withdrawing support as students become more able to complete tasks independently.

Should Speaking Activities Focus on Texts or Sentences?

There may be good reasons for focusing on sentence-level study. Cook (1989: 4ff) lists the following:

- Formal grammatical knowledge and skills that provide the basis for communication can be taught.
- Proficiency in specific aspects of pronunciation, grammar and vocabulary can be easily diagnosed and assessed.
- 'Abstract' sentences are still the best material for language instruction as they isolate the language from the complexities of a particular context.
- Formal language rules underpin well-formed sentences and need to be understood and recognized.
- The treatment of language as sentences has been successful in language learning in revealing how language works.
- It is more difficult to establish rules and constraints about what is communicatively effective beyond sentence-level.

By way of contrast, the following are some of the arguments that have been advanced for a focus on text:

- Communicative competence requires more than producing and understanding sentences.
- Texts, in the form of scripted dialogues, are commonly used in language teaching.
- If dialogues are to be used, they should also introduce learners to some of the features of 'real-life' discourse, such as generic structure, associated grammatical choices and the role of pronunciation in creating meaning.
- Focusing on discourse and text helps students to notice and analyse authentic and appropriate usage of language.
- Discourse-based activities enable students to extend their communicative repertoire and prepare them more effectively for communication in the target language outside the classroom.

How Can a Discourse-based Approach be Applied in Classroom Practice?

Both teachers and students can benefit from an awareness of the discourse features of different texts. Developing awareness of these features suggests a consciousness-raising approach, rather than implying that students should follow 'recipe' type models in a slavish fashion (Burns and Joyce, 1997).

At a macro-level, students can be sensitized to:

- Functional purpose: identifying whether a text is primarily transactional or interactional.
- Generic structure: highlighting the typical ways that different text types 'unfold' in spoken interaction. This may help to clarify reasons for cross-cultural miscommunication where different expectations may be at play; intercultural differences in genres can also be compared.
- 'Gate-keeping' contexts: identifying situations where speakers may have unequal power relations and how language is used to confirm or contest these roles.

At a micro-level the following patterns can be explored:

- Exchange structure: showing how speakers position themselves to hold the floor and the strategies they use to do this (challenges, dispreferred responses, clarification checks, etc.).
- Turn-taking: highlighting what kinds of turns are likely to go together and how speakers can take up or modify different kinds of turns.
- Conversational moves: enabling learners to practise expressions realizing conversational openings, closings, evaluative follow-ups, back-channelling and so on.

Should we use only 'Authentic' Texts?

In responding to this question, we support in general Lynch and Mendelssohn's comments on authenticity in text and task (*see* Chapter 11, *Listening*). 'Authentic' texts may not be always be the most available or feasible, but teachers can potentially offer students a a continuum of spoken text samples from single sentences to scripted dialogues to semi-scripted dialogues to completely natural speech. We have already commented on the use of single sentences. There are also advantages and disadvantages to each of the other options.

- Scripted dialogues constructed specifically for the purposes of language teaching are common in many published course books. They are valuable for students at lower levels because they often control the vocabulary and grammatical structures introduced. Usually the dialogue is a vehicle for practising particular patterns that have already been introduced through word- or sentence-level exercises. However, they may present spoken discourse as unrealistic and unproblematic and they rarely reflect the grammar, discourse features and idiomatic uses of the language in natural speech. If used exclusively, they represent a 'restricted diet' of speaking and pronunciation development.

- Semi-scripted texts are increasing in more recently published materials. They are sometimes based on recordings where speakers are given a general outline of a dialogue and asked to include features of natural discourse (de Silva Joyce and Burns, 1999). The resulting dialogues is less fragmented and 'messy' than authentic discourse and therefore lends itself to language teaching with a focus on particular topics, vocabulary, grammar, discourse features and pronunciation. Although it can be a 'transition' to authentic speech, it may suffer from some of the same restrictions as scripted dialogues.

- Authentic texts can introduce students to a full range of transactional and interpersonal speech, as well as the reality, unpredictability and complexity of spoken communication. They can highlight language variation and choice rather than fixed and formal sets of rules. However, authentic texts are highly context-dependent and may assume substantial cultural and social knowledge (Carter, 1997). They may also be fragmented (hesitations, false starts, overlaps, interruptions, unclear utterances) and include too many different grammatical and other features for focused language pattern practice in the classroom.

What Procedures are there Specifically for Pronunciation Teaching?

The teacher's decision as to what kind of activities to use in any specific context will, of course, depend on an analysis of learner needs and variables such as learning purpose, learners' age and setting. Procedures range on a continuum from either fairly mechanical or analytic/cognitive exercises drawing attention to specifics of the language code on the one end to communication tasks on the other.

Elicited Mechanical Production

Manipulation of sound patterns without apparent communicative reason and without offering learners an opportunity for making motivated choices of sounds, stress patterns, etc. Examples: manipulation of stress for prominence, as in 'How about dinner with us tonight? How about dinner with US tonight? How about dinner with us tonight?'. For individual sounds, tongue twisters of the 'she sells sea shells on the sea shore' kind. Another time-honoured technique is 'listen and repeat', which involves learners in imitating chunks of language provided by the teacher or a recording; still widely used in course-books which are accompanied by a tape, and particularly popular as a language laboratory exercise.

Ear Training for Sound Contrasts

For instance, reading contrasting sounds or words aloud to a class and asking them to decide what has been uttered. This can take the form of a bingo-like game, as in Bowen and Marks's (1992: 36f) 'sound discrimination exercise'. An interesting variation of this particularly suitable for monolingual classes is 'bilingual minimal pairs' (Bowen and Marks, 1992: 21), which asks learners to listen out for differences in articulatory settings in lists of L1–L2 word pairs, such as German *Bild* and English *build*.

Sounds for Meaning Contrasts

Although 'listen and repeat' is very drill-like, there are numerous ways in which such exercises can be modified to make them more meaningful for the learner while retaining a focus on sounds. Most recent textbooks offer such variations. What they have in common is that they endeavour to relate linguistic form to pragmatic meaning and action. This can be achieved through more active involvement of the part of the learner, a clearer specification of purpose, and a stronger element of choice. Minimal pairs (pairs of words distinguished by one phoneme only) can be embedded in sentences such as 'This BED is not BAD'; ideally, minimal pairs can be used for listening for differences and giving appropriate responses, a technique in which Gilbert (1993) is unsurpassed, for example:

> 'a. He wants to buy my boat. / b. He wants to buy my vote.' is to be matched with 'a. Will you sell it? / b. That's against the law!'

The same principle can be applied for teaching how to employ pitch height for contrast, for example when emphasizing the correct word *composer* versus the incorrect word *author*: 'The AUTHOR of the concerto is Mozart. – The COMPOSER of the concerto is Mozart'. Similarly, chunking into tone units can be practised with effective information gap activities, such as arithmetic pair practice, where the correct answers depend on correct grouping, and students thus get immediate evidence of the importance of chunking, as in:

> '$(2 + 3) \times 5 = 25 -$ // two plus three // times five // equals twenty-five' // vs.
> '$2 + (3 \times 5) = 17 -$ // two plus // three times five // equals seventeen'
> (Gilbert, 1993: 109)

Peer dictation activities also challenge learners as both listeners and speakers.

Cognitive Analysis

Many learners, in particular more mature ones, welcome some overt explanation and analysis. These notions include a wide range of methodological options, such as:

- 'Talking about it', for example discussing stereotypic ideas about 'correct' and 'sloppy' speech for introducing assimilation and elision as crucial features of connected speech.
- Phonetic training: explanations of how particular sounds are articulated, with the help of videos and head diagrams, and conscious exploration and analysis by learners how they themselves articulate L1 and L2 sounds.
- Teaching learners phonemic script: controversial, but appreciated by many students as it better enables them to conceptualize the L2 sound system, to use pronunciation dictionaries, to record pronunciation themselves, and to draw comparisons with their L1.
- Giving rules, especially when they are simple and comprehensive, for example for the pronunciation of the -ed past tense marker and the -s inflectional ending (Celce-Murcia, Brinton and Goodwin, 1996: Chapter 8).
- Comparison of L1 and L2 sound systems: since learners tend to hear the sounds of a new language through the filter of their L1, it can be very helpful for them not to be taught just the articulation of the new sounds, but the system of phonemes, that is, the relevant oppositions.
- Analysis of sounds in texts: Dalton and Seidlhofer (1994: 55, 58, 91, 159f) demonstrate how dialogues not designed for pronunciation work can be used for awareness-raising of the functions of stress and intonation, for example, pitch height for smooth turn-taking.
- Looking up the pronunciation of new words in a dictionary: a good investment in learner autonomy.

Whole Brain Activities, Communication Activities and Games

These are intended to activate the right brain hemisphere and often involve music, poetry, guided fantasies, relaxation techniques such as yoga breathing, and kinaesthetic experiences (Laroy 1995). Whilst many of the techniques already mentioned can contain a game-like element, there are activities which are primarily focused on a particular communicative purpose or outcome, such as mini-plays whose interpretation depends entirely on the learners' use of voice quality and intonation (Dalton and Seidlhofer, 1994: 162) or many of the games in Hancock (1996).

Learning Strategies

Learner training with the aim of fostering learner autonomy and enabling students to develop strategies for coping on their own and for continuing to learn is perhaps the most valuable thing that can be developed in learners. Ways of working towards these goals include awareness-raising questionnaires, learner diaries, recording of learners' production, dealing with incomprehensibility and employing correction strategies such as soliciting repetition, paraphrasing and checking feedback.

In conclusion, however ambitious the learning objectives may be, it might be helpful to think about the different aspects of pronunciation along a teachability–learnability scale. Some things, such as the distinction between voiced and voiceless consonants, are fairly easy to describe and to generalize – they are teachable. Other aspects, notably the attitudinal function of intonation, are extremely dependent on individual circumstances and therefore nearly impossible to isolate out for direct teaching. In other words, some aspects might better be left for learning (or not) without teacher intervention (Dalton and Seidlhofer, 1994: 72ff).

Further Reading

- Burns, A., Joyce, H., Gollin, S. (1996) *'I see what you mean' Using Spoken Discourse in the Classroom: A Handbook for Teachers.* Sydney: National Centre for English Language Teaching and Research. This book contains an introduction to key theoretical approaches for analysing spoken discourse, offers advice on collecting and transcribing spoken texts, provides sample analyses of a range of transactional and interactional texts, and provides frameworks and guidelines for adopting a discourse-based approach to teaching speaking.
- Carter, R., McCarthy, M. (1997) *Exploring Spoken English.* Cambridge: Cambridge University Press. This is a useful collection of 20 samples of authentic spoken data based on the Cambridge Nottingham Corpus of Discourse in English (CANCODE). It guides teachers and learners in analysing spoken discourse and provides a good basis for pedagogical language awareness-raising activities.
- Riggenbach, H. (1999). *Discourse Analysis in the Language Classroom. Vol 1. The Spoken Language.* Ann Arbor, MI: The University of Michigan Press. Students as discourse analysts is a major focus of this book. The author encourages teachers to develop their students' skills as researchers in acquiring their new language. Numerous useful awareness-raising activities are presented including techniques for training students to be researchers, methods for using discourse analysis tools in the classroom and options for incorporating discourse analysis for different teaching situations and student groups.
- Celce-Murcia, M., Brinton, D., Goodwin, J. (1996) *Teaching Pronunciation. A Reference for Teachers of English to Speakers of Other Languages.* Cambridge and New York: Cambridge University Press. This is a comprehensive reference book on the theory and practice of pronunciation

teaching. It focuses on North American English, and an accompanying training cassette is available for practising the transcription of sounds and assessing learners' pronunciation.

- Dalton, C., Seidlhofer, B. (1994) *Pronunciation (Language Teaching: A Scheme for Teacher Education)*. Oxford: Oxford University Press. This book forms part of the series 'Language Teaching: A Scheme for Teacher Education'. It explains the basic principles and terminology of pronunciation, and its main objective is to help teachers understand and evaluate the pronunciation materials available to them and so approach the teaching of pronunciation with more confidence. It includes over 120 classroom tasks which readers can use to develop their pronunciation teaching.
- Jenkins, J. (2000) *The Phonology of English as an International Language*. Oxford: Oxford University Press. This innovative and controversial book is a must for those concerned with mutual intelligibility among 'non-native' speakers in contexts where English is used as an international lingua franca. The author proposes a new pronunciation syllabus, the 'Lingua Franca Core', as an alternative to traditional approaches based on imitation of native speakers.

Hands-on Activity

Doing hands-on work on spoken language is a challenge if you only have the printed text in front of you. However, it is an activity that does happen in the 'real world': for instance, in courts of law minutes are taken during trials, and these then constitute the only record of 'what was said' – which means that people reading the minutes in an attempt to find out 'what happened' in a sense have to reconstruct *how* things were said: for example, a witness can say *'Her husband telephoned me on the Friday'*, and depending on which word is made most prominent, this utterance will carry different implications – compare, for instance:

> // her HUSBAND telephoned me on the friday// (not anybody else)
> // her husband TELEPHONED me on the friday// (he did not talk to me face to face)
> // her husband telephoned ME on the friday// (not anybody else)
> // her husband telephoned me on the FRIDAY// (not on another day)

Similarly, when we read, say, a bedtime story to a child, we enact and bring to life all the meanings conveyed by the use of sounds, all from the inert printed words in front of us – by the way we use intonation, pauses, voice quality, stress and segmental sounds.

It is in a similar spirit that readers are invited to bring the record of the interaction below to life. Since this chapter deals with speaking and pronunciation in second or foreign language learning and teaching, it seemed appropriate to focus on an instructional setting and on protagonists who are (intermediate/ low advanced) learners of English.

Read the conversation transcript below and answer the questions following it. The conversation took place in the following context: A and B are students at a London college, studying for an examination in advanced spoken English (as a foreign language). They are engaged in a communication task: B, a Japanese female student is describing an alpine scene to her male Swiss-German interlocutor, A. He has the same set of six pictures as her, although in a different order. His task is to identify in his set the picture being described.

B1: Mm there are a lot of cars around the hotel and the cars, some cars are f-covered with snow, and I can see three red [pronounced /led/] cars in front of the hotel

A1: Pardon, three?

B2: Three red /led/ cars in front of hotels. And there are some people who are going to skiing I think. And it's quite shi-mm it's very sh-sun the sun is shining very brightly . . . and I can see the mark, 'P' on the wall of the first floor of the hotel [laughs]

A2: Ah yeah . . . Do you see the sky on the picture?

B3: Yes, yes.

A3: Okay, then I know which one it is [identifies the picture to B]

B4: Yeah, yes xx [unintelligible]

A4: I didn't understand the let cars. What do you mean with this?

B5: Let cars? Three red [pronounced /red/] cars.

A5: Ah red.

B6: Red.

A6: Now I understand. I understood car to hire, to let. Ah red, yeah I see.

(From Jenkins, 2000: 81; supplemented by more co-text provided by J. Jenkins.)

Questions

- How does the text unfold? Does it have an overall generic structure?
- How do the speakers' choices of grammar and vocabulary reflect the various stages of the text?
- What features of 'online' processing of speech are evident?
- What strategies does A use to manage and negotiate the topic?
- Where are follow-up turns made? What do you notice about them?

- On which level (segmental or suprasegmental) does the main pronunciation problem seem to be? How do you explain this problem, and what
  would you do as a teacher to try and help with it? Would you only work
  on the pronunciation or also on the perception aspects of this problem?
  How would an understanding of phonology help you in your teaching
  task?

13

Reading

Patricia L. Carrell
Georgia State University

William Grabe
Northern Arizona University

Introduction

Interest in second language reading research and practice has increased dramatically in the past 15 years. Part of this interest is due to the increasing recognition that reading abilities are critical for academic learning, and that L2 reading represents the primary way that L2 students can learn on their own beyond the classroom. Part of the interest is due to the increasing recognition that we all live in a multi-lingual and multi-cultural world, one that is becoming more interconnected through global media and the new global economy. Part of this interest evolves out of increasing numbers of immigrant and language minority students in mainstream L1 educational systems around the world and efforts to address their needs appropriately. Without a doubt, L2 reading research and instruction will grow in importance in the coming decade.

Reading, as is true of all aspects of language knowledge and use, is complex and the development of fluent reading abilities by L2 students is a challenging undertaking. In this chapter we outline some of the complexities involved with L2 reading, key issues concerning L2 reading processes and learning, and some of the implications of these issues for instructional practice.

What is Reading?

Because we read for a variety of purposes, we often vary the cognitive processes and knowledge resources that we use. Therefore, it is not straight-forward to identify one purpose for reading as the single way to interpret what we mean by 'reading'. The many purposes for reading, although drawing on the same cognitive processes and knowledge resources, do so in differing combinations and with varying emphases on these processes and resources.

For example, when we want information from a manual, we will search for that information by some combination of scanning for key terms and skimming small segments for meaning to see if we are in the right area of the text. When we read a newspaper we read headlines and often skim news stories to see if we want to slow down and read more carefully. When we read a good novel at night, we generally do not skim (unless we get bored), but we usually do not read carefully to remember details either. When we are trying to learn new information, we read more slowly, thinking about how information fits with prior information in the text and with our own background knowledge. As we read for all of these different purposes, we shift how we employ our cognitive processes and knowledge resources.

It is possible to talk about a number of these purposes with general labels, such as scanning, skimming, reading for general understanding, reading to learn, reading to integrate information and reading to evaluate critically. To understand these purposes better, we need to determine how the underlying cognitive processes and resources systematically relate to the ability to achieve these purposes. Thus, in line with Carver (1992), scanning is a reading process that requires recognition of a visual form (number, word or phrase) that can be matched to forms in the text. It does not require semantic processing and it can usually be carried out at a rate of 600 words per minute (wpm). Reading for understanding is a process requiring visual and semantic processing and the construction of the summary version of what the text means. It is usually carried out by fluent readers at about 250–300 wpm. Reading to learn is a process that requires, in addition to a summary version of what the text means, an array of elaborated relations created among the sets of information being processed. These relations form hierarchies of text interpretation and they need to be combined with the reader's prior topical knowledge. For fluent readers, such a process seems to be carried out at about 200 wpm. (Younger readers do not read fluently, but progress in efficiency through school grades. By the middle to end of secondary level education, most students read fluently at the rates noted above.)

For this chapter, we will assume that L2 readers in academic settings most often need to develop 'reading for understanding' and 'reading to learn'. Under both reading purposes, it is possible to say that reading is 'the process of receiving and interpreting information encoded in language form via the medium of print' (Urquhart and Weir, 1998: 22). At the same time, this definition does not indicate the many components of the required cognitive processing or the knowledge bases being integrated during the reading process. Thus, a definition of reading requires some recognition that a reader engages in processing at the phonological, morphological, syntactic, semantic and discourse levels, as well as engages in goal setting, text-summary building, interpretive elaborating from knowledge resources, monitoring and assessment of goal achievement, making various adjustments to enhance comprehension, and making repairs to comprehension processing as needed. Moreover, these processes are carried out by the integration of activated processes and resources (in working memory) under intense processing-time constraints.

With this more elaborate definition of reading, it becomes apparent that the tasks of understanding the nature and development of L2 reading is complex. It is also apparent that developing fluent L2 readers is a challenging task requiring much time, resources and effort.

Reading in a Second Language

Aside from the complexity involved in understanding the nature of reading, there are added complexities for L2 readers. L2 readers exhibit the full range of variation that can be found for L1 readers (variation in training, age, schooling, motivation, socio-economic level, as well as individual cognition). In addition, these L2 readers are usually acquiring a complex cognitive ability that is in some ways distinct from L1 reading. L2 readers do not have the same language resources as L1 readers at the outset of learning; they do not share all the social and cultural assumptions and knowledge bases that L1 readers use when reading in their own language; they do not share all the background knowledge that is often assumed about 'how the world works'; they often are learning in the second language for various reasons – to return to their home country, to integrate in the L2 society, to build on an educational base that is already in place from earlier L1 schooling – and they are working with cognitive resources and processing that involve two different languages.

These differences have at least three consequences. First, research in L2 reading will need to examine the potential impact of these differences and cannot simply assume that results of research on L1 reading will apply in L2 contexts. Second, these differences suggest that L2 readers may employ cognitive resources in somewhat different ways from L1 readers, especially where there are clear differences between the L1 and the L2 (for example, the mapping of sounds and graphemic or orthographic forms may differ in two languages). Third, the actual cognitive processes themselves may be somewhat different simply as a result of working with more than one language (for example, L1 and L2 words may be stored and accessed differently in the lexicon; transfer from the L1 may affect L2 reading) and these possibilities need to be explored. The recognition that L2 reading is in some ways similar to and in some ways different from L1 reading deserves attention because the differences represent a major reason for carrying out L2 reading research.

L2 Reading Versus L1 Reading

In some cases, the differences between L1 and L2 reading contexts are matters of degree; in other cases there are strong qualitative differences between the two that motivate important research questions and instructional practices. Major differences between L1 and L2 reading can be categorized according to three groupings: linguistic and processing differences; other individual and experiential differences; and socio-cultural and institutional differences (Grabe and Stoller, in press). Within these groupings, the following 12 differences represent important elements in understanding the nature of L2 reading development, which also serve to drive L2 reading research.

Key Linguistic and Processing Differences

1. Differing amounts of lexical, grammatical, and discourse knowledge at beginning stages of L1 and L2 reading. L1 students usually know several thousand words orally in their L1 before starting to read. They also implicitly know most of the basic syntactic structures of the language, and they have already had experiences with the way stories and other genres are structured.

2. Varying linguistic differences across any two languages and varying language-transfer influences. L2 students often come from languages that use different orthographies or different ways to encode information in orthography. These differences across languages also may generate significant differences in the way the print is processed and in the types of transfer that may or may not occur.

3. Interacting influences of working with two languages. L2 students build and use a bilingual mental lexicon of some type (*see* Chapter 8, *Psycholinguistics*); they engage in bilingual processing of language structures and semantic interpretations; they engage in translating; they have relatively varying fluencies in the two languages; they make varying uses of each language in differing sociolinguistic domains. They also learn their L2 at different times in their lives and they experience varying degrees of interdependence between the two languages.

4. Varying L2 proficiencies as a foundation for L2 reading. L2 students come to reading tasks with a wide range of L2 proficiencies. The obvious consequences of this variation is demonstrated by their abilities to carry out different reading tasks successfully and to read for multiple purposes. Less obvious consequences also involve motivation, the role of language transfer, socio-cultural factors and several other issues (many noted below).

Key Individual and Experiential Differences

This second set of factors that separate L1 and L2 reading are less commonly investigated, but the results available suggest that these differences play important roles in L2 reading development. In particular, they suggest that L1 reading findings and their implications need to be examined in light of L2 research findings rather than be assumed to apply to L2 instruction.

5. Differing levels of L1 reading abilities among the L2 students.
6. Differing amounts of exposure to L2 print.
7. Differing motivations for reading in the L2.
8. Differing kinds of texts in L2 settings.
9. Differing language learning resources for L2 readers.

Key Socio-cultural and Institutional factors

These topics are relatively unexplored except for the work under contrastive rhetoric and further research is needed. The L2 research to date suggests that these differences can influence the development of L2 reading abilities above and beyond the differences noted above.

10 Differing socio-cultural backgrounds of L2 readers.
11 Differing ways to organize discourse and texts in L1 and L2 settings.
12 Differing expectations of educational institutions in L1 and L2 settings.

Issues in L2 Reading

Automaticity and Word Recognition

Word recognition is at the centre of reading fluency and automaticity. Given the importance of words in reading, it is not surprising that much of the research in second or foreign language reading has focused on vocabulary issues (*see below*; *see also* Chapter 3, *Vocabulary*). An increasing amount of L2 research has focused more specifically on processes of L2 word recognition, with the findings having real implications for instruction.

Koda (1996: 453) makes the case that word recognition in second language reading must be viewed as a 'significant phenomenon in its own right' and not just as a facet of overall second language proficiency. She argues that L2 word recognition is affected by the amount of L2 orthographic processing experience, the distance between the orthographies of the L1 and L2, and the interaction between L1 and L2 orthographic knowledge.

Recent word recognition studies have shown differences in word recognition efficiency among learners with different amounts of L2 experience. Favreau and Segalowitz (1983) showed that even for otherwise fluent bilinguals, if a second language is weaker than the first language and reading is slower in the second language, word recognition in the L2 is less automatic than in the L1. In a follow-up study of the development of automaticity in French speakers learning ESL, Segalowitz and Segalowitz (1993) showed that practice on word recognition tasks leads to faster and more stable (less variable) responses. These faster and more stable responses indicated that processing had not merely become faster across the board, but that a qualitative change or restructuring of processing had occurred. They maintained that this reflected the attainment of automatization, not just a simple speeding up of the processing mechanisms.

Although Segalowitz's various studies have examined mature, literate adult readers, Geva, Wade-Woolley and Shany (1997) have focused on younger learners learning to read simultaneously in English (L1) and Hebrew (L2). Geva *et al.* (1997) conclude that steps associated with the development of L1 reading efficiency (that is, accuracy attained before speed) may be applicable to the development of word recognition skills in L2, but they do not emerge concurrently in both languages. They also conclude that linguistic features, such as 'orthographic depth' (the degree to which the written system of a language corresponds to its spoken system) and morphosyntactic complexity 'may interact with more global L2 proficiency effects' (Geva *et al.*, 1997: 119) to determine the course of early L2 reading development.

> *Implications: Word recognition exercises are probably useful for both older and younger L2 readers, enhancing fluency and raising student awareness of the processing demands of extended independent reading.*

L2 Word Recognition Differences across L1s

According to the orthographic depth hypothesis (Feldman and Turvey, 1983), pre-lexical phonology (the immediate and automatic matching of graphemes and phones) plays a more important role in lexical access in 'shallow orthographies', where the correspondences of graphemes to phonemes are more direct and consistent (for example, Finnish, Spanish, Turkish) than in 'deep orthographies', where the mapping of letters to sounds is less direct and less consistent (for example, English, unmarked Arabic, Chinese). Cross-linguistic research comparing L2 learners with different L1 backgrounds has consistently demonstrated superior word recognition performance for those with L1 orthographic backgrounds more similar to the L2. For example, Koda (1989) found better word recognition for L2 learners of Japanese with related L1 backgrounds (Chinese and Korean) than she did for unrelated ones (English). Muljani, Koda and Moates (1998) showed this effect again for ESL learners from related (Indonesian [Roman alphabet]) versus unrelated (Chinese [logographic]) L1 orthographic backgrounds.

Green and Meara (1987) showed differences between three groups of ESL learners with contrasting L1 orthographic backgrounds: Spanish speakers (Roman alphabetic orthography), Arabic speakers (non-Roman alphabetic orthography) and Chinese speakers (non-alphabetic orthography). The researchers concluded that the three groups used different visual processing strategies when pursuing a search task not only in their L1s but also in their L2s. Green and Meara (1987) concluded that L1 writing systems have a deep and lasting effect on the ways in which L2 materials are processed. Ryan and Meara (1991) investigated the hypothesis that Arabic speakers learning English, because of the emphasis on consonants in the lexical structure and orthography of their L1, would also tend to rely heavily on consonants when attempting to recognize English words. In a task that required participants to detect missing vowels, the researchers found that Arabic ESL learners were considerably slower and less accurate than non-Arabic counterparts. Ryan and

Meara (1991) conclude that their findings confirm the earlier results that L1 orthography has a long and lasting impact on L2 processing.

In addition to the influences of L1 orthography, researchers have also investigated the influences of L1 phonology on L2 word recognition, and consequently, on L2 reading. L1 learners show preferences for acquiring new vocabulary (in their L1) with phonological patterns ('phonotactics') that are already familiar to them or that are already in their repertoire. They tend to avoid or acquire less readily words with unfamiliar sound patterns (Gathercole and Baddeley, 1989). In L2 contexts, Feldman and Healy (1998) reported an interesting experiment designed to test whether L2 students might actually avoid learning the meanings of L2 words with phonotactic patterns unfamiliar to them from their L1. These authors studied a group of native speakers of Japanese at intermediate levels of ESL instruction and found that the learning of common, high-frequency English words was affected by the similarity or difference of the phonological patterns of those words from phonological patterns in Japanese. Meanings of common English words with familiar L1 phonotactic patterns were easier to acquire than the meanings of common English words with unfamiliar L1 phonotactic patterns.

> *Implications: Teachers need to be aware that L2 learners coming from an L1 with a different orthographic system may be disadvantaged not only because they have to learn a new orthographic system but because they may also need to develop new processing mechanisms more suitable to the L2.*

Vocabulary

Issues in Vocabulary and L2 Reading Development

There are a number of issues that center on the contributing role of vocabulary knowledge for L2 reading abilities:

- The number of words needed to read L2 texts independently and for instructional uses.
- The role of context in L2 vocabulary acquisition and in the guessing/guessability of word meaning in L2 reading.
- The role of dictionaries of various kinds and the use of cognates in L2 vocabulary acquisition and in L2 reading.
- The ways L2 learners go about the task of acquiring vocabulary in the L2.
- The role of extensive or pleasure reading in the 'incidental' acquisition of L2 vocabulary and the role of vocabulary instruction.
- The impact of various kinds of vocabulary instruction on L2 vocabulary development.

The first three issues above are surveyed briefly in this section. (*See* Chapter 3, *Vocabulary*, for more on these issues and for discussion of the last three issues.)

How Much L2 Lexis is Needed?

Several researchers have addressed the issue of how much vocabulary is necessary for L2 reading, from different perspectives. Laufer (1989) addressed the question in terms of percentage of text-lexis necessary for comprehension of academic literature by native speakers of Hebrew and Arabic in a university EAP course. She found significant differences at the 95 per cent level of text coverage, and concluded that L2 readers had a significantly higher chance of being a 'reader' if they understood 95 per cent of the text's word tokens. Hu and Nation (2000) found that the percentage necessary might be closer to 98 per cent. Hirsh and Nation (1992) addressed the question in terms of the vocabulary size needed to read short, unsimplified novels for pleasure. Their results showed that in order to achieve 97–98 per cent coverage of the running words in such texts, that a vocabulary size of about 5000 word families would be needed.

The hallmark study in this area was conducted by Hazenberg and Hulstijn (1996). In a very carefully designed and executed study with Dutch native speakers reading first-year university level materials, Hazenberg and Hulstijn (1996) first assessed the representativeness of more than 23,000 words (lemmas) taken from a dictionary to cover a 42 million-word corpus of contemporary written Dutch. They found that, with frequency as a criterion, text coverage substantially increased with up to 11,123 words but not beyond. Next, Hazenberg and Hulstijn (1996) assessed the representativeness of the same 23,000 words to cover first-year university reading materials. They found that the coverage of the academic corpus did not differ from the coverage of the larger general corpus. In the third part of the study, they developed and administered a vocabulary test aimed at measuring receptive knowledge of more than 18,000 content words of the 23,000 words. From these results they concluded that the minimal size vocabulary needed for university study is 10,000 base words, clearly a larger vocabulary size than required for reading everyday unsimplified texts such as newspapers or novels.

The Role of Context in Guessing/Guessability of Word Meaning in L2 Reading

Bensoussan and Laufer (1984) investigated use of context by university-level EFL students in translating words into their native language. Through analysis of student answering patterns they determined that context helped lexical guessing in only 13 per cent of the responses and for only 24 per cent of the words. Moreover, word guessability was shown to be less a function of using the context than of applying 'preconceived notions'. And, although more proficient students knew more words than less proficient students, they were not any more effective in the use of context. Haynes (1984) also has shown that students make greater use of local, rather than global, contextual clues in their contextual guessing of word meanings, and that what may appear to be transparent, 'guessable' contexts to native speakers are often incomprehensible contexts to non-native speakers.

In a study which examined both guessing from context as well as retention, Mondria and Wit-de Boer (1991) found that factors such as 'subject,' 'verb' and 'function' contribute to the guessability of a word in a sentence context, and that correctly guessing a word did not lead to improved retention as compared with guessing a word incorrectly. In fact, retention of correctly guessed words was sometimes even worse than it was for incorrectly guessed words. Mondria and Wit-de Boer (1991) conclude that factors that are conducive to guessing are not conducive to retention.

Dictionary Use and L2 Reading

The role of dictionaries in both word learning as well as in reading comprehension in second language reading has been of much interest. The seminal Bensoussan, Sim and Weiss (1984) study of relatively proficient first-year university-level EFL students in Israel found that use of dictionaries during reading had no significant effect on multiple-choice comprehension test scores. More recently, Hulstijn (1993) found that students with high inferencing ability (that is, were able to guess word meaning from context) used a dictionary to the same extent as students with low inferencing ability, suggesting that some students may use a dictionary when it may not be necessary for comprehension. Thus, these two studies together suggest that dictionary use during reading may not be facilitative of second language reading comprehension, and possibly unnecessary for higher-proficiency students and ineffective for lower-proficiency students.

By contrast, Knight (1994) studied university-level students of Spanish as a foreign language (both high and low verbal abilities), and found that reading comprehension (as measured by the amount of information recalled) was significantly better for the group who had access to a computerized dictionary than for the group with no access to the dictionary. This result directly contradicts the results of Bensoussan *et al.* (1984). However, Knight's (1994) students were of much lower proficiency in the L2 than were those of Bensoussan et al. (1984). Moreover, when Knight (1994) examined the reading comprehension scores according to verbal ability, no significant difference was found between the dictionary and no-dictionary conditions for high verbal ability learners, a result similar to that of Bensoussan et al (1984). However, for the lower verbal ability group, there was a significant difference. Thus, dictionary access was significant only for the lower verbal ability group. Moreover, although the higher group performed better than the lower group both with and without the dictionary, the two groups performed more similarly to each other when they had access to the dictionary, suggesting the dictionary use can help weaker students close the gap between themselves and higher ability students.

> *Implications: In order for L2 learners to read well, they must have an adequately sized vocabulary and must be able to recognize the words in that vocabulary quickly and accurately. Guessing from context and dictionary use can help in acquiring this vocabulary, but these skills are not automatic. Rather, they need to be developed and practised in order to be used effectively in conjunction with reading.*

Reading Rate

In L1 reading research studies, there is considerable evidence that fluent readers read at rates between 200 wpm and 300 wpm for most types of texts (Carver, 1992). Moreover, evidence demonstrated that this fluency develops consistently across age and grade levels. Unfortunately, L2 students typically do not have 12 years to develop fluent reading rates, so recommendations are regularly made to use speed reading and reading rate activities in L2 reading classes (*see* Anderson, 1999; Jensen, 1986, for examples). However, there are few published studies of the relationship between reading rate development or training and foreign or second language reading comprehension. Moreover, those studies which are available have significant research design flaws. Only Anderson (1991) included both aspects of what are normally considered minimal components for a training study. During a 14-week semester in a university-level intensive ESL programme, Anderson (1991) worked with students to increase reading rate, and measured student's comprehension scores as well. Students in the experimental group significantly increased their reading rate (from 161 wpm to 275 wpm), whereas readers in the control group showed an insignificant increase (from 160 wpm to 167 wpm). Although students in the experimental group did not make significant comprehension gains, whilst students in the control group did, the good news was that these students' comprehension did not suffer while their reading rate increased dramatically. The results from this study suggest that it is indeed possible to help students improve their reading rate.

Weigle and Jensen (1996), although not including a control group, similarly found significant increases in reading rate after training, but slight decreases in comprehension for another university-level ESL sample. In analysing differences between a sub-group with lower proficiency and one with higher proficiency, and noting that the higher-proficiency group experienced more dramatic rate gains while their comprehension levels suffered less dramatically, Weigle and Jensen (1996) speculate that reading rate development training may have been more effective for students who were already somewhat strong L2 readers. In contrast, weaker readers may need to develop their 'bottom-up' skills of word recognition and vocabulary development before rate development exercises can be maximally beneficial.

> *Implications: Exercises aimed at improving reading rate seem to help L2 learners, in particular those who have already developed their word recognition skills.*

Language Threshold

A major research topic for L2 reading is the extent to which L2 language proficiency is needed as a support for L2 reading before L1 reading strategies and skills can be used effectively in an L2 context. Alderson (1984) posed the question most cogently in a book chapter entitled 'Reading in a foreign language: a reading problem or a language problem?' Research results at that time pointed in both directions, and led to the formulation of two apparently contradictory positions: the so-called 'language threshold' or 'short-circuit hypothesis' and the 'linguistic interdependence hypothesis'. The language threshold hypothesis maintained that some minimal threshold of proficiency in the L2 must be attained in order for the reader's first language reading skills to transfer to reading in the second language. The linguistic interdependence hypothesis maintained that reading or learning to read is accomplished only once, and that once learners have matured in their ability to read in the first language, the awareness of the reading process transfers to the second language and does not need to be relearned. Thus, reading performance in the second language was claimed to share a common underlying proficiency with reading ability in the first language (Cummins, 1979).

In the first widely available empirical study to use a cross-linguistic research design with learners of varying L1 reading ability, L2 language proficiency and L2 reading ability, and utilizing multiple regression analyses, Carrell (1991) investigated two groups of second language learners in the USA: native speakers of Spanish learning English, and native speakers of English learning Spanish. Results showed that both independent variables (L1 reading ability and L2 proficiency), when taken together, were statistically significant predictors of second language reading ability, together accounting for 35 per cent (for the native Spanish group) and 53 per cent (for the native English group) of the variance in second language reading. However, in the native Spanish group (whose L2 proficiency was higher than the native English group), L1 reading ability appeared to be the more important predictor of L2 reading. Conversely, in the native English group (with lower overall L2 proficiency), second language proficiency appeared to be the more important predictor of L2 reading.

Bernhardt and Kamil (1995) further tested the language threshold and language interdependence hypotheses with adult native English speakers learning Spanish as the L2 at university level in the USA. Proficiency levels consisted of beginning freshmen, intermediate juniors and seniors who had had up to five semesters of Spanish study, and advanced learners who had had up to seven semesters of Spanish. Bernhardt and Kamil (1995) were able to account for 48 per cent of the variance in L2 reading by both L1 reading and L2 proficiency. Between 10 per cent and 16 per cent of the 48 per cent was due to L1 reading; between 32 per cent and 38 per cent was due to L2 proficiency. For these learners, as with the similar group in Carrell's (1991) study, second language proficiency was a stronger predictor of second language reading than was first language reading ability.

Lee and Schallert (1997) were the most recent to test the language threshold hypothesis, and did so in an EFL context, with a large sample ($n = 809$) of Korean middle and high school students exhibiting a wide range of abilities in both their L1 and L2 English reading, and in their L2 proficiency. Basic results yielded a squared multiple correlation coefficient indicating 62 per cent of the variance in L2 reading due to the two independent variables. Approximately twice as much of the variance in L2 reading was due to L2 proficiency as was due to L1 reading (57 per cent versus 30 per cent).

Although all the findings of the studies summarized above are consistent with the existence of a language threshold, the evidence is complicated and is also interpretable in terms of a continuously changing relationship as L2 proficiency increases, not necessarily in terms of the existence of a specific 'threshold'. Moreover, assuming that a threshold exists, it is not likely that it could be determined in absolute terms, even for a given population of learners.

Implications: It seems that a certain level of L2 proficiency is necessary before L1 reading strategies and skills can be utilized effectively in L2 reading. Therefore, L2 reading development must take place in a learning context that also promotes overall L2 language proficiency, at least for lower-level students.

The Role of Background Knowledge in Reading

Work done in the 1970s and 1980s (Steffensen, Joag-dev, and Anderson, 1979; Johnson, 1981) clearly established the role of background knowledge in second language reading. Further training studies showed that for students who lacked appropriate cultural background knowledge (or 'content schemata') for particular texts, explicit teaching of appropriate background information could facilitate second language reading (Floyd and Carrell, 1987).

Bernhardt (1991) was one of the first to caution against a predictive relationship between background knowledge and second or foreign language reading comprehension. Whilst finding that the effects of background knowledge were statistically significantly correlated with recall protocols scores on the topic (Pearson's $r = 0.27$; $p<0.05$), Bernhardt (1991) pointed out the weak nature of the correlation. Moreover, when results were broken out by individual texts, which had been controlled for similarity in style and text-readability, correlations ranged from 0.11 to 0.59, all moderate correlations.

Thus, there were definite text content effects above and beyond prior knowledge effects.

More recent research has continued to show strong effects for background knowledge, but has also shown that there are complex interactions between background knowledge and other factors in second or foreign language reading. For example, Pritchard (1990) demonstrated the interaction of cultural content schemata and reading strategies, with students using different sets of strategies for culturally familiar than for culturally unfamiliar passages. Carrell and Wise (1998), exploring the relationship between background knowledge and topic interest, found a significant interaction between the two. If either prior knowledge or topic interest is high, students perform better than if both prior knowledge and topic interest are low.

> *Implications: Appropriate background knowledge about the topic being read helps learners understand the reading better. It is an important element in reading comprehension, but only one of many.*

Knowledge of Text Structure and Discourse Cues

Beyond background knowledge of the content domain of a text, empirical research has confirmed that texts have particular rhetorical organizational patterns and that readers' background knowledge of text structure and discourse cues significantly affect their reading in a second or foreign language (Geva, 1983; Carrell, 1984a, b). Moreover, training studies have also been conducted which show the facilitating effects on foreign or second language reading of teaching students to recognize and use text mapping strategies to represent the rhetorical structure of texts (Carrell, 1985; Carrell, Pharis and Liberto, 1989; Raymond, 1993; Tang, 1992).

More recent research has replicated earlier studies, yielding the same basic results, but adding additional considerations. In a study of university-level ESL students' awareness (recognition and use) of text structure and reading comprehension, Carrell (1992) found that those students who used the structure of the original passages to organize their written recalls remembered significantly more total ideas from the original passage than did those who did not. Thus, this study shows that students who possess a specialized kind of background knowledge – awareness of different patterns used by authors to organize expository texts – are more likely to use a structure strategy when they read, and therefore, are also more likely to understand and remember more of what they read.

> *Implications: L2 readers can benefit from an understanding of the text structures which organize L2 texts, and can profit from making those structures explicit through the use of text mapping strategies.*

Meta-cognition and Reading Strategies

As Brown, Armbruster and Baker (1986: 49) have asserted, 'metacogntion plays a vital role in reading'. One's 'knowledge' (for example, of strategies for learning from texts, of the differing demands of various reading tasks, of text structures, and of one's own strengths and weaknesses as a reader and learner) as well as 'control' or 'regulation' of one's own actions while reading for different purposes are two different aspects of meta-cognition. Successful readers demonstrate higher levels of meta-cognitive knowledge as well as control of their reading; less successful and novice readers show less sophistication in meta-cognition (Paris, Lipson and Wixson, 1983).

One important aspect of metacognition is controlling one's reading process through the use of strategies (*see* Chapter 10, *Focus on the Language Learner: Motivation, Styles and Strategies*, for more on strategies). It has been a long-standing tenet of first-language reading research that expert readers use a variety of reading strategies to aid comprehension (Baker and Brown, 1984), and that 'strategic reading is a prime characteristic of expert readers' (Paris, Wasik and Turner, 1991). Block (1986), in a study of generally non-proficient L1 and L2 English readers, found that four characteristics seem to differentiate the more successful from the less successful:

- Ability to integrate information.
- Ability to recognize aspects of text structure.
- Ability to use general knowledge, personal experiences, and associations.
- Ability to address information in the text rather than respond personally.

Later studies showed a more complex situation, where the use of certain reading strategies does not always lead to successful reading comprehension, whereas use of other strategies does not always result in unsuccessful reading comprehension. It may be the skilful use of clusters of strategies that is most important: Anderson (1991) found that subjects who utilized more strategies tended to score higher on reading comprehension tasks. He concluded successful strategic reading was not only 'a matter of knowing what strategy to use, but also . . . know[ing] how to use a strategy successfully and [to] orchestrate its use with other strategies' (Anderson, 1991: 468–469).

In addition, it seems that L2 readers can be successfully trained in strategy use. Learners who were taught mapping strategies to recognize and use the rhetorical structure of texts (Carrell, 1985; Raymond, 1993), strategies for word, sentence and discourse analysis (Kern, 1989) and strategies relating to Experience–Text–Relationship (ETR) and semantic mapping (Carrell, Pharis and Liberto, 1989) all improved their reading skills. Moreover, the improvements may prove to be durable; Carrell (1985) still found evidence of the training three weeks later. Strategy training may be especially helpful for weaker students, as Kern's (1989) study showed that the strategy instruction benefited low-proficiency students to a greater extent than middle and high proficiency students.

> *Implications: Better learners actively control their reading and strategy use. Fortunately, it seems that these meta-cognitive skills can be taught, with lower proficiency students gaining the most. Therefore, reading instruction should include some training in these 'management' skills.*

Extensive Reading/Impact of Exposure to Print

Day and Bamford (1998) provide an overview of a number of studies that have investigated the impact of extensive reading on second language reading. Unfortunately, many of these studies have limitations; in particular, due to the nature of the extensive reading treatment which usually runs over some extended period of time, it is difficult to control a number of other factors and variables (for example, contamination from other courses students are taking). However, what seems clear from the research is that second or foreign language readers at various ages and proficiency levels can benefit from extensive reading (Elley, 1991). For example, Hafiz and Tudor (1989) found that a three-month extensive reading programme yielded significant improvement in secondary school ESL students' reading and writing, whereas two control groups failed to show significant improvement over the same three-month period. In addition, groups of Japanese EFL learners using extensive reading performed better than similar traditionally instructed control groups (Mason and Krashen, 1997). (It should also be noted that the L1 evidence for extensive reading is now overwhelming.) Although there are good reasons to believe in the importance of extensive reading, what is not clear from these studies is the extent to which extensive reading should be balanced with an intensive reading programme containing well-considered reading instruction/pedagogy (for example, in reading strategies, in vocabulary, etc.).

> *Implications: Extensive reading should be a component of almost any reading programme.*

Further Issues

This review of specific areas of second language research does not purport to exhaust the many other studies that have contributed important insights into L2 reading. Moreover, due to space limitations, there are other areas that have not been covered but which deserve important attention and much continued research. Some of these other areas include: models of L2 reading and reading development, the interplay between higher and lower level processes, motivation in L2 reading, reading and writing relations, social context factors influencing L2 reading, assessment practices in L2 reading, and the increasing similarities of L2 reading processes across languages as students reach advanced levels. There are assuredly other issues that also deserve further attention.

Implications of L2 Research for Instruction

L2 reading research findings, when combined with appropriate L1 reading research, highlight important implications for instructional practices. While it is true that each instructional context has local factors that make it unique, and therefore not fully amenable to a generalized set of recommendations, it is also true that the research to date suggests general implications and guidelines as a starting point for planning L2 reading curricula. Based on the research reported in this chapter, we would like to propose the following ten implications for L2 reading instruction, at least as a starting point for curriculum planning.

- The need to develop reading fluency and word-recognition automaticity.
- The need to develop a large recognition vocabulary.
- The importance of discourse structure and the instructional benefits of using graphic representations.
- The need for language awareness and attention to language (structure) and genre form (meta-linguistic knowledge).
- The importance of meta-cognitive awareness and strategic reading.
- The importance of specific reading strategies to support word learning and reading to learn goals.
- The need for extensive reading.
- The importance of motivation.
- The benefits of integrated skills instruction and content-based instruction.
- The need for a supportive (classroom and institutional) environment for reading.

Suggesting implications for reading instruction represents part of the bridge to an effective reading curriculum. A second part is a needs analysis for each instructional context. Issues that a needs analysis might address include: What are the reading goals and why? Do the goals fit with institutional expectations? Are the goals achievable given students' L2 proficiency levels? Are there sufficient resources and sufficient time to achieve instructional goals? These and other questions need to be considered to establish viable goals for instruction and determine the extent to which L2 reading abilities can be developed.

A third part, once a curriculum plan and customized goals are established, is to determine priorities for specific instructional practices to achieve these goals. It is beyond the scope of this chapter to comment on the numerous specific practices themselves, though there are many sources that provide useful suggestions for instruction (Grellet, 1981; Carrell, Devine and Eskey,

1988; Carrell *et al.*, 1989; Mickulecky, 1990; Day, 1993; Silberstein, 1994; Anderson, 1999; Grabe and Stoller, 2001, in press). There are also many excellent and appropriate ideas for instruction that can be drawn from L1 resources (Pressley, 1998; Thompson and Nicholson, 1999; Vacca and Vacca, 1999).

Further Reading

- Alderson, J. (2000). *Reading Assessment.* New York: Cambridge University Press. Although focusing on assessment, this book provides important discussions of L2 reading theory, covering many common topics and issues. The focus on assessment also offers insights into assessment tasks and practices that are not only useful for testing purposes but also reading research purposes.
- Anderson, N. (1999). *Exploring Second Language Reading.* Boston, MA: Heinle & Heinle. The volume offers a concise and coherent interpretation of reading research for L2 reading instruction. The book is very accessible, but covers a wider range of key topics than other books devoted to reading instruction.
- Grabe, W., Stoller, F. (2001). *Researching and Teaching Reading.* New York: Longman. This volume addresses current reading research from both L1 and L2 contexts and develops a set of general principles for reading instruction and action research inquiry. The book presents an explanation for how reading comprehension works, how L2 reading is different from L1 reading, and the issues for instruction that are created by these differences. It also outlines 30 possible action research projects on a range of topics.
- Kamil, M., Mosenthal, P., Pearson, P.D., Barr, R. (eds). (2000). *Handbook of Reading Research.* Volume III. Mahwah, NJ: Lawrence Erlbaum. This major edited collection summarizes current thinking by leading reading and education researchers in English L1 contexts. Although the chapters in this volume focus less on the cognitive aspects of reading, in comparison to Volume II (1991), there are many important chapters that anyone seeking greater knowledge about reading would need to review.
- Pressley, M. (1998). *Reading Instruction that Works.* New York: Guilford. This is the best L1 reading volume on issues in translating reading research into implications for reading instruction. It is both authoritative and very accessible. It presents a coherent balanced perspective on English L1 reading issues and instructional practices.
- Stanovich, K. (2000). *Progress in Understanding Reading: Scientific Foundations and New Frontiers.* New York: Guilford. This volume is a recent compilation of major articles by Keith Stanovich, one of the world's leading reading researchers. While the gathering of his major articles is worth the effort to read by itself, fully one-half of the book is new material, representing Stanovich's latest thinking on all of the key issues in reading that he has explored over the past 20 plus years. It is not the easiest book to

read, but it may be the most important one for anyone interested in understanding reading research.

- Urquhart, S., Weir, C. (1998). *Reading in a Foreign Language: Process, Product and Practice*. New York: Longman. This volume represents an important contribution to our understanding of L2 reading research and its implications for both instruction and assessment practices. It complements the Alderson book (*see above*) well in the coverage of standard topics in L2 reading theory and practice. It also presents an important discussion of reading assessment and issues to be addressed by future research.

Hands-on Activity

Text: Select a substantial text (two to three pages) excerpt from a textbook or other reading resource in the social sciences (for example, psychology, economics, sociology).

Students: Imagine a group of high-intermediate or low-advanced students of English from either heterogeneous or homogeneous L1 backgrounds (you decide which), whose language requirements include reading skills in the social sciences (for example, in an EAP programme).

Activity: The activity focuses on reading strategies to comprehend the text and to use the information for other tasks. These strategies may include setting a purpose for reading, previewing the text, predicting key information, skimming the text to determine main ideas, note-taking, summarizing, clarifying difficult concepts, identifying supporting ideas and evidence.

Task for the reader:

- How might you model the application of the reading strategies listed above (and others) to the selected text?
- How can you help students make their use of each strategy 'meta-cognitive,' to include student awareness of *what* the strategy is, *how* to use the strategy, *why* the strategy should be used, *when* and *where* to use the strategy, and *how* to help students *evaluate* their use of the strategy?

14

Writing

Tony Silva
Purdue University

Paul Kei Matsuda
University of New Hampshire

Introduction

Writing has always been part of applied linguistics. Even before the 1960s, when writing was considered as a mere representation of speech, it provided a way of monitoring students' language production and of providing linguistic material because the technology for sound recording was not widely available. For researchers, it has always provided a source of tangible and relatively stable data for analysis as well as a way of recording speech. However, in the early years of applied linguistics, writing was not considered to be one of the proper goals of language learning. Writing was used only to the extent that it assisted the learning of speech. It was assumed that anyone who had the knowledge of spelling and grammar would be able to write.

In the latter half of the twentieth century, writing, or written discourse, and the teaching of writing began to receive significant attention as a legitimate area of inquiry within applied linguistics. With the growth of composition studies in the USA and the parallel development of the field of second language writing, the act of writing also became an important focus of research and instruction in L1 and L2 writing. More recently, prompted by the recognition of the complexity of writing and the teaching of writing, the study and teaching of L2 writing have evolved into interdisciplinary fields of inquiry involving many related fields, including applied linguistics and composition studies, which are themselves highly interdisciplinary.

Although applied linguists have come to recognize the importance of writing in its own right as well as its complexity, writing remains one of the least well-understood, if not misunderstood, subjects in applied linguistics in general. One reason is the ambiguity of the term 'writing' – which has been used in referring to orthography, written discourse, the act of writing or even literature – and the prevalence of the definition of writing as mere orthography in linguistic sciences during the last two centuries. Although the body of research in applied linguistics focusing on writing and writing instruction has grown exponentially over the last few decades, writing continues to be marginalized in mainstream second language acquisition research (Harklau, 2000; Leki, 2000) and many popular introductory linguistics textbooks still perpetuate the view of writing as an orthographic representation of speech, if writing is discussed at all. For this reason, we need to begin by demystifying writing.

Demystifying Writing

Many of the assumptions that have limited the place of writing in applied linguistics were formed in the late nineteenth century, when phonetics was at the heart of the emerging field of linguistic sciences and the literacy rate was rather low – the highest literacy skill required for most people was letter writing (Matsuda, 2001a). As the importance of literacy has grown in contemporary societies, and as the complexity of literacy has become widely recognized, the traditional view of writing that informed early applied linguistics has become obsolete, especially for the purpose of writing teachers and researchers.

One of the traditional views is the notion of writing as transcribed speech. In its early years, applied linguistics inherited the view of language as speech and writing as an orthographic – and many would say inaccurate – representation of speech. It was often assumed that the acquisition of spoken proficiency had to take precedence over the learning of written language, and that students would be able to write once they 'mastered' spoken language and orthographic conventions. One of the pedagogical implications of these assumptions was that language teachers refrained from introducing writing early in the process of language learning because they were afraid that the discrepancy between speech sounds and orthography would interfere with the proper learning of speech, which was considered to be the only appropriate goal of language learning. On the contrary, the acquisition of L2 literacy can take place alongside the acquisition of L2 proficiency; moreover, L2 literacy can facilitate rather than hinder the development of general linguistic competence for adult learners (Weissberg, 2000).

Another problematic assumption is that writing is 'decontextualized' (Ellis, 1994: 188). This view of writing is simplistic, if not outdated, because it assumes that written communication never takes place in the presence of the writer and the reader. People can and sometimes do communicate face-to-face in writing, for example students passing notes to each other in the classroom or speakers of mutually unintelligible Chinese dialects communicating in written Chinese. The advent of the Internet and computer-mediated communication technology has also made it a common practice to carry real-time written conversations with other people in distant locations. Even in more conventional types of written communication, writing is far from decontextualized because every writing task is situated in a rhetorical context, involving complex interrelationships among various elements of writing: the writer, the reader, the text and reality (Grabe and Kaplan, 1996; Matsuda, 1997).

For teachers and researchers of writing, then, it is more productive to define writing as one of the three modes of linguistic expression and communication – along with speaking and signing – rather than secondary or subservient to speech. It is a manifestation of, as well as the process of manifesting, sociolinguistic, strategic and grammatical competences (Canale and Swain, 1980) mediated by the use of orthographic systems. In the next section, we consider theoretical perspectives on the three aspects of writing competence, including relational, strategic and textual, that correspond roughly to Canale and Swain's (1980) conception of communicative competence.

Aspects of Writing

Relational Aspect of Writing

Writing does not happen in a vacuum; it is always embedded in a rhetorical situation – a complex web of relationships among the elements of writing (Moffett, 1968/1983; Kinneavy, 1971). The relationships between the writer, the reader, the text and reality are constantly changing, and it is quite possible for writers and readers to develop different perceptions of any particular rhetorical situation. For this reason, the writer's task is not as simple as constructing an accurate representation of reality; the writer also has to negotiate, through the construction of text, his or her own view of these elements of writing with the views held by the readers (Matsuda, 1997).

The rhetorical situation refers to a combination of various elements of writing that comprise the context of writing; it is a particular social and material arrangement in which written expression and communication take place. No two rhetorical situations are exactly the same, but similar situations do tend to recur. This gives rise to typified responses (that is, genre as typified rhetorical action) that are developed and shared by a network of writers who work in a particular discourse community (Miller, 1984; Bakhtin, 1986). 'Genre knowledge', that is, the knowledge of typified responses in particular rhetorical situations, functions as a scaffolding that assists writers in managing the complex task of understanding and responding to the rhetorical situation (*see* Bazerman, 1988; Swales, 1990; Berkenkotter and Huckin, 1995).

The writer's task is complicated by the varying and ever-changing nature of the elements of writing. The notion of the writer is more complex than it first appears because the writer is more than just the physical person who creates texts. Writers are not only presenting their view of reality but also constructing their discursive identity (Goffman, 1959; Ivanic, 1998), which may affect the way the text is read and responded to. A writer's self-construction may also be constrained by his or her past self-constructions, especially if the writer is writing in the same discourse community – a sudden change in self-representation can be highly marked and even distracting. Writers who are learning to write in new rhetorical situations (for example, first-year college students writing a research paper or international ESL students writing in US higher education) may struggle because conventional self-representation in the particular situation may not be compatible with the writer's self-image. A piece of written discourse may also be co-authored by two or more writers – or sometimes even by a committee. Even when the author is singular, the text may have been shaped by feedback and interventions from peers, tutors, teachers, mentors and editors. (When those interventions override the writers' intentions, it becomes 'appropriation'.)

The reader is not a simple concept either. Like the writer, the reader may be one person or many. In most cases, the writer is the first reader who provides comments, asks questions and makes suggestions for revision; in some cases, such as private diaries, the writer may be the only intended reader (Murray, 1982). Readers may play different roles, such as that of a friend, critic, coach, evaluator, learner or bystander. Those roles may belong to real audiences addressed by the writer but they may also be imagined roles invoked in the text (Ede and Lunsford, 1984). For example, this chapter addresses beginning applied linguists – perhaps graduate students in an introductory applied linguistics course. At the same time, this chapter invokes readers who may not be familiar with writing issues but are certainly intelligent and inquisitive, wanting to understand theory and research as well as pedagogy. This imagined audience role is invoked by the 'content' (for example, the choice of topics, the amount of and type of explanations and examples) as well as the 'form' (for example, the use or non-use of certain technical terms, strategies for referencing sources).

The text is also complicated. Although each text is unique in some ways, a text cannot be understood only in terms of itself because the text is always situated in a network of other texts, to which it may respond explicitly or implicitly (Bakhtin, 1986). Other texts also provide a pool of discursive features that may be appropriated by the writer in order to achieve similar rhetorical effects and by the reader in interpreting the text. In many cases, each local 'discourse community' develops its own network of texts that are shared by its members. However, the formal and functional features of those texts continue to evolve as members of local discourse communities bring in practices from other discourse communities. When new rhetorical situations arise, writers often draw on practices in existing discourse communities in developing hybrid discourses (Berkenkotter and Huckin, 1995; Hyland, 2000).

Reality may seem stable, but it can be interpreted in many ways. Although there is a reality people can interact with physically, reality is also socially and discursively constructed to the extent that people understand, communicate and agree upon versions of reality through language (*see* Berger and Luckmann, 1966). Because people conceive of and relate to reality in various ways, and because writers and readers have varying degrees of access to different aspects of reality, the writer has to use the text to construct a version of reality and negotiate it with readers within the local and historical context of interaction.

As we have seen, writing is a complex phenomenon because writers have to negotiate all the above elements of writer, reader, text and reality, and construct written discourse accordingly. In order to manage this complex process, writers adopt, develop and use various strategies.

Strategic Aspect of Writing

Writers draw on various strategies (or 'heuristics') to assess the rhetorical situation and respond to it by developing written text. Those strategies are often internalized; some writers may have acquired them so naturally through practice that they may not even be aware of some of the strategies they use. For most writers – especially less experienced ones – it is often helpful to have an explicit understanding of some of the strategies that can be internalized through practice. Understanding the strategic aspect of writing is important for writing teachers because it enables them to teach 'writing' rather than teach 'about writing'.

In order for the process of writing to begin, the writer has to assess the rhetorical situation and identify the primary purpose or aim of writing, with an emphasis on one of the elements of writing. The aim of writing may be 'expressive' (emphasis on the writer), 'persuasive' (emphasis on the reader), 'referential' (emphasis on reality) or 'literary' (emphasis on the text) (Kinneavy, 1971). The writer may also identify and develop ideas for writing by focusing on one or more of the elements, such as:

- Exploring or discovering what the writer already knows, feels or believes through techniques such as clustering, listening and free writing (focus on the writer).
- Looking for dissonance or conflict (focus on the reader).
- Examining reality through reading or observation (focus on reality).
- Choosing a form of writing, such as sonnet, personal narrative or conference proposal (focus on the text).

Once the topic is identified, the writer needs to explore, develop and sometimes redefine the topic. One of the most commonly known heuristics for exploration is journalists' '5W1H' (*who, what, when, where, why* and *how*). Burke's (1969) 'pentad' (*act, scene, agent, agency* and *purpose*) is a similar heuristic designed to aid the exploration process. Another example of an exploration heuristic is 'tagmemics' (Young, Becker and Pike, 1970) which facilitates the exploration of the topic by focusing on its distinctive features, on changes over time and on classification. Reading may also be a way of exploring topics. Visually oriented writers may map out their ideas on paper in order to explore and organize as well as present various aspects of the topic. The writer's intuitive sense of what is to be discussed in a certain rhetorical situation – an aspect of genre knowledge – can also guide the writer as an implicit exploration heuristic. For example, in empirical studies, writers' methods of exploration are often directly guided by accepted research procedures and conventionalized ways of reporting that research.

Writers also need to identify, develop and assess rhetorical appeals. The Aristotelian conception of 'ethos' (ethical or credibility appeal), 'pathos' (emotional or affective appeal) and 'logos' (logical or rational appeal) have been widely taught in writing classrooms. They have also been used in text analysis (Connor and Lauer, 1985). Although ethos and pathos are especially important when the primary aim of writing is persuasive, they also contribute, to varying degrees, to the success of discourse with other aims. Traditional approaches to the analysis of logos focused on the evaluation of arguments according to the rules of formal logic and the identification of logical fallacies. More recently, writing teachers have come to use situationally based theories of argumentation that consider audience and discourse communities as important criteria in generating and evaluating arguments (Toulmin, 1958; Perelman, 1982).

'Drafting' can be a challenge for writers because factors such as the writer's self-image and anxiety about writing can make the writing task overwhelming, sometimes resulting in writing inhibition, commonly referred to as 'writer's block' (Rose, 1980). Various strategies have been suggested for reducing anxiety levels and facilitating the production of written text. Writers may choose to ignore one or more of the elements of writing, such as grammar and audience, in the early stages of drafting (Flower, 1979; Elbow, 1987). Some writers may draw on their spoken language or their knowledge of other genres to develop and revise written texts. Second language writers may also translate from texts generated in their L1, although the effectiveness of this strategy may be limited for advanced L2 writers (Kobayashi and Rinnert, 1992).

'Revision' is an important part of the writing process. Writers often revise based on comments and suggestions from peers and teachers. The writer may also be able to revise the text by letting it sit for a while, which allows the writer to see the text from a somewhat different perspective. Editing and proofreading – the processes of checking and changing grammatical and stylistic features – is also an important part of the revision process. In the writing classroom, students are often advised to focus on content before focusing on form.

These strategies are not always used consciously by writers. Furthermore, writers do not always go through these stages (planning, drafting and revising) in a linear and orderly fashion; rather, the process of writing is often 'recursive' (Flower and Hayes, 1981). Most writers go through numerous revisions – both during the process of drafting and after the draft is completed. Some of the revisions are invisible because they take place in writers' minds as they rehearse particular passages. In fact, experienced writers writing in a familiar rhetorical situation may be able to rehearse so extensively in their heads that their first drafts require relatively few revisions. Genre knowledge also functions heuristically to assist the writers in planning, developing and organizing ideas as well as in choosing appropriate linguistic features for the specific rhetorical context.

Textual Aspect of Writing

We discuss the textual aspect of writing last, not because it is least important but because it is the material realization of the other two aspects of writing. It is through written text that the writer constructs, represents and negotiates his or her conceptions of the writer, the reader, the text and reality. Writers do not simply encode 'ideational meaning' (the meaning of their ideas); they also create 'textual meaning' (the meaning that helps the readers navigate through the text) as well as 'interpersonal meaning' (the meaning about the relationship between the writer and the reader) (Halliday, 1973). The knowledge of how these meanings can be constructed through the use of particular written discourse features is therefore an important part of the writer's competence.

Whereas spoken discourse represents additional meaning through prosodic features such as tone, pitch, intonation, volume and pauses (*see* Chapter 12, *Speaking and Pronunciation*), written discourse achieves similar functions through typographical features such as punctuation marks, capitalization, italics, bold face, font sizes and indentation. In formalized writing situations, where the use of typographical features is constrained by stylistic conventions established by publishers and academic societies, writers have to rely more heavily on structural means (for example, topicalization, nominalization) as well as discursive features such as the use of hedges (for example, *may*, *probably*) and boosters (for example, *must*, *definitely*) (Hyland, 2000). Writers also construct – intentionally or unintentionally – their discursive identity or 'voice' by using various written discourse features and by aligning themselves with certain discourse communities (Ivanic, 1998; Matsuda, 2001b).

Although the ability to write presupposes some level of morphological, lexical and syntactic as well as idiomatic knowledge, such knowledge alone does not guarantee the ability to write well because writing involves much more than constructing grammatical sentences. Sentences need to be 'cohesive', that is, they have to be connected by cohesive devices in ways that can be followed by readers (Halliday and Hasan, 1976). The whole text also needs to be 'coherent', that is, various parts of the text have to work together conceptually in the particular rhetorical context. Although cohesion and coherence are related concepts, cohesive text is not necessarily coherent (Witte and Faigley, 1981; Carrell, 1982). Furthermore, coherence is not universal; rather, what is considered coherent differs from one discourse community to another. Research in 'contrastive rhetoric' has shown, for example, that the standard of coherence may vary across languages and cultures (Connor and Johns, 1990; Leki, 1991, Connor, 1996), although the differences cannot simply be attributed to language or culture alone (Mohan and Lo, 1985; Kubota, 1997; Matsuda, 1997). For this reason, the assessment of the quality of writing requires an understanding of the context in which it was written and especially the audience for which it was intended.

Second Language Writing: Theory, Research and Pedagogy

This section will, drawing on Silva (1990), survey major developments during the last 50 years or so in second language writing with regard to theory, research and pedagogy. (For alternative perspectives, *see* Raimes, 1991; Blanton, 1995.) We have limited our attention to second language writing here because applied linguists interface primarily with professionals in second language studies; we focus on ESL writing because, to date, most of the research on second language writing has been done in this area.

Although developments in second language writing have been influenced by work in mainstream composition studies, the unique contexts of second language writing require distinct perspectives, models and practices. In the recent history of second language writing, a number of approaches or orientations (more or less specific to second language writing) have vied for the attention of second language writing professionals. These approaches or traditions will be addressed below in order of their appearance on the second language writing stage.

Controlled Composition

'Controlled composition' can be seen as offshoot of the audiolingual approach to second language teaching in that it shares two of its central tenets: the idea that language is speech (from structural linguistics) and that learning is habit formation (from behaviourist psychology). Thus, it is not difficult to understand why, within this tradition, writing is regarded essentially as reinforcement for oral habits and as a secondary concern (*see* Fries, 1945; Rivers, 1968; for theoretical background for this approach).

Linguistic analysis dominated the research in this tradition and is still a major focus, though it has become more functional and less formal over the years. Early work in the linguistic analysis of second language writers' texts involved 'contrastive analysis' (comparing the grammatical structures of two languages, for example, Spanish and English, in an attempt to ascertain structural differences, which were believed to pose the greatest problems for second language writers) and 'error analysis' (locating, counting and categorizing errors to discern patterns of error in written texts). Formal features examined include primarily lexical and syntactic phenomena; features such as number of words per t-unit and clause structure have been used to measure fluency, accuracy, and complexity in second language writers' texts.

In the controlled composition classroom the primary focus is on formal accuracy. The teacher employs a controlled programme of systematic habit formation in an attempt to avoid errors (presumed to be related to first language interference) and to reinforce appropriate second language behaviour. Practice with previously learned discrete units of language is privileged over concerns about ideas, organization and style; imitation and manipulation of carefully constructed and graded model passages is the central activity. Overall, in the controlled composition tradition, writing functions as a service activity, reinforcing other language skills. The goal of writing instruction is habit formation. Students manipulate familiar language structures; the teacher is an editor, privileging linguistic features over ideas. The text is seen as a collection of vocabulary and sentence patterns; there is negligible concern for audience or purpose. (For accounts of this pedagogical approach, *see* Dykstra and Paulston, 1967; Paulston and Dykstra, 1973.)

The Paragraph Pattern Approach

Increasing awareness of second language writers' need to produce extended written texts led to the realization that there was more to writing than constructing grammatical sentences. The result of this realization was what Raimes (1983b: 7) has called the 'paragraph pattern approach', which emphasized the importance of organization at the above-sentence level. This approach owes much to Kaplan's (1966) notion of 'contrastive rhetoric' – the notion that writers' different cultural and linguistic backgrounds will be reflected in their 'rhetoric', with rhetoric typically seen as primarily a matter of textual structure. Thus, first language interference was believed to extend beyond the sentence to paragraphs and longer stretches of text.

The basic concern in this tradition was the logical construction and arrangement of discourse forms. Of primary interest, especially in the early years, was the paragraph, where the focus was on its elements (for example, topic sentences) as well as options for its development (for example, comparison and contrast). Another important concern was 'essay' development, actually an extrapolation of paragraph principles to complete texts. This involved larger structural entities (for example, introductions) and organizational patterns or modes (for example, exposition).

By far, the largest single concern in second language writing research has been 'contrastive rhetoric' (for overviews, *see* Leki, 1991; Connor, 1996; Purves, 1988). The focus of this work has been on characterizing how first language 'cultural thought patterns' are reflected in second language writers' texts, how some cultures put the responsibility for successful written communication on the writer and others on the reader, and how differences between 'collectivist' and 'individualist' tendencies manifest themselves in second language writing. The most commonly compared linguistic or cultural backgrounds have been Arabic, Chinese, English, Japanese and Spanish. Contrastive rhetoric has been and still is a controversial issue, with some of its critics arguing that the notion can lead to stereotypes (Kubota, 1997, 1998; Spack, 1997) and others suggesting that the differences seen between groups are a matter of development rather than transfer (Mohan and Lo, 1985). A number of other specific rhetorical features have been addressed in the literature. These include assertions, hedging, indirectness, reader orientation, introductions, meta-discourse, rhetorical preferences and voice (*see* Hyland, 2000).

Classroom procedures associated with this tradition have tended to focus students' attention primarily on 'form'. At the most basic level, students are asked to choose among alternative sentences within the context of a provided paragraph or text. At a higher level, learners are instructed to read and analyse a model text and then apply the knowledge gleaned from this analysis to a parallel piece of original writing. At their most complex, exercises require students (already given a topic to write on) to list and group relevant facts, develop topic and supporting sentences on the basis of these facts, put together an outline and compose their text from that outline.

In short, this tradition sees writing as basically a matter of arranging sentences and paragraphs into particular patterns; learning to write requires developing skills in identifying, internalizing and producing these patterns. The writer uses provided or self-generated data to fill out a pattern; thus, the reader is not confused by an unfamiliar pattern of expression. The text is made up of increasingly complex discourse structures (that is, sentences, paragraphs, sections and so on), each embedded in the next largest form; and all of this takes place within an academic context, wherein the instructor's evaluation is assumed to reflect a community of educated native speakers.

The Process Approach

Dissatisfaction with controlled composition and the paragraph-pattern approach, due to the belief that neither adequately engendered thought or its expression and to their perceived linearity and prescriptivism, paved the way for the process approach, another import from mainstream composition studies. This tradition saw the composing process as a recursive, exploratory and generative process wherein ideas were discovered and meaning made. It was believed that guidance through and intervention in the process was preferable to the imposition of organizational patterns or syntactic or lexical constraints, and that, where there was a need or desire to communicate, content would determine form so as to convey meaning successfully. (For early work in second language composing, *see* Zamel, 1976, 1982; Raimes, 1983a, 1985.)

The advent of the 'process approach' prompted research on composing that focused on the person (that is, the writer) and the process (that is, strategies) involved in writing. Many variables affecting second language writers have been identified and addressed in the literature. The second language writer has been looked at primarily in terms of the extent of transfer of first language proficiency or writing ability to second language writing and the relationship between general second language proficiency and second language writing ability. Also of interest are the possible connections between second language writing ability and first language writing experience and expertise, writing apprehension, gender, learning style, language and instructional background, the second language writer's perceptions with regard to writing and writing instruction, and the amount of reading (in both first and second languages) a second language writer engages in. Research in this area has gone from seeing writer variables as simple and relatively discrete to very complex and greatly intertwined.

There is also a substantial body of scholarship on second language writers' composing processes (for overviews, *see* Krapels, 1990; Sasaki, 2000; Manchón, in press). Predominant in this area are general 'composing process' studies, that is, research that looks at second language writing processes holistically. There are also studies that focus on particular sub-processes and elements of the composing process. The most common of these are studies of planning, drafting, revising and editing. However, a number of other elements have also been examined. These include translating, backtracking, restructuring, formulating, monitoring, the use of the first language when writing in the second, language switching and the use of dictionaries and background texts when composing.

In the classroom, the process tradition calls for providing and maintaining a positive, encouraging and collaborative workshop environment, and for providing ample time and minimal interference so as to allow students to work through their composing processes. The objective is to help students develop viable strategies for getting started, drafting, revising and editing. From a process perspective, then, writing is a complex, recursive and creative process that is very similar in its general outlines for first and second language writers; learning to write requires the development of an efficient and effective composing process. The writer is engaged in the discovery and expression of meaning; the reader, on interpreting that intended meaning. The product (that is, the written text) is a secondary concern, whose form is a function of its content and purpose. In the process tradition it is up to the writer to identify a task and an audience and to make the response to the former meet the needs of the latter.

English for Academic Purposes

Perceiving theoretical and practical problems and omissions with regard to the process approach, critics suggested that the emphasis in ESL composition research and instruction be shifted from the writer to the reader, in particular academic and professional discourse communities. Most of the aforementioned criticism of the process approach came from proponents of an English for academic purposes orientation wanting to consider more seriously issues such as developing schemata for academic discourse, deriving insights from research on contrastive rhetoric, understanding what constitutes realistic preparation for academic work, learning about the nature of high stakes academic writing tasks, giving students a better idea of how university writing is evaluated, and, generally, understanding the socio-cultural context of academic writing (Reid, 1984; Horowitz, 1986).

Research in writing English for academic purposes has looked primarily at the issues of audience and, more recently, 'genre'. The audience research has focused primarily on one particular readership: the academic discourse community, in particular college and university professors (Vann, Meyer and Lorenz, 1984; Santos, 1988) and, to a lesser extent, on editors of scholarly journals (Gosden, 1992). This research has been done primarily through surveys and addresses academics' beliefs, practices, expectations and reactions with regard to errors, literacy skills and writing problems. The question of whether and how students should be initiated into the academic discourse community has also been debated.

In recent years, the study of genre in second language writing has become very popular. In addition to general treatments of genre, many studies of particular written genres have appeared. Some address general types or modes of writing, such as narrative, descriptive and argumentative writing as well as personal, academic, business, technical and legal texts. A number of more specific text types addressed include summaries, essay examinations, laboratory reports, research papers, theses, dissertations, research articles, experimental research reports and letters of reference.

Instruction in writing English for academic purposes focuses primarily on academic discourse genres and the range and nature of academic writing tasks (Swales, 1990; Hyon, 1996). This instruction is meant to help students work successfully within the academic context. The instructional methodology suggested aims at recreating, as well as is possible, the conditions under which actual university writing takes place and involves closely examining and analysing academic discourse genres and writing task specifications; selecting and intensively studying materials appropriate for a given task; evaluating, screening, synthesizing and organizing relevant information from these sources; and presenting these data in a form acceptable to the academy.

To sum up, in the English for academic purposes tradition, the emphasis is placed on the production of texts that will be acceptable at an English-medium institutions of higher education; learning to write is part of becoming socialized into the academic community. The writer is pragmatic and interested primarily in meeting the standards necessary for academic success; the reader is a player in the academic community who has clear and specific expectations for academic discourse. The text is viewed as a more or less conventional response to a particular writing task that fits a recognizable genre; the context is the academic discourse community. Although the English for academic purposes tradition has grown and prospered, some have questioned its emphasis on writing in various disciplines (particularly in scientific and technical fields), pointing out the difficulty of academic discourses (Spack, 1988; Zamel, 1993).

Issues that Transcend Traditions

There are a number of important issues in second language writing that transcend the traditions described above and need to be touched upon in even the most cursory survey of this research area. These include programmatic, contextual, disciplinary and political issues.

A number of 'programmatic' issues have been addressed in the research. These include second language writing programmes and programme administration, needs analyses and placement. A great deal has been written on specific instructional practices and issues. These include writing conferences and workshops, the use of model texts, peer and teacher response, peer tutoring, the use of journals, writing about literature, sentence combining, reformulation, plagiarism, sequenced writing assignments and content-based instruction (see Reid, 1993; Grabe and Kaplan, 1996; Ferris and Hedgcock, 1998).

However, the programmatic issue that has received by far the most recognition is the assessment of second language writing (*see* Hamp-Lyons, 1991, 2001; Hamp-Lyons and Kroll, 1996). Second language writing assessment has been written about from a number of perspectives. These include test types, specifically 'indirect' or 'objective' (wherein no written text is produced or examined) and 'direct' tests (wherein a text is produced and examined), for example, holistic, analytic/multiple trait and primary trait tests. Another basic issue is 'text rating' or grading; here issues such as rater training, rater judgements and the difference between rating done by individuals with and without experience with second language writers. Also central are questions of test validity and reliability. In addition, a number of variables that could potentially affect ratings have been explored. These include 'linguistic variables' (primarily lexical and syntactic); 'rhetorical variables' and the writer's subject matter knowledge, cultural expectations, nationality, reading comprehension and amount of reading done in both the first and second languages. Elements such as writing prompts, topics and time constraints have also been explored. Different types of tests, for example, writing proficiency exams, entrance and exit exams, and placement exams have been described. Finally, some specific second language writing tests: the Test of Written English (TWE), the English as a Second Language Composition Profile (Jacobs, Zinkgraf, Wormuth, Hartfiel and Hughey, 1981) and the writing sub-test of the International English Language Testing Service (IELTS) test have been developed, deployed and critiqued.

A number of instructional contexts have been described in the literature. These include, most generally, the academic discourse community (at both the graduate and undergraduate levels) and a number of specific programme or course types therein: basic or 'remedial' writing courses, bilingual education programmes, immersion and submersion programmes, sheltered ESL courses, mainstream (native English speaker dominant) courses, cross-cultural composition courses, writing across the curriculum programmes, intensive language programmes and writing centres. Also addressed are particular instructional contexts in academia (engineering, natural sciences, science and technology, and sociology courses) or in the private sector (corporate and medical contexts) (*see* Belcher and Braine, 1995).

In recent years, and following from work in L1 composition, interest has grown in disciplinary matters; for example, the nature of L2 writing as a discipline or area of research; its standing in relation to fields like rhetoric, composition studies, second language studies/acquisition and linguistics; and the future direction of research in second language writing (Matsuda, 1998, 1999; Santos, Atkinson, Erickson, Matsuda and Silva, 2000). The last ten years or so have also seen increased interest in and explicit treatment of matters of politics and ideology growing out of post-modern thought, social constructionist inquiry and critical theory and pedagogy (Santos, 1992, 2001; Severino, 1993; Benesch (2001).

The current situation in second language writing studies is one of reflection on and re-examination of basic assumptions about the nature of second language writing and writing instruction, of rejecting easy answers to complex problems, of taking stock of what has been learned and trying to put it together as a coherent whole, of synthesis and model building, of realizing that there will be no magic bullet, no particular approach or procedure that will work with all people in all places at all times. It is a situation in which second language writing professionals are beginning to seize the opportunity to escape the confines of a particular tradition, to resist simplistic methods of 'teacher training', to reflect critically on 'what the research means', to discard off-the-shelf instructional approaches, to use their knowledge of theory and the results of inquiry to decide for themselves what makes sense for their students, for their objectives and teaching styles and for their instructional contexts. In short, it is an exciting time to be involved in such a vital, vibrant and evolving area of research and instruction.

Further Reading

Here we provide some basic works on second language writing and writing instruction. For a more extensive listing, *see* the annotated bibliographies of Tannacito (1995), Silva, Brice and Reichelt (1999) and the brief bibliographies that appear in each issue of the *Journal of Second Language Writing*.

- Belcher, D., Braine, G. (eds). (1995). *Academic Writing in a Second Language: Essays on Research and Pedagogy*. Norwood, NJ: Ablex. This collection seeks to enrich readers' understanding of non-native English-speaking students and the sociopolitical diversity of the academic discourse communities within which they must function. Part 1 (Issues) explores 'isolationist tendencies in higher education' with respect to non-native speakers. Part 2 (Research) presents studies on the writing of native English-speaking and non-native English-speaking students in a variety of academic disciplines and Part 3 (Pedagogy) describes writing curricula and assignments developed by the authors.
- Ferris, D., Hedgcock, J. (1998). *Teaching ESL Composition: Purpose, Process, and Practice*. Mahwah, NJ: Erlbaum. This book presents approaches to teaching ESL composition that are informed by current theoretical perspectives on second language writing and writers. The authors provide a comprehensive review of theoretical and research issues and discuss various pedagogical matters, including reading–writing relations, course design, teaching materials, teacher response, peer response, grammar, assessment and technology.
- Grabe, W., Kaplan, R.B. (1996). *Theory and Practice of Writing: An Applied Linguistic Perspective*. London: Longman. Taking an interdisciplinary perspective, this book discusses major issues in L1 and L2 writing

research and current directions in writing instruction, proposing a framework for a theory of writing. Later chapters, organized around 75 themes for writing instruction, explore connections between theory and practice in a variety of instructional contexts.

- Leki, I. (1992). *Understanding ESL Writers: A Guide for Teachers.* Portsmouth, NH: Boynton-Cook. To help teachers better understand ESL writers and their writing and make informed decisions about methods and materials, the author discusses the context of ESL writing instruction (its history and relation to L2 acquisition research), ESL writers (their characteristics and expectations) and their writing behaviours (composing processes and rhetorical and linguistic patterns).

- Silva, T., Matsuda, P.K. (eds). (2001). *Landmark Essays on ESL Writing.* Mahwah, NJ: Erlbaum. This volume attempts to provide a sense of how ESL writing scholarship has evolved over the last four decades. It brings together 15 articles that address various issues in second language writing in general and ESL writing in particular. The works, presented in chronological order, mirror the state of the art when they were published and represent a wide variety of perspectives, contributions and issues in the field.

- Silva, T., Matsuda, P.K. (eds). (2001). *On Second Language Writing.* Mahwah, NJ: Erlbaum. This collection brings together 15 internationally recognized second language writing scholars in a collection of original articles that, collectively, systematically delineate and explore central issues in second language writing with regard to theory, research, instruction, assessment, politics, articulation with other disciplines and standards.

Hands-on Activity

The texts below are a call for proposals for a professional conference and a proposal submitted for consideration. Read the proposal and answer the questions that follow.

Call for Proposals

We are pleased to announce that the Second Symposium on Second Language Writing will be held at Purdue University, West Lafayette, Indiana, USA, on September 15–16, 2000. We invite proposals for papers (20 minutes) and poster sessions. Any topic related to second language writing is welcome. We especially encourage proposals that focus on second or foreign languages other than English, English as a foreign language, and instructional contexts other than higher education. We also encourage proposals from non-native speakers of English.

Effective Teaching of English for Specific Purposes Writing

Teachers of English for Specific Purposes (ESP) work with speakers of other languages (Internationals) who write for various professional writing communities such as business, management, marketing and engineering. Different rhetorical situations require different criteria: conventions or rules, approaches, formats and genres. It is impossible for the TESOL professional to know all the forms, document designs, and stylistic and grammatical conventions governing the various rhetorical situations in which the international professionals and students with whom she works will need to write. It is possible, however, to know a smaller set of rationales and values underlying these conventions and to learn who are the individuals or institutions that determine these rationales.

The presenter will discuss the findings of her study into various professional and educational writing rhetorical situations using primary texts, textbooks, scholarly research, and teaching practices. She will present the rationales and values behind the criteria of the various writing communities, and she will reveal the individuals or institutions responsible for promoting or continuing those values. She will also show how to use the rationales underlying the criteria and the knowledge of those responsible for determining the criteria to help non-native speakers of English to write an actual text.

Teachers of English to speakers of other languages will leave the session with strategies that use the rationales and values underlying the criteria of various professional writing communities in order to better help professional and student internationals to write more effectively in English for Specific Purposes.

Questions

- Describe the rhetorical situation for this writing task.
- Identify parts of the proposal that are particularly effective and explain why you think they are effective.
- Identify parts of the proposal that are not effective and explain why you think they are ineffective.
- Suppose the writer of the proposal has asked you to read and comment on the proposal before submitting it. Provide one page of written feedback for the writer.

15

Assessment

Carol A. Chapelle
Iowa State University

Geoff Brindley
Macquarie University

What is Language Assessment?

In the context of language teaching and learning, 'assessment' refers to the act of collecting information and making judgements about a language learner's knowledge of a language and ability to use it. Although some people consider 'testing' and 'assessment' to be synonymous (Clapham, 1997), many use the latter term in a broader sense to include both formal measurement tools which yield quantifiable scores and other types of qualitative assessment, such as observation, journals and portfolios (Davies, Brown, Elder, Hill, Lumley and McNamara, 1999: 11). What unifies the variety of tests and assessments is that they all involve the process of making inferences about learners' language on the basis of 'observed performance'.

Despite this common feature, assessment practices vary according to the purpose for which assessment information is required. One purpose-related distinction is conventionally made between 'proficiency assessment', which is concerned with measuring a person's general ability, typically for gatekeeping decisions, and 'achievement assessment', which focuses on determining what has been learned as part of a specific programme of instruction, usually for assigning marks. In language programmes, Broadfoot (1987) identifies a number of assessment purposes:

- 'Assessment for curriculum' (providing diagnostic information and motivating learners).
- 'Assessment for communication' (informing certification and selection).
- 'Assessment for accountability' (publicly demonstrating achievement of outcomes).

Assessment purpose is closely tied to the 'stakes' attached to testing, and it therefore governs the type of assessment tool that is used and the resources that are invested in its development. In 'high-stakes' situations where the results of assessment may have a significant effect on test-taker's lives (for example, selection for university entry), the instrument should have been developed with great care by suitably qualified professionals and subjected to rigorous piloting and validation. In this and other testing situations, many stakeholders are involved in language assessment, either as those who construct and/or research tests and assessment tools (for example, test development agencies, curriculum developers, teachers, university researchers), as test-takers (students hoping to be certified for a job) or as 'consumers' of assessment information (for example, policy-makers, government officials, educational administrators, parents, employers and the media). These groups are likely to have different and, at times, conflicting perspectives on the role and purpose of assessment in language programmes, which, according to some writers, can lead to a dispro-portionate emphasis on assessment for accountability (Moore, 1996; McKay, 2000). For this reason, it has been suggested that the process of test develop-ment needs to involve a wide range of stakeholders so as to ensure fairness to all (Shohamy, 1993; Brindley 1998). However, the ideal of involvement needs to be balanced against the realities of implementation and the need for tests and assessments to demonstrate acceptable levels of validity and reliability.

Fundamental issues in Language Assessment

Figure 15.1 illustrates the relationships assumed to apply in the process of test interpretation and use. The learners' language capacities (that is, their

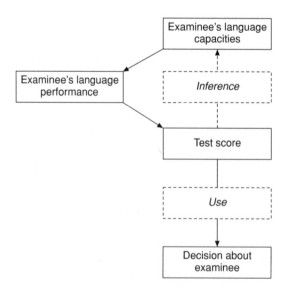

Figure 15.1 Fundamental components of testing.

knowledge and abilities) are assumed to be responsible for their language performance on a test. Test performance is, in turn, quantified by assigning it a score that summarizes the quality of the performance. That test score is used, for some purpose, typically for making decisions about examinees, but it might also be used for other purposes such as to allow examinees to make decisions about their own subsequent study or to classify participants for research on second language acquisition. These relationships correspond to three fundamental concepts which underpin the whole process of language assessment. The examinee's language capacities refer to the 'construct' (the examinee's underlying knowledge and abilities) that the test is assessing. Language performance occurs within the context of a 'test method' that has been specified to elicit a particular type of performance from the examinee. The test score, which serves as a summary of performance, requires 'validation', which refers to the justification of the inferences made from test scores and their use. Let us look at each of these three concepts in turn.

Construct Definition

On the surface, terms such as 'language proficiency' may make the construct of language ability seem simple and easily defined. However, researchers who develop and validate language tests find that such a general term is of little use. They confront issues such as whether or not examinees' selection of the correct verb tense on a multiple-choice question should be considered to reflect language proficiency, writing ability, grammatical competence or knowledge of verb tense. In other words, language testing researchers need to be precise about what a test is intended to measure, and so they develop the conceptual apparatus to do so.

Ability/Performance Constructs

Construct definition is closely related to the inference that is illustrated in Figure 15.1 because the construct refers to what is being inferred on the basis of test scores. The process of inference involves drawing conclusions about language ability or subsequent language performance on the basis of evidence from test performance. For example, an inference might be made about test-takers' 'grammatical competence' on the basis of their responses to questions such as the verb tense question above, as well as questions on other linguistic features such as relative clauses, placement of adverbs and subordinating conjunctions. The fact that an inference is made on the basis of a test score denotes a critical fact in language testing: that the score itself is not the object of interest to test users. What is of interest is what a test-taker might be expected to be capable of in non-test settings. If the concept of a construct definition is viewed in this way, it is possible to see the two distinct approaches that have been taken to construct definition by the language testing researchers.

The first is the 'ability' approach, which defines the construct as an unobservable concept that is not tied to any particular context of language use.

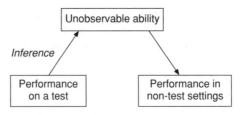

Figure 15.2 The conceptualization of inference in ability testing.

Ability testing is based on the point of view that performance on a test is the result of some underlying capacities, which are also responsible for performance in non-test settings, as illustrated in Figure 15.2. Constructs such as grammatical ability appear to reflect an ability perspective toward construct definition because they clearly refer to something which is not observable directly and which is therefore not tied to a context of performance. Other ability constructs would be reading comprehension and vocabulary knowledge.

The second is the 'performance' approach, as illustrated in Figure 15.3, which aims to make inferences more 'directly' from test performance to performance outside the test setting. 'A defining characteristic [of a performance test] is that actual performances of relevant tasks are required of candidates, rather than more abstract demonstration of knowledge' such as that required by tests of ability (McNamara, 1996: 6). Tests used to measure writing and speaking are often referred to as 'performance tests' because examinees are asked to use language with a simulated purpose, and the inference is made about their probable success in speaking or writing in other similar situations.

Figure 15.3 The conceptualization of inference in performance testing.

An ability test is sometimes referred to as 'indirect' because of the abstract relationship between what examinees do on the test and their potential future performance. Performance tests, in contrast, are sometimes called 'direct' because of the relative directness of the inference. However, this dichotomy is misleading because as Bachman (1990) pointed out, all test performance bears an indirect relationship to what is being assessed. Test users are always interested not in test performance and test scores themselves, but in what test scores mean, that is, the inferences that can be drawn from them and what they can do with the scores.

Specific/General Purpose Constructs

A second important distinction drawn among various types of construct definitions is their degree of specificity, as illustrated by the continuum in Figure 15.4. On the left end is the type of construct underlying a specific purpose test for which:

> . . . content and methods are derived from an analysis of a specific purpose target language use situation, so that test tasks and content are authentically representative of tasks in the target situation. Such a test allows [test users] to make inferences about a test taker's capacity to use language in a specific purpose domain. (Douglas, 2000: 19)

Figure 15.4 Degree of specificity in construct definition.

An example comes from a project whose purpose was to develop the Occupational English Test in Australia (McNamara, 1996). One of the testing procedures on this language test required the examinee to play the role of a physiotherapist who was interacting with a patient. The construct of interest in this test was the ability to use English for speaking with patients. The detailed construct definition would consist of the many questions and statements of advice that physiotherapists would need to give as well as the lexico-grammatical constructions required to interact in this context. Such a test would not require the examinee to listen to the daily news about animals in the wildlife preserve west of Melbourne, nor would the examinee be asked to read materials from a textbook on brain surgery. The construct of speaking for particular types of medical interactions would define the test tasks.

A general purpose construct definition, in contrast, is intended to assess language without reference to a particular context of language use. For example, the Vocabulary Levels Test (Schmitt, Schmitt and Clapham, 2001) is intended to assess developmental level of vocabulary knowledge in general and therefore words were chosen on the basis of their frequencies of occurrence across a wide range of linguistic registers. At a mid-point on the continuum would be a test of academic English such as the TOEFL, which includes materials that have been drawn from a variety of topics but within academic registers.

Construct Perspective and Specificity

At first it may appear that specific purpose constructs and performance type constructs may be a natural match, whereas general purpose constructs naturally go with ability constructs. In the examples provided above, the

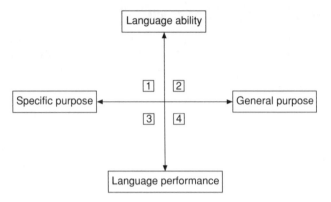

Figure 15.5 Dimensions defining the options for construct definition.

Occupational English and the Vocabulary Levels Test, this was the case. These two tests would be examples for numbers '3' and '2' in Figure 15.5, but one can also find examples of tests of specific purpose ability (1) and those intended to assess general purpose through performance (4).

An example of the former would be ChemSPEAK (Douglas and Selinker, 1993) a test that requires examinees to perform tasks that use the lexico-grammatical constructions from chemistry in order to test ability to speak about chemistry. The test does not, however, ask examinees to simulate the performance of 'doing' chemistry. An example of a 'general performance' test would be the oral proficiency interview of the American Council for Teachers of Foreign Languages (ACTFL). It requires examinees to engage in conversation about themselves and family that might come up in a social situation. In contrast to the specific language content of the various modules of the Occupational English Test, this test avoids requiring the examinee to talk about field specific topics so that the test score can be used to indicate capacity for speaking performance in general.

Construct theory is obviously slippery conceptual business, which needs to be anchored in the practices of test design and empirical research. Some steps toward understanding construct theory from the perspective of test design have appeared recently (Read and Chapelle, 2001), but perhaps the most sweeping impact on rethinking construct definition is coming from the use of technology for developing test methods. Bachman's (2000) review of the state of the art of language testing at the turn of the century includes the following observation on the contribution of technology in language testing, '. . . the new task formats and modes of presentation that multi-media computer-based test administration makes possible . . . may require us to redefine the very constructs we believe we are assessing' (Bachman, 2000: 9). In other words, the resources available for constructing test methods will push construct theory forward.

Test Methods

Having defined assessment as 'the act of collecting information and making judgements', we can define test methods as the systematic procedures set out for collecting information and making judgements for a particular assessment event. Language testers consider test methods as a set of procedures and describe them as sets of characteristics rather than by cover-all terms such as 'multiple-choice'. Multiple-choice refers only to one characteristic of a test – the manner by which the examinee responds – but any given testing event is composed of a number of other factors which should be expected to affect performance. Ideally, the three components of test performance, the underlying capacities which are supposed to be responsible for it and how the performance is summarized into a score (as outlined earlier in Figure 15.1) would be free from any outside influence. However, test methods do affect test performance in various ways, and this has been the source of much concern and interest in the testing world.

Douglas (1998) theorizes how test methods affect test performance, suggesting a series of processes though which the test-taker perceives cues in the test method, interprets them and uses them to set goals for task completion, as illustrated in Figure 15.6. Consistent with Bachman (1990) and Bachman and Palmer (1996), Douglas (1998) suggests that these strategies are key to the manifestation of particular language abilities. In short, the test-taking process outlined earlier in Figure 15.1 shows a simplified view of the factors that are responsible for test performance. Figure 15.6 gives a more realistic view, showing both language capacity and test method as responsible for test performance. Testing experts differ on how to interpret and deal with the fact of test method influence on performance; however, most agree that it is essential to identify those aspects of test method that may play a role.

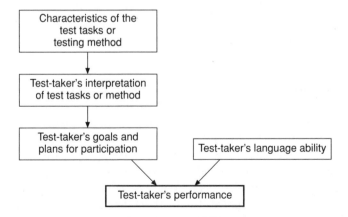

Figure 15.6 Factors involved in the relationship between a test method and performance as outlined by Douglas (1998).

The most encompassing framework for describing test methods has been developed in two stages, first as 'test method facets' (Bachman, 1990) and, more recently, 'test task characteristics' (Bachman and Palmer, 1996). Test task characteristics are defined as:

- The test 'setting', such as the physical specifications of the room and the participants.
- The testing 'rubrics', including the instructions, test structure, allotted time, response evaluation and calculation of scores.
- The 'input' to the test-taker, such as test length and grammatical and topical characteristics of test questions.
- The 'output' expected from the learner, such as the length and grammatical and topical features of responses.
- The relationship between input and output, such as whether or not the answers to questions the examinee is asked depend on previous responses.

These test task characteristics provide the analytic tools needed for both construction and analysis of language tests, and therefore have played a role in test validation research.

Validation

The term 'validity' carries some meaning for almost everyone, but in educational measurement, including language testing, this term has an extensive technical sense about which volumes have been written. Many applied linguists learned at one time that validity was defined as consisting of three sub-types:

- 'Content validity' (whether the content of the test questions is appropriate).
- 'Criterion-related validity' (whether other tests measuring similar linguistic abilities correlated with the test in question).
- 'Construct validity' (whether research shows that the test measures the 'construct' discussed above).

In addition, many people think of validity of a test being established by measurement experts through statistical analysis of test scores. Although current perspectives retain traces of these ideas, both the theory and practice of validation are now markedly different from this view. The change is typically associated with a seminal paper by Messick (1989), even though that paper collected, summarized and expanded on work that had been in progress over the prior 15 years. A brief historical account of validity in language assessment demonstrates important changes for the language testing researcher and test users alike (Chapelle, 1999) because validation is now seen as the process of constructing an argument about the inferences and uses made from test scores. As an 'argument', rather than a black and white 'proof', validation may draw upon a number of different types of data, and it is likely to be interpreted differently depending on the audience.

Such an argument is made on the basis of both qualitative and quantitative research, and it relies on the perspectives obtained from technical work on language testing and the perspectives of applied linguists, language teachers and other test users. An example of an ESL reading test provides an example of how these perspectives worked together. A publishing company contracted testing researchers to develop an ESL test to be delivered on the world-wide web to ESL learners at a wide variety of proficiency levels. Because the test-takers would have a great deal of variation in their reading ability, the test developers decided to include three modules in the test, one with beginning level texts for the examinees to read, one with somewhat simplified texts and a third with advanced-level texts. Once this decision had been made, however, the test developers needed to be able to show that the tests on the texts actually represented the intended differences in levels and therefore three types of evidence were used.

One type of evidence was the judgement of ESL teachers. Teams of ESL teachers were formed and they worked together to form an understanding of what they should be looking for in texts of various levels in ESL books. Then each passage that had been selected for its potential as a reading text on the test was evaluated by two members of the team to give it a rating of 'beginning', 'intermediate' or 'advanced'. An interesting finding during this part of the work was that the two ESL teachers did not always agree on the level of the text, nor did they always agree with the original author's assignment of the text to a particular level. This part of the test development process resulted in a pool of texts about which two raters agreed. In other words, if two raters thought that a text was a beginning level one, it was retained in the pool of possible texts of the test, but if one rater thought it was a beginning level one and the other rater thought it was intermediate, it was eliminated. The text agreed upon then proceeded to the next stage of analysis.

The second type of analysis drew on the expertise of a corpus linguist, who did a quantitative analysis of the language of each of the texts. The texts were scanned to copy them into electronic files, which were then tagged and analysed by use of a computer program, that quantified characteristics of the texts that signal difficulty, such as word length, sentence length and syntactic complexity. The corpus linguist set cut scores for each of these features and then selected texts that, on the basis of these characteristics, were clear examples of each level. These texts formed the basis of the reading comprehension modules at the three levels of difficulty. Test writers developed questions to test comprehension as well as other aspects of reading comprehension and then the three module tests were given to a group of examinees.

The third type of analysis was quantitative. The researchers wanted to see if the texts that had been so carefully selected as beginning level actually produced test items that were easier than those that had been selected as intermediate and advanced. The question was whether or not the predicted number of examinees got test questions correct for the beginning, intermediate and advanced level tests. As Table 15.1 shows, the researchers predicted that a high percentage of examinees would obtain correct responses on the beginning level texts and so on. The table also shows the results that were obtained when a group of 47 learners took the tests. In fact the percentages of correct responses turned out as anticipated.

Table 15.1 Summary of predictions and results in a quantitative validity argument

Predicted and actual results	Intended test level		
	Beginning	**Intermediate**	**Advanced**
Predicted	High percentage	Medium percentage	Low percentage
Actual mean percentage of correct responses	85%	74%	68%

These three types of evidence about the reading test modules are obviously not all that we would want to know about their validity as tests of reading, but these data form one part of the validity argument. The many types of qualitative and quantitative analysis that are used in validity research would be too much to describe in this introduction, but the idea of how testing researchers evaluate test data can be illustrated through the description of two basic test analysis procedures.

Test Analysis

Two types of analysis form the basis for much of the quantitative test analysis: 'difficulty analysis' and 'correlational analysis'. Difficulty analysis refers to the type of analysis that was described above, in which the concern is to determine how difficult the items on the test are. Correlational analysis is a means of obtaining a statistical estimate of the strength of the relationship between two set of test scores. Computationally, each of these analyses is straightforward. The challenge in language testing research is to design a study in which the results of the analysis can be used to provide information about the questions that are relevant to the validity of test use.

Item Difficulty

In the example above, the researchers were concerned that their intended levels of text difficulty would actually hold true when examinees took the three modules of the reading test. In the description of the results, we summarized the item difficulties of each of the tests. However, in the actual study the researchers also examined the item difficulties of each item on each of the tests. The item difficulty is defined as the percentage of examinees who answered the item correctly. To obtain this percentage, the researchers divided the number who scored correctly by the total number who took the test and multiplied by 100. On the reading test described above, if 40 correct responses were obtained on an item, that would be $(40/47 = 0.85$, and then $0.85 \times 100 = 85)$. People who write tests professionally use this and other item statistics to decide which items are good and which ones should be revised or deleted from a test during test development.

As illustrated above, the concept of difficulty can be used several different ways, but it is best used in view of the construct that the test is intended to measure, and the use of the test. If all of the items on a test have high values for item difficulty, for example, the person analysing the test knows that the test is very easy. But whether or not this means that the items should be changed depends on the test construct, the examinees tested and the test use. In this regard, testing researchers distinguish between 'norm-referenced' tests, which are intended to make distinctions among examinees, and 'criterion-referenced' decisions, which are intended to be used to make decisions about an individual's knowledge of the material reflected on the test. A test that is easy for a group of examinees would not be successful in distinguishing between examinees, but it may have shown correctly that individuals in that group knew the material tested. Moreover, when difficulty is interpreted in view of the construct that an item of a test is intended to measure, it can be used as one part of a validity argument.

Correlation

A second statistical analysis used in validation research is 'correlation'. When testing researchers or teachers look at how similar two tests are, they are considering the correlation between tests. For example, if a group of students takes two tests at the beginning of the semester, their scores can be lined up next to each other and, if the number of students is small, the degree of relationship between them may be apparent, as shown in Table 15.2. With this

Table 15.2 The use of correlation in validation research

Examinees	Test 1	Test 2
Student 1	35	35
Student 2	25	26
Student 3	30	26
Student 4	34	32
Student 5	17	16

small number, it is evident that the student who preformed well on the first test also did so on the second. Student 5, scored the lowest on both tests, and the others line up in between. The correlation allows for an exact number to be used to express the observation that the students scored approximately the same on the two tests. The correlation is 0.97.

A correlation can range from 1.00 to –1.00, indicating a perfect positive relationship or a perfect negative relationship. A correlation of 0.00 would indicate no relationship. Table 15.3 illustrates two sets of scores that show a negative relationship. The correlation among the scores in Table 15.3 is –0.79. Typically, in language testing, correlations in the positive range are found when tests of different language skills are correlated. However, like the analysis of difficulty, the analysis of correlations requires an understanding of the constructs and test uses of the tests investigated.

Table 15.3 Two sets of scores that show a negative relationship

Examinees	Test 1	Test 2
Student 1	35	17
Student 2	25	26
Student 3	30	26
Student 4	34	28
Student 5	17	35

The direction and strength of a correlation depend on many factors, including the number of subjects and the distributions of scores, and therefore correlations should be interpreted in view of both the construct that the test is intended to measure and the data used to do the analysis. Correlational techniques are the conceptual building blocks for many of the complex test analyses that are conducted, which also require a clear understanding of the basic principles outlined in the first part of the chapter.

Language Assessment and Language Teaching

The relationships between assessment and teaching are as multifaceted as the contexts and purposes of assessment; however, some trends are worth noting. The first is an increased interest in social and political influences on assessment (*see* McNamara, 1998, for an overview). In this context, most professional language testers, under the influence of Messick's (1989) argument that validation should 'trace the social consequences' of a test, have embraced the idea that tests should be designed and used so as to have a positive impact on teaching and learning. In recent years, researchers have begun to study this impact in a range of educational contexts. Another notable shift in the assessment landscape is the move towards greater alignment of curriculum and instruction through the adoption by teachers of new forms of performance assessment and a corresponding loss of faith in the capacity of 'traditional' forms of educational measurement to capture learning outcomes accurately. A third aspect of language assessment which is found in recent literature is the way in which governments in many countries, under increasing pressure to demonstrate accountability and measurable outcomes, are using assessment as a policy tool. Let us look at each of these trends in more detail.

Washback

One result of Messick's (1989) expansion of the concept of validity to include the social consequences of test use has been an increased focus on 'washback', a term commonly used by writers on language assessment to denote the influence of testing on teaching (Hughes, 1989: 1). This influence often tends to be presented as harmful – it has been claimed, for example, that tests (particularly large-scale multiple-choice proficiency tests) exercise a negative influence due to the temptation for teachers to spend time on activities that will help students to succeed in the test (for example, test-taking strategies) rather than to develop the skills and knowledge which should be the object of instruction (Alderson and Hamp-Lyons, 1996: 280–281). Conversely, it is also believed that 'positive washback' can be brought about through the intro-duction of tests that target the skills needed by language learners in real life (Cheng, 1998: 279). Seen in this way, a test could be considered more or less valid according to how beneficial its washback effects were thought to be.

Alderson and Wall (1993), however, reject such a view of washback as simplistic and unsupported by evidence. They argue that 'washback, if it exists . . . is likely to be a complex phenomenon which cannot be related to a test's validity' (Alderson and Wall, 1993: 116). The findings of research into washback in language teaching contexts support Alderson and Wall's (1993) contention that washback effects are complex. In a study of the impact of two national tests used in Israel, Shohamy, Donitsa-Schmidt and Ferman (1996) found that washback patterns 'can change over time and that the impact of tests is not necessarily stable'. Wall and Alderson's (1993) study of the intro-duction of a new examination into the Sri Lankan educational system showed that a range of constraints may influence the intended effects of an examina-tion, including inadequate communication of information by educational authorities, low levels of teacher awareness and lack of professional develop-ment support. These authors conclude that 'an exam on its own cannot reinforce an approach to teaching the educational system has not adequately prepared its teachers for' (Wall and Alderson, 1993: 67). Cheng's (1998) research into the introduction of a new task-based examination into the Hong Kong examination system suggests that the impact of assessment reform may be limited unless there is genuine change in 'how teachers teach and how textbooks are designed'.

The role of the teacher emerges as a major factor in many washback studies. Alderson and Hamp-Lyons (1996) investigated teacher attitudes and behaviour in TOEFL preparation classses and concluded that washback effects may vary significantly according to individual teacher characteristics. Burrows (forthcoming) reached a similar conclusion in a study of adult ESL teachers' reactions to the introduction of a new competency-based assessment system in the Adult Migrant English Program in Australia. She concluded that teachers' responses are related to their attitudes towards and experiences of the implementation of the assessment, their perceptions of the quality of the assessment; the extent to which the assessment represented a departure from their previous practices; and their attitudes to change itself. All of these findings suggest that the nature and extent of washback are governed by a wide range of individual, educational and social factors. These include the political context in which a test or assessment system is introduced, the time that has elapsed since adoption, the knowledge, attitudes and beliefs of teachers and educational managers, the role of test agencies and publishers, the relationships between participants and the resources available. An adequate model of impact, according to Wall (1997: 297) needs to include all of these influences and to describe the relationships between them.

'Alternative' Assessment

The close interrelationship between teaching and assessment which is depicted in many of the washback studies described above has not always been reflected in the language testing literature. In comparison to standardized proficiency testing, the pedagogical role of assessment has until recently received relatively little attention (Rea-Dickins and Gardner, 2000; Brindley, 2001). However, in recent years, language educators have become progressively disenchanted with the capacity of standardized tests to provide fair and accurate information on learners' achievement (Huerta-Macias, 1995). At the same time, there has been a growing acknowledgement of the need for closer links between assessment and instruction (Shohomy, 1992; Genesee and Hamayan, 1994). This has led to the widespread adoption of various forms of 'alternative' assessment which directly reflect learning activities and which are carried out by practitioners in the context in which learning takes place (Brown and Hudson, 1998). Some of the more commonly used methods include the following.

Observation

Informal observation of learners' language use is one of the most widely used methods of assessment in language classrooms (Brindley, 2001). Information derived from teacher observations may be used in a variety of ways to inform classroom decision-making (for example, whether learners have achieved the learning objectives for a particular unit of instruction and are ready to progress to the next unit). Types of observation that can be used to monitor progress and identify individual learning difficulties range from anecdotal records to checklists and rating scales.

In some educational systems, teachers' observations of learner performance may form an important part of the evidence that is used for external reporting (Barrs, 1992) and may thus require careful and detailed recording of classroom language use. In this context, Rea-Dickins and Gardner (2000) have identified a number of sources of potential unreliability in teachers' transcription and interpretation of classroom language samples that may affect the validity of the inferences that are made. They call for more research into the validity and reliability of observational assessment and highlight the need to include classroom observation skills in teacher professional development programmes (Rea-Dickins and Gardner, 2000: 238–239).

Portfolios

A portfolio is a purposeful collection of students' work over time that contains samples of their language performance at different stages of completion, as well as the student's own observations on his or her progress.

Three types of portfolio have been identified, reflecting different purposes and features (Valencia and Calfee, 1991). These are first, the 'showcase' portfolio which represents a collection of student's best or favourite work. The entries in the showcase portfolio are selected by the student and thus portray an individual's learning over time. No comparison with external standards or with other students is involved. Second, there is the 'documentation' portfolio which contains systematic ongoing records of progress. The documentation portfolio may include observations, checklists, anecdotal records, interviews, classroom tests and performance assessments. The selection of entries may be made by either the teacher or the student. According to Valencia and Calfee (1991: 337), 'the documentation resembles a scrapbook, providing evidence but not judging the quality of the activities'. Finally, the 'evaluation' portfolio which is used as public evidence of learners' achievement is more standardized than either the showcase or documentation portfolio because of the need for comparability. The contents of the evaluation portfolio and the assessment criteria used are largely determined by external requirements, although there is some room for individual selection and reflection activities.

The use of portfolios as a means of recording and assessing progress offers a number of advantages to both teachers and learners. Not only does it provide a way of relating assessment closely to instruction and motivating learners (Fulcher, 1997) but it also enables learners the opportunity to reflect on their learning goals and strategies, thus promoting learner independence (Gottlieb, 1995). Another claimed advantage of assessment portfolios is that they provide concrete evidence of development that can be used to demonstrate tangible achievement to external stakeholders in language programmes (Genesee and Upshur, 1996: 100).

However, the introduction of portfolio assessment has not been without problems. There has been considerable debate in the research literature concerning issues such as the type and amount of student work that should be included in a portfolio, the extent to which students should be involved in selection of the entries and the amount of external assistance they should be allowed (Fulcher, 1997; Brown and Hudson, 1998). In addition, research studies have highlighted both technical and practical difficulties associated with portfolio use, including low levels of agreement between assessors on the quality of language samples (Koretz, McCaffrey, Klein, Bell and Stecher, 1992), lack of comparability between the samples submitted (Hamp-Lyons and Condon, 1993) and the time and expense associated with collecting and grading large numbers of student texts on a continuing basis (Belanoff, 1997). In this context, it has become apparent that the systematic use of portfolio assessment is not only costly and time-consuming but also makes considerable demands on teachers' skills.

In spite of these potential difficulties, however, it has been argued that the positive impact of portfolios on both teachers and learners is in itself sufficient reason to continue their use, even if it cannot be demonstrated that portfolio assessment is technically more reliable than more traditional means of assessment (Hamp-Lyons and Condon, 1993; Fulcher, 1997).

Self-Assessment

The process of self-assessment involves learners in making judgements of their language ability and/or their achievement of learning goals and objectives. Self-assessment is an integral part of learner-centred approaches to instruction which aim to encourage the active participation of the learner in each stage of the teaching or learning process, including assessment (Ekbatani, 2000). Proponents of self-assessment have argued that using self-assessment can help learners to become skilled judges of their own strengths and weaknesses and to set realistic goals for themselves, thus developing their capacity to become self-directed (Oscarson, 1997). Self-assessment techniques that are commonly used in language programmes include self-corrected tests and exercises, rating scales, learner progress grids, standardized questionnaires and self-assessment test batteries (*see* Oscarson, 1984; Brindley, 1989, for discussion and a range of examples). These procedures can be used by learners to estimate their general level of ability (for example, at the beginning of a course of instruction) or as a means of monitoring their progress relative to particular instructional objectives during the course.

Research into the use of self-assessment in a variety of educational contexts has provided a number of insights that can usefully inform language teaching practice. First, it has become apparent that the ability to carry out self-assessment cannot be taken for granted and that it is important to provide learners with adequate training in the use of self-assessment techniques (*see* Cram, 1995, for an example of such a programme). Second, the ability of learners to self-assess accurately appears to be related to the transparency of the instruments used. In this regard, the findings of a study by Bachman and Palmer (1989) suggest that learners find it easier to say what they 'cannot' do or what they have difficulty doing than what they 'can' do. This finding has clear implications for the design of self-assessment instruments, since most self-assessment scales are typically presented as 'can do' statements. Third, research studies indicate that self-assessment scales work best when the self-assessment statements are situation-specific and closely related to learners' personal experience (Oscarson, 1997; Ross, 1998). Finally, there is some evidence to suggest that cultural factors affect both learners' willingness to self-assess and the accuracy of their self-assessments (von Elek, 1985; Blue, 1994). However, there is relatively little research evidence available on this question and there is a need for further research into the effects of cultural background on learners' use of self-assessment (Oscarson 1997: 183).

Other types of alternative assessment include learning journals, project work, teacher-developed tasks and simulations and peer-assessment. In many education systems, evidence from alternative assessments is being used increasingly, sometimes in combination with external tests, as a basis for reporting student progress and achievement against pre-specified outcomes statements or standards (Brindley, 1998; Snow, 2000).

The various kinds of 'non-test' assessment listed above offer a number of potential benefits for all stakeholders in language learning programmes. First, they allow teaching and curriculum goals to be closely aligned, thus improving communication between teachers, students and other external stakeholders (Katz, 2000). Second, the detailed diagnostic information yielded by such assessments can motivate learners to set their own goals and become more involved in their own learning. Third, the close observation of individual learner performance which accompanies some forms of qualitative monitoring and assessment can provide rich insights into student learning processes and thus serve a useful professional development function for teachers (Mohan and Low, 1995). Fourth, the use of various forms of alternative assessment in combination enables teachers to obtain a wide sample of learners' language performance in a range of contexts, thus providing more valid and dependable evidence of progress and achievement (Shohamy, 1998). Finally, since alternative assessment is less threatening to learners than formal tests that are administered under controlled conditions, it is more likely to elicit their optimal level of performance.

Despite these advantages, however, a range of concerns has been expressed about the use of alternative assessment as the basis for reporting student outcomes, particularly in high-stakes contexts. These concerns relate to:

- The validity and reliability of the assessment tools that are used.
- Their administrative feasibility and cost effectiveness.

Research in both general education and language learning contexts suggests that using a small number of context-specific assessment tasks results in low levels of generalizability, thus severely limiting the inferences that can be made about a learner's ability (Gao, Shavelson and Baxter, 1994; Brindley, 2000a). At the same time, considerable variability has been identified in teacher-developed assessment tasks (Wigglesworth, 2000). This makes comparability across tasks difficult, thus potentially diminishing the value of information on student learning outcomes. Other reliability issues which have been identified include the difficulties of obtaining acceptable levels of agreement between raters on the quality of student writing portfolios (Hamp-Lyons, 1996) and inconsistencies in teachers' observations of student performance (Rea-Dickins and Gardner, 2000). In terms of practicality, research studies have consistently demonstrated that alternative assessment is more time-consuming and expensive to conduct than more traditional testing and requires higher levels of skill on the part of teachers (Hardy, 1995; Breen, Barrett-Pugh, Derewianka, House, Hudson, Lumley and Rohl, 1997; Hardy 1995).

Outcomes-based Assessment

In recent years, the shift towards alternative assessment has been paralleled by a move towards greater accountability. Under increasing pressure to demonstrate 'value for money' to taxpayers, governments world-wide have developed system-wide indicators for monitoring the outcomes of educational programmes. This has led to the widespread adoption of 'outcomes-based' approaches to assessment and reporting, whereby the results of teacher-developed performance assessments are used as the basis for reporting student learning outcomes against pre-specified attainment standards, known variously as 'curriculum profiles', 'attainment targets', 'benchmarks', 'bandscales' or 'competencies' (Norton Peirce and Stewart, 1997; Brindley, 1998; McKay 2000).

The implementation of outcomes-based approaches has raised many of the issues in relation to the use of alternative assessment that are mentioned above (*see* Brindley, 1998, for an overview). In addition, the history of their adoption shows that language assessment is increasingly being used as a policy tool (McNamara, 1998), in some cases to the detriment of student learning (Brindley, 2000b). This situation has prompted the emergence of the discipline of 'critical language testing' which questions the ideologies and assumptions that underlie language assessment and calls for a radical re-examination of the power structures involved (Shohamy, 1997).

Conclusion

The fundamental concepts, beliefs and practices in language assessment have changed in recent years, in part because of the shifting relationship between assessment and teaching. Previously, assessment tended to take the form of proficiency testing, based on general ability constructs, which was largely unconnected to the curriculum. Now there is a widespread recognition of the need for close links between the desired outcomes of instruction, curriculum content and assessment, and this new emphasis is increasingly reflected in assessment policies, materials and methods. However, although the integration of assessment and learning is supported by strong educational arguments, as yet little research has been conducted to determine whether or not 'embedded' assessment results in improved learning. This important question will need to be investigated through the study of washback, which is seen as one of several approaches to language testing research. At the same time, in order to ensure that the tests and assessments that are used in language programmes are optimally fair and valid, a continuing research effort will be required to clarify the nature of the constructs that underlie them.

Further Reading

- Bachman, L.F. (1990). *Fundamental Considerations in Language Testing*. Oxford: Oxford University Press. This classic work on language assessment develops issues of construct definition, test method, and validation in depth. It connects work in applied linguistics (for example, communicative competence theory) with the fundamentals of educational measurement.
- Bachman, L.F., Palmer, A.S. (1996). *Language Testing in Practice*. Oxford: Oxford University Press. This book takes readers through test development and formative evaluation – detailing each step of the way in view of the theoretical and practical concerns that should inform decisions. The book contributes substantively to current discussion of validity by proposing a means for evaluating language tests which incorporates current validation theory but which is framed in a manner which is sufficiently comprehensible, and appropriately slanted toward language testing.
- Chapelle, C.A. (1998). Construct definition and validity inquiry in SLA research. In Bachman, L.F., Cohen, A.D. (eds), *Second Language Acquisition and Language Testing Interfaces*. Cambridge: Cambridge University Press. Focusing on the significance of construct definition in the process of validation, this paper outlines three ways of defining a construct and explains the implications of one of these perspectives for framing validation studies. The three perspectives on constructs – trait (for example, ability), behaviourist (for example, performance) and interactionalist (a combination of the two) – are illustrated through definitions of vocabulary ability.
- McNamara, T. (1996). *Measuring Second Language Performance*. London: Longman. This book is an in-depth examination of the issues and problems involved in assessing language performance. The first half of the book looks at approaches and theories in performance assessment and identifies the dimensions of an adequate model of language performance. The second half of the book is concerned with ways in which Rasch measurement technology can be used to model variability in language performance and rater behaviour.
- Alderson, J.C., Wall, D. (1993). Does washback exist? *Applied Linguistics* 14: 115–129. This paper introduces the concept of washback to the broader field of applied linguistics and problematizes the simplistic view of washback as an effect which projects directly from a test to the classroom. A series of 'washback hypotheses' is advanced and the authors explore the extent to which washback can be said to exist. An agenda for research into washback is proposed.
- Bachman, L.F., Alderson, J.C. (eds), *Cambridge Language Assessment*

Series. This series offers authoritative treatments of practical issues in areas of language assessment, such as reading (Alderson, 2000), vocabulary (Read, 2000), language for specific purposes (Douglas, 2000), listening (Buck, 2001) and writing (Weigle, 2001). Each volume contains an up to date overview of theory and research, accompanied by useful discussion and examples of testing principles and techniques.

Hands-on Activity

Question 1

In an short ESL vocabulary test, the test developers wanted to be sure to include vocabulary items at a wide variety of difficulty levels, and so they included items such as the following: 'The main <u>focus</u> of the course', 'People's <u>stereotypes</u> of other social groups' and 'My <u>name</u> is Sandy'. The examinee had to select the correct word (the underlined one) from four choices. Since the items were intended to reveal different ability levels, the test developers looked at the item difficulty of each of the items. They found a range of difficulties for the three items (100, 74 and 42). Complete Table 15.4 with your analysis of where each item fits, the level of predicted item difficulties (low, medium, high) and actual item difficulties.

Table 15.4 Summary of predictions and results for ESL vocabulary items

Item, predicted and actual results	Beginning	Intermediate	Advanced
Item			
Predicted			
Actual item difficulty			

Question 2

Test developers were attempting to develop two forms of a language test that they could claim measured the same thing. They started by developing three forms of the test, each of which had the same types of items. They gave the three tests to a group of students and they found that the correlation between Form 1 and Form 2 was 0.74. The correlation between Form 1 and Form 3 was 0.75, and the correlation between Form 2 and Form 3 was 0.85. Which two forms should the test developers choose?

Question 3

Test developers were attempting to write a test of ESL Business English, and therefore as one part of the validity study they needed to find evidence that the test was measuring this construct. They did this, in part, by examining the scores obtained on the tests by four different groups of examinees. The four groups were chosen because of their predicted differences in ability in Business English. Can you predict which group the researchers hoped would perform the best on the test, the second best, etc? Place each of the four groups in the appropriate place in Table 15.5:

- Native speakers of English, business majors (NSBM).
- Non-native speakers of English, business majors (NNSBM).
- Native speakers, non-business majors (NSNBM).
- Non-native speakers, non-business majors (NNSNBM).

Table 15.5 Developing a test of ESL Business English

Predicted test performance	Lowest scores	Third-highest scores	Second-highest scores	Highest scores
Group				

Question 4

In order to improve their testing of language ability, many testing programmes are attempting to develop tests that are delivered and scored by computer, and as a part of the development process, validation studies are conducted. One type of validation study looks at the correlation of performance on the computer-delivered test with performance on a similar paper and pencil test. If the purpose of the computer-delivered test is to assess language ability better than has been possible with paper and pencil tests, what kind of relationship should be expected as the ideal outcome from such a study and why? (A strong correlation would be approaching 1 (for example, Pearson's $r = 0.92$), and a low correlation would approach 0 (for example, Pearson's $r = 0.23$).)

Question 5

In a large test revision project, testing researchers were hoping to develop a better test of academic language ability. To do so they tested several different tests, including tests of listening, vocabulary, grammar and reading. They found that they only had enough time to include either the reading or the grammar test in the final version, and they found that the correlations of the grammar test with the other language tests were somewhat stronger than those between the reading test and other tests, but in the end they chose to include the reading test rather than the grammar test. Why do you think they would do this?

Question 6

As a teacher in a language programme, you have developed an achievement test for your course that helps you to focus your teaching on particular reading strategies throughout the semester, and that seems to assess your students in a manner that is fair and useful as input to the grading process. In looking for a means of reporting outcomes to an external agency, your programme administrator takes a look at your test and then starts questioning its validity for the purpose that she is concerned about. She wants you to do a correlational study of your final exam with another reading test to see if it is valid. What should you tell her?

16 Suggested Solutions

Chapter 2, *Grammar*

1. Form. In English, a specific number or number-like phrase in English used as an adjective is always singular before the noun it modifies.
2. Meaning. This sentence is accurate and meaningful, but it is not likely the meaning that the student intends. The *-ing* participle refers to the cause, not the experiencer of the emotion.
3. Use. It is not as acceptable to use a stative verb (for example, *want*) with the passive voice as it is to use a verb denoting physical action (for example, *score*).
4. Meaning. The logical connector 'on the contrary' usually denies a proposition. A connector like 'in contrast', to compare two things, would be better.
5. Use. The historical present modal form, that is, *will*, is likely to be used in a response to a request, for example, '*Of course, I will*'.
6. Meaning. *Few* has a negative connotation. *Although* signals a contrast. One would therefore expect either a quantifier with a positive connotation to be used, such as *a few* or a causal connector, such as *because*. Thus we would expect either: '*Although he had a few close friends, he was very lonely*' or '*Because he had few close friends, he was very lonely*'.
7. Form. The direct object (*a house*) precedes the indirect object (*my parents*) when the indirect object is in a prepositional phrase. Without the preposition, this sentence would have been accurate.

Here is an example of an activity that would *promote noticing* of number phrases used in singular form before a noun (*see* Question 1).

> Bring into class some advertisements from the real estate section of the newspaper. Such advertisements contain phrases such as '3-bedroom house', 'two-car garage', 'two-bathroom apartment', '5-acre lot', etc. See how many of these number phrases before nouns students can find. They may need help with any abbreviations that are used.

Here is an example of a *practice* activity that would help students work on the order of direct and indirect objects (*see* Question 7).

> Think of five friends or relatives that you have. What gifts would you buy for each?
>
> For example, I would buy a book for my sister. OR I would buy my sister a book.

Chapter 3, *Vocabulary*

Research has shown that vocabulary size is directly related to the ability to use English in various ways. Around 2000 word families should supply the bulk of the lexical resources required for basic everyday conversation (chat). About 3000 word families is the threshold which should allow learners to begin to read authentic texts. Most research indicates that knowledge of around 5000 word families should provide enough vocabulary to enable learners to read authentic texts without lexical problems. Of course, many words will still be unknown, but this level of knowledge should allow learners to infer the meaning of many of the novel words from context, and to understand most of the communicative content of the text. Second language learners with a knowledge of the most frequent 10,000 words in English can be considered to have a wide vocabulary, which should allow them to operate in a university environment (*see* Chapter 13, *Reading*).

It is important to note that these sizes are approximations, and the ability to accomplish the things in English also depends on many other factors, including speaking and reading skills, background knowledge and strategy use. However, they do provide useful 'rules of thumb' which can be used as lexical goals by both teachers and learners.

Chapter 4, *Discourse Analysis*

Both these texts are about the same topic – cockroaches – but they are clearly different in many respects. Perhaps the most obvious difference between the two texts, is that the first text is a written text about cockroaches (taken from the *Encyclopaedia Britannica*, Volume 5, p 909) and the second text is an anecdote told by a woman to her friends during an informal chat over lunch at work.

Text 1 is characterized by the following features typical of written discourse:

- *Context independent*: as the written text must be able to make sense away from the physical context in which it was produced, it must be self-explanatory and the reader needs to be able to access the meanings from the text itself (*see* Burns and Joyce, 1997).
- *Lexical density*: In Text 1 the lexical words have been underlined. There are nine clauses, with 29 lexical items, giving a lexical density of 3.2 items

per clause; whereas in Text 2, there are 10 clauses, with 18 lexical items, giving a lexical density of 1.8. The information is therefore more densely packed in written discourse.

- *Formal and specialized vocabulary*: for example: *eminently tropical, species, widely disseminated, cosmopolitan.*

On the other hand, Text 2 displays features typical of spoken English. These are:

- *Context dependent*: spoken discourse is more context dependent, in that speakers constantly refer to things in the context, for example *'there was this cockroach like this'.*
- *Lexically sparse*: spoken discourse is lexically less dense.
- *Grammatical intricacy*: the text is made up mainly of simple main clauses connected to one another by *and*. However, sentence grammar in speech can be very complex with clause after clause being added on, with extensive use of conjunctions, such as *and, because, then,* to link the clauses. For example in Text 2, Turn 3, there are 16 clauses in one clause complex (totalling 95 words).
- Use of *paralinguistic features* (for example, Pat's hand gesture of size of cockroach).
- Because spoken language is produced as 'process' not as a completed product, it contains spontaneity phenomena, such as false starts, hesitations, incomplete clauses.

These differences between spoken and written discourse are summarized in Table 16.1 below.

Table 16.1 Differences between spoken and written discourse

Spoken discourse	Written discourse
Context dependent: relies on shared knowledge between participants; greater use of exophoric (external context) reference	*Context independent*: must recreate the context for readers
Less explicit/relies strongly on shared knowledge between participants	Quite explicit marking out of what is going to be said (for example, *in the first place, firstly, finally*)
Spontaneous and therefore displays spontaneity phenomena, such as false starts, hesitations, incomplete clauses	Planned, edited and redrafted

Table 16.1 – *continued*

Spoken discourse	Written discourse
All interactants are engaged in the creation of the text, so there is turntaking, interruptions, overlaps, etc.	Written text is only implicitly interactive (reader is assumed but not involved in the creation of the text)
Multilogue (casual conversation very often involves more than two speakers, that is, it is usually multilogue rather than dialogue)	*Dialogic*: Writer engages in a dialogue with the projected reader
Grammatical complexity: in terms of the chaining of clauses and the inclusion of non-linguistic support to the construction of meaning	*Grammatical complexity*: in terms of density of structure within sentences
Lexically sparse	Lexically dense
Vocabulary is everyday/ non-specialized	Vocabulary more specialized

Chapter 5, *Pragmatics*

Reference

There are numerous deictic expressions that need interpreting (for example, *it* [03], *that* [05, 06]), as well as the expression *the South* [05] meaning *the South of the United States*. However, none of them pose any significant interpretation problems.

Illocutionary Force

For example, *Everything's ready now* [03] is an invitation to come to the table to eat; *but that's so much that is FAR TOO MUCH rice* [06] functions as a complaint. Both of these speech acts are performed indirectly. Although they are interpreted with ease in this dialogue, they could carry a different force in a different context. For example, if the 'complaint' was uttered with soft intonation and in a country where polite refusals are expected out of modesty, this could function as a ritualistic expression of modesty.

Agreement/Disagreement

Andi does not adhere to Leech's politeness maxim of agreement, and this disturbs the social equilibrium.

Face-threatening behaviour

Brian was hoping to please Andi [03], so Andi's complaint is likely to be face-threatening to him (threatening to his positive face).

Context

In a retrospective interview, Brian commented that in this communicative activity (a social dinner) he was expecting to indulge in 'small talk' rather than to be 'talked at'. If they had known each other better, or if they were in a different context (for example, in a university seminar), a debate of this kind might have seemed more appropriate to Brian.

Conversational Pattern/Structure

Andi took longer turns than Brian and interrupted him when Brian attempted to speak. This pattern of turn-taking was not what Brian was expecting in this context, and made him feel he was being talked at.

Chapter 6, *Corpus Linguistics*

First, it is important to remember that these concordance lines do not represent an exhaustive study. However, there are several interesting observations that can be made from the patterns seen in the concordance lines. Although *think of* and *think about* do have some overlap in use and meaning, there are situations when there is a strong preference for one form over the other. Here are some of the observations that can be made from the concordance lines presented in the activity.

- *Think of* is often used with indefinite references (for example, *something*, *nothing*). However, the words *something* and *nothing* never occur with *think about* (for example, *think about nothing*).
- Although *it* occurs after both *think of* and *think about*, *think of* continues its preference for a non-referential use. The concordance lines show that *think of it* is a non-referential use of *it*, whereas the *it* reference in *think about it* is usually referring back to a specific reference in the text. This may be difficult to see from the limited text available. However, if you were actually carrying out this exploration with a concordance program you could increase the 'window' of words available to help you find out the reference patterns.
- *Come to think of it* is quite common and quite idiomatic, yet *come to think about it* does not occur.
- *Think about it* is often preceded by the pronoun *you* (that is, *you think about it*).

- The examples of *think about* + *that* also demonstrate the preference for *think about* to be used with referential situations (for example, *Think about that train. Think about that sort of place*).

Chapter 7, *Second Language Acquisition*

	Student A	Student B	Student C
1.	3	2	3
2.	5	2	5
3.	5	4	5
4.	4	5	3
5.	5	4	3
6.	N/A	2	3
7.	5	2	3
8.	4	2	3
9.	3	3	3
10.	4	4	3
11.	4	3	4

Who is the Most/Least Advanced?

Student A is the most advanced. He uses several stage 5 questions that appear to be original rather than formulaic. In addition, he shows the ability to use his sense of humour while completing the task, suggesting that he is at ease with his English language use.

Student B is the least advanced. Many of his questions are stage 2 questions. He is able to use some more advanced questions, including one stage 5 question. This may be an example of a formulaic question, that is, one that he has learned from classroom activities. On the other hand, it may be an original question, but the fact that most of his questions are from lower stages suggests that it is more difficult for him to produce these advanced questions.

Student C's questions are mostly stage 3 questions, but there is evidence that he is able to create more advanced questions. It is never possible to be sure whether a particular question is formulaic when it is correct. Sometimes, a question which seems a little odd or which contains an error is a clearer indication of the fact that the learner has created the sentence rather than repeating something heard elsewhere. Thus, a question such as 'Can I know witch one is my trunk?' suggests that the learner is putting the pieces together himself.

Written versus Oral Interaction Task

A written task permits learners to take the time to recall what they have learned in class. These more advanced questions may be either chunk-learned items or they may reflect the learners' meta-linguistic ability, which may be in advance of the language they use spontaneously. On an oral task, there is pressure to respond more quickly and there is no opportunity to review what has been produced and to make changes. Therefore, their oral performance is more likely to reflect their true level of development.

Interlanguage Features

The use of *Mrs* and *Mister*, without a family name, as a polite form of address matches French usage of *Madame* and *Monsieur*.

The use of questions without inversion is typical of spoken or informal French, and students were clearly writing what they considered to be appropriate for informal oral interaction. Recall, however, that even learners whose L1 requires inversion with questions will nevertheless pass through stages of development at which they do not use inversion.

Chapter 8, *Psycholinguistics*

Evidence in Data

Yes, the data show that the less proficient learners were significantly slower and less accurate to judge form-related pairs than unrelated control pairs. The more proficient learners also show some sensitivity to lexical form in that it took them longer to reject form-related pairs than controls and they were significantly less accurate than in the control condition. However, the magnitude of the form interference effect was larger for less than for more proficient learners.

Support for the Prediction

The results for the semantically related pairs are almost the reverse of those for the form-related pairs. Here, the more proficient group appears to be more vulnerable to semantic interference, particularly if we focus on the response latencies where only the more proficient group is significantly longer to reject semantically related pairs relative to controls. However, for both groups there is evidence in the accuracy data that they were sometimes fooled by the presentation of a second word that was semantically related to the correct translation.

Characterizing L2 Lexical Development

The overall pattern of results supports a general characterization of L2 lexical development as proceeding from reliance on lexical form to reliance on meaning (Kroll and Stewart, 1994). However, the course of development does not appear to be discrete; there is evidence that even less skilled learners are sensitive to the semantics of L2 words to some degree (Dufour and Kroll,

1995) and that even more skilled learners are still vulnerable to consequences of competition among lexical form relatives. The changes with increasing proficiency appear to reflect a change in the relative activation of different lexical codes.

Implications of Observed Form Interference

The presence of form interference for even the more skilled group is consistent with the evidence for non-selective lexical access in fluent bilinguals reviewed in the chapter. Although the magnitude of the form interference effect is smaller for the more proficient participants, the fact that it is still present suggests that it reflects a basic property of the developed lexicon.

Chapter 9, *Sociolinguistics*

Middlesbrough English	Standard English
Phonological examples	
Ee	*Oh* (but also to indicate scandalization, exasperation, surprise)
eh?	Tag inviting agreement
yer	*you*
Hey	Attention-grabbing tag
wanna	*want to*
fest	*first*
Lexical examples	
like	Informality tag
class	*excellent*
reckon	Used more than *think*
rubbishy	*bad*
mucky	*dirty, rude*
smart	*good, cool*
anyroad	*anyway*
mind	*however*
Our Lass	*my wife/girlfriend*
Our Tony	*my brother Tony*
Our House	*my house*
right cob on	*is in a mood*
learning	*teaching*
owt/nowt	*anything/nothing*
gadgie	*man*, like *codger*
parmo	a *parmesan*, as explained
eggheads	Educated people
choice	swearing (euphemistically)
gobsmacked	*surprised*

plonked	*placed*
croggie/tan	different words for giving someone a ride on a bicycle

Grammatical examples

us	Nominatively used for *we*, accusatively meaning *me*
we only get a mention	*only* for *actually*
I didn't know there were that many words in the world, me	*me* as reflexive intensifier
what it is, right	Topic introduction
there's this	*there is a*
way what we talk	*what* for subordinating particle *that*
ones what all the eggheads underlined in red, and that	As above
and so on	
on the news and everything	Tag phrase as intensifier
them rubbishy efforts	*them* (for demonstrative *those*)
this dictionary, it's huge	Topicalization
don't give a hoot about no Italian cars	Multiple negation
I swear down dead	Emphatic idiom
down Oxford	*down* (meaning anywhere southwards)
get yerselves round	Imperative *get*
had a right chew on	*complained loudly*

Discoursal examples

Questions	*Did yer see it?*
Elicitations	*eh?*
Exclamations	*honest*
	that's rubbish, that is
	so anyroad like
Empathy markers	*get this*
	way what we talk, eh?

Chapter 10, *Focus on the Language Learner: Motivation, Styles and Strategies*

The following are general descriptions of your learning style preferences. It does not describe you all of the time, but gives you an idea of your tendencies when you learn.

Part 1: How I Use my Physical Senses

If you are a visual person, you rely more on the sense of sight, and you learn best through visual means (books, video, charts, pictures). If you are an auditory person, you prefer listening and speaking activities (discussions, debates, audio tapes, role-plays, lectures). If you are a tactile/kinesthetic person, you benefit from doing projects, working with objects and moving around the room (games, building models, conducting experiments).

Part 2: How I Expose Myself to Learning Situations

If you are extroverted, you enjoy a wide range of social, interactive learning tasks (games, conversations, discussions, debates, role-plays, simulations). If you are introverted, you like to do more independent work (studying or reading by yourself or learning with the computer) or enjoy working with one other person you know well.

Part 3: How I Handle Possibilities

If you are a random-intuitive, you are more future-oriented, prefer what can be over what is, like to speculate about possibilities, enjoy abstract thinking and avoid step-by-step instruction. If your preference is concrete-sequential, you are present-oriented, prefer one-step-at-a-time activities, and want to know where you are going in your learning at every moment.

Part 4: How I Approach Tasks

If you are more closure-oriented, you focus carefully on all learning tasks, meet deadlines, plan ahead for assignments and want explicit directions. If you are more open in your orientation, you enjoy discovery learning (in which you pick up information naturally) and prefer to relax and enjoy your learning without concern for deadlines or rules.

Part 5: How I Deal with Ideas

If you are a synthesizing person, you can summarize material well, enjoy guessing meanings and predicting outcomes, and notice similarities quickly. If you are analytic, you can pull ideas apart, do well on logical analysis and contrast tasks, and tend to focus on grammar rules.

Part 6: How I Deal with Input

If you are a global person, you enjoy getting the main idea and are comfortable communicating even if you don't know all the words or concepts. If you are a particular person, you focus more on details, and remember specific information about a topic well.

Chapter 11, *Listening*

Question 1: Listening Sub-skills

Examples of cases where the learner found it difficult to discriminate between the sounds include: *conversing/convergent*, *context/contact* and *doubts/done*. Examples of misperceived word boundaries are: *on seventy* (for *uncertainty*) and *everywhere* (for *every word*). As far as tackling unfamiliar words is concerned, he produced a plausible alternative, *decide*, for the unusual word *decipher*, but was totally confused by *catch the words*, which he interpreted as *catch the dog*.

Question 2: Overall Comprehension

One way of assessing what the listener made of the text as a whole is to focus on the right-hand version and treat it as a text in its own right. What does it seem to be about? When you do that, it is hard to see any overall coherence. Although some of his versions of sentences (2, 9 and perhaps 10) are relatively accurate, they all have some detail missing. Others (for example, 3, 5 and certainly 7) make no obvious sense to the reader. Although the class was told in advance that the topic of the text was the problems of talking to native speakers, it seems clear that the Japanese learner either did not understand that or did not hear it, because it is only in the final two sentences that he seems to have been writing about language.

The learner was an undergraduate in economics. There is some lexical evidence of that in his version: *convergent* (sentence 1) and *consumption* (sentence 6), and also perhaps in his hearing the nouns *demand* and *benefit* (sentence 10) instead of their respective adjectives.

Question 3: Intercultural Misunderstanding

Although the language of this extract was simple, it still provided the opportunity for conflicting interpretations. The reporter said the food was *hot*, (meaning too spicy for his taste), which the interviewee changed to *tasty* (spicy enough) and justified (you want plenty of spice when you are celebrating). The reporter then picked up the word *tasty*, but with a slight pause and a glance at the camera, suggesting that he felt the need to be polite. His next sentence is the most interesting, for our purposes: *'I don't suppose you have a carry-out do you?'* The reporter seemed to be looking for a polite excuse not to eat any more of the food: his *'I don't suppose you have a carry-out?'* implied that he was asking for a portion to take away with him to eat later. But the interviewee seems to have interpreted what he said as *'I don't suppose you have a take-away restaurant?'* and so replied that he was a doctor, and not a restaurateur.

This could be seen as a simple lexical misinterpretation. On the other hand, Pakistani immigrants in the UK may be so used to being stereotyped as working in certain occupations, such as catering, that the doctor here assumes that the reporter assumes just that. This extract seems to carry echoes of many other conversations the doctor has had with British people! Real-life misunderstandings like this can provide valuable material for discussion with L2 listeners, especially when the examples come from interaction between competent users of a language, as was the case here. Adult L2 learners, in particular, can gain confidence (perhaps paradoxically) from analysing the problems that arise in listening, even in their own L1.

Chapter 12, *Speaking and Pronunciation*

Question 1

The first part of the interaction (B1–B4) is mediated by the fact that this is a pedagogical task requiring description of a picture. The text unfolds as:

> Description (B1)^(Clarification)(A1)^Description (B2)^(Reaction) (A2-B3)^Task closure (A3)

Clarification and Reaction can be regarded as Optional stages. The second part (A4–A6) is a kind of Coda, a commentary on the overall interaction, which clears up the central misunderstanding.

Question 2

Many of the lexico-grammatical choices in the Description stage reflect the goal of the task – describing and identifying a picture. The major human and material participants are named – *cars, hotel, snow, people, sun, mark, first floor* – as well as the location circumstances – *around the hotel, in front of the hotel, on the wall of the first floor of the hotel.* The main verb choice, reflecting the existence of the things or people in the picture is the verb 'to be' and the tense used is present simple. In some instances present continuous – *are going to skiing* – is used, reflecting the still ongoing nature of the actions portrayed.

Other choices, outside the stage of Description reflect the fact that the speakers are involved in a joint 'here and now' task. Personal pronouns *I, you* are used to refer to each other, whilst major verb choices refer to the conduct of the task – *see, know, understand, mean, understood.*

Question 3

B1 is a fluent speaker; in her initial turns (B1, B2), she uses a series of independent clauses linked by the conjunction *and.* There are some examples of backtracking (*'the cars, some cars are f-'*) and false starts (*'And it's quite shi-mm it's very sh-sun the sun'*) as she searches for an appropriate structure. The laughter that ends B2 may be to relieve the ongoing pressure to speak, to signal a turn to A, or to allow her time to think further about what she can say. There are no examples of ellipsis in the text, but A uses 'substitution' in *'I know which one it is'*, where *one* refers out into the shared context of the task and the materials (pictures) they are using.

Question 4

A uses clarification checks (A1), backchannels (*'Ah, yeah'* ... A2), the turn type of question (A2) (a question usually 'obliges' the person questioned to respond), and repetition (A4, A5, A6) to negotiate the topic and achieve his purpose.

Question 5

Unlike the three-part exchange we noted in the spider text, this interaction has an example of a more extended series of follow-ups (B5, A5, B6) where the two speakers go on checking each others utterances (by echoing) until they are sure they have reached a common understanding. The last turn (A6) is a final confirmation that this understanding has been reached.

Question 6

Segmental: the Japanese student pronounces /red/ as /led/. This is because /l/ and /r/ are not distinct phonemes in Japanese, but are perceived as allophones. It is only from her interlocutor's reaction that B knows she needs to correct the initial consonant in *red*. Interestingly, also, A does not hear *led* but *let* (another minimal pair) – which may be due to a tendency in German speakers to pronounce the final consonant with more force (for example, /t/ rather than /d/). This problem illustrates very clearly that generally speaking, in pronunciation learning the perception of significant differences needs to be in place before students can successfully work on production.

An understanding of phonology is extremely helpful to teachers as it enables them to analyse and describe the systematic sound pattern of the language they teach, and, ideally, to contrast it with the phoneme inventories of their students' first language(s). Such an understanding is also useful for the setting up of teaching tasks, for example, work on contextualized minimal pairs which are relevant given the students' L1.

Chapter 13, *Reading*

An Example of a Response by the Authors

Reading strategy: previewing and predicting.

- *What*: the reader examines the title, headings, sub-headings and any graphics, and makes predictions about what the text (as a whole) or the next section, will be about.

- *How*: the reader guesses (sometimes in the form of questions, sometimes in the form of statements) what the text will be about. For example: 'I see from the title that this chapter is about the "other economy" and the subtitle says something about the "unofficial untaxed sector".' So I think that the next section is going to talk about parts of a country's economy that do not get reported officially.
- *Why*: the goal is to prepare the reader for the upcoming text information and to enhance comprehension. It also allows the reader to form a mental picture, or model, of the text's development and overall meaning.
- *When* and *Where*: the reader can use this strategy before beginning to read, and at the beginnings and ends of paragraphs and sections. In fact, the reader can use this strategy throughout the reading. Explicit use of this strategy may work best with academic texts and other information texts. Implicit use of this strategy may be sufficient when reading for pleasure, with texts intended to be enjoyed and not remembered in detail.
- *Evaluation*: the reader should ask herself whether this strategy is working for her, to help enhance her understanding of the text's meaning, and whether it is worth the effort being exerted.

Chapter 14, *Writing*

Rhetorical Situation

The rhetorical situation is writing a conference proposal for the Symposium on Second Language Writing. The purpose of this proposal is to demonstrate that the writer has identified an important issue, question or problem in the field and to persuade the reader that this presentation will provide useful insights, answers or solutions. The writer has to portray herself as a competent researcher who is familiar with the ongoing discussion and has something significant to contribute to the field. The audience includes the conference organizers as well as a few outside reviewers. Since this is a conference focusing on second language writing, they are probably specialists in the field who are familiar with L2 writing literature in general. The discourse community is the field of second language writing, but the call for proposals suggests that the conception of the field is broad and inclusive.

The Proposal

This proposal addresses a classic dilemma for many ESP writing teachers – that they cannot possibly have an insider's knowledge into the discourse practices of all academic and professional discourse communities. Her proposed solution – identifying the values and criteria that are used by various discourse communities – is intriguing. The statement of what this presentation contributes to the audience at the end is also effective.

Ineffective Parts of the Proposal

Although the writer refers to a study she has conducted as a main source of support for her argument, she does not explain what the study was about, how it was designed and conducted, and what specific findings might be. Without more specific information, the reviewer will not be able to determine whether the writer will be able to substantiate her arguments with her study.

Written Feedback

Thank you for sharing your proposal with me. Seems like you have found a perfect conference for your interest!

I think you have identified an important issue in ESP instruction. As you point out, it is difficult for any teacher to know all conventions or rules, approaches, formats and genres that students will encounter because rules and expectations vary widely from one context to another and are constantly changing. I am especially intrigued by your proposed solution, which is to learn 'a smaller set of rationales and values underlying these conventions' and to learn about 'the individuals or institutions that determine these rationales'. I also like how you conclude your proposal by emphasizing what teachers are going to gain by attending your session.

One way to strengthen your proposal may be to provide more specific details. Although you mention your 'study into various professional and educational writing rhetorical situations using primary texts, textbooks, scholarly research, and teaching practices', you don't seem to explain the design of your study or how you used the sources you mention. Without knowing more about the design of the study, it would be difficult for the reviewers to assess its potential.

Similarly, you don't seem to describe what some of the specific findings of the study are, nor do you provide any support for the claim that the 'rationales' you have identified can help students. In other words, the reader is left without a clear idea of how your suggested solution might actually work.

In your revision, you might consider describing the design of the study, providing a summary of major 'rationales' that you have identified, and explaining how knowing these rationales can help ESL writers in the ESP classroom.

Also, your title seems somewhat generic. Can you think of a title that emphasizes the unique contribution your study is trying to make?

Feel free to call me if you want to talk about these comments. Best of luck!

Chapter 15, *Assessment*

Question 1

Summary of predictions and results in a quantitative validity argument

Item, predicted and actual results	Beginning	Intermediate	Advanced
Item	My <u>name</u> is Sandy	The main <u>focus</u> of the course	People's <u>stereotypes</u> of other social groups
Predicted	High	Medium	Low
Actual item difficulty	100	74	42

Question 2

The correlations suggest that forms 2 and 3 are the most similar of the three tests and therefore these are the ones that should be chosen, all other things being equal.

Question 3

Placing predicted differences in ability in Business English

Predicted test performance	Lowest scores	Third-highest scores	Second-highest scores	Highest scores
Group	NNSNBM	NNSBM	NSNBM	NSBM

NNSNBM = Non-native speakers of English, non-business majors; NNSBM = Non-native speakers of English, business majors; NSNBM = Native speakers of English, non-business majors; NSBM = native speakers of English, business majors.

Question 4

We would hope for a correlation of around 0.70–0.80. We do not want the tests to correlate near perfectly, because the hope is that the tests will not measure exactly the same language abilities. The computer-based test is supposed to be better.

Question 5

They were concerned not only with the correlations but also with the construct that the test measured and the influence that the test would have on students studying English for the test.

Question 6

Your test is a criterion-referenced test that is appropriate for your grading purposes, but there is no reason to expect that it would correlate with a test for another purpose. You do not want your test judged on the basis of a single analysis that is affected in ways that neither you nor your administrator understand.

References

Chapter 1, *An Overview of Applied Linguistics*

Biber, D., Johansson, S., Leech, G., Conrad, S., Finegan, E. (1999) *Longman Grammar of Spoken and Written English*. Harlow: Longman.

Brown, C.M., Hagoort, P. (1999) *The Neurocognition of Language*. New York: Oxford University Press.

Carter, R., Nunan, D. (eds). (2001) *The Cambridge Guide to Teaching English to Speakers of Other Languages*. Cambridge: Cambridge University Press.

Chomsky, N. (1959) Review of 'Verbal Behavior' by B.F. Skinner. *Language* 35: 26–58.

Chomsky, N. (1965) *Aspects of the Theory of Syntax*. Cambridge, MA: MIT Press.

Cook, V. (1996) *Second Language Learning and Language Teaching*. London: Arnold.

Cole, M. (1996) *Cultural Psychology*. Cambridge, MA: Belknap Press.

Crystal, D. (1987) *The Cambridge Encyclopedia of Language*. Cambridge: Cambridge University Press.

Crystal, D. (1995) *The Cambridge Encyclopedia of the English Language*. Cambridge: Cambridge University Press.

Doughty, C., Williams, J. (eds). (1998) *Focus on Form in Classroom Second Language Acquisition*. Cambridge: Cambridge University Press.

Egbert, J.E., Hanson-Smith, E. (eds). (1999) *CALL Environments: Research, Practice, and Critical Issues*. Alexandria, VA: TESOL.

Ellis, N. (1998) Emergentism, connectionism, and language learning. *Language Learning* 48: 631–644.

Ellis, N.C. (in press, a) Frequency effects in language processing: a review with implications for theories of implicit and explicit language acquisition. *Studies in Second Language* 24 (2).

Ellis, N.C. (in press, b) Reflections on frequency effects in language processing. *Studies in Second Language* 24 (2).

Halliday, M. (1973) *Explorations in the Functions of Language*. London: Edward Arnold.

Halliday, M.A.K. (1978) *Language as Social Semiotic*. London: Arnold.

Howatt, A.P.R. (1984). *A History of English Language Teaching*. Oxford: Oxford University Press.

Howatt, A.P.R. (1999) History of second language teaching. In Spolsky, B. (ed.). *Concise Encyclopedia of Educational Linguistics*. Amsterdam: Elsevier; 618–625.

Hymes, D. (1972) On communicative competence. In Pride, J.B., Holmes, J. (eds). *Sociolinguistics: Selected Readings*. Harmondsworth: Penguin Books; 269–293.

Kelly, L.G. (1969) *25 Centuries of Language Teaching*. Rowley, MA: Newbury House.

Krashen, S. (1982) *Principles and Practice in Second Language Acquisition*. Oxford: Pergamon.

Labov, W. (1970) The study of language in its social context. *Studium Generale* **23**: 30–87.

Littlewood, W. (1981) *Communicative Language Teaching: An Introduction*. Cambridge: Cambridge University Press.

Littlewood, W. (1996) Autonomy: an anatomy and a framework. *System* **24**: 427–435.

McCarthy, M., Carter, R. (1997) Written and spoken vocabulary. In Schmitt, N., McCarthy, M. (eds). *Vocabulary: Description, Acquisition, and Pedagogy*. Cambridge: Cambridge University Press; 20–39.

Messick, S. (1989) Validity. In Linn, R. (ed.). *Educational Measurement* (third edition). New York: Macmillan; 13–103.

Moon, R. (1997) Vocabulary connections: multi-word items in English. In Schmitt, N., McCarthy, M. (eds). *Vocabulary: Description, Acquisition, and Pedagogy*. Cambridge: Cambridge University Press; 40–63.

Naiman, N., Fröhlich, M., Stern, H.H., Todesco, A. (1978) *The Good Language Learner*. Research in Education Series 7. Toronto, Ontario: Ontario Institute for Studies in Education.

O'Malley, J.M., Chamot, A.U. (1990) *Learning Strategies in Second Language Acquisition*. Cambridge: Cambridge University Press.

Oxford, R.L. (1990) *Language Learning Strategies: What Every Teacher Should Know*. Boston, MA: Newbury House.

Pawley, A., Syder, F.H. (1983) Two puzzles for linguistic theory: native like selection and native like fluency. In Richards, J., Schmidt, R. (eds). *Language and Communication*. London: Longman; 191–225.

Richards, J., Platt, J., Weber, H. (1985) *Longman Dictionary of Applied Linguistics*. Harlow: Longman.

Saussure, F. de. (1966) (transl. Baskin, W.). *Course in General Linguistics*. New York, NY: McGraw-Hill.

Schmitt, N. (2000) *Vocabulary in Language Teaching*. Cambridge: Cambridge University Press.

Schumann, J. (1998) *The Neurobiology of Affect in Language*. Oxford: Blackwell.

Sinclair, J. (1996) The search for units of meaning. *Textus* **IX**: 75–106.

Tarone, E. (1979). Interlanguage as chameleon. *Language Learning* **29**: 181–192.

van Ek, J.A. (1976) *The Threshold Level for Modern Language Learning in Schools*. Council of Europe, London: Longman.

van Ek, J.A., Trim, J.L.M. (1998) *Threshold 1990*. Council of Europe, Cambridge: Cambridge University Press.

Vygotsky, L.S. (1987) *The Collected Works of L.S. Vygotsky*. Volume 1. Thinking and Speaking. New York, NY: Plenum Press.

West, M. (1953) *A General Service List of English Words*. London: Longman, Green & Co.

Wenden, A. (1991) *Learner Strategies for Learner Autonomy*. Englewood Cliffs, NJ: Prentice Hall.

Wilkins, D.A. (1999) Applied linguistics. In Spolsky, B. (ed.). *Concise Encyclopedia of Educational Linguistics*. Amsterdam: Elsevier; 6–17.

Wundt, W. (1877). *Völkerpsychologie. Vol. 1: Die Sprache*. Leipzig: Wilhelm Engelmann Verlag.

Chapter 2, *Grammar*

Adair-Hauck, B., Donato, R., Cumo-Johanssen, P. (2000) Using a story-based approach to teach grammar. In Shrum, J., Glisan, E. (eds). *Teacher's Handbook* (second edition). Boston, MA: Heinle & Heinle.

Aljaafreh, A., Lantolf, J. (1994) Negative feedback as regulation and second language learning in the zone of proximal development. *Modern Language Journal* **78**: 465–483.

Bygate, M., Tonkyn, A., Williams, E. (eds) (1994) *Grammar and The Language Teacher*. Hemel Hempstead: Prentice Hall International.

Carter, R., McCarthy, M. (1995) Grammar and the spoken language. *Applied Linguistics* **16**: 141–158.

Celce-Murcia, M. (1998) Discourse analysis and grammar instruction. In Oaks, D.D. (ed.). *Linguistics at Work: A Reader of Applications*. Fort Worth, TX: Harcourt Brace College Publishers.

Celce-Murcia, M., Larsen-Freeman, D. (1999) *The Grammar Book: An ESL/EFL Teacher's Course* (second edition). Boston, MA: Heinle & Heinle.

Chomsky, N. (1957) *Syntactic Structures*. The Hague: Mouton.

Chomsky, N. (1965) *Aspects of the Theory of Syntax*. Cambridge, MA: MIT Press.

Chomsky, N. (1992) *A Minimalist Program for Linguistic Theory*. MIT Occasional Papers in Linguistics, no. 1.

Collins COBUILD English Grammar. (1990) London: HarperCollins.

DeCarrico, J.S. (1998) Syntax, lexis, and discourse: issues in redefining the boundaries. In Haastrup, K., Viberg, A. (eds). *Perspectives on Lexical Acquisition in a Second Language*. Lund: Lund University Press.

DeCarrico, J.S. (2000) *The Structure of English: Studies in Form and Function for Language Teaching*. Ann Arbor, MI: University of Michigan Press.

Donato, R. (1994) Collective scaffolding in second language learning. In Lantolf, J., Appel, G. (eds). *Vygotskian Approaches to Second Language Research*. Norwood, NJ: Ablex Publishing Corporation.

Doughty, C., Williams, J. (eds) (1998) *Focus on Form in Classroom Second Language Acquisition*. Cambridge: Cambridge University Press.

Ellis, N. (1998) Emergentism, connectionism, and language learning. *Language Learning* **48**: 631–644.

Ellis, R. (1993) The structural syllabus and second language acquisition. *TESOL Quarterly* **27**: 91–113.

Fotos, S., Ellis, R. (1991) Communicating about grammar: a task-based approach. *TESOL Quarterly* **25**: 605–628.

Halliday, M.A.K. (1973) *Explorations in the Functions of Language*. London: Edward Arnold.

Hughes, R., McCarthy, M. (1998) From sentence to discourse: discourse grammar and English language teaching. *TESOL Quarterly* **32**: 263–287.

Hymes, D. (1972) On communicative competence. In Pride, J.B., Holmes, J. (eds). *Sociolinguistics*. New York, NY: Penguin; 269–293.

Krashen, S., Terrell, T. (1983) *The Natural Approach*. New York, NY: Pergamon.

Larsen-Freeman, D. (1991a) Teaching grammar. In Celce-Murcia, M. (ed.). *Teaching English as a Second or Foreign Language* (second edition). New York, NY: Newbury House.

Larsen-Freeman, D. (1991b). Second language acquisition: staking out the territory. *TESOL Quarterly* **25**: 315–349.

Larsen-Freeman, D. (1995) On the teaching and learning of grammar: challenging the myths. In Eckman, F., Highland, D., Lee, P., Mileham, J., Rukowski Weber, R. (eds). *Second Language Acquisition Theory and Pedagogy*. Mahwah, NJ: Lawrence Erlbaum.

Larsen-Freeman, D. (1997) *Grammar Dimensions* (second edition). Boston, MA: Heinle & Heinle.

Larsen-Freeman, D. (2001a) *Teaching Language: From Grammar to Grammaring*. Boston, MA: Heinle & Heinle.

Larsen-Freeman, D. (2001b) Teaching grammar. In Celce-Murica, M. (ed.). *Teaching English as a Second or Foreign Language* (third edition). Boston, MA: Heinle & Heinle.

Larsen-Freeman, D. (Forthcoming) The grammar of choice. In Hinkel, E., Fotos, S. (eds.). *New Perspectives on Grammar Teaching*. Mahwah, N.J.: Lawrence Erlbaum Associates.

Leech, G., Svartvik, J. (1975) *A Communicative Grammar of English*. London: Longman.

Long, M. (1991) Focus on form: a design feature in language teaching methodology. In De Bot, K., Ginsberg, R., Kramsch, C. (eds). *Foreign Language Research in Cross-Cultural Perspective*. Amsterdam: John Benjamins.

Loschky, L., Bley-Vroman, R. (1993) Grammar and task-based methodology. In Crookes, G., Gass, S. (eds). *Tasks and Language Learning: Integrating Theory and Practice*. Clevedon: Multilingual Matters.

Lyster, R., Ranta, L. (1997) Corrective feedback and learner uptake: negotiation of forms in communicative classrooms. *Studies in Second Language Acquisition* 19: 37–66.

McCarthy, M. (1998) *Spoken Language and Applied Linguistics*. Cambridge: Cambridge University Press.

McCarthy, M., Carter, R. (1994) *Language as Discourse: Perspectives for Language Teaching*. London: Longman.

Nattinger, J.R., DeCarrico, J.S. (1992) *Lexical Phrases and Language Teaching*. Oxford: Oxford University Press.

Odlin, T. (1994) *Introduction to Perspectives on Pedagogical Grammar*. Cambridge: Cambridge University Press.

Pawley, A., Syder, F.H. (1983) Two puzzles for linguistic theory: nativelike selection and nativelike fluency. In Richards, J., Schmidt, R. (eds). *Language and Communication*. London: Longman.

Peters, A. (1983) *The Units of Language Acquisition*. Cambridge: Cambridge University Press.

Pienemann, M. (1984) Psychological constraints on the teachability of languages. *Studies in Second Language Acquisition* 6: 186–214.

Quirk, R., Greenbaum, S., Leech, G., Svartvik, J. (1972) *A Grammar of Contemporary English*. London: Longman.

Rutherford, W. (1987) *Second Language Grammar: Learning and Teaching*. London: Longman.

Rutherford, W., Sharwood Smith, M. (eds) (1988) *Grammar and Second Language Teaching*. New York, NY: Newbury House.

Schmidt, R. (1990) The role of consciousness in second language learning. *Applied Linguistics* 11: 129–158.

Sharwood Smith, M. (1993) Input enhancement in instructed SLA. Theoretical bases. *Studies in Second Language Acquisition* 15: 165–179.

Spada, N., Lightbown, P. (1993) Instruction and the development of questions in the L2 classroom. *Studies in Second Language Acquisition* 15: 205–221.

Sinclair, J.M. (1985) Selected issues. In Quirk, R., Widdowson, H.G. (eds). *English in the World*. Cambridge: Cambridge University Press.

Swain, M., Lapkin, S. (1998) Interaction and second language learning: two adolescent French immersion students working together. *The Modern Language Journal* **82**: 320–337.

Thompson, S. (1985) Grammar and written discourse: initial vs. final purpose clauses in English. *Text* **5**: 56–84.

Tomasello, M., Herron, C. (1989) Feedback for language transfer errors. *Studies in Second Language Acquisition* **11**: 384–395.

Van Patten, B. (1996) *Input Processing and Grammar Instruction in Second Language Acquisition*. Norwood, NJ: Ablex Publishing Corporation.

White, L. (1987) Against comprehensible input. *Applied Linguistics* **8**: 95–110.

Widdowson, H.G. (1979) *Explorations in Applied Linguistics*. Oxford: Oxford University Press.

Widdowson, H.G. (1989) Knowledge of language and ability for use. *Applied Linguistics* **10**: 128–137.

Widdowson, H.G. (1990) *Aspects of Language Teaching*. Oxford: Oxford University Press.

Chapter 3, *Vocabulary*

Baddeley, A. (1990) *Human Memory*. London: Lawrence Erlbaum Associates.

Bauer, L., Nation, I.S.P. (1993) Word families. *International Journal of Lexicography* **6**: 253–279.

Beck, I.L., McKeown, M.G., Omanson, R.C. (1987) The effects and uses of diverse vocabulary instructional techniques. In McKeown, M.G., Curtis, M.E. (eds). *The Nature of Vocabulary Acquisition*. Mahwah, NJ: Lawrence Erlbaum Associates; 147–163.

Brown, G.D.A., Ellis, N.C. (1994) *Handbook of Spelling*. Chichester: John Wiley and Sons.

Corson, D. (1995) *Using English Words*. Dordrecht: Kluwer Academic.

Coxhead, A. (2000) A new academic word list. *TESOL Quarterly* **34**: 213–238.

Day, R.R., Bamford, J. (1998) *Extensive Reading in the Second Language Classroom*. Cambridge: Cambridge University Press.

Elley, W.B. (1989) Vocabulary acquisition from listening to stories. *Reading Research Quarterly* **24**: 174–187.

Ellis, R. (1994) Factors in the incidental acquisition of second language vocabulary from oral input: a review essay. *Applied Language Learning* **5**: 1–32.

Ellis, R. (1995) Modified oral input and the acquisition of word meanings. *Applied Linguistics* **16**: 409–441.

Ellis, R., He X. (1999) The roles of modified input and output in the incidental acquisition of word meanings. *Studies in Second Language Acquisition* **21**: 285–301.

Ellis, R., Heimbach, R. (1997) Bugs and birds: children's acquisition of second language vocabulary through interaction. *System* **25**: 247–259.

Fountain, R.L., Nation, I.S.P. (2000) A vocabulary-based graded dictation test. *RELC Journal* **31**: 29–44.

Fukkink, R.G., de Glopper, K. (1998) Effects of instruction in deriving word meaning from context: a meta-analysis. *Review of Educational Research* **68**: 450–469.

Goulden, R., Nation, P., Read, J. (1990). How large can a receptive vocabulary be? *Applied Linguistics* **11**: 341–363.

Higa, M. (1963) Interference effects of intralist word relationships in verbal learning. *Journal of Verbal Learning and Verbal Behavior* 2: 170–175.

Hu, M. and Nation, I.S.P. (2000) Vocabulary density and reading comprehension. *Reading in a Foreign Language* 13, 1: 403–430.

Joe, A., Nation, P., Newton, J. (1996) Speaking activities and vocabulary learning. *English Teaching Forum* 34: 2–7.

Kuhn, M.R., Stahl, S.A. (1998) Teaching children to learn word meanings from context. *Journal of Literacy Research* 30: 119–138.

Laufer, B., Kimmel, M. (1997) Bilingualised dictionaries: how learners really use them. *System* 25: 361–369.

Laufer, B., Hadar, L. (1997) Assessing the effectiveness of monolingual, bilingual and 'bilingualised' dictionaries in the comprehension and production of new words. *Modern Language Journal* 81: 189–196.

Laufer, B., Nation, P. (1999) A vocabulary size test of controlled productive ability. *Language Testing* 16: 36–55.

Laufer, B., Osimo, H. (1991). Facilitating long-term retention of vocabulary: the second-hand cloze. *System* 19: 217–224.

Meara, P., Jones, G. (1990) *Eurocentres Vocabulary Size Test 10KA*. Zurich: Eurocentres.

Miller, G.A., Fellbaum, C. (1991) Semantic networks in English. *Cognition* 41: 197–229.

Nagy, W.E., Anderson, R.C., Schommer, M., Scott, J.A., Stallman, A. (1989) Morphological families in the internal lexicon. *Reading Research Quarterly* 24: 263–282.

Nagy, W.E., Herman, P., Anderson, R.C. (1985) Learning words from context. *Reading Research Quarterly* 20: 233–253.

Nation, I.S.P. (2001) *Learning Vocabulary in Another Language*. Cambridge: Cambridge University Press.

Nation, P. (2000) Learning vocabulary in lexical sets: dangers and guidelines. *TESOL Journal* 9: 6–10.

Nation, P., Wang, K. (1999) Graded readers and vocabulary. *Reading in Foreign Language* 12: 355–380.

Newton, J. (1995) Task-based interaction and incidental vocabulary learning: a case study. *Second Language Research* 11: 159–177.

Pawley, A., Syder, F.H. (1983) Two puzzles for linguistic theory: nativelike selection and nativelike fluency. In Richards, J.C., Schmidt, R.W. (eds). *Language and Communication*. London: Longman; 191–225.

Read, J. (2000) *Assessing Vocabulary*. Cambridge: Cambridge University Press.

Ringbom, H. (1983) On the distinctions of item learning vs. system learning, and receptive vs. productive competence in relation to the role of L1 in foreign language learning. In Ringbom, H. (ed.). *Psycholinguistics and Foreign Language Learning*. Åbo: Åbo Akademi.

Schmidt, R. (1995) *Attention and Awareness in Foreign Language Learning*. University of Hawaii: Second Language Teaching and Curriculum Center.

Schmitt, N. (2000) *Vocabulary in Language Teaching*. Cambridge: Cambridge University Press.

Schmitt, N., McCarthy, M. (eds), (1997). *Vocabulary: Description, Acquisition and Pedagogy*. Cambridge: Cambridge University Press.

Schmitt, N., Schmitt, D., Clapham, C. (2001) Developing and exploring the behaviour of two new versions of the Vocabulary Levels Test. *Language Testing* 18: 55–88.

Stahl, S.A., Fairbanks, M.M. (1986) The effects of vocabulary instruction: a model-based meta-analysis. *Review of Educational Research* 56: 72–110.

Tinkham, T. (1997) The effects of semantic and thematic clustering on the learning of second language vocabulary. *Second Language Research* **13**: 138–163.

Waring, R. (ed.) (1997a) Special issue on extensive reading. *The Language Teacher* **21**: 5.

Waring, R. (1997b) The negative effects of learning words in semantic sets: a replication. *System* **25**: 261–274.

Watanabe, Y. (1997) Input, intake and retention: effects of increased processing on incidental learning of foreign vocabulary. *Studies in Second Language Acquisition* **19**: 287–307.

West, M. (1953) *A General Service List of English Words*. London: Longman, Green & Co.

Wijk, A. (1966) *Rules of Pronunciation for the English Language*. London: Oxford University Press.

Venezky, R.L. (1970) *The Structure of English Orthography*. Janua Linguarum Series Minor 82, The Hague: Mouton.

Chapter 4, *Discourse Analysis*

Beattie, G. (1983) *Talk: An Analysis of Speech and Non-Verbal Behaviour in Conversation*. Milton Keynes: Open University Press.

Biber, D., Johansson, S., Leech, G., Conrad, S., Finegan, E. (1999) *Longman Grammar of Spoken and Written English*. Harlow: Longman.

Biber, D., Conrad, S., Reppen, R. (1998) *Corpus Linguistics: Investigating Language Structure and Use*. Cambridge: Cambridge University Press.

Carter, R.A., McCarthy, M.J. (1995) Grammar and the spoken language. *Applied Linguistics* **16**: 141–158.

Carter, R., Hughes R., McCarthy, M.J. (2001) *Exploring Grammar in Context*. Cambridge: Cambridge University Press.

Cook, G. (1989) *Discourse*. Oxford: Oxford University Press.

Coulthard, M. (1985) *An Introduction to Discourse Analysis*. London: Longman.

Eggins, S., Slade, D. (1997) *Analysing Casual Conversation*. London: Cassel.

Fairclough, N. (1989) *Language and Power*. London: Longman.

Fairclough, N. (1992) *Discourse and Social Change*. Cambridge: Polity Press.

Fairclough, N. (1995) *Critical Discourse Analysis*. London: Longman.

Francis, G., Hunston, S. (1992) Analysing everyday conversation. In Coulthard, R. (ed.) *Advances in Spoken Discourse*. London: Routledge; 123–161.

Gardner, R. (1987) The identification and role of topic in spoken interaction. *Semiotica* **65**: 129–141.

Garfinkel, H. (1967) *Studies in Ethnomethodology*. Englewood Cliffs, NJ: Prentice Hall.

Goffman, E. (1974) *Frame Analysis: An Essay on the Organisation of Experience*. New York, NY: Harper & Row. [Reprinted by Northeastern University Press, Boston, MA, 1986.]

Goffman, E. (1981) *Forms of Talk*. Oxford: Blackwell.

Gumperz, J., Hymes, D. (eds) (1972) *Directions in Sociolinguistics*. Winston, NY: Holt, Rinehart & Winston.

Halliday, M.A.K. (1966) Lexis as a linguistic level. In Bazell, C.E., Catford, J.C.

Halliday, M.A.K., Robins, R.H. (eds). *In Memory of J.R.Firth*. London: Longman; 148–162.

Halliday, M.A.K. (1978) *Language as Social Semiotic: The Social Interpretation of Language and Meaning*. London and Baltimore, MD: Edward Arnold and University Park Press.

Halliday, M.A.K. (1985) *Spoken and Written Language*. Geelong, Australia: Deakin University Press. [Republished by Oxford University Press, 1989.]

Halliday, M.A.K. (1994) *An Introduction to Functional Grammar* (second edition). London: Edward Arnold.

Hoey, M.P. (1991) Some properties of spoken discourse. In Bowers, R., Brumfit, C. (eds). *Applied Linguistics and English Language Teaching*. Basingstoke: Macmillan/MEP.

Hughes, R. (1996) *English in Speech and Writing*. London: Routledge.

Hymes, D. (1972a) Towards ethnographies of communication: the analysis of communicative events. In Giglioli, P. (ed.). *Language and Social Context*. Harmondsworth: Penguin Books; 21–33.

Hymes, D. (1972b) Models of the interaction of language and social life. In Gumperz, J., Hymes, D. (eds). *Directions in Sociolinguistics: The Ethnography of Communication*. New York, NY: Holt, Rinehart & Winston; 35–71.

Hymes, D. (1974) *Foundations in Sociolinguistics*. Philadelphia, PA: University of Pennsylvania Press.

Jefferson, G. (1972) Side sequences. In Sudnow, D. (ed.). *Studies in Social Interaction*. New York, NY: The Free Press; 294–338.

Labov, W. (1972) *Sociolinguistic Patterns*. Philadelphia, PA: University of Pennsylvania Press.

Labov, W., Waletzky, J. (1967) Narrative analysis: oral versions of personal experiences. In Helm, J. (ed.). *Essays on the Verbal and Visual Arts*. American Ethnological Society, Proceedings of Spring Meeting 1966. Washington DC: University of Washington Press.

Levinson, S. (1983) *Pragmatics*. Cambridge: Cambridge University Press.

McCarthy, M.J. (1988) Some vocabulary patterns in conversation. In Carter, R.A., McCarthy, M.J. *Vocabulary and Language Teaching*. London: Longman; 181–200.

McCarthy, M.J. (1991) *Discourse Analysis for Language Teachers*. Cambridge: Cambridge University Press.

McCarthy, M. (1998) *Spoken Language and Applied Linguistics*. Cambridge: Cambridge University Press.

McCarthy, M.J. (2001) I*ssues in Applied Linguistics*. Cambridge: Cambridge University Press.

Miller, C.R. (1984) Genre as social action. *Quarterly Journal of Speech* 70: 151–167.

Pomeranz, A. (1984) Agreeing and disagreeing with assessments: some features of preferred/dispreferred turn shapes. In Atkinson, J., Heritage, J. (eds) *Structures of Social Action*. Cambridge: Cambridge University Press; 57–101.

Sacks, H. (1992a) *Lectures on Conversation*. Volumes I and II. Cambridge, MA: Blackwell.

Sacks, H., Schegloff, E.A., Jefferson, G. (1974) A simplest systematics for the organisation of turn-taking for conversation. *Language* 50: 696–735.

Saville-Troike, M. (1989) *The Ethnography of Communication: An Introduction* (second edition). Oxford: Blackwell.

Schegloff, E.A. (1972) Notes on a conversational practice: formulating place. In Sudnow, D. (ed.). *Studies in Social Interaction*. New York, NY: Free Press; 75–117.

Schegloff, E.A., Sacks, H. (1973) Opening up closings. *Semiotica* 8: 289–327.

Schegloff, E.A., Jefferson, G., Sacks, H. (1977) The preference for self-correction in the organisation of repair in conversation. *Language* 53: 361–382.

Schiffrin, D. (1994) *Approaches to Discourse*. Cambridge, MA: Blackwell.

Schmitt, N. (2000) *Vocabulary in Language Teaching*. Cambridge: Cambridge University Press.

Sinclair, J.McH. (1966) Beginning the study of lexis. In Bazell, C.E., Catford J.C., Halliday M.A.K., Robins, R.H. (eds). *In Memory of J.R.Firth*. London: Longman; 410–430.

Sinclair, J. McH., Coulthard, R.M. (1975) *Towards an Analysis of Discourse*. Oxford: Oxford University Press.

Tannen, D. (1984) *Conversational Style: Analyzing Talk Among Friends*. Norwood, NJ: Ablex.

Tannen, D. (1989) *Talking Voices: Repetition, Dialogue and Imagery in Conversational Discourse*. Cambridge: Cambridge University Press.

Yngve, V.H. (1970) On getting a word in edgewise. In *Papers from the 6th Regional Meeting, Chicago Linguistic Society*. Chicago, IL: Chicago Linguistic Society.

Chapter 5, *Pragmatics*

Austin, J. (1975) *How to Do Things with Words* (second edition). Oxford: Clarendon Press.

Blakemore, D. (1987) *Semantic Constraints on Relevance*. Oxford: Blackwell.

Brown, P., Levinson, S.C. (1987) *Politeness. Some Universals in Language Usage*. Cambridge: Cambridge University Press. (Originally published as 'Universals in language usage: politeness phenomenon'. In: Goody, E. (ed.) (1978) *Questions and Politeness: Strategies in Social Interaction*. New York: Cambridge University Press.

Grice, P. (1967) Logic and Conversation (William James Lectures), published in Grice, P. (1989) *Studies in the Way of Words*. Cambridge MA: Harvard University Press. (pp. 22–143).

Grice, P. (1989) *Studies in the Way of Words*. Harvard, MA: Harvard University Press.

Hacking, I. (1995) The looping effects of human kinds. In Sperber, D., Premack, D., Premack, A.J. (eds) *Causal Cognition*. Oxford: Clarendon Press; 351–384.

House, J. (2000) Understanding misunderstanding: a pragmatic-discourse approach to analysing mismanaged rapport in talk across cultures. In: Spencer-Oatey, H. (ed.). (2000) *Culturally Speaking. Managing Rapport through Talk across Cultures*. London: Continuum; 145–164.

Kasper, G. (1992) Pragmatic transfer. *Second Language Research* 8: 203–231.

Kasper, G. (2000) Data collection in pragmatics research. In: Spencer-Oatey, H. (ed.). (2000) *Culturally Speaking. Managing Rapport through Talk across Cultures*. London: Continuum; 316–341.

Kasper, G., Blum-Kulka, S. (eds). *Interlanguage Pragmatics*. Oxford: Oxford University Press.

Leech, G. (1983) *Principles of Pragmatics*. London: Longman.

Mey, J. (1993) *Pragmatics. An Introduction*. Oxford: Blackwell.

Mey, J. (2000) *Pragmatics. An Introduction* (second edition). Oxford: Oxford University Press.

Morris, C. (1938) Foundations of the theory of signs was originally published in Neurath, O., Carnap, R., and Morris, C. (eds) (1938) *International Encyclopaedia of Unified Science*. Chicago, IL: University of Chicago Press. (pp. 77–138). The paper was also reprinted in: **Morris, C.** (1971) Writings on the general theory of signs. The Hague: Mouton. The quote we have used in the text of the chapter is on page 30 of the (1971) publication.

Munby, J. (1978) *Communicative Syllabus Design*. Cambridge: Cambridge University Press.

Searle, J. (1969) *Speech Acts: An Essay in the Philosophy of Language*. Cambridge: Cambridge University Press.

Sifianou, M. (1992) *Politeness Phenomena in England and Greece. A Cross-Cultural Perspective*. Oxford: Clarendon Press.

Sperber, D., Wilson, D. (1986/1995) *Relevance: Communication and Cognition*. Oxford: Blackwell.

Thomas, J. (1983) Cross-cultural pragmatic failure. *Applied Linguistics* 4: 91–112.

Thomas, J. (1995) *Meaning in Interaction. An Introduction to Pragmatics*. London: Longman.

Verschueren, J. (1999) *Understanding Pragmatics*. London: Arnold.

Yule, G. (1996) *Pragmatics*. Oxford: Oxford University Press.

Wilkins, D.A. (1986) *Notional Syllabuses*. Oxford: Oxford University Press.

Žegarac, V., Pennington, M. (2000) Pragmatic transfer in intercultural communication. In: Spencer-Oatey, H. (ed.) *Culturally Speaking. Managing Rapport through Talk across Cultures*. London: Continuum; 165–190.

Chapter 6, *Corpus Linguistics*

Barnbrook, G. (1996). *Language and Computers: A Practical Introduction to the Computer Analysis of Language*. Edinburgh: Edinburgh University Press.

Biber, D. (1988). *Variation across Speech and Writing*. New York, NY: Cambridge University Press.

Biber, D. (1990) Methodological issues regarding corpus-based analyses of linguistic variation. *Literary and Linguistic Computing* 5: 257–269.

Biber, D. (1993a) Representativeness in corpus design. *Literary and Linguistic Computing* 8: 243–257.

Biber, D. (1993b) Using register-diversified corpora for general language studies. *Computational Linguistics* 19: 219–241.

Biber, D. Conrad, S., Reppen, R. (1998) *Corpus Linguistics: Investigating Language Structure and Use*. Cambridge: Cambridge University Press.

Biber, D., Johansson, S., Leech, G., Conrad, S., Finegan, E. (1999). *The Longman Grammar of Spoken and Written English*. London: Longman.

Carter, R., McCarthy, M. (1997). *Exploring Spoken Language*. Cambridge: Cambridge University Press.

Cook, G. (1998). The uses of reality: a reply to Ronald Carter. *English Language Teaching Journal* 52: 57–63.

Donley, K.M., Reppen, R. (2001) Using corpus tools to highlight academic vocabulary in sustained content language teaching. *TESOL Journal* 10: 2–3.

Edwards, J.A., Lampert, M.D. (eds) (1993). *Talking Data: Transcription and Coding in Discourse Research*. Hillsdale, NJ: Lawrence Erlbaum.

Flowerdew, L., Tong, A. (eds) (1994). *Entering Text*. Hong Kong: Language Centre.

Johns, T. (1994) From printout to handout: grammar and vocabulary teaching in the context of data-driven learning. In Odlin, T. (ed.). *Perspectives on Pedagogical Grammar*. Cambridge: Cambridge University Press.

Sinclair, J. (1991) *Corpus Concordance and Collocation*. Oxford: Oxford University Press.

Simpson, R., Swales, J. (eds) (2001) *Corpus Linguistics in North America: Selections from the 1999 Symposium*. Ann Arbor, MI: University of Michigan Press.

Wichmann, A., Fligelstone, S., McEnery, T., Knowles, G. (eds) (1997) *Teaching and Language Corpora*. London: Longman.

Chapter 7, *Second Language Acquisition*

Bley-Vroman, R. (1989) What is the logical problem of foreign language learning? In Gass, S., Schachter, J. (eds). *Linguistic Perspectives on Second Language Acquisition.* Cambridge: Cambridge University Press; 41–68.

Brown, R. (1973) *A First Langauge: The Early Stages.* Cambridge, MA: Harvard University Press.

Chomsky, N. (1968) *Language and Mind.* New York, NY: Harcourt Brace Jovanovich.

Corder, S.P. (1967) The significance of learners' errors. *International Review of Applied Linguistics* 5: 161–169.

Dulay, H., Burt, M. (1974) Natural sequences in child second language acquisition. *Language Learning* 24: 37–53.

Dulay, H., Burt, M. (1976) Creative construction in second language learning and teaching. *Language Learning* Special Issue No. 4: 65–79.

Dulay, H., Burt, M., Krashen, S. (1982) *Language Two.* Oxford: Oxford University Press.

Ellis, N. (1999) Cognitive approaches to SLA. *Annual Review of Applied Linguistics* 19: 22–42.

Ellis, N., Schmidt, R. (1997) Morphology and longer distance dependencies: laboratory research illuminating the A in SLA. *Studies in Second Language Acquisition* 19: 145–71.

Ellis, R. (1994) *The Study of Second Language Acquisition.* Oxford: Oxford University Press.

Elman, J.L., Bates, E., Johnson, M., Karmiloff-Smith, A., Parisi, D., Plunkett, K. (1996) *Rethinking Innateness: A Connectionist Perspective on Development.* Cambridge, MA: A Bradford Book.

Gass, S., Selinker, L. (2000) *Second Language Acquisition: An Introductory Course* (second edition). Hillsdale, NJ: Lawrence Erlbaum Associates.

Hakuta, K. (1976) A case study of a Japanese child learning English as a second language. *Language Learning* 26: 321–351.

Hamilton, R.L. (1994) Is implicational generalization unidirectional and maximal? *Language Learning* 44: 123–157.

Harley, B., Swain, M. (1984) The interlanguage of immersion students and its implications for second language teaching. In Davies, A., Criper, C., Howatt, A.P.R. (eds). *Interlanguage.* Edinburgh: Edinburgh University Press; 291–311.

Kellerman, E. (1986) Crosslinguistic constraints on the development of the L2 lexicon. In Kellerman, E., Sharwood Smith, M. (eds). *Crosslinguistic Influence in Second Language Acquisition.* New York, NY: Pergamon, 35–48.

Kellerman, E., Sharwood Smith, M. (eds) (1986) *Crosslinguistic Influence in Second Language Acquisition.* New York, NY: Pergamon.

Krashen, S. (1982) *Principles and Practice in Second Language Acquisition.* Oxford: Pergamon.

Kupferberg, I., Olshtain, E. (1996) Explicit contrastive instruction facilitates the acquisition of difficult L2 forms. *Language Awareness* 5: 149–165.

Lado, R. (1964) *Language Teaching: A Scientifc Approach.* New York: McGraw-Hill.

Lantolf, J.P. (2000) *Sociocultural Theory and Second Language Learning.* Oxford: Oxford University Press.

Larsen-Freeman, D. (1976) An explanation for the morpheme acquisition order of second language learners. *Language Learning* 26: 125–134.

Larsen-Freeman, D., Long, M.H. (1991) *An Introduction to Second Language Acquisition*. New York, NY: Longman.

Lightbown, P.M. (1985) Input and acquisition for second-language learners in and out of classrooms. *Applied Linguistics* 6: 263–273.

Lightbown, P.M. (1998) The importance of timing in focus on form. In Doughty, C., Williams, J. (eds). *Focus on Form in Classroom Second Language Acquisition*. Cambridge: Cambridge University Press; 177–196.

Lightbown, P.M., Spada, N. (1990) Focus-on-form and corrective feedback in communicative language teaching: effects on second language learning. *Studies in Second Language Acquisition* 12: 429–448.

Lightbown, P.M., Spada, N. (1999) *How Languages are Learned*. Oxford: Oxford University Press.

Long, M.H. (1985) Input and second language acquisition theory. In Gass, S.M., Madden, C.G. (eds). *Input in Second Language Acquisition*. Rowley, MA: Newbury House, 377–393.

Long, M.H. (1996) The role of the linguistic environment in second language acquisition. In Ritchie, W., Bhatia, T. (eds) *Handbook of Research on Second Language Acquisition*. New York, NY: Academic; 413–468.

Lyster, R. (1994) The effect of functional-analytic teaching on aspects of French immersion students' sociolinguistic competence. *Applied Linguistics* 15: 263–287.

Mackey, A., Philp, J. (1998) Conversational interaction and second language development: recasts, responses and red herrings? *Modern Language Journal* 82: 338–356.

McLaughlin, B. (1987) *Theories of Second Language Learning*. London: Edward Arnold.

McLaughlin, B., Heredia, J.L.C. (1996) Information-processing approaches to research on second language acquisition and use. In Ritchie, W.C., Bhatia, T. (eds). *Handbook of Second Language Acquisition*. New York, NY: Academic.

Mitchell, R., Miles, R. (1998) *Second Language Learning Theories*. London: Edward Arnold.

Norris, J.M., Ortega, L. (2000) Effectiveness of L2 instruction: a research synthesis and quantitative meta-analysis. *Language Learning* 50: 417–528.

Odlin, T. (1989) *Language Transfer: Cross-Linguistic Influence in Language Learning*. Cambridge: Cambridge University Press.

Ohta, A. (2000) Rethinking recasts: a learner-centered examination of corrective feedback in the Japanese classroom. In Hall, J.K., Verplaeste, L. (eds). *The Construction of Second and Foreign Language Learning Through Classroom Interaction*. Mahwah, NJ: Erlbaum; 47–71.

Pienemanm, M. (1989) Is language teachable? Psycholinguistic experiments and hypotheses. *Applied Linguistics* 10: 52–79.

Richards, J. (1974) A non-contrastive approach to error analysis. In Richards, J. (ed.). *Error Analysis: Perspectives on Second Language Acquisition*. London: Longman; 172–188.

Ringbom, H. (1986) Crosslinguistic influence and the foreign language learning process. In Kellerman, E., Sharwood Smith, M. (eds). *Crosslinguistic Influence in Second Language Acquisition*. New York, NY: Pergamon; 150–162.

Rumelhart, D., McClelland, J. (1986) On learning the past tense of English verbs. In McClelland, J., Rumelhard, D. (eds). *Parallel Distributed Processing: Explorations in the Microstructure of Cognition: Volume 2. Psychological and Biological Models*. Cambridge, MA: MIT Press; 216–217.

Schmidt, R. (1990) The role of consciousness in second language learning. *Applied Linguistics* **11**: 129–156.

Selinker, L. (1972) Interlanguage. *International Review of Applied Linguistics* **10**: 209–231.

Sharwood Smith, M. (1981) Consciousness-raising and the second language learner. *Applied Linguistics* **2**: 159–168.

Skinner, B.F. (1957) *Verbal Behavior*. New York, NY: Appleton–Century–Crofts.

Slobin, D. (1973) Cognitive prerequisites for the acquisition of grammar. In Ferguson, C., Slobin, D. (eds). *Studies of Child Language Development*. New York, NY: Holt, Rinehart & Winston; 175–208.

Spada, N. (1997) Form-focussed instruction and second language acquisition: a review of classroom and laboratory research. *Language Teaching* **30**: 73–87.

Spada, N., Lightbown, P.M. (1999) Instruction, L1 influence and developmental readiness in second language acquisition. *Modern Language Journal* **83**: 1–22.

Swain, M. (1988) Manipulating and complementing content teaching to maximize second language learning. *TESL Canada Journal* **6**: 68–83.

Swain, M. (2000) The output hypothesis and beyond: mediating acquisition through collaborative dialogue. In Lantolf, J.P. (ed.). *Sociocultural Theory and Second Language Learning*. Oxford: Oxford University Press; 97–114.

Tarone, E., Swain, M. (1995) A sociolinguistic perspective on second language use in immersion classrooms. *Modern Language Journal* **79**: 166–178.

Towell, R., Hawkins, R. (1994) *Approaches to Second Language Acquisition*. Clevedon: Multilingual Matters.

Vygotsky, L.S. (1987) *The Collected Works of L.S. Vygotsky. Volume 1. Thinking and Speaking*. New York, NY: Plenum Press.

White, L. (1989) *Universal Grammar and Second Language Acquisition*. Amsterdam: John Benjamins.

White, L. (1991) Adverb placement in second language acquisition: some effects of positive and negative evidence in the classroom. *Second Language Research* **7**: 133–161.

Wode, H. (1981) *Learning a Second Language: An Integrated View of Language Acquisition*. Tübingen: Gunter Narr Verlag.

Wray, A. (1999) Formulaic language in learners and native speakers. *Language Teaching* **32**: 213–231.

Zobl, H. (1980) The formal and developmental selectivity of L1 influence on L2 acquisition. *Language Learning* **30**: 43–57.

Chapter 8, *Psycholinguistics*

Altarriba, J., Mathis, K.M. (1997) Conceptual and lexical development in second language acquisition. *Journal of Memory and Language* **36**: 550–568.

Anderson, J. (1983) *The Architecture of Cognition*. Cambridge, MA, Harvard University Press.

Bijeljac-Babic, R., Biardeau, A., Grainger, J. (1997) Masked orthographic priming in bilingual word recognition. *Memory & Cognition* **25**: 447–457.

Brown, R., McNeill, D. (1966) The 'tip of the tongue' phenomenon. *Journal of Verbal Learning and Verbal Behavior* **5**: 325–337.

Carroll, D.W. (1999) *Psychology of Language* (third edition). Belmont, CA: Wadsworth Publishing.

Chen, H.-C., Leung, Y.-S. (1989) Patterns of lexical processing in a nonnative language. *Journal of Experimental Psychology: Learning, Memory, and Cognition* **15**: 316–325.

Costa, A., Miozzo, M., Caramazza, A. (1999) Lexical selection in bilinguals: do words in the bilingual's two lexicons compete for selection? *Journal of Memory and Language* **41**: 365–397.

de Bot, K. (1996) Language attrition. In Nelde, P., Wölck, W. *Handbuch Sprach Kontakt*. Berlin, Mouton; 579–585.

de Bot, K. (2000) Psycholinguistics in applied linguistics: trends and perspectives. *Annual Review of Applied Linguistics* **20**: 224–237.

de Bot, K., Stoessel, S. (2000) In search of yesterday's words: reactivating a long forgotten language. *Applied Linguistics* **21**: 364–388.

de Groot, A.M.B. (1992) Determinants of word translation. *Journal of Experimental Psychology: Learning, Memory, and Cognition* **18**: 1001–1018.

de Groot, A.M.B., Kroll, J.F. (eds) (1997) *Tutorials in Bilingualism: Psycholinguistic Perspectives*. Mahwah, NJ: Lawrence Erlbaum Associates.

de Groot, A.M.B., Delmaar, P., Lupker, S.J. (2000) The processing of interlexical homographs in a bilingual and a monolingual task: support for nonselective access to bilingual memory. *Quarterly Journal of Experimental Psychology* **53A**: 397–428.

Dijkstra, A., De Bruijn, E., Schriefers, H., Ten Brinke, S. (2000) More on interlingual homograph recognition: language intermixing versus explicitness of instruction. *Bilingualism: Language and Cognition* **3**: 69–78.

Dijkstra, A., Grainger, J., Van Heuven, W.J.B. (1999) Recognizing cognates and interlingual homographs: the neglected role of phonology. *Journal of Memory and Language* **41**: 496–518.

Dijkstra, A., Van Heuven, W.J.B. (1998) The BIA model and bilingual word recognition. In Grainger, J., Jacobs, A. (eds). *Localist Connectionist Approaches to Human Cognition*. Hillsdale, NJ: Lawrence Erlbaum Associates; 189–225.

Dijkstra, A., Van Heuven, W.J.B., Grainger, J. (1998). Simulating cross-language competition with the Bilingual Interactive Activation model. *Psychologica Belgica* **38**: 177–197.

Dijkstra, A., Van Jaarsveld, H., Ten Brinke, S. (1998) Interlingual homograph recognition: effects of task demands and language intermixing. *Bilingualism: Language and Cognition* **1**: 51–66.

Dufour, R., Kroll, J.F. (1995) Matching words to concepts in two languages: a test of the concept mediation model of bilingual representation. *Memory & Cognition* **23**: 166–180.

Gerard, L.D., Scarborough, D.L. (1989) Language-specific access of homographs by bilinguals. *Journal of Experimental Psychology: Learning, Memory, and Cognition* **15**: 305–315.

Gollan, T., Forster, K.I., Frost, R. (1997) Translation priming with different scripts: masked priming with cognates and noncognates in Hebrew–English bilinguals. *Journal of Experimental Psychology: Learning, Memory, and Cognition* **23**: 1122–1139.

Green, D.W. (1998) Mental control of the bilingual lexico-semantic system. *Bilingualism: Language and Cognition* **1**: 67–81.

Hakuta, K. (1986) *Mirror of Language. The Debate on Bilingualism*. New York, Basic Books.

Hansen, L. (2001) Language attrition: the fate of the start. *Annual Review of Applied Linguistics* **21**: 60–73.

Harley, B. (1994) Maintaining French as a second language in adulthood. *Canadian Modern Language Review* 50: 688–713.

Hermans, D. (2000) Word Production in a Foreign Language. Unpublished doctoral dissertation, University of Nijmegen, Nijmegen, The Netherlands.

Hermans, D., Bongaerts, T., de Bot, K., Schreuder, R. (1998). Producing words in a foreign language: can speakers prevent interference from their first language? *Bilingualism: Language and Cognition* 1: 213–230.

Jared, D., Kroll, J.F. (2001) Do bilinguals activate phonological representations in one or both of their languages when naming words? *Journal of Memory and Language* 44: 2–31.

Jescheniak, J.D., Schriefers, K.I. (1998) Discrete serial versus cascading processing in lexical access in speech production: further evidence from the coactivation of near-synonyms. *Journal of Experimental Psychology: Learning, Memory, and Cognition* 24: 1256–1274.

Jiang, N. (1999) Testing processing explanations for the asymmetry in masked cross-language priming. *Bilingualism: Language and Cognition* 2: 59–75.

Jones, G., Langford, S. (1987) Phonological blocking in the tip of the tongue state. *Cognition* 26: 115–122.

Kroll, J.F., Curley, J. (1988) Lexical memory in novice bilinguals: the role of concepts in retrieving second language words. In Gruneberg, M., Morris, P., Sykes, R. (eds). *Practical Aspects of Memory, Volume 2*. London: John Wiley and Sons; 389–395.

Kroll, J.F., Stewart, E. (1994) Category interference in translation and picture naming: evidence for asymmetric connections between bilingual memory representations. *Journal of Memory and Language* 33: 149–174.

La Heij, W., Kerling, R., Van der Velden, E. (1996) Nonverbal context effects in forward and backward translation: evidence for concept mediation. *Journal of Memory and Language* 35: 648–665.

Levelt, W.J.M. (1989) *Speaking. From Intention to Articulation*. Cambridge, MA: MIT Press.

Levelt, W. (1993) Language use in normal speakers and its disorders. In Blanken, G., Dittman, E., Grimm, H., Marshall, J., Wallasch, C. *Linguistic Disorders and Pathologies. An International Handbook*. Berlin: Walther de Gruyter; 1–15.

Levelt, W. (1999) Producing spoken language. In Brown, C., Haagoord, P. (eds). *The Neurocognition of Language*. Oxford: Oxford University Press; 83–122.

Levelt, W.J.M., Roelofs, A., Meyer, A.S. (1999) A theory of lexical access in speech production. *Behavioral and Brain Sciences* 22: 1–75.

Levelt, W.J.M., Schriefers, H., Vorberg, D., Meyer, A.S., Pechman, T., Havinga, J. (1991) The time course of lexical access in speech production: a study of picture naming. *Psychological Review* 98: 122–142.

Nicol, J.L. (ed.). *One Mind, Two Lanugages: Bilingual Language Processing*. Cambridge, MA: Blackwell Publishers.

Paradis, M. (1981) Neurolinguistic organization of a bilingual's two languages. In Copeland, J.E., Davis, P.W. *The Seventh LACUS Forum*. Columbia, SC: Hornbeam Press; 486–494.

Peterson, R.R., Savoy, P. (1998). Lexical selection and phonological encoding during language production: evidence for cascaded processing. *Journal of Experimental Psychology: Learning, Memory, and Cognition* 24: 539–557.

Potter, M.C., So, K.-F., Von Eckardt, B., Feldman, L.B. (1984) Lexical and conceptual representation in beginning and more proficient bilinguals. *Journal of Verbal Learning and Verbal Behavior* 23: 23–38.

Poulisse, N. (1997) Language production in bilinguals. In de Groot, A.M.B., Kroll, J.F. (eds). *Tutorials in Bilingualism: Psycholinguistic Perspectives*. Mahwah, NJ: Lawrence Erlbaum; 201–224.

Poulisse, N. (1999) *Slips of the Tongue: Speech Errors in First and Second Language Production*. Amsterdam/Philadelphia, PA: John Benjamins.

Poulisse, N., Bongaerts, T. (1994) First language use in second language production. *Applied Linguistics* 15: 36–57.

Schneider, W., Shiffrin, R. (1977) Controlled and automatic human processing. I: Detection, search, and attention. *Psychological Review* 84: 1–66.

Schreuder, R., Weltens, B. (eds). *The Bilingual Lexicon*. Amsterdam/Philadelphia, PA: John Benjamins.

Schriefers, H., Meyer, A.S., Levelt, W.J.M. (1990) Exploring the time-course of lexical access in production: picture–word interference studies. *Journal of Memory and Language* 29: 86–102.

Starreveld, P.A. (2000) On the interpretation of onsets of auditory context effects in word production. *Journal of Memory and Language* 42: 497–525.

Starreveld, P.A., La Heij, W. (1995) Semantic interference, orthographic facilitation, and their interaction in naming tasks. *Journal of Experimental Psychology: Learning, Memory, and Cognition* 21: 686–698.

Talamas, A., Kroll, J.F., Dufour, R. (1999) From form to meaning: stages in the acquisition of second language vocabulary. *Bilingualism: Language and Cognition* 2: 45–58.

Chapter 9, *Sociolinguistics*

Ball, M., Rahilly, J. (1999) *Phonetics: The Science of Speech*. London: Arnold.

Bell, R.T. (1976) *Sociolinguistics: Goals, Approaches and Problems*. London: Batsford.

Bex, A.R., Watts, R. (eds) (1999) *Standard English: The Widening Debate*. London: Routledge.

Cameron, D. (1995) *Verbal Hygiene*. London: Routledge.

Celce-Murcia, M., Brinton, D.M., Goodwin, J.M. (1996) *Teaching Pronunciation*. Cambridge: Cambridge University Press.

Chambers, J.K. (1995) *Sociolinguistic Theory: Linguistic Variation and Its Social Significance*. Oxford: Blackwell.

Chambers, J.K., Trudgill, P. (1998) *Dialectology* (second edition). Cambridge: Cambridge University Press.

Coates, J. (1993) *Women, Men and Language* (second edition). London: Longman.

Coates, J., Cameron, D. (eds) (1986) *Women in Their Speech Communities*. London: Longman.

Coulmas, F. (1997) *The Handbook of Sociolinguistics*. Oxford: Blackwell.

Coupland, N., Jaworski, A. (1997) *Sociolinguistics: A Reader and Coursebook*. Basingstoke: Macmillan.

Crawford, M. (1995) *Talking Difference: On Gender and Language*. London: Sage.

Downes, W. (1984) *Language and Society*. London: Fontana.

Foulkes, P., Docherty, G.J. (1999) *Urban Voices: Accent Studies in the British Isles*. London: Arnold.

Holm, J. (1988, 1989) *Pidgins and Creoles* (two volumes). Cambridge: Cambridge University Press.

Holms, J. (2001) *An Introduction to Sociolinguistics* (second edition). London: Longman.

Hudson, R. (1996) *Sociolinguistics* (second edition). Cambridge: Cambridge University Press.

Jackson, H., Stockwell, P. (1996) *An Introduction to the Nature and Functions of Language*. Cheltenham: Nelson Thornes.

Kochman, T. (1981) *Black and White Styles in Conflict*. Chicago, IL: University of Chicago Press.

Labov, W. (1972) *Language in the Inner City: Studies in the Black English Vernacular*. Philadelphia, PA: University of Pennsylvania Press.

Labov, W. (1994) *Principles of Linguistic Change: Volume 1 Internal Factors*. Oxford: Basil Blackwell.

Labov, W. (2001) *Principles of Linguistic Change: Volume 2 Social Factors*. Oxford: Basil Blackwell.

Lippi-Green, R. (1997) *English with an Accent: Language, Ideology and Discrimination in the United States*. London: Routledge.

Kerswill, P., Llamas, C., Upton, C. (1999) The First SuRE Moves: early steps towards a large dialect project. *Leeds Studies in English Volume XXX*: 257–269.

Llamas, C. (2000) Middlesbrough English: convergent and divergent trends in a 'part of Britain with no identity'. *Leeds Working Papers in Linguistics and Phonetics* 8.

Llamas, C. (2001) The sociolinguistic profiling of (r) in Middlesbrough English. In Van de Velde, H., van Hout, R. (eds). *r-atics: Sociolinguistic, Phonetic and Phonological Characteristics of /r/*. Brussels: ILVP; 123–139.

Mills, S. (1995) *Language and Gender*. London: Longman.

Milroy, J. (1992) *Linguistic Variation and Change: On the Historical Sociolinguistics of English*. Oxford: Blackwell.

Milroy, J., Milroy, L. (eds) (1993) *Real English: The Grammar of English Dialects in the British Isles*. London: Longman.

Milroy, J., Milroy, L. (1999) *Authority in Language: Investigating Standard English* (third edition). London: Routledge.

Milroy, L. (1987) *Language and Social Networks* (second edition). Oxford: Basil Blackwell.

Pennycook, A. (1994) *The Cultural Politics of English as an International Language*. London: Longman.

Romaine, S. (1988) *Pidgin and Creole Languages*. London: Longman.

Sebba, M. (1997) *Contact Languages: Pidgins and Creoles*. London: Macmillan.

Stockwell, P. (2002) *Sociolinguistics: A Resource Book for Students*. London: Routledge.

Trudgill, P. (1983) *Sociolinguistics: An Introduction to Language and Society* (revised edition). Harmondsworth: Penguin.

Wardhaugh, R. (1998) *An Introduction to Sociolinguistics* (third edition). Oxford: Blackwell.

Wolfram, W., Schilling-Estes, N. (1998) *American English: Dialects and Variation*. Oxford: Blackwell.

Chapter 10, *Focus on the Language Learner: Motivation, Styles and Strategies*

Alison, J. (1993) *Not Bothered? Motivating Reluctant Language Learners in Key Stage 4*. London: CILT.

Benson, P. (2001) *Teaching and Researching: Autonomy in Language Learning*. Harlow: Pearson.

Brown, H.D. (1994) *Teaching by Principles*. Englewood Cliffs, NJ: Prentice-Hall.

Chamot, A.U. (1987) The learning strategies of ESL students. In Wenden, A., Rubin, J. (eds). *Learner Strategies in Language Learning*. Englewood Cliffs, NJ: Prentice-Hall; 71–84.

Clément, R. (1980) Ethnicity, contact and communicative competence in a second language. In Giles, H., Robinson, W.P., Smith, P.M. (eds). *Language: Social Psychological Perspectives*, Oxford: Pergamon; 147–154.

Clément, R., Gardner, R. (2001) Second language mastery. In Giles, H., Robinson, W.P. (eds). *The New Handbook of Language and Social Psychology* (second edition). New York, NY: John Wiley & Sons; 489–504.

Clément, R., Dörnyei, Z., Noels, K.A. (1994) Motivation, self-confidence and group cohesion in the foreign language classroom. *Language Learning* 44: 417–448.

Cohen, A.D. (1990) *Language Learning: Insights for Learners, Teachers, and Researchers*. New York, NY: Newbury House/Harper & Row.

Cohen, A.D. (1998) *Strategies in Learning and Using a Second Language*. Harlow: Longman.

Corno, L., Kanfer, R. (1993) The role of volition in learning and performance. *Review of Research in Education* 19: 301–341.

Covington, M. (1999) Caring about learning: the nature and nurturing of subject-matter appreciation. *Educational Psychologist* 34: 127–136.

Dörnyei, Z. (1995) On the teachability of communication strategies. *TESOL Quarterly* 29: 55–85.

Dörnyei, Z. (2001a) *Teaching and Researching Motivation*. Harlow: Longman.

Dörnyei, Z. (2001b). *Motivational Strategies in the Language Classroom*. Cambridge: Cambridge University Press.

Dörnyei, Z., Csizér, K. (1998) Ten commandments for motivating language learners: results of an empirical study. *Language Teaching Research* 2: 203–229.

Dörnyei, Z., Scott, M.L. (1997) Communication strategies in a second language: definitions and taxonomies. *Language Learning* 47: 173–210.

Dörnyei, Z., Skehan, P. (in press). Individual differences in second language learning. In Doughty, C.J., Long, M.H. (eds). *Handbook of Second Language Acquisition*. Oxford: Blackwell.

Ehrman, M.E. (1996) *Understanding Second Language Learning Difficulties*. Thousand Oaks, CA: Sage.

Faerch, C., Kasper, G. (1983) Plans and strategies in foreign language communication. In Faerch, C., Kasper, G. (eds). *Strategies in Interlanguage Communication*. London: Longman; 20–60.

Gardner, R.C. (1985) *Social Psychology and Second Language Learning: The Role of Attitudes and Motivation*. London: Edward Arnold.

Kasper, G., Kellerman, E. (1997) *Communication Strategies: Psycholinguistic and Sociolinguistic Perspectives*. Harlow: Longman.

Kuhl, J. (1987) Action control: the maintenance of motivational states. In Halish, F., Kuhl, J. (eds). *Motivation, Intention, and Volition*. Berlin: Springer; 279–291.

Noels, K.A. (2001) Learning Spanish as a second language: learners' orientations and perceptions of their teachers' communication style. *Language Learning* 51: 107–144.

Noels, K.A., Clément, R., Pelletier, L.G. (1999) Perceptions of teachers' communicative style and students' intrinsic and extrinsic motivation. *Modern Language Journal* 83: 23–34.

Oxford, R.L. (1990) *Language Learning Strategies: What Every Teacher Should Know*. New York, NY: Newbury House/Harper Collins.

Oxford, R.L. (1995) Style Analysis Survey (SAS): assessing your own learning and working styles. In Reid, J.M. (ed.). *Learning Styles in the ESL/EFL Classroom*. Boston, MA: Heinle & Heinle; 208–215.

Oxford, R.L., Shearin, J. (1994) Language learning motivation: expanding the theoretical framework. *Modern Language Journal* 78: 12–28.

Poulisse, N. (1990) *The Use of Compensatory Strategies by Dutch Learners of English*. Dordrecht: Foris.

Reid, J.M. (ed.) (1995) *Learning Styles in the ESL/EFL Classroom*. Boston, MA: Heinle & Heinle.

Rubin, J. (1975) What the 'good language learner' can teach us. *TESOL Quarterly* 9: 41–51.

Schumann, J.H. (1997) *The Neurobiology of Affect in Language*. Oxford: Blackwell.

Singleton, D. (2001) Age and second language acquisition. *Annual Review of Applied Linguistics* 21: 77–89.

Tarone, E., Yule, G. (1989) *Focus on the Learner*. Oxford: Oxford University Press.

Ushioda, E. (1996) *Learner Autonomy 5: The Role of Motivation*. Dublin: Authentik.

Weaver, S.J., Cohen, A.D. (1997) *Strategies-based Instruction: A Teacher-training Manual*. Minneapolis, MN: Center for Advanced Research on Language Acquisition, University of Minnesota.

Williams, M. (1994) Motivation in foreign and second language learning: an interactive perspective. *Educational and Child Psychology* 11: 77–84.

Williams, M., Burden, R. (1997) *Psychology for Language Teachers*. Cambridge: Cambridge University Press.

Chapter 11, *Listening*

Anderson, A., Lynch, T. (1988) *Listening*. Oxford: Oxford University Press.

Anderson J.R. (1985) *Cognitive Psychology and Its Implications*. New York, NY: Freeman.

Barsalou, L. (1999) Language comprehension: archival memory or preparation for situated action? *Discourse Processes* 28: 61–80.

Berne, J.E. (1996) Current trends in L2 listening comprehension research: are researchers and language instructors on the same wavelength? *Minnesota Language Review* 24: 6–10.

Berne, J.E. (1998) Examining the relationship between L2 listening research, pedagogical theory, and practice. *Foreign Language Annals* 31: 169–190.

Bond, Z., Garnes, S. (1980) Misperceptions of fluent speech. In Cole, R. (ed.). *Perception and Production of Fluent Speech*. Hillsdale, NJ: Erlbaum; 115–132.

Bremer, K., Roberts, C., Vasseur M., Simonot, M., Broeder, P. (1996) *Achieving Understanding: Discourse in International Encounters*. London: Longman.

Brown, G. (1986) Investigating listening comprehension in context. *Applied Linguistics* 7: 284–302.

Brown, G. (1990) *Listening to Spoken English* (second edition). London: Longman.

Brown, G. (1995a) Dimensions of difficulty in listening comprehension. In Mendelsohn, D.J., Rubin, J. (eds) *A Guide for the Teaching of Second Language Listening*. San Diego, CA: Dominie Press; 59–73.

Brown, G. (1995b) *Speakers, Listeners and Communication*. Cambridge: Cambridge University Press.

Brown, G., Anderson, A., Shillcock, R., Yule, G. (1984) *Teaching Talk*. Cambridge: Cambridge University Press.

Brown, G., Yule, G. (1983) *Teaching the Spoken Language: An Approach Based on the Analysis of Spoken English*. New York: Cambridge University Press.

Byrnes, H. (1984) The role of listening comprehension: a theoretical base. *Foreign Language Annals* 17: 317–329.

Chamot, A.U. (1987) The learning strategies of ESL students. In Wenden, A., Rubin, J. (eds). *Learning Strategies in Language Learning*. Englewood Cliffs, NJ: Prentice-Hall; 71–83.

Chaudron, C., Richards, J. (1986) The effect of discourse markers on the comprehension of lectures. *Applied Linguistics* 7: 113–127.

Cutler, A. (1997) The comparative perspective on spoken language processing. *Speech Communication* 21: 3–15.

Delabatie, B., Bradley, D. (1995) Resolving word boundaries in spoken French: native and nonnative strategies. *Applied Psycholinguistics* 16: 59–81.

Field, J. (1998) Skills and strategies: towards a new methodology for listening. *ELT Journal* 52: 110–118.

Flowerdew, J. (1994) Research of relevance to second language lecture comprehension – an overview. In Flowerdew, J. (ed.). *Academic Listening: Research Perspectives*. Cambridge: Cambridge University Press; 7–29.

Geddes, M., White, R. (1979) The use of semi-scripted simulated authentic speech and listening comprehension. *British Journal of Language Teaching* 17: 137–145.

Kasper, G. (1997) Beyond reference. In Kasper, G., Kellerman, E. (eds). *Communicative Strategies: Psycholinguistic and Sociolinguistic Perspectives*. London: Longman; 345–360.

Kasper, G., Kellerman, E. (eds). (1997) *Communication Strategies: Psycholinguistic and Sociolinguistic Perspectives*. London: Longman.

Licklider, J., Miller, G. (1951) The perception of speech. In Stevens, S. (ed.). *Handbook of Experimental Psychology*. New York, NY: Wiley.

Lynch, T. (1995) The development of interactive listening strategies in second language academic settings. In Mendelsohn, D.J., Rubin, J. (eds). *A Guide for the Teaching of Second Language Listening*. San Diego, CA: Dominie Press; 166–185.

Lynch, T. (1996) *Communication in the Language Classroom*. Oxford: Oxford University Press.

Lynch, T. (1997) Life in the slow lane: observations of a limited L2 listener. *System* 25: 385–398.

Mendelsohn, D.J. (1994) *Learning to Listen: A Strategy-based Approach for the Second-Language Learner*. San Diego, CA: Dominie Press.

Mendelsohn, D.J. (1998) Teaching listening. *Annual Review of Applied Linguistics* 18: 81–101.

Mendelsohn, D.J. (2001) Listening Comprehension: We've Come a Long Way, but . . . . Proceedings of Research Symposiums held at the TESL Ontario Conference, Toronto, November 2000. *CONTACT* 27 (Special issue): 33–40.

Mendelsohn, D.J., Rubin, J. (eds) (1995) *A Guide to the Teaching of Second Language Listening*. San Diego, CA: Dominie Press.

Ohta, A. (2000) Rethinking interaction in second language acquisition: developmentally appropriate assistance in the zone of proximal development and the acquisition of L2 grammar. In Lantolf, J. (ed.). *Sociocultural Theory and Second Language Learning*. Oxford: Oxford University Press; 51–78.

O'Malley, J.M., Chamot, A.U. (1990) *Learning Strategies in Second Language Acquisition*. Cambridge: Cambridge University Press.

O'Malley, J.M., Chamot, A.U., Stewner-Manzanares, G., Russo, R.P., Kupper, L. (1985) Learning strategies used by beginning and intermediate ESL students. *Language Learning* 35: 21–46.

Oxford, R. (1990) *Language Learning Strategies: What Every Teacher should Know.* New York, NY: Newbury House.

Porter, D., Roberts, J. (1981) Authentic listening activities. *ELT Journal* **36**: 37–47.

Richards, J.C. (1983) Listening comprehension: approach, design, procedure. *TESOL Quarterly* **17**: 219–240.

Rings, L. (1986) Authentic language and authentic conversational texts. *Foreign Language Annals* **19**: 203–208.

Ross, S. (1997) An introspective analysis of listener inferencing on a second language listening test. In Kasper, G., Kellerman, E. (eds). *Communication Strategies: Psycholinguistic and Sociolinguistic Perspectives.* London: Longman; 216–237.

Rost, M. (1990) *Listening in Language Learning.* London: Longman.

Rubin, J. (1975) What the 'good language learner' can teach us. *TESOL Quarterly* **9**: 41–51.

Rubin, J. (1994) A review of second language listening research. *Modern Language Journal* **78**: 199–221.

Shannon, C., Weaver, W. (1949) *The Mathematical Theory of Communication.* Urbana, IL: University of Illinois.

Sperber, D., Wilson, D. (1995) *Relevance: Communication and Cognition* (second edition). Oxford: Blackwell.

Thompson, I., Rubin, J. (1996) Can strategy instruction improve listening comprehension? *Foreign Language Annals* **29**: 331–342.

Tsui, A., Fullilove, J. (1998) Bottom-up or top-down processing as a discriminator of L2 listening performance. *Applied Linguistics* **19**: 432–451.

van Lier, L. (1996) *Interaction in the Language Curriculum: Awareness, Autonomy and Authenticity.* London: Longman.

van Lier, L. (2000) From input to affordance: social-interactive learning from an ecological perspective. In Lantolf, J. (ed.). *Sociocultural Theory and Second Language Learning.* Oxford: Oxford University Press; 245–259.

Wenden, A., Rubin, J. (eds.) (1987) *Learning Strategies in Language Learning.* Englewood Cliffs, NJ: Prentice Hall.

Wesche, M., Ready, D. (1985) Foreigner talk in the university classroom. In Gass, S., Madden, C. (eds). *Input in Second Language Acquisition.* Rowley, MA: Newbury House; 89–114.

White, G. (1998) *Listening.* Oxford: Oxford University Press.

Wu, Y. (1998) What do tests of listening comprehension test? A retrospection study of EFL test-takers performing a multiple-choice task. *Language Testing* **15**: 21–44.

Yule, G., Powers, M. (1994) Investigating the communicative outcomes of task-based interaction. *System* **22**: 81–91.

Chapter 12, *Speaking and Pronunciation*

Abercrombie, D. (1972) Paralanguage. In Laver, J., Hutcheson, S. (eds). *Communication in Face-to-face Interaction.* Harmondsworth: Penguin; 64–70.

Bowen, T., Marks, J. (1992) *The Pronunciation Book. Student-centred Activities for Pronunciation Work.* London: Longman.

Brazil, D. (1997) *The Communicative Value of Intonation in English.* Cambridge: Cambridge University Press.

Brazil, D., Coulthard, M., Johns, C. (1980) *Discourse Intonation and Language Teaching.* London: Longman.

Burns, A. (2001) Analysing spoken discourse: Implications for TESOL. In Burns, A., Coffin, C. (eds). *Analysing English in a Global Context*. London: Routledge; 123–148.

Burns, A., Joyce, H. (1997) *Focus on Speaking*. Sydney: National Centre for English Language Teaching and Research.

Burns, A., Joyce, H., Gollin, S. (1996) *'I see what you mean' Using Spoken Discourse in the Classroom: A Handbook for Teachers*. Sydney: National Centre for English Language Teaching and Research.

Carter, R. (1997). Speaking Englishes, speaking cultures, using CANCODE. *Prospect* 12: 4–11.

Carter, R., McCarthy, M. (1997) *Exploring Spoken English*. Cambridge: Cambridge University Press.

Celce-Murcia, M., Brinton, D., Goodwin, J. (1996) *Teaching Pronunciation. A Reference for Teachers of English to Speakers of Other Languages*. Cambridge and New York, NY: Cambridge University Press.

Cook, G. (1989) *Discourse. (Language Teaching: A Scheme for Teacher Education)*. Oxford: Oxford University Press.

Dalton, C., Seidlhofer, B. (1994) *Pronunciation (Language Teaching: A Scheme for Teacher Education)*. Oxford: Oxford University Press.

de Silva Joyce, H., Burns, A. (1999) *Focus on Grammar*. Sydney: National Centre for English Language Teaching and Research.

Eggins, S., Slade, D. (1997) *Analysing Casual Conversation*. London: Cassell.

Gilbert, J. (1993) *Clear Speech. Pronunciation and Listening Comprehension in American English* (second edition). Cambridge: Cambridge University Press.

Grice, H. (1975) Logic and conversation. In Cole, P., Morgan, J. (eds). *Syntax and Semantics 3: Speech Acts*. New York, NY: Academic; 41–58.

Halliday, M.A.K. (1989) *Spoken and Written Language*. Oxford: Oxford University Press.

Hancock, M. (1996) *Pronunciation Games*. Cambridge: Cambridge University Press.

Jenkins, J. (2000) *The Phonology of English as an International Language*. Oxford: Oxford University Press.

Labov, W., Waletzky, J. (1967) Narrative analysis: oral versions of personal experiences. In Helm, J. (ed.). *Essays on the Verbal and Visual Arts*. American Ethnological Society, Proceedings of the Spring Meeting 1966. Washington, DC: University of Washington Press; 12–44.

Laroy, C. (1995) *Pronunciation*. Oxford: Oxford University Press.

Levelt, W.J.M. (1989) *Speaking: From Intention to Articulation*. Cambridge, MA: MIT Press.

Martin, J.R. (2001) Language, register and genre. In Burns, A., Coffin, C. (eds). *Analysing English in a Global Context*. London: Routledge; 149–166.

Martin, J.R., Rothery, J. (1980–1981) *Writing Project Reports 1 & 2* (Working Papers in Linguistics). Department of Linguistics, Sydney University.

McCarthy, M. (1998) *Spoken Language and Applied Linguistics*. Cambridge: Cambridge University Press.

McCarthy, M., Carter, R. (1994) *Language as Discourse: Perspectives for Language Teachers*. Cambridge: Cambridge University Press.

O'Connor, J.D., Arnold, G.F. (1973) *Intonation of Colloquial English* (second edition). London: Longman.

Painter, C. (2001) Understanding genre and register: implications for language teaching. In Burns, A., Coffin, C. (eds). *Analysing English in a Global Context*. London: Routledge; 167–180.

Riggenbach, H. (1999) *Discourse Analysis in the Classroom. Volume 1. The Spoken Language.* Ann Arbor, MI: The University of Michigan Press.

Sacks, H., Schegloff, E., Jefferson, G. (1974) A simplest systemic for the organisation of turn-taking for conversation. *Language* 50: 696–735.

Seidlhofer, B. (2001) Pronunciation. In Carter, R., Nunan, D. (eds). *The Cambridge Guide to Teaching English to Speakers of Other Languages.* Cambridge: Cambridge University Press; 56–65.

Sinclair, J., Coulthard, R.M. (1975) *Towards an Analysis of Discourse.* Oxford: Oxford University Press.

Slade, D. (1997) Stories and gossip in English: the micro-structure of casual talk. *Prospect* 12: 43–71.

Widdowson, H.G. (1979) *Explorations in Applied Linguistics 1.* Oxford: Oxford University Press.

Chapter 13, *Reading*

Alderson, J.C. (1984) Reading in a foreign language: a reading problem or a language problem? In Alderson, J.C., Urquhart, A.H. (eds). *Reading in a Foreign Language.* London: Longman; 1–24.

Alderson, J. (2000) *Reading Assessment.* New York, NY: Cambridge University Press.

Anderson, N.J. (1991) Individual differences in strategy use in second language reading and testing. *Modern Language Journal* 75: 460–472.

Anderson, N.J. (1999). *Exploring Second Language Reading.* Boston, MA: Heinle & Heinle.

Baker, L., Brown, A.L. (1984) Metacognitive skills and reading. In Pearson, P.D., Kamil, M., Barr, R., Mosenthal, P. (eds) *Handbook of Reading Research, Volume I.* New York: Longman; 353–394.

Bensoussan, M., Laufer, B. (1984) Lexical guessing in context in EFL reading comprehension. *Journal of Research in Reading* 7: 15–32.

Bensoussan, M., Sim, D., Weiss, R. (1984) The effect of dictionary usage on ESL text performance compared with student and teacher attitudes and expectations. *Reading in a Foreign Language* 2: 262–276.

Bernhardt, E.B. (1991) *Reading Development in a Second Language: Theoretical, Empirical, and Classroom Perspectives.* Norwood, NJ: Ablex.

Bernhardt, E.B., Kamil, M.L. (1995) Interpreting relationships between L1 and L2 reading: consolidating the linguistic threshold and the linguistic interdependence hypotheses. *Applied Linguistics* 16: 15–34.

Block, E. (1986) The comprehension strategies of second language readers. *TESOL Quarterly* 20: 463–494.

Brown, A.L., Armbruster, B.B., Baker, L. (1986) The role of metacognition in reading and studying. In Orasanu, J. (ed.). *Reading Comprehension: From Research to Practice.* Hillsdale, NJ: Erlbaum; 49–75.

Carrell, P.L. (1984a) Evidence of a formal schema in second language comprehension. *Language Learning* 34: 87–112.

Carrell, P.L. (1984b) The effects of rhetorical organization on ESL readers. *TESOL Quarterly* 18: 441–469.

Carrell, P.L. (1985) Facilitating ESL reading by teaching text structure. *TESOL Quarterly* 19: 727–752.

Carrell, P.L. (1991) Second language reading: reading ability or language proficiency? *Applied Linguistics* 12: 159–179.

Carrell, P.L. (1992) Awareness of text structure: effects on recall. *Language Learning* **42**: 1–20.

Carrell, P.L., Devine, J., Eskey, D.E. (1988) *Interactive Approaches to Second Language Reading*. Cambridge: Cambridge University Press.

Carrell, P.L., Pharis, B.G., Liberto, J.C. (1989) Metacognitive strategy training for ESL reading. *TESOL Quarterly* **23**: 647–678.

Carrell, P.L., Wise, T.E. (1998) The relationship between prior knowledge and topic interest in second language reading. *Studies in Second Language Acquisition* **20**: 285–309.

Carver, R. (1992) Reading rate: Theory, research, and practical implications. *Journal of Reading* **36**: 84–95.

Cummins, J. (1979) Linguistic interdependence and the development of bilingual children. *Review of Educational Research* **49**: 222–251.

Day, R. (ed.). (1993) *New Ways in Teaching Reading*. Washington, DC: TESOL.

Day, R.R., Bamford, J. (1998) *Extensive Reading in the Second Language Classroom*. New York, NY: Cambridge University Press.

Elley, W.G. (1991) Acquiring literacy in a second language: the effect of book-based programs. *Language Learning* **41**: 375–411.

Favreau, M., Segalowitz, N.S. (1983) Automatic and controlled processes in the first- and second-language reading of fluent bilinguals. *Memory & Cognition* **11**: 565–574.

Feldman, A., Healy, A.F. (1998) Effect of first language phonological configuration on lexical acquisition in a second language. In Healy, A.F., Bourne, A.E. Jr. (eds). *Foreign Language Learning: Psycholinguistic Studies on Training and Retention*. Mahwah, NJ: Erlbaum; 57–76.

Feldman, L.B., Turvey, M.T. (1983). Word recognition in Serbo-Croatian is phonologically analytic. *Journal of Experimental Psychology: Human Perception and Performance* **9**: 414–420.

Floyd, P., Carrell, P.L. (1987) Effects on ESL reading of teaching cultural content schemata. *Language Learning* **37**: 89–108.

Gathercole, S.E., Baddeley, A.D. (1989) Evaluation of the role of phonological STM in the development of vocabulary in children: a longitudinal study. *Journal of Memory and Language* **28**: 200–213.

Genesee, F., Upshur, J. (1996) *Classroom-based Evaluation in Second Language Education*. Cambridge: Cambridge University Press.

Geva, E. (1983) Facilitating reading comprehension through flowcharting. *Reading Research Quarterly* **18**: 384–405.

Geva, E., Wade-Woolley, L., Shany, M. (1997) Development of reading efficiency in first and second language. *Scientific Studies of Reading* **1**: 119–144.

Grabe, W., Stoller, F. (2001) Reading for academic purposes: guidelines for the ESL/EFL teacher. In Celce-Murcia, M. (ed.). *Teaching English as a Second or Foreign Language* (third edition). New York, NY: Heinle & Heinle; 187–203.

Grabe, W., Stoller, F. (in press) *Teaching and Researching Reading*. New York, NY: Longman.

Green, D.W., Meara, P. (1987) The effects of script on visual search. *Second Language Research* **3**: 102–117.

Grellet, F. (1981) *Developing Reading Skills*. New York: Cambridge University Press.

Hafiz, F. M., Tudor, I. (1989) Extensive reading and the development of language skills. *ELT Journal* **43**: 4–13.

Haynes, M. (1984). Patterns and perils of guessing in second language reading. In Handscombe, J., Orem, R., Taylor, B. (eds). *On TESOL '83: The Question of Control*. Washington, DC: TESOL; 163–176.

Hazenberg, S., Hulstijn, J.H. (1996) Defining a minimal receptive second-language vocabulary for non-native university students: an empirical investigation. *Applied Linguistics* 17: 145–163.

Hirsch, D., Nation, P. (1992) What vocabulary size is needed to read unsimplified texts for pleasure? *Reading in a Foreign Language* 8: 689–696.

Hu, H.M., Nation, P. (2000) Unknown vocabulary density and reading comprehension. *Reading in a Foreign Language* 13: 403–430.

Hulstijn, J.H. (1993) When do foreign-language readers look up the meaning of unfamiliar words? The influence of task and learner variables. *Modern Language Journal* 77: 139–147.

Jensen, L. (1986) Advanced reading skills in a comprehensive course. In Dubin, F., Eskey, D., Grabe, W. (eds). *Teaching Second Language Reading for Academic Purposes*. Reading, MA: Addison-Wesley; 103–124.

Johnson, P. (1981) Effects on reading comprehension of language complexity and cultural background knowledge of a text. *TESOL Quarterly* 15: 169–181.

Kamil, M., Mosenthal, P., Pearson, P.D., Barr, R. (eds) (2000) *Handbook of Reading Research*. Volume III. Mahwah, NJ: Lawrence Erlbaum.

Kern, R.G. (1989). Second language reading strategy instruction: its effects on comprehension and word inference ability. *Modern Language Journal* 73: 135–148.

Knight, S. (1994). Dictionary use while reading: the effects on comprehension and vocabulary acquisition for students of different verbal abilities. *Modern Language Journal* 78: 285–299.

Koda, K. (1989) The effects of transferred vocabulary knowledge on the development of L2 reading proficiency. *Foreign Language Annals* 22: 529–542.

Koda, K. (1996) L2 word recognition research: a critical review. *Modern Language Journal* 80: 450–460.

Laufer, B. (1989) What percentage of text-lexis is essential for comprehension? In Lauren, C., Nordman, M. (eds). *Special Language: From Humans Thinking to Thinking Machines*. Clevedon and Philadelphia, PA: Multilingual Matters; 316–323.

Lee, J-W., Schallert, D.L. (1997) The relative contribution of L2 language proficiency and L1 reading ability to L2 reading performance: a test of the threshold hypothesis in an EFL context. *TESOL Quarterly* 31: 713–739.

Mason, B., Krashen, S. (1997) Extensive reading in English as a foreign language. *System* 25: 91–102.

Mikulecky, B. (1990) *A Short Course in Teaching Reading Skills*. Reading, MA: Addison-Wesley.

Mondria, J.-A., Wit-de Boer, M. (1991) The effects of contextual richness on the guessability and the retention of words in a foreign language. *Applied Linguistics* 12: 249–267.

Muljani, D., Koda, K., Moates, D.R. (1998) The development of word recognition in a second language. *Applied Psycholingustics* 19: 99–113.

Paris, S.G., Lipson, M.Y., Wixson, K.K. (1983) Becoming a strategic reader. *Contemporary Educational Psychology* 8: 293–316.

Paris, S.G., Wasik, B.A., Turner, J.C. (1991) The development of strategic readers. In Barr, R., Kamil, M.L., Mosenthal, P.B., Pearson, P.D. (eds). *Handbook of Reading Research, Volume II*. New York: Longman; 609–640.

Pressley, M. (1998) *Reading Instruction That Works*. New York: Guilford.

Pritchard, R.H. (1990) The effects of cultural schemata on reading processing strategies. *Reading Research Quarterly* 25: 273–295.

Raymond, P.M. (1993) The effects of structure strategy training on the recall of expository prose for university students reading French as a second language. *Modern Language Journal* 77: 445–458.

Ryan, A., Meara, P. (1991) The case of the invisible vowels: Arabic speakers reading English words. *Reading in a Foreign Language* 7: 531–540.

Segalowitz, N.S., Segalowitz, S.J. (1993) Skilled performance, practice, and the differentiation of speed-up from automatization effects: evidence from second language word recognition. *Applied Psycholinguistics* 14: 369–385.

Silberstein, S. (1994) *Techniques and Resources in Teaching Reading*. New York, NY: Oxford University Press.

Steffensen, M.S., Joag-dev, C., Anderson, R.C. (1979) A cross-cultural perspective on reading comprehension. *Reading Research Quarterly* 1: 10–29.

Tang, G. (1992) The effect of graphic representation of knowledge structures on ESL reading comprehension. *Studies in Second Language Acquisition* 14: 177–195.

Thompson, G.B., Nicholson, T. (eds). (1999) *Learning to Read: Beyond Phonics and Whole Language*. New York: Teacher's College Press.

Urquhart, S., Weir, C. (1998) *Reading in a Foreign Language: Process, Product and Practice*. New York: Longman.

Vacca, R., Vacca. J. (1999) *Content Area Reading* (sixth edition). New York, NY: Longman.

Weigle, S.C., Jensen L. (1996) Reading rate improvement in university ESL classes. *The CATESOL Journal* 9: 55–71.

Chapter 14, *Writing*

Bakhtin, M. (1986) (McGee, V.W., trans., Emerson, C., Holquist, M. (eds)). *Speech Genres and Other Late Essays*. Austin, TX: University of Texas Press.

Bazerman, C. (1988) *Shaping Written Knowledge: The Genre and Activity of the Experimental Article in Science*. Madison, WI: University of Wisconsin Press.

Belcher, D., Braine, G. (eds) (1995) *Academic Writing in a Second Language: Essays on Research and Pedagogy*. Norwood, NJ: Ablex.

Benesch, S. (2001) Critical pragmatism: a politics of L2 composition. In Silva, T., Matsuda, P.K. (eds). *On Second Language Writing*. Mahwah, NJ: Erlbaum; 161–172.

Berger, P.L., Luckmann, T. (1966) *The Social Construction of Reality: A Treatise in the Sociology of Knowledge*. Garden City, NY: Doubleday.

Berkenkotter, C., Huckin, T. (1995) *Genre Knowledge in Disciplinary Communication: Cognition/Culture/Power*. Hillsdale, NJ: Lawrence Erlbaum Associates.

Blanton, L. (1995) Elephants and paradigms: conversations about teaching writing. *College ESL* 5: 1–21.

Burke, K. (1969) *A Grammar of Motives*. Berkeley, CA: University of California Press.

Canale, M., Swain, M. (1980) Theoretical bases of communicative approaches to second language teaching and testing. *Applied Linguistics* 1: 1–47.

Carrell, P. (1982) Cohesion is not coherence. *TESOL Quarterly* 16: 479–488.

Connor, U. (1996) *Contrastive Rhetoric: Cross-cultural Aspects of Second Language Writing*. New York, NY: Cambridge University Press.

Connor, U., Johns, A. (eds) (1990) *Coherence in Writing: Research and Pedagogical Perspectives*. Alexandria, VA: TESOL.

Connor, U., Lauer, J.M. (1985) Understanding persuasive essay writing: linguistic/rhetorical approach. *Text* **5**: 309–326.

Dykstra, G., Paulston, C. (1967) Guided composition. *English Language Teaching* **21**: 136–141.

Ede, L., Lunsford, A. (1984) Audience addressed/audience invoked: the role of audience in composition theory and pedagogy. *College Composition and Communication* **35**: 155–171.

Elbow, P. (1987) Closing my eyes as I speak: an argument for ignoring audience. *College English* **49**: 50–69.

Ellis, R. (1994) *The Study of Second Language Acquisition*. Oxford: Oxford University Press.

Ferris, D., Hedgcock, J. (1998) *Teaching ESL Composition: Purpose, Process, and Practice*. Mahwah, NJ: Erlbaum.

Flower, L. (1979) Writer-based prose: a cognitive basis for problems in writing. *College English* **41**: 19–37.

Flower, L., Hayes, J.R. (1981) A cognitive process theory of writing. *College Composition and Communication* **32**: 365–387.

Fries, C. (1945) *Teaching and Learning English as a Second Language*. Ann Arbor, MI: University of Michigan Press.

Goffman, E. (1959) *The Presentation of Self in Everyday Life*. New York, NY: Anchor/Doubleday.

Gosden, H. (1992) Research writing and NNSs: from the editors. *Journal of Second Language Writing* **1**: 123–139.

Grabe, W., Kaplan, R.B. (1996) *Theory and Practice of Writing: An Applied Linguistic Perspective*. London: Longman.

Halliday, M.A.K. (1973) *Explorations in the Functions of Language*. London: Arnold.

Halliday, M.A.K., Hasan, R. (1976) *Cohesion in English*. London: Longman.

Hamp-Lyons, L. (ed.) (1991) *Assessing ESL Writing in Academic Contexts*. Norwood, NJ: Ablex.

Hamp-Lyons, L. (2001) Fourth generation writing assessment. In Silva, T., Matsuda, P.K. (eds). *On Second Language Writing*. Mahwah, NJ: Erlbaum; 117–127.

Hamp-Lyons, L., Kroll, B. (1996) Issues in ESL writing assessment: an overview. *College ESL* **6**: 52–72.

Harklau, L. (2000) Writing Literacy into Second Language Acquisition Theory: Lessons from US High School Classrooms. Paper presented at the Symposium on Second Language Writing, Purdue University, West Lafayette, Indiana, USA, September.

Horowitz, D. (1986) Process, not product: less than meets the eye. *TESOL Quarterly* **20**: 141–144.

Hyland, K. (2000) *Disciplinary Discourses: Social Interactions in Academic Writing*. New York, NY: Addison-Wesley Longman.

Hyon, S. (1996) Genre in three traditions: implications for ESL. *TESOL Quarterly* **30**: 693–722.

Ivanic, R. (1998) *Writing and Identity: The Discoursal Construction of Identity in Academic Writing*. Amsterdam: John Benjamins.

Jacobs, H., Zinkgraf, S., Wormuth, D., Hartfiel, V., Hughey, J. (1981) *Testing ESL Composition: A Practical Approach*. Rowley, MA: Newbury House.

Kaplan, R. (1966) Cultural thought patterns in intercultural education. *Language Learning* **16**: 1–20.

Kinneavy, J. (1971) *A Theory of Discourse: The Aims of Discourse*. New York, NY: Norton.

Kobayashi, H., Rinnert, C. (1992) Effects of first language on second language writing: translation versus direct composition. *Language Learning* **42**: 183–215.

Krapels, A.R. (1990) An overview of second language writing process research. In Kroll, B. (ed.). *Second Language Writing: Research Insights for the Classroom*. New York, NY: Cambridge University Press; 37–56.

Kubota, R. (1997) A reevaluation of the uniqueness of Japanese written discourse: implications for contrastive rhetoric. *Written Communication* **14**: 460–480.

Kubota, R. (1998) An investigation of L1–L2 transfer in writing among Japanese university students: implications for contrastive rhetoric. *Journal of Second Language Writing* **7**: 69–100.

Leki, I. (1991) Twenty-five years of contrastive rhetoric: text analysis and writing pedagogies. *TESOL Quarterly* **25**: 123–143.

Leki, I. (1992) *Understanding ESL Writers: A Guide for Teachers*. Portsmouth, NH: Boynton–Cook.

Leki, I. (2000) Writing, literacy, and applied linguistics. *Annual Review of Applied Linguistics* **20**: 99–115.

Leki, I., Silva, T. (eds). *Journal of Second Language Writing*. New York, NY: Elsevier Science. <http://www.jslw.org/>

Manchón, R. (in press). Second language learners' composing strategies: a review of the research. In Manchón, R. (ed.). *Writing in the L2 Classroom: Issues in Research and Pedagogy*. Murcia, Spain: Universidad de Murcia.

Matsuda, P.K. (1997) Contrastive rhetoric in context: a dynamic model of L2 writing. *Journal of Second Language Writing* **6**: 45–60.

Matsuda, P.K. (1998) Situating ESL writing in a cross-disciplinary context. *Written Communication* **15**: 99–121.

Matsuda, P.K. (1999) Composition studies and ESL writing: a disciplinary division of labor. *College Composition and Communication* **50**: 699–721.

Matsuda, P.K. (2001a) Reexamining audiolingualism: on the genesis of reading and writing in L2 studies. In Belcher, D., Hirvela, A. (eds). *Linking Literacies: Perspectives on Second Language Reading/Writing Connections*. Ann Arbor, MI: University of Michigan Press; 84–105.

Matsuda, P.K. (2001b) Voice in Japanese written discourse: implications for second language writing. *Journal of Second Language Writing* **10**: 1–19.

Miller, C. (1984) Genre as social action. *Quarterly Journal of Speech* **70**: 151–167.

Moffett, J. (1968/1983) *Teaching the Universe of Discourse*. Portsmouth, NH: Boynton/Cook.

Mohan, B.A., Lo, W.A. (1985) Academic writing and Chinese students: transfer and developmental factors. *TESOL Quarterly* **19**: 515–534.

Murray, D. (1982) Teaching the other self: the writer's first reader. *College Composition and Communication* **33**: 140–147.

Paulston, C., Dykstra, G. (1973) *Controlled Composition in English as a Second Language*. New York, NY: Regents.

Perelman, C.H. (1982) *The Realm of Rhetoric* (W. Kluback, trans.). Notre Dame, IN: University of Notre Dame Press.

Purves, A. (1988) *Writing across Languages and Cultures: Issues in Contrastive Rhetoric*. Newbury Park, CA: Sage.

Raimes, A. (1983a) Anguish as a second language? Remedies for composition teachers. In Freedman, A., Pringle, I., Yalden, J. (eds). *Learning to Write: First Language/Second Language*. London: Longman; 258–272.

Raimes, A. (1983b) Techniques in Teaching Writing. New York, NY: Oxford University Press.

Raimes, A. (1985) What unskilled writers do as they write: a classroom study of composing. *TESOL Quarterly* 19: 229–258.

Raimes, A. (1991) Out of the woods: emerging traditions in the teaching of writing. *TESOL Quarterly* 25: 407–430.

Reid, J. (1984) The radical outliner and the radical brainstormer: a perspective on composing processes. *TESOL Quarterly* 18: 529–533.

Reid, J.M. (1993) *Teaching ESL Writing*. Englewood Cliff, NJ: Regents/Prentice Hall.

Rivers, W. (1968) *Teaching Foreign Language Skills*. Chicago, IL: University of Chicago Press.

Rose, M. (1980) Rigid rules, inflexible plans, and the stifling of language: a cognitivist analysis of writer's block. *College Composition and Communication* 31: 389–400.

Santos, T. (1988) Professors' reaction to the academic writing of nonnative speaking students. *TESOL Quarterly* 22: 69–90.

Santos, T. (1992) Ideology in composition: L1 and ESL. *Journal of Second Language Writing* 1: 1–15.

Santos, T. (2001) The place of politics in second language writing. In Silva, T., Matsuda, P.K. (eds). *On Second Language Writing*. Mahwah, NJ: Erlbaum; 173–190.

Santos, T., Atkinson, D., Erickson, M., Matsuda, P.K., Silva, T. (2000) On the future of second language writing: a colloquium. *Journal of Second Language Writing* 9: 1–20.

Sasaki, M. (2000) Toward an empirical model of EFL writing processes: an exploratory study. *Journal of Second Language Writing* 9: 259–291.

Severino, C. (1993) The sociopolitical implications of response to second language and second dialect writing. *Journal of Second Language Writing* 2: 181–201.

Silva, T. (1990) Second language composition instruction: developments, issues, and directions in ESL. In Kroll, B. (ed.). *Second Language Writing: Research Insights for the Classroom*. New York, NY: Cambridge University Press; 11–23.

Silva, T., Matsuda, P.K. (eds) (2000) *Landmark Essays on ESL Writing*. Mahwah, NJ: Erlbaum.

Silva, T., Matsuda, P.K. (eds) (2001) *On Second Language Writing*. Mahwah, NJ: Erlbaum.

Silva, T., Brice, C., Reichelt, M. (eds) (1999) *Annotated Bibliography of Scholarship in Second Language Writing: 1993–1997*. Stamford, CT: Ablex.

Spack, R. (1988) Initiating ESL students into the academic discourse community: how far should we go? *TESOL Quarterly* 22: 29–51.

Spack, R. (1997) The rhetorical construction of multilingual students. *TESOL Quarterly* 31: 765–774.

Swales, J. (1990) *Genre Analysis: English in Academic and Research Settings*. New York, NY: Cambridge University Press.

Tannacito, D. (ed.) (1995) *A Guide to Writing in English as a Second or Foreign Language: An Annotated Bibliography of Research and Pedagogy*. Alexandria, VA: Teachers of English to Speakers of Other Languages.

Toulmin, S. (1958) *The Uses of Argument*. Cambridge: Cambridge University Press.

Vann, R., Meyer, D., Lorenz, F. (1984) Error gravity: a study of faculty opinion of ESL errors. *TESOL Quarterly* 18: 427–440.

Weissberg, B. (2000) Developmental relationships in the acquisition of English syntax: writing vs. speech. *Learning and Instruction* **10**: 37–53.

Witte, S., Faigley, L. (1981) Coherence, cohesion, and writing quality. *College Composition and Communication* **32**: 189–204.

Young, R.E., Becker, A.L., Pike, K.L. (1970) *Rhetoric: Discovery and Change.* New York, NY: Harcourt Brace Jovanovich.

Zamel, V. (1993) Questioning academic discourse. *College ESL* **3**: 28–39.

Chapter 15, *Assessment*

Alderson, C. (2000) *Assessing Reading.* Cambridge: Cambridge University Press.

Alderson, J.C., Wall, D. (1993) Does washback exist? *Applied Linguistics* **14**: 115–129.

Alderson, J.C., Hamp-Lyons, L. (1996) TESOL preparation courses: a study of washback. *Language Testing* **13**: 280–297.

Bachman L.F. (1990) *Fundamental Considerations in Language Testing.* Oxford: Oxford University Press.

Bachman, L.F. (2000) Modern language testing at the turn of the century: assuring that what we count counts. *Language Testing* **17**: 1–42.

Bachman, L.F., Palmer, A.S. (1989) The construct validation of self-ratings of communicative language ability. *Language Testing* **6**: 14–25.

Bachman, L.F., Palmer, A.S. (1996) *Language Testing in Practice.* Oxford: Oxford University Press.

Barrs, M. (1992) The Primary Language Record: what we are learning in the UK. In Bouffler, C. (ed.). *Literacy Evaluation: Issues and Practicalities.* Sydney: Primary English Teaching Association; 53–62.

Belanoff, P. (1997) *Portfolios.* Upper Saddle River: Prentice Hall Regents.

Blue, G. (1994) Self-assessment of foreign language skills: does it work? *CLE Working Papers* **3**: 18–35.

Breen, M., Barratt-Pugh, C., Derewianka, B., House, H., Hudson, C., Lumley, T., Rohl, M. (1997) *Profiling ESL Children. Volume 1: Key Issues and Findings.* Canberra: Department of Employment, Education, Training and Youth Affairs.

Brindley, G. (1989) *Assessing Achievement in the Learner-centred Curriculum.* Sydney: National Centre for English Language Teaching and Research, Macquarie University.

Brindley, G. (1998) Outcomes-based assessment and reporting in language programs: a review of the issues. *Language Testing* **15**: 45–85.

Brindley, G. (2000a) Task difficulty and task generalisability in competency-based writing assessment. In Brindley, G. (ed.). *Issues in Immigrant English Language Assessment.* Sydney: National Centre for English Language Teaching and Research, Macquarie University; 45–80.

Brindley, G. (2000b) Implementing Alternative Assessment. Paper presented at AAAL annual conference, Vancouver, Canada, March 11–14.

Brindley, G. (2001) Language assessment and professional development. In Elder, C., Brown, A., Hill, K., Iwashita, N., Lumley, T., McNamara, T., O'Loughlin, K. (eds). *Experimenting with Uncertainty: Essays in Honour of Alan Davies.* Cambridge: Cambridge University Press; 126–136.

Broadfoot, P. (1987) *Introducing Profiling.* London: Macmillan.

Brown, J.D., Hudson, T. (1998) The alternatives in language assessment. *TESOL Quarterly* **32**: 653–675.

Buck, G. (2001) *Assessing Listening.* Cambridge: Cambridge University Press.

Burrows, C. (Forthcoming) Searching for washback in the Certificates in Spoken and Written English. In Brindley, G., Burrows, C. (eds). *Issues in Immigrant English Language Assessment. Volume 2.* Sydney: National Centre for English Language Teaching and Research, Macquarie University.

Chapelle, C. (1998) Construct definition and validity enquiry in SLA research. In Bachman, L.F., Cohen, A.D. (eds). *Second Language Acquisition and Language Testing Interfaces.* Cambridge: Cambridge University Press.

Chapelle, C. (1999) Validity in language assessment. *Annual Review of Applied Linguistics* 19: 254–272.

Cheng, L. (1998) Impact of a public English examination change on students' perceptions and attitudes toward their English learning. Studies in Educational Evaluation, 24, 3: 279-301.

Clapham, C. (1997) Introduction. In Clapham, C., Corson, D. (eds). *Encyclopedia of Language and Education. Volume 7: Language Testing and Assessment.* Dordrecht: Kluwer Academic Publishers; xiii–xix.

Cram, B. (1995) Self-assessment: from theory to practice. Developing a workshop guide for teachers. In Brindley, G. (ed.). *Language Assessment in Action.* Sydney: National Centre for English Language Teaching and Research, Macquarie University; 271–305.

Davies, A., Brown, A., Elder, C., Hill, K., Lumley, T., McNamara, T. (1999) *Dictionary of Language Testing.* Cambridge: Cambridge University Press.

Douglas, D. (2000) *Testing Language for Specific Purposes: Theory and Practice.* Cambridge: Cambridge University Press.

Douglas, D. (1998) Testing methods in context-based second language research. In Bachman, L.F., Cohen, A.D. (eds). *Interfaces between Second Language Acquisition and Language Testing Research.* Cambridge: Cambridge University Press; 141–155.

Douglas, D., Selinker, L. (1993) Performance on general vs. field-specific tests of speaking proficiency. In Douglas, D., Chapelle, C. (eds) *A New Decade of Language Testing Research.* Alexandria, VA: TESOL Publications; 235–256.

Ekbatani, G. (2000) Moving towards learner-directed assessment. In Ekbatani, G., Pierson, H. (eds). *Learner-directed Assessment in ESL.* Mahwah, NJ: Lawrence Erlbaum Associates; 1–11.

Fulcher, G. (1997) Assessing writing. In Fulcher, G. (ed.). *Writing in the English Language Classroom.* Hemel Hempstead: Prentice Hall ELT/The British Council; 91–107.

Gao, X., Shavelson, R., Baxter, G. (1994) Generalizability of large-scale performance assessments in science: promises and problems. *Applied Measurement in Education* 7: 323–342.

Genesee, F., Hamayan, E. (1994) Classroom-based assessment. In Genessee, F. (ed.). *Educating Second Language Children.* New York, NY: Cambridge University Press; 212–239.

Genesee, F., Upshur, J. (1996) *Classroom-based Evaluation in Second Language Education.* Cambridge: Cambridge University Press.

Gottlieb, M. (1995) Nurturing student learning through portfolios. *TESOL Journal* 5: 12–14.

Hamp-Lyons, L. (1996) Applying ethical standards to portfolio assessment. In Milanovic, M., Saville, N. (eds). *Performance Testing, Cognition and Assessment.* Cambridge: Cambridge University Press; 151–164.

Hamp-Lyons, L., Condon, W. (1993) Questioning assumptions about portfolio-based assessment. *College Composition and Communication* 44: 176–190.

Hardy, R.A. (1995) Examining the costs of performance assessment. *Applied Measurement in Education* 8: 121–134.

Huerta-Macias, A. (1995) Alternative assessment: responses to commonly asked questions. *TESOL Journal* 5: 8–11.

Hughes, A. (1989) *Testing for Language Teachers*. Cambridge: Cambridge University Press.

Katz, A. (2000) Changing paradigms for assessment. In Snow, M.A. (ed.). *Implementing the ESL Standards for Pre-K-12 Students through Teacher Education*. Alexandria, Virginia: TESOL, Inc.; 137–166.

Koretz, D., McCaffrey, D., Klein, S., Bell, R., Stecher, B. (1992) *The Reliability of Scores from the 1992 Vermont Portfolio Assessment Program: Interim Report*. Santa Monica, CA: Rand Institute.

McKay, P. (2000) On ESL standards for school-age learners. *Language Testing* 17: 185–214.

McNamara, T.F. (1996) *Measuring Second Language Performance*. London: Longman.

McNamara, T.F. (1998) Policy and social considerations in language assessment. *Annual Review of Applied Linguistics* 18: 304–319.

Messick, S. (1989) Validity. In Linn, R. (ed.). *Educational Measurement* (third edition). New York, NY: Macmillan; 13–103.

Mohan, B., Low, M. (1995) Collaborative teacher assessment of ESL writers: conceptual and practical issues. *TESOL Journal* 5: 28–31.

Moore, H. (1996) Telling what is real: competing views in assessing English as a Second Language development. *Linguistics and Education* 8: 189–228.

Norton Peirce, B., Stewart, G. (1997) The development of the Candian Language Benchmarks Assessment. *TESL Canada Journal* 14: 17–31.

Oscarson, M. (1984) *Self-assessment of Foreign Language Skills: A Survey of Research and Development*. Strasbourg: Council for Cultural Co-operation, Council of Europe.

Oscarson, M. (1997) Self-assessment of foreign and second language proficiency. In Clapham, C., Corson, D. (eds). *Encyclopedia of Language and Education. Volume 7: Language Testing and Assessment*. Dordrecht, The Netherlands: Kluwer Academic Publishers; 175–187.

Read, J. (2000) *Assessing Vocabulary*. Cambridge: Cambridge University Press.

Read, J., Chapelle, C.A. (2001) A framework for second language vocabulary assessment. *Language Testing* 18: 1–32.

Rea-Dickins, P., Gardner, S. (2000) Snares and silver bullets: disentangling the construct of formative assessment. *Language Testing* 17: 215–243.

Ross, S. (1998) Self-assessment in language testing: a meta-analysis and analysis of experiential factors. *Language Testing* 15: 1–20.

Schmitt, N., Schmitt, D., Clapham, C. (2001) Developing and exploring the behaviour of two new versions of the Vocabulary Levels Test. *Language Testing* 18: 55–88.

Shohamy, E. (1992) Connecting testing and learning in the classroom and on the program level. In Phillips, J. (ed.). *Building Bridges and Making Connections*. Lincolnwood, IL: National Textbook Company/ACTFL; 154–176.

Shohamy, E. (1993) The exercise of power and control in the rhetorics of testing. *Carleton Papers in Applied Language Studies* 10: 48–62.

Shohamy, E. (1997. Critical Language Testing and Beyond. Plenary address presented at AAAL annual conference, Orlando.

Shohamy, E. (1998) Alternative assessment in language testing. In Li, E., James, G. (eds). *Testing and Evaluation in Second Language Education*. Hong Kong: Language Centre, Hong Kong University of Science and Technology; 99–114.

Shohamy, E., Donitsa-Schmidt, S., Ferman, I. (1996) Test impact revisited: washback effect over time. *Language Testing* **13**: 298–317.

Snow, M.A. (ed.) (2000) *Implementing the ESL Standards for Pre-K-12 Students through Teacher Education.* Alexandria, Virginia: TESOL, Inc.

Valencia, S.W., Calfee, R. (1991) The development and use of literacy portfolios for students, classes and teachers. *Applied Measurement in Education* **4**: 333–345.

von Elek, T. (1985) A test of Swedish as a second language: an experiment in self-assessment. In Lee, Y.P., Fok, A.C.Y.Y., Lord, R., Low, G. (eds). *New Directions in Language Testing.* Oxford: Pergamon; 47–57.

Wall, D. (1997) Impact and washback in language testing. In Clapham, C., Corson, D. (eds). *Encyclopedia of Language and Education. Volume 7. Language Testing and Assessment.* Dordrecht: Kluwer Academic Publishers; 291–302.

Wall, D., Alderson, J.C. (1993) Examining washback: the Sri Lankan impact study. *Language Testing* **10**: 41–69.

Weigle, S.C. (2001) *Assessing Writing.* Cambridge: Cambridge University Press.

Wigglesworth, G. (2000) Issues in the development of oral tasks for competency-based assessments of second language performance. In Brindley, G. (ed.). *Issues in Immigrant English Language Assessment.* Sydney: National Centre for English Language Teaching and Research, Macquarie University; 81–123.

Index